LONDON

LONDON

THE SECRETS AND THE SPLENDOUR

BY NICK YAPP
PHOTOGRAPHS BY RUPERT TENISON

KÖNEMANN

Contents

Contents

Frontispiece: A summer's day in Kensington Gardens
Background: Household Cavalry moves out from Knightsbridge Barracks

© 1999 Könemann Verlagsgesellschaft mbH
Bonner Straße 126, D – 50968 Cologne

Art Direction and Project Management: Peter Feierabend
Editor: Elizabeth Ingles, London
Managing Editor: Bettina Kaufmann
Assistant: Alex Morkramer
Design: Samantha Finn, Mark Thomson,
International Design UK Ltd., London
Production Manager: Detlev Schaper
Production: Mark Voges
Reproduction: Omniascanners, Milan and divis GmbH, Cologne
Printing and Binding: Imprimerie Jean Lamour, Maxéville

Printed in France
ISBN 3–8290–0484–2
10 9 8 7 6 5 4 3 2 1

Introduction

This is not a guide book. It contains little information about opening times, prices of admission, what you would pay for a meal for two at the latest cult restaurant, or where the nearest camp sites are (there are two in London, as a matter of fact – one at Crystal Palace, the other at Alexandra Palace). It is more like a book about cooking than a cookery book. It lists plenty of ingredients but leaves the reader to devise the recipes. For you will make of London what you like, or what you don't like – there are those who hate the place.

But those who dislike London do so more because of what it isn't than what it is. Jetsetters claim it isn't as romantic as Paris, as energetic as Hong Kong, as sharp as New York, as ancient as Rome. Country folk criticize it because it doesn't have log fires, paddocks or the sound of church bells across the meadows. Much of the rest of Britain regards London as a giant parasite, producing nothing but feeding off the wealth of the nation.

They may all be right, though I suspect that they know little indeed about London. To those of us who love it, it is a delight. Never dull, never empty, never even half-explored. Walking through what may at first sight appear the most humdrum streets, you will suddenly come across something that causes you to halt, laugh, wonder, shake your head in amazement – a tiny front garden stuffed with gnomes (in Camberwell New Road), a showroom of beautifully preserved cars from the 1920s and 1930s (in Queen's Gate Mews), a fine Victorian drinking fountain (at the Gloucester Gate entrance to Regent's Park).

For London will always be full of surprises – a trumpeter serenading his love at 9.30 in the morning in one of the back streets of Soho, an ancient Italian harvesting figs in the yard of a terraced house in Catford, two policemen asking a policewoman where they are in Ladbroke Grove, an off-duty angler in a smart City suit trying out a new fishing rod in a shopping arcade. It is simply in an attempt to celebrate all this and much more that I have written this book.

The Structure of the Book

The book contains eight chapters, roughly but not entirely arranged geographically. In each chapter I have tried to include something to whet the appetite or build up a thirst, for London is full of wonderful places to eat and drink. The two chapters that explore the centre of London are The West End and Westminster – the one a land of pleasure, the other of duty. The River Thames, The City of London and Historical London are self-explanatory. The Villages of London sets out to explore the further-flung suburbs – a vast area often wrongly sneered at and full of good things. The Heart of London and London's Character and Characters are both attempts to look at some of the less often explored facets of life in the city.

There is no need to read the book through from cover to cover (though I should feel greatly flattered if you did so). This is a book to dip into. My hope is that in so doing, you will find something that takes your fancy, arouses your curiosity and causes you to visit a part of London that you might otherwise have overlooked.

Note: throughout the book the "City" means what is now the City of London, the Square Mile of the old walled settlement. The "city" simply means the great metropolis, the whole of London. Though many Londoners may distinguish "northwest London" from "northeast London" and, indeed, "north London", I have used the phrases "north London" and "south London" simply to mean the whole of London north or south of the Thames respectively.

Nick Yapp

The West End

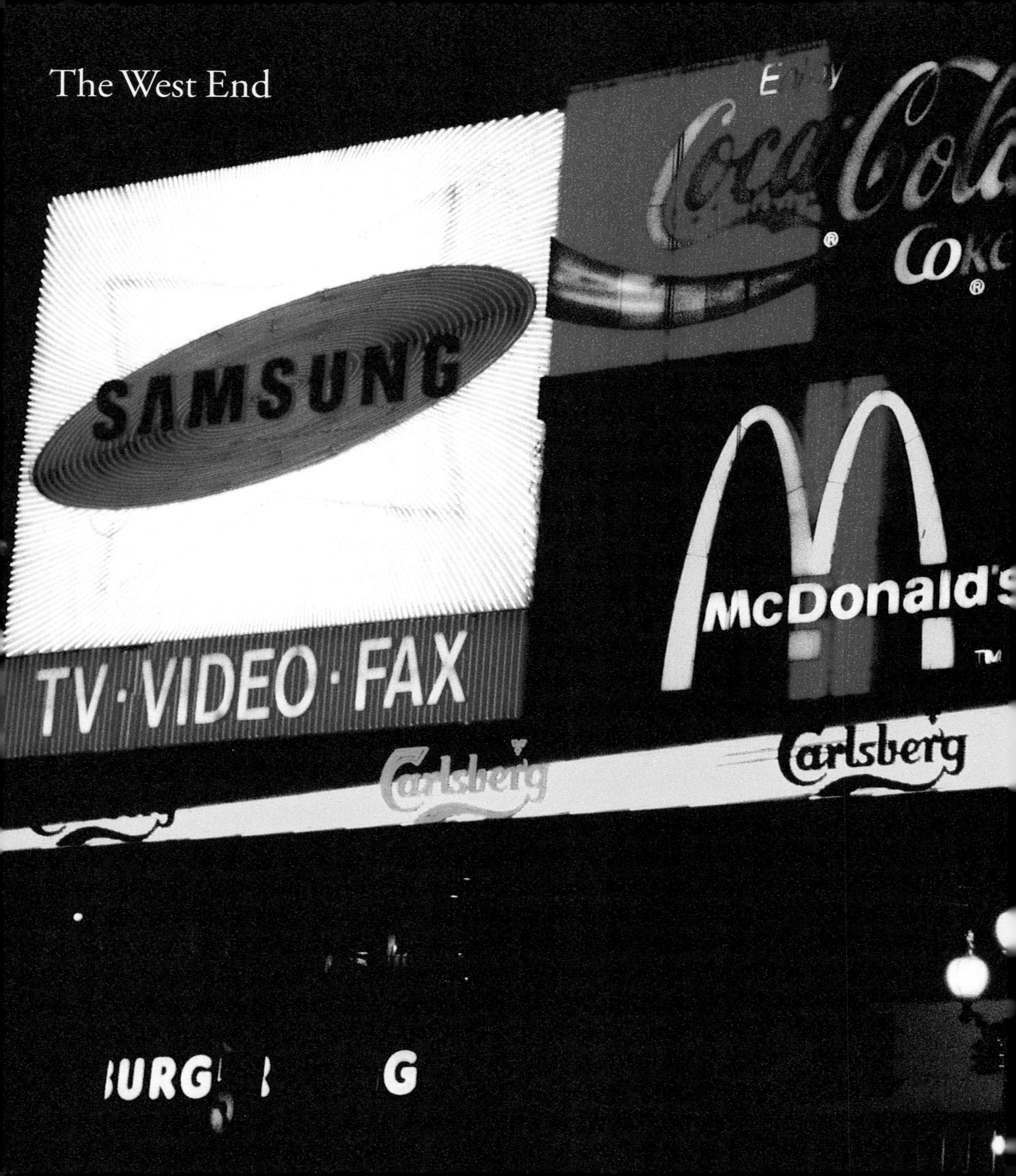

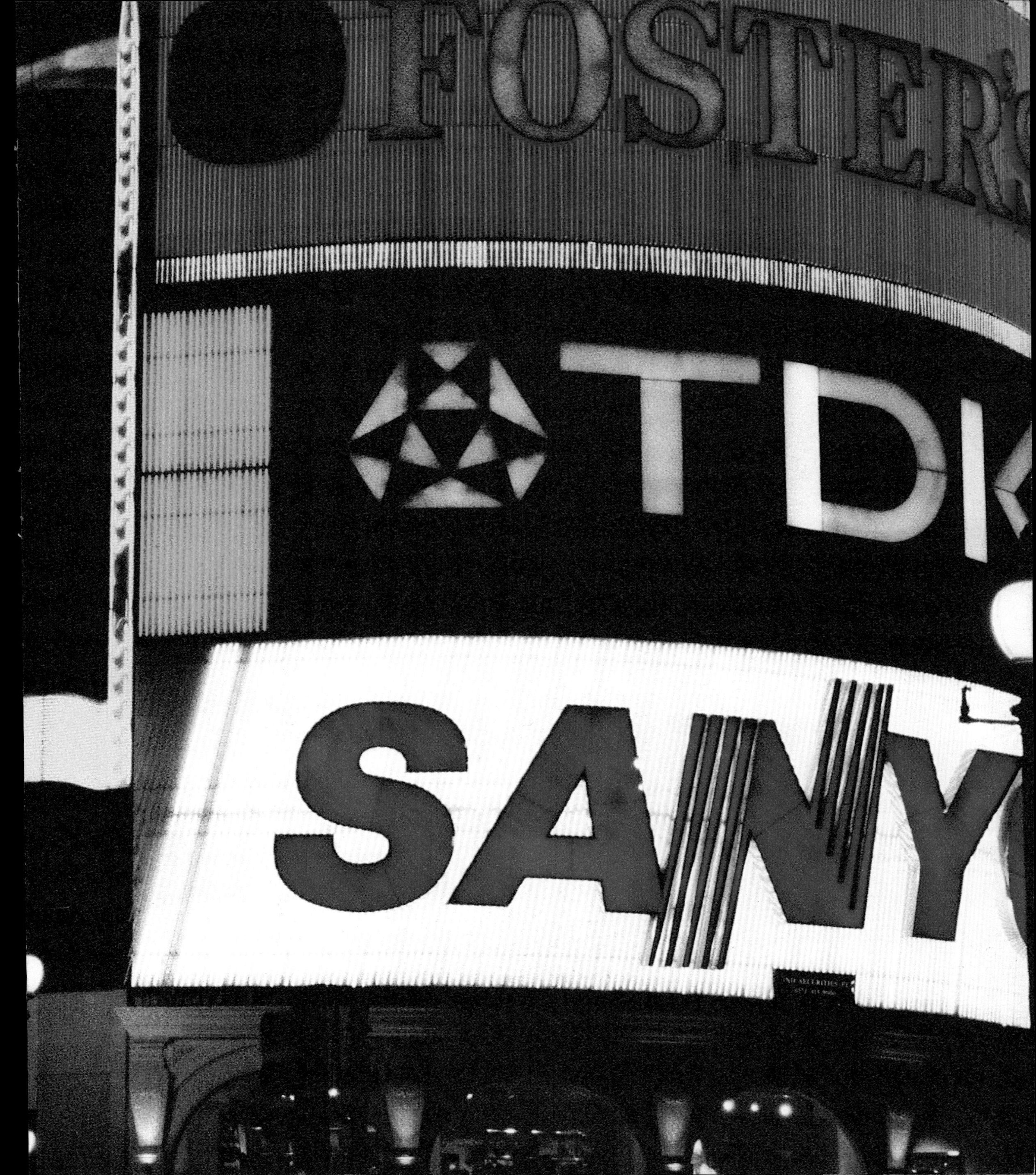
FOSTER'S
TDK
SANY

Theatreland

The heart of London's theatreland is an area of less than a square mile to the east of Piccadilly Circus. Its main thoroughfares are Shaftesbury Avenue, Charing Cross Road, The Haymarket and The Strand. There are hundreds of other theatres dotted all over London, some of them large and famous, but, theatrically speaking, this is London's "West End". This is where you can see spectacular musicals, classy revivals of classic plays from the 1920s and 1930s, imported or home-bred farce, the latest transfers from Broadway, and *The Mousetrap*, which has been running in London for 45 years.

The finest theatres in the West End were built in the late 19th and early 20th centuries, following the last great slum clearance in central London. As the rotten, rat-infested houses were pulled down, impresarios rushed forward, cheque books in hand, to grab the best sites. Between 1880 and 1913 the most ornate and beautiful of London's theatres opened: the London Pavilion, the Lyric, the Prince's, the Palace (where Nijinsky nightly performed his famous leap in *Le Spectre de la Rose*), the Garrick, Wyndham's, the Coliseum and many others. The Coliseum rivalled its Roman predecessor. When it opened, the stage had three revolving platforms to accommodate spectacles that included chariot races, a re-enactment of the Derby, and elephants playing cricket. The proprietor, Oswald Stoll, lured Sarah Bernhardt to

the Coliseum to play Hamlet for £1000 a week – an enormous sum of money in 1910. After each night's performance, the Divine Sarah made Stoll pay her personally – in gold. The dressing room in which these transactions took place is small and surprisingly dingy, with hardly enough room to swing her wooden leg round.

In 1916 Stoll took over the London Opera House, which had been built at the foot of Kingsway as a rival to Covent Garden but had gone bankrupt. He renamed it the Stoll Theatre and turned it into a successful cinema. In the Forties and Fifties it reverted to a theatre, staging ice shows, ballet, the first London performance of *Porgy and Bess*, and Ingrid Bergman's London debut as *Joan of Arc at the Stake*. It was pulled down in 1957, and a hideous office block now occupies the site. There is, however, the consolation of the Peacock Theatre in the bowels of the building, lacking in atmosphere, but comfortable and modern.

To enjoy the red plush and decadent ornamentation of London's theatre, go to Her Majesty's in The Haymarket, the little Fortune Theatre near Covent Garden, the amazing Palace Theatre in Cambridge Circus, or any one of a dozen other Victorian and Edwardian showpieces. If they seem too expensive, go east to the Hackney Empire, and climb the 90 steps to the gallery, where, almost starved of oxygen, you can gaze giddily down into the well of the theatre, or look across at the virulently coloured plaster grapes and trumpets that decorate the walls and ceiling.

The London Palladium

It used to be the ambition of every comedian, variety artist and singer from California to the Caucasus to play the London Palladium. It is vast, built in 1910 on the site of Hengler's Circus. Its most famous days were as the home of variety and revues. In the 1930s it was the home of the Crazy Gang, a collection of British comedians headed by Bud Flanagan and Chesney Allen, much loved by Londoners for their mad, anarchic humour. And every Christmas time, Barrie's *Peter Pan* was staged here. In the 1940s and 1950s the Palladium became the showcase for the finest American talent: Bob Hope, Danny Kaye, Frankie Laine, Bing Crosby, and hundreds more. Today it's the venue for large-scale, bright, brash musicals.

Theatre Royal, Drury Lane

For many Londoners, this is the finest theatre in the capital. It's certainly the oldest still in use. The first theatre on the site was destroyed by fire in 1672, with the loss of all its costumes and scenery. There were many fires in

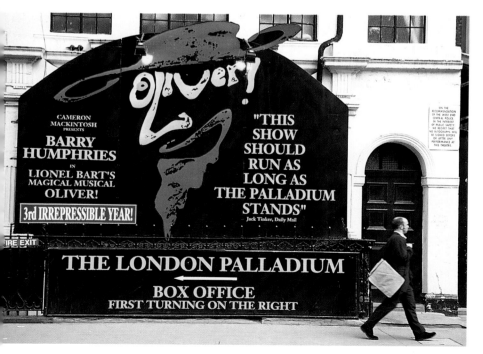

The Palladium in Argyll Street is the most glamorous of all London's variety theatres.

London in those days. Like so much of the capital, the theatre was rebuilt by Sir Christopher Wren.

It was always a lively place. There was an attempted assassination of George III there in 1800. Lavish melodramas were staged, and "spectacles" with herds of elephants and troupes of performing dogs. Despite the introduction of an iron safety curtain in 1794, Wren's theatre burnt down in 1809.

Once again it was rebuilt, this time with funds provided by the London brewer Samuel Whitbread. For much of the early part of the 19th century, the staple diet for playgoers was a series of melodramas. What Londoners enjoyed at that time is revealed in the titles of the various plays: *The Murder in the Red Barn, The Bleeding Nun* and *I Have Eaten My Friend*. By the late 1870s, however, too much Shakespeare had reduced the

company running the Theatre Royal to bankruptcy, and it closed for a year.

Since then, all has been well. Shakespeare proved more profitable in the early 20th century, and Frank Benson, the company manager, was knighted in the royal box of the theatre by George V, using a property sword. From the 1930s onwards, the theatre was home to a string of hit musicals, from Coward's *Cavalcade* and Ivor Novello's *Glamorous Night* to *South Pacific, The King and I, My Fair Lady* and *Hello Dolly!*

It's a very beautiful theatre, and if you can't afford a ticket, at least penetrate the foyer as far as the box office, and pretend you can.

The main auditorium of the Theatre Royal, Drury Lane. The theatre has a long tradition of staging many great musicals.

Going to The Theatre

Theatre tickets in the West End are expensive, though going to the theatre isn't the dressy business it was a couple of generations ago. Whatever the fashion world says, whatever devotees of opera may insist, it's perfectly acceptable to go to almost any West End theatre in smart casual and comfortable dress.

How you behave when you get there does matter. In the last 20 or 30 years theatregoers have become more talkative and ever more prone to rustle packets of sweets, crisps or biscuits. It may be that, once they have become absorbed in a play, they forget they are not at home watching television, and feel free to chat to each other about the plot, the characters and even the costumes. It may be that they simply don't become absorbed in the play. Either way, actors would prefer audiences to be respectfully quiet.

If the price of a seat is intimidating, then it's worth paying a visit to the cut-price ticket booth in Leicester Square. You can't book for anything in advance, but you can pick up some half-price bargains on the day of performance itself. Queues begin to form at the booth in the late afternoon, when the starlings start to screech in the autumn, and when the setting sun's rays slant along Panton Street (home of the charming 1881 Comedy Theatre) in the spring and early summer. Many London theatres are architecturally delightful, inside and out, particularly the Fortune in Russell Street, the two theatres facing each other across the bottom of the Haymarket (Her Majesty's and the Haymarket Theatre), the Duke of York's in St Martin's Lane, Wyndham's and the Garrick in Charing Cross Road.

Nell of Old Drury

Charles II loved the theatre and was a lascivious connoisseur of actresses. His most famous mistress was Nell Gwyn, a young woman who began her career selling oranges to the crowds at the Theatre Royal, Drury Lane. She was illiterate, but had a good sense of comedy. Samuel Pepys described her as "witty, pretty Nell", and with the patronage of first Lord Buckhurst and then King Charles, Nell became a leading actress. She also became the mother of two of Charles's illegitimate sons – the elder was Charles Beauclerk, Duke of St Albans. She was a kindly soul who urged Charles to establish the Chelsea Hospital for war veterans.

Unlike most of his other mistresses, Charles loved Nell until his death. Indeed, some say his last words were "Don't let poor Nellie starve". Nell, for her part, was grief-stricken when Charles died, and she outlived him by only two years, dying in 1687 at the age of 37.

If you are emotionally overwhelmed by this touching story, you may need to go to the pub opposite the Theatre Royal in Drury Lane. It's called *Nell of Old Drury*, and it's one of the oldest and most charming pubs in Covent Garden.

London's Music Halls

In Victorian times, hundreds of music hall theatres were opened in London. The city was so crowded with them that it was possible to attend two or three in an evening. Popular artistes like Marie Lloyd often managed to give five performances in different venues in a single night, clattering over the cobbles from theatre to theatre in hansom cabs.

The forerunners of the music halls were the Penny Gaffs, shops turned into temporary theatres at night. The admission fee was one penny ("*Ladies and Gentlemen to the Front Places must Pay Two Pence*"), and for this the audience was treated to singing and dancing, and the projection of rude pictures on the bare walls of the shop. The biggest Penny Gaffs could accommodate an audience of up to 200 people, including many children. They were primitive places with reputations for licentious performances. The women were said to "show their legs and all, prime!" But they were one step up from the street, where one showman at least ate live cats, outside a music hall near St Katharine's Dock.

Most music halls began life as the back-rooms of pubs, where drinkers and smokers enjoyed a nightly bill of comics, ballad-singers, acrobats and jugglers. The rooms in which these shows were staged became bigger and bigger, and in 1848 the first purpose-built music hall opened in London. It was the Canterbury in Lambeth, built on the site of an old skittle alley. Others, more famous, soon sprang up: the Alhambra, the Holborn Empire, the London Pavilion (the shell of which you can still see in Piccadilly Circus), the Metropolitan in the Edgware Road, and the Tivoli.

Happily, one or two still remain, carefully restored or miraculously surviving. One of the finest, well worth a visit, is Wilkins' Music Hall in the East End.

The Mousetrap
The British may be creatures of habit who worship tradition, but this isn't enough to explain why Agatha Christie's *The Mousetrap* has been running in the West End every night since November 1952. The play opened at the Ambassador's Theatre and after 8862 performances moved down the road to the St Martin's Theatre. It's a competent enough piece – a detective story with twists and turns in the plot, and an ending that you're not to divulge to the three or four people left in Britain who haven't yet seen it.

Dick Whittington and the Pantomime

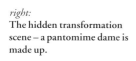

right:
The hidden transformation scene – a pantomime dame is made up.

Richard ("Dick") Whittington was a mercer or dealer in the silks and velvets used for noble dress. Originally, he came from Pauntley in Gloucestershire, but he became MP for London and four times Lord Mayor in the early 15th century. He married Alice, daughter of the very rich Sir Ivo Fitzwaryn (be patient – the reasons for this surfeit of information will be apparent later). Whittington in turn became rich enough to advance loans to Richard II, Henry IV and Henry V (probably safe enough with Henry IV, but definitely risky with the other two). In his lifetime, Whittington established a library at Greyfriars' monastery, an unmarried mothers' home at St Thomas's, and a vast public lavatory – revolutionary in that it was flushed by the Thames. When he died, Whittington left money for the rebuilding of Newgate Prison, the foundation of an almshouse, and the establishment of Whittington College, which was suppressed by Henry VIII over 100 years later.

But the reason why Dick Whittington is known and remembered by every Londoner is because he is the hero of a pantomime. Nobody knows when the legend of Dick Whittington was first written, but it was probably around 1605. And the legend is that the very young and penniless Dick worked as a servant in the Fitzwaryn household. There he fell in love with Alice, but there was no way he could be considered as her suitor unless he made a fortune.

This proved impossible in London. So Dick left, taking with him his trusty cat. He trudged northwards. When he got as far as Highgate Hill, he heard the bells of Bow church, and they seemed to be saying: "Turn again,

who wrote several pantomimes; colourful mixtures of romance, song and dance, slapstick comedy, and speciality acts that really had nothing to do with the main plot. The mixture is much the same today.

The Pantomime Dame

A disturbing number of British men like dressing up as women. Apart from those who are declared transvestites and, it is said, an alarming number of Conservative MPs, there are lots of comedians and actors who love to put on frocks and stockings, high heels and lipstick, and prance about as grotesque caricatures of the opposite sex.

The pantomime Dame may well be responsible for a lot of this. Every panto has a Dame, the leading comedy role – always a female character, always played by a man. In *Aladdin*, it's Widow Twankey. In *Jack and the Beanstalk*, it's Dame Trot. In *Cinderella* there are two dames – the ugly sisters – or sometimes three, if Cinderella's step-mother is similarly cast. In *Dick Whittington*, it's the Cook, the scourge of poor Dick's life when he's a servant in the kitchen. Although all pantomime Dames are presented as monsters of fashion, and are outrageously dressed in costumes of almost blinding brilliance, they are much loved. No other characters have such rapport with audiences. It is always the Dame who encourages children on to the stage to take part in silly competitions, and who reassures them that pantomime is only a bright and brash fairy story.

Bill Sikes and the Whittington Stone

At the foot of Highgate Hill, on the right as you go down, is the Whittington Stone. It's supposed to mark the site of the spot where Dick Whittington heard Bow Bells calling him back to his destiny as Lord Mayor.

It is not the original stone. That was probably put there some 250 years after Whittington died, and removed to Queen's Head Lane, Islington, in 1795. Nor is it the second stone. That was removed in 1821 and nobody knows what happened to it. So the present stone is Number 3. The first half of the inscription on it is wrong for two reasons. Whittington was never knighted, and he was Lord Mayor *four* times, not three. The second half, which explains who placed the figure of the cat on the stone in 1964, is correct.

In Dickens's *Oliver Twist*, the stone played a part in luring Bill Sikes back to London, back to his destruction.

Whittington, thrice Lord Mayor of London." It would seem the prediction of the bells was right in principle, but wrong in detail. Hearing this, Dick resolved to go back to London. He took ship to Morocco, where his cat chased away all the rats that were plaguing the Sultan. In gratitude, the Sultan gave Dick a fortune in goods to be sold on the London market. Dick returned, married Alice, and they lived happily ever after.

The Pantomime

This is the legend that is re-enacted every year somewhere or other in London – and indeed all over Britain – in the pantomime *Dick Whittington and his Cat*. From time to time people try to invent new pantomime stories, but the standard old favourites apart from this one are *Cinderella*, *The Sleeping Beauty*, *Jack and the Beanstalk*, *The Babes in the Wood*, *Aladdin* and *Sinbad the Sailor* – almost all of them stories of rags to riches.

Although they owe something to both the Italian *commedia dell'arte* and the Paris *Arlequin*, pantomimes are a truly English theatre form. They were pioneered by John Weaver in London in the late 17th and early 18th centuries. Weaver was a Drury Lane dancing-master

Commemorative plaque to Dick Whittington on the wall of St Michael Paternoster Royal, College Hill.

Leicester Square and the London Cinema

Charlie Chaplin

The bronze statue of Charlie Chaplin bears the legend: "The comic genius who gave pleasure to so many." Chaplin was a Londoner, born in Kennington in 1889. His father died when he was a child, leaving the family in great poverty, and Chaplin's education was largely at the Hanwell Poor Law Institution. The cocky character he played in numerous films was a comic caricature of a London down-and-out, and he took the little "Tramp" with him when he went to Hollywood in 1914.

Once upon a time, Leicester Square was common Lammas land, on which parishioners could dry clothes and pasture their cattle after Lammas Day (12 August). Today it's a pedestrian area, with a tiny garden. In the middle there's a badly eroded statue, generally thought to be of Shakespeare (who had no connections with Leicester Square), but at one time so labelled that many thought it was of Albert Grant, who bought the square in the 1870s and then handed it over to the Metropolitan Board of Works.

The square is the West End home of the cinema in London. To the north, east and south of it there are four large cinemas: the Empire, Warner West End, the Odeon and the Odeon West End. They were all built between 1900 and 1940, and the architecture is heavily influenced by D.W. Griffith and Hollywood itself. The Odeon Leicester Square was built of black granite in 1937, replacing the Alhambra Theatre – home of such acts as Blondin, Leotard ("the daring young man on the flying trapeze"), George Robey and the Diaghilev Ballet.

There are offices to the west, one expensive hotel (the Hampshire), a couple of unremarkable restaurants and some snack bars. At the northwest tip of the square is the Swiss Centre, with excellent food in its very clean café, and an extravagant clock – which may remind you of Harry Lime's famous wisecrack in *The Third Man*.

Until the Reformation, the land was owned by St Peter's Westminster, but Henry VIII pinched it in 1536. The connection with the Leicester family goes back to 1630. In that year Robert Sidney, the second Earl (weak son of a strong father, weak father of a strong son who was executed for his republican views), bought the land from the Crown. Robert built a large house (on the site of the present Empire), and initiated the building of a fine square faced by terraces of imposing houses with not a shop in sight. The artist William Hogarth lived at No. 30, and produced some of his best London work there (*Rake's Progress, Beer Street, Gin Lane, Industry and Idleness*).

In the 19th century, the houses gave way to hotels, theatres, Turkish baths, oyster bars, music halls and James Wyld's Great Globe – a model of the world 60 feet (18 metres) high built for the 1851 Exhibition. The square became the centre of the *demi-monde*, no place for unescorted ladies, and in the song *It's a Long Way to Tipperary* there are wistful echoes of a way of life that ended abruptly with the First World War.

Most film premières and Royal Command film performances are held here. Crowds gather to scream at the stars and politely cheer and applaud members of the Royal Family. The lights are bright, the dinner jackets gleam, the tiaras sparkle, the flashlights flicker, even the police are all smart and tidy. For a moment or two Leicester Square seems like a muted version of Hollywood. But reality presses much harder on life in the heart of London, and it's difficult to get completely carried away. Anyway, it's almost impossible to manoeuvre a stretch-limo in the West End.

A Leicester Square Oddity

In November 1726 Nathaniel St André, surgeon of Westminster Hospital and anatomist to King George I, brought a young woman named Mary Tofts to his house at 27 Leicester Square. Mary was of a "healthy strong constitution, small size, fair complexion, a very stupid and sullen temper, and unable to read or write". She claimed that she gave birth to litters of rabbits. It caused a panic among butchers – people stopped eating rabbits on moral grounds, and the price of letting a rabbit warren plummeted. Something had to be done. Mary was threatened with a gruesome exploratory operation and confessed. She had invented the whole thing, simply in

the hope of making money. She was sent to Tothill Fields' Bridewell, the prison used by Hogarth as his model for *The Rake's Progress*. To date, no one has made a film of Mary's story.

Power to the People

In the early 1990s, a large electricity substation was built under Leicester Square to supply electricity to the square itself, and to Piccadilly, the National Gallery, the theatres of The Strand and Shaftesbury Avenue, and Covent Garden. The entrance to it is at the corner of the square and Panton Street, but its owners do not encourage visitors. Maybe it's just as well. Though only a few years old, the substation is already home to a great many of the ten million brown rats that scuttle about underneath London.

opposite:
Crowds gather in Leicester Square for a film premiere.
below:
The Odeon, Leicester Square in all its 1930's glory.

Covent Garden

The Punch and Judy Festival

Covent Garden is also the site of the annual Punch and Judy Festival. Puppeteers and puppet masters parade with their Mr Punches through the streets and the piazza, accompanied by bands and a town crier. A commemorative address is delivered – to squawky heckling from the puppets. A service is then held in St Paul's Church, also much enjoyed by the puppets, and then Punch and Judy is performed all afternoon. There are traditional shows, modern variations, politically correct versions, given by old hands and hopeful apprentices. For some puppeteers it's a chance to take the Punch and Judy examination, to prove to the judges that they should be allowed to style themselves official Punch and Judy men and women, and to show that they know "That's the way to do it!"

Despite its origins as the garden of a convent, Covent Garden has long been associated with fun and frolics. It's yet another slab of London pinched from the Church by Henry VIII, but the seven acres of garden were given by the king to John Russell, first Earl of Bedford. Francis Russell, the fourth Earl, successfully drained the East Anglian fens, unsuccessfully attempted to mediate between Charles I and Parliament, and in the early 17th century most successfully laid out the main square of Covent Garden, much as we know it today. He appointed Inigo Jones, then King's Surveyor of Works, initially to build a number of houses "fitt for the habitacions of *Gentlemen* and men of ability." Jones did all this and more, designing one of the finest of all London churches on the west side of the square.

It was also Francis Russell who paid to have sheds built for the fruiterers and greengrocers coming daily to London to sell their produce. For 100 years the market remained a hotch-potch collection of stalls and storerooms, selling herbs, snails, parrots and live hedgehogs (kept as pets to catch the beetles that infested people's homes), as well as fruit and vegetables. There were frequent complaints from the local residents about the noise and the litter, both of which grew worse with the

closure of the Stocks Market in the City in 1737, and the Fleet Market in 1820.

So the young sixth Duke of Bedford, Edward Russell, developed the square, and the large buildings in the middle of the piazza were put up in 1830 to house a much larger market. It was a lively place: Edward Gibbon enjoyed four "costly and dangerous frolics" there, but added that "I was too young and bashful to enjoy the taverns and bagnios of Covent Garden".

From the late 19th century until the 1930s, the area was famous for its supper-rooms, where the wealthy would eat a far from vegetarian meal after a visit to the theatre or the nearby Royal Opera House. At its height, the market employed 1000 porters, scurrying to and fro, with baskets of fruit piled high on their heads. At the annual championships, the most experienced porters could balance 20 or more, in a crazy-looking wicker tower. The market used to open at midnight and close at around nine in the morning. It was at its busiest at 8 am, when retailers were loading their lorries, costers trundled their barrows, and the flower-women were making their way to their pitches with arms full of blooms.

It all came to an end when the market moved to Nine Elms, where it's now a much tamer affair; a succession of low flat sheds, with uniform loading bays – efficient and characterless. And the pubs that used to open at 6 am to quench the porters' thirsts are now but a beery memory.

Modern Covent Garden

But the fun goes on. When the market moved out in 1974, there were some doubts as to the future of the piazza. Developers were poised to wreck the area and turn it into a bland collection of offices. The Greater London Council took over, and Fowler's Market (the central block) was converted into an upper and lower alley of small shops, selling everything from food to books. The old Flower Market has become the home of the London Transport Museum, and the Jubilee Market is now a covered general street market.

Every day street performers parade in front of the east end of the church of St Paul's. The church itself is a gem, built by Inigo Jones. The fourth Earl, who didn't like spending money, asked Jones for a building "not much better than a barn". Jones replied: "You shall have the handsomest barn in England." It's an actors' church – the ashes of Ellen Terry are kept there – so it's appropriate that so much entertainment takes place beside it.

Oxford Street and Its Origins

Oxford Street doesn't get its name because it leads to Oxford, although it does run vaguely westwards in that direction. It used to be called "The Waye from Uxbridge" (running eastwards, as it were), "The King's Highway", "The Acton Road", and "The Road to Tyburn" – more about Tyburn later. "Oxford Street" became its title in the 18th century, when Robert Harley, Earl of Oxford, acquired much of the land on the north side of the road. He married into the Cavendish family; his daughter married into the Portland family. So, to the north of Oxford Street you will find Harley Street (the business centre for London's richest medical practices), Cavendish Square and Portland Place. You will also find Wigmore Street (named after yet another of Robert Harley's titles – Baron Wigmore of Herefordshire) and the Wigmore Hall, in which many world-renowned musicians have made their London debut.

Oxford Street isn't smart. It's a hustling, bustling stretch of shops, just under a mile long, running west from Tottenham Court Road to Marble Arch. In many ways the stretch east of Oxford Circus is the nearest thing London has to an oriental bazaar. There's a feeling of cut-price furtiveness about it – the Street of a Thousand Sales. Architecturally, it's neither pretty nor impressive. Apart from Selfridges there's no building of any stature. It's half a mile of shops: only one pub (the Tottenham), no smart restaurants, no fine churches. And the shops have a piecemeal, ramshackle look about them, as if they have all been bought from a catalogue by people with widely different tastes. At any one time you may find up to 300,000 wads of old chewing gum stuck to the pavements.

But every week an average four million people crowd those pavements, pouring out of tube stations, leaping off buses. And they come for only one reason – to spend their money in its five million square feet (half a million square metres) of retail space. For Oxford Street is the shopping Mecca of London: there isn't anywhere in Britain to touch it for clothes, shoes, CDs and videos, tacky souvenirs or dodgy goods (the favourites at the moment are illicit Calvin Klein perfume, Armani jeans and Ray-Bans). Every year the annual turnover amounts to £5 billion.

It's noisy. Hundreds of buses grind past. Music seeps out of the bargain boutiques. The amplified urgings of sharp salesmen can be heard from across the road. A Scots bagpipe wails outside a department store. The

A Holbein of the streets.
A pavement artist paints Henry in chalk on the pavements of Oxford Street.

Hare Krishna followers pad up and down, ringing their finger cymbals and chanting endlessly. It's crowded. There are foreign students from the numerous schools of English dotted along the street. There are office workers, grabbing the chance offered by their short lunch break to buy a pair of Reeboks or a shirt or a dress. There are delivery vans, feeding the hungry shops with yet more merchandise. And it smells – not altogether unpleasantly. It's true there are traffic fumes, but there are also the aromas of fast food (pizza slices, hamburgers and onions, Euro-croissants). And there's the heady scent that slinks from the department stores – all of which have their perfume counters on the ground floor, right on the street.

For those who live in the Home Counties, immediately around London, the glory of Oxford Street has always been the big stores – Selfridges, John Lewis, Debenhams, D.H. Evans. A later generation would add Marks and Spencer (Marks and Sparks to the British), and C & A. The more middle-class you are, the fewer shops you patronize in Oxford Street. It's not just a question of convenience. There's tradition here, and an unconscious feeling that swathes of Oxford Street are a little bit seedy. It is here that the "three card trick" is used to fleece some poor provincial, up from the country. A small crowd gathers to watch him lose his money to a gang who look terrifyingly like modern day pirates. Nobody shows any sympathy. I think they all see it as part of the Oxford Street norm.

And one last word of warning: there are only seven public toilets in Oxford Street – three conventional, three automatic and one for the disabled.

Tyburn

At the western end of Oxford Street, where the Edgware Road joins the Bayswater Road, you will find a stone set in a traffic island. It marks the site of the gallows at Tyburn, the most used venue for public executions in London from 1388 to 1783. The condemned wretches were driven to Tyburn in open carts for all to see. Often they were dressed in all their finery, and they had the right to a drink at every pub they passed. But, cruelly, there were no pubs in Oxford Street, for the very reason that the hangman wanted his victims to arrive sober at the gallows. So they took a last drink at St Giles-in-the-Fields. Even Earl Ferrers, hanged for killing his steward in 1760, was refused a second drink and had to make do with pigtail tobacco. The hangman had his drink after the execution, at a pub in Fleet Street, where he sold the deadly rope at sixpence an inch for curative purposes.

A good hanging at Tyburn was a public holiday, the idea being that the more people who witnessed it, the

An Oxford Street shopper picks his way carefully through spent chewing gum.

more it would serve as a deterrent. It didn't work. Henry Fielding, the 18th century magistrate who wrote *Tom Jones*, declared: "The day appointed by law for the thief's shame is the day of glory in his own opinion. His procession to Tyburn and his last moments there are all triumphant; attended with the compassion of the weak and tender-hearted, and with the applause, admiration and envy of all the bold and hardened."

Bargain or rip-off? Sometimes it's hard to tell in Oxford Street.

above:
Christmas lights on the façade
of Selfridges store.

Selfridges and Marble Arch

In 1902 Harry Gordon Selfridge was bored with Chicago, where he had made a fortune, and decided to try Europe. Seven years later, he opened his store in Oxford Street. It was a monster, enormous, brazen, triumphant. London had never seen anything like it.

Inside there were a hundred different departments, including an American soda fountain and a barber's shop. The façade was one window display after another, a glazed extravagance that attracted thousands of shoppers to what had previously been considered the disaster area of Oxford Street. On the roof were a golf range, a dance floor and an ice-rink. And the lifts were just magnificent.

The well-to-do flocked to Selfridges. In 1917 Lady Cynthia Asquith, whose husband had only just given up being Prime Minister, paid a visit. "Michael walked to Selfridges with me and there I took the great step of buying a bicycle, having decided on that as my method of transport in London. I rode it home in triumph and found it delightful, and much less alarming than I anticipated. Of course, there is only about a third of the traffic there used to be and one can always dismount to cross Oxford Street or to meet any crisis." Those were the days...

Selfridges Today

From the outside, Selfridges (it lost its apostrophe years ago) remains a glorious department store. Its magnificent 1909 façade has happily escaped damage by war and desecration by developers. The window displays are always worth inspection, and at Christmas time are often the best in London.

But inside, things are not what they were. Apart from

the food halls, it has to be said that Selfridges has lost some of its glamour. The glorious Art Deco lifts have been replaced by inferior modern descendants, though you can still see one of the beautiful originals in the Museum of London. There's a sad lack of sparkle. The American Soda Fountain that captured every young Londoner's appetite for Hollywood allure in the 1950s is no longer there.

There's a sad lack, comparatively speaking, of demonstrators – one of the best pieces of entertainment in London used to be to stand and watch and listen to the slick salesmen demonstrating kitchen gadgets in the basement at Selfridges. With luck, however, you may yet come across a knife-sharpener who will put a razor edge on a set of carvers, and a chef who will create a mouth-watering salad before your very eyes.

And you still can't buy furniture there. Gordon Selfridge was backed at that time by Waring and Gillow, another London store, when he applied to build his vast emporium, on the understanding that he would never sell furniture.

Marble Arch

Marble Arch was built in 1827 by John Nash. He based his design on the Arch of Constantine in Rome, and it cost £10,000. But originally it stood in front of Buckingham Palace, and it wasn't moved to its present site until 1851, the year of the Great Exhibition, when Hyde Park became the focus of the entire country. Now it stands in the middle of a large traffic island, a pleasant enough venue in the summer, but decidedly chilly and exposed in winter.

Surprisingly, the arch has three little rooms inside, which used to be an emergency police station. In the Hyde Park riots of 1855 the police hid inside, and then suddenly rushed out, Trojan-horse-like, taking the rioters unawares. Don't worry if you wish to riot in Hyde Park today: the police abandoned their station in 1950. But you mustn't walk through the arch. That's a privilege reserved for senior members of the Royal Family and the King's Troop of the Royal Horse Artillery. Junior members of the Royal Family don't appear particularly bothered, but you never know.

Oxford Street and the Eternal Soul

For some unknown reason, Oxford Street attracts those who wish to express their concern for our eternal well-being. There used to be a man who patrolled Oxford Circus with a vast sandwich board that condemned (among other things) meat, nuts and protein in general, and "too much sitting". Alas, he is no longer with us, but a spiritual descendant still pounds the pavements of Oxford Street with a sign that reads "Ye Must Be Born Again of the Spirit". And there's always the Hare Krishna Marching Band.

Marble Arch – originally one of the entrances to the grounds of Buckingham Palace – now marooned amid the traffic of Oxford Street.

The London Salesman

Almost everyone in London has something to sell – a house, a car, a skill, an unwanted exercise bicycle, a pushchair their child has outgrown. Among the millions of amateur salespeople, however, there are tens of thousands of professionals – people who sell for a living. They range from the smartly attired flunkeys of Fortnum's or Harrods to the wideawake boys who sell illegally from trays in Oxford Street; from suave experts in car showrooms to shivering market stallholders out in all weathers; from bored money-takers at the entrance to a Soho clip joint to enthusiastic "wannabees" in the box office of a West End theatre.

At the top end of the market, the technique of selling is polished, assured, unthreatening. There is no need to "sell" luxuries, they almost sell themselves. If someone wants a Rolls Royce and has the necessary money, the only thing likely to stop the transaction would be a complete collapse of the Stock Exchange. Down at street level, however, all is different. It's cut and thrust, hurly-burly, and hustle, hustle, hustle.

Fleecing the Punter

Stop for a moment outside one of the shops in Oxford Street that sell fire-damaged goods or allegedly bankrupt stock. These shops usually have quaintly old-fashioned names ("Tankerton and Goodbody", "Painsworthy and Buccleuch") in olde worlde lettering above their wide open doors. The suggestion is that they are thoroughly respectable and reliable. The reality is that they are fly-by-night organizations that settle for a month or two, take a lot of money for a load of junk, and then vanish – to reappear under another name a few doors away, a few weeks later.

Here the selling technique is simple and crude. What seems an almost ludicrous bargain is offered – a television set for £5. There are only a few of them, the salesman says, so the shoppers begin to panic and compete. "Who wants one?" Hands shoot up. The spending spree is under way. The salesman singles out a dozen or so customers, and then says that since this chosen few have been so obliging, he's prepared to offer them another bargain – a food mixer for £25. This is far less of a bargain, but the salesman's patter and the competitive atmosphere that has been created work their magic. The shoppers are almost intoxicated. No one wants to be left out. No one wants to miss a chance to buy such smart-looking goods in such shiny new boxes.

Some of the shoppers may be lucky. They may buy a walkman or a CD player that works. Most will end up with shoddy goods in possibly dangerous condition. Anyone who starts to complain in the shop will be per-suaded – perhaps quite forcefully – to leave. The money rolls in. The customers stagger out.

On the Street

If you have time, pause for a while and watch the gangs who sell watches, perfume or lighters from suitcases or baker's trays on the street.

They usually work in groups of three, near a litter bin on which they can rest their case or tray. One of the gang does the actual selling, while the other two hover nearby, keeping watch for signs of approaching police. When the police appear, the look-outs signal to the salesman, who snatches up his tray and darts down a nearby alley. The look-outs may then leap on a passing bus, just to remove themselves from the scene. The police arrive and find no sign of any illegal trading. They move on. The look-outs return. The salesman brings his tray out of the alley, and business starts again.

It's a very smooth operation. Capitalism at its competitive best.

Cleaning Rugs in the Lower Marsh

Stallholders in markets are legitimate traders, and their skill as salespeople is a joy to behold. In Lower Marsh, tucked behind Waterloo station, you may come across a stall that has nothing on it but a dirty rug – indeed, a rug so multi-stained that it looks as though Jack the Ripper ate his breakfast off it and wiped his feet on it.

Out of nowhere comes a voice. "If I could just have a moment of your time…"

You turn towards the voice, and the performance begins. The salesman has a wonder cleaner. It will remove every stain, every spot, every tiny smear from this deeply encrusted rug. He slaps a bottle of this wonder cleaner on the stall, extols its virtues. Then he produces a rival product, which is dismissed as rubbish.

All the time, the humour keeps bubbling out of him. He selects a woman in the small crowd that has gathered. "You know how hard a sponge gets, love, when you use it for this sort of work? Not with this product! Have a feel, love – no, no! The sponge! Did you see what she was going to do there…?"

As he wipes away at the rug, he keeps talking. Blood, gravy, oil, treacle, wine and lipstick succumb to his foaming cleaner. Now is the time to promise special offers for the first six to buy a bottle. Now is the time to reveal that you cannot buy this cleaner in any shop, that it would cost three times the price if you bought it through telesales. Now is the time to rinse and exhibit the rug. Not a trace of a stain. No wonder they never caught Jack the Ripper.

Drumming up a crowd at
Waterloo – a street trader
in action.

Shopping for Toys

Hamley's

Londoners like to champion Hamley's of Regent Street as "The Most Famous Toy Shop in the World", and for anyone who finds growing up difficult, Hamley's is a cross between Aladdin's Cave and Shangri-La. It's a large shop – six floors stuffed with toys, playthings, games and puzzles. The best time to visit, if you're feeling strong, is in winter, during the grim days that lead up to Christmas, when the store is crowded, the windows are at their best, and the atmosphere is inspiringly frenzied. As you plunge in off the street one of the first things you see are the demonstrators, showing off their skills with anything from the simplest yo-yo to the latest radio-controlled stratocruiser or miniature fighting machine.

Each floor has its own special enticements. On the first floor you are in the land of old favourites – train sets, planes, cars, boxes of Meccano, jigsaw puzzles. Toy soldiers are on parade in glass cabinets, led by a complete scale replica of the regimental band of the First Battalion of the Gordon Highlanders.

The second floor is quieter. This is the land of marble-runs, construction kits, toy musical instruments, computer games and toys for very young children. On the third floor you enter the world of dolls, dolls' houses, Barbie, Action Man, and fantasy War Lord toys. Two floors to go. You may join the queues for the video consoles on the fourth floor, or relive the frustration of being unable to manipulate Rubik's Cube successfully, or buy yet another edition of Monopoly, Cluedo or Scrabble (or any one of a hundred other games). There are chess and draught sets, three-dimensional jigsaw puzzles, and yet more CD and computer games. Finally, on the top floor, you can pick up a model yacht, a pair of in-line (rollerblade) skates, a football, or a pool table.

Struggling out of the store, weighed down with parcels, you may experience one or two doubts. There is a kind of gluttony that attaches to buying toys. The sight of all those half-remembered or endlessly longed-for delights makes many drool, and all tend to lose their self-control. Never mind – whatever the cost, there is still to come the joy of watching someone we love unwrapping those same parcels – or of unwrapping them ourselves.

The Story of Hamley's and "Cossima"

John Hamley first opened a toyshop called Noah's Ark in High Holborn in 1760. The family business prospered, and Hamley's bought other premises in Regent Street (near the Café Royal) and Oxford Street. The present store opened in 1906.

Over the years, many inventors of toys and games have come to Hamley's with the prototypes of their genius. Around 100 years ago a man walked into one of their stores with a game he had invented, called "Cossima". Hamley's liked the game. It was simple, great fun, and could be enjoyed by young and old alike. They became the first company to sell it. However, they didn't think much of the name, so they changed it to the more onomatopoeic "Ping Pong". More formally, the world knows it as table tennis.

Pollock's

Tucked away in the streets to the west of Tottenham Court Road (at 1 Scala Street, to be precise), is Pollock's. You can't mistake it – it's bright and welcoming, but charmingly aged at the same time. It is three premises in one – a toy shop, a theatrical print warehouse and a toy museum. Inside, the floors are bare boards, the shelves old and crowded. There are still traces of the old gaslights on the wooden ceilings, and there's a solid, ancient till that registers the pre-1971 pounds, shillings and pence.

One room is full of clockwork tin toys – trains, motorbikes, motor boats, ferris wheels, ice-cream tricycles – and jack-in-the-boxes, teddy bears, dolls, furniture and equipment for dolls' houses, puzzles and tricks. Another room is festooned with "penny plain and twopence coloured" toy theatres, complete with scenery, characters and scripts for dozens of old plays and pantomimes.

These are the joys on which Pollock's has built its name. The shop was founded by Benjamin Pollock in the 19th century. "If you love art, folly, or the bright eyes of

Hope eternal – a child's eyes gaze in wonder at the delights of Hamley's.

children," wrote Robert Louis Stevenson, "speed to Pollock's." The museum was started much later, in 1956. It consists of half a dozen rooms, spread higgledy-piggledy on three floors and connected by a narrow twisting staircase. An air of fairytale pervades the whole place, with ancient toys from all over the world. There are 100-year-old American alphabet boards, jointed wooden dolls of the 1870s from Vermont, "Saucy Fräulein" brooches of Weimar days, wax dolls from the 1840s and a teddy bear that was born in 1905.

As you climb the stairs you will find train sets from the 1900s, venerable rocking horses, magic lanterns, toy soldiers that were cast from lead when the British Empire was at its height, farm animals, trucks, carts, Punch and Judy puppets, miniature toy shops – every conceivable childhood favourite (although lead soldiers are no longer sold to children for fear of poisoning).

It is a corner of London that gladdens the heart.

above:
All the joys of childhood – the interior of Pollock's toy shop in Scala Street.
left:
The pleasures of times past – outside Pollock's toy shop.

Old Shops

Paxton and Whitfield have been selling cheese here for over 200 years.

One of the joys of strolling around London is coming across one of the old shops that have traded in much the same goods for centuries. With a bit of care you can find them all over the capital. There are some in the City, a cluster in the West End, and individual oddities scattered throughout the inner suburbs: hatters, chemists, snuff shops, bookshops, bootmakers and wine merchants, and even gentlemen's hairdressers.

The row of shops at Staple Inn, Holborn, is housed in the last surviving example of Elizabethan domestic architecture in London. They were built in 1586, but these days are inhabited by more modern concerns. There is "Ye Olde Tobacco Shoppe", but that's a mere upstart, established in 1864. An old noticeboard, in the archway that leads from High Holborn, reads: "The porter has orders to prevent old clothes men and others from calling articles for sale. Also rude children playing &c. No horses allowed within this Inn." Go through this archway into the little courtyard beyond. It's one of the prettiest courtyards in London, and if you're lucky you may get there when the lights are still on in Staple Inn Hall, illuminating the stained-glass windows.

A couple of hundred yards west from Piccadilly Circus, on the north side of Piccadilly, is the Burlington Arcade, built in 1819 to prevent London louts throwing oyster shells and other rubbish into the garden of Lord George Cavendish. It's a dull place for shopping, full of very English clothes of good quality and unimaginative design, but it's famous for the beadles who patrol it. The beadles, who are all ex-servicemen, make sure that shoppers uphold the very particular laws of the Burlington Arcade – it is illegal to carry an open umbrella or "a very large parcel", whistle, sing or run.

Paxton and Whitfield

There are lots of fine shirtmakers in Jermyn Street, many of them well over 100 years old, but good shirts are not hard to find in London. The best reason for going to Jermyn Street is to visit Paxton and Whitfield, cheesemongers since 1797. It's a narrow, dark shop, with a discreet black-painted façade and a large window, temptingly dressed with whole Cheddars, Stiltons, wines, biscuits and mustards. The small inside is ripely appetizing – these are real, breathing cheeses, not the filmwrapped, waxy copies to be found in most supermarkets.

James Smith and Sons

This is the most famous walking stick and umbrella shop in the world, established in 1830. It's very near the British Museum, at the junction of New Oxford Street and Bloomsbury Street. Originally it was a dairy, but James Smith moved his vast collection of sticks and canes, riding crops and whips, Irish blackthorns (wrongly but romantically called "shillelaghs"), shooting sticks and Malacca canes here in 1856. If you haven't time to go inside, at least pause to read the details on the shop fascia.

The Old Curiosity Shop

There really is still a second-hand clothes shop – which says it sells "Antique and Modern Art" – on the site of Dickens's Old Curiosity Shop. It's in Portsmouth Street, just off Lincoln's Inn Fields. It claims to have been built in 1567, and is said to have been the model for the birthplace of Little Nell. It certainly looks ancient, though its appealing scruffiness is let down by a thick coating of what looks like bright red cement on its roof.

How the old shop has survived is perhaps the most curious thing about it. It is overwhelmed by its unattractive immediate surroundings, ugly even by 20th-century standards. Inside, however, all is attractively gloomy. It's full of old coats and jackets, grubby shoes and the accumulated bric-à-brac of centuries. The air is musty, dusty and saturated with the aroma of age.

Tessier's of Bond Street

Tessier's, Silversmiths and Goldsmiths, at 26 New Bond Street, isn't particularly old. It was established in 1851. But it is a charming shop, with an ornate exterior in dark green, and an appropriately antique-looking interior of exquisite proportions. Should you feel in the mood to buy something precious, this is the place to visit. Shopping here would be a pleasant experience.

Cigars and Snuff

Until recently, some of the oldest surviving shops in London were those that sold tobacco in its various forms. Cancer scares and government health warnings have led to a reduction in smoking by the rich, who were the main patrons of shops that made up their own cigarettes and mixed their own snuffs. Although their pretty 18th-century bow windows remain, Fribourg and Treyer in The Haymarket is now sadly a paper and greetings card shop called "Fancy That", and what was a fiery and fumey den in Greenwich Market is now a harmless gift shop. But Smith's remains in the Charing Cross Road ("Snuff Supplier since 1869"), and at 18 St James's Street you will find James J. Fox, Cigar Merchants, established 1881 in premises built in 1787. This is hunting ground much favoured by American connoisseurs of cigars, for here London can supply that which cannot be found in the United States – the finest Havanas.

left:
A small selection of sticks with carved heads in James Smith and Sons. From left to right: unknown dog and frog, Bach, Berlioz and Chopin.
below:
Like the entrance to Ali Baba's Cave... the doors of Tessier's of Bond Street.

Hunting in Mayfair

Mayfair was once a pretty little village, taking its name from the original May Fayre held near the Shepherd's Tavern in Hertford Street in the 17th century. Nowadays, Mayfair is a fashionable residential and commercial area, with outrageously expensive houses and apartments, a very comfortable cinema, and two or three charming, café-lined little squares.

Nothing in Mayfair is cheap. The very names of the streets (Grosvenor, Berkeley, Curzon) reek of wealth and privilege. It's the place to go to if you want to buy a Rolls Royce or a Bentley, a house with a swimming pool in the basement and a ballroom on the first floor, or London's most expensive and exclusive wallpaper – try Zoffany's in South Audley Street.

It's also the place to go to if you want to buy some prime ready-slaughtered meat, or the means to slaughter your own.

R. Allen of Mount Street

On a corner site at the end of a parade of shops at the Carlos Place end of Mount Street is R. Allen and Company, Butchers. The outside of the shop may not be particularly impressive – two shop windows, neither of which is festooned with poultry or stuffed with racks of lamb or barons of beef. Allen's has never been that sort of shop. The meat is all at the back, in store. At Allen's they expect the customer to know exactly what he or she wants, and to demand it, so that they can go and find it.

Inside, there are no counters, just huge free-standing

The imposing façade of Holland and Holland, riflemakers of Bruton Street.

butchers' blocks, on which the finest of joints will be trimmed, the best steaks lovingly sliced, the juiciest of kidneys prised from their protective shells of shiny white fat. It is an old-fashioned shop where you do not buy what's on offer, but ask the experts to meet your requirements.

The craftsmen whose knives have cunningly created the tournedos and fillets, the half-shoulders and topsides, the loin chops and cutlets do not, of course, handle any money. That is done by the cashier in the booth to the rear of the shop, as it used to be in the good old days. The price of your purchase is called out by the butcher, and you move across to the cashier to make your payment. Meanwhile, your parcel of meat is being neatly wrapped, and by the time you've finished paying, it's ready for you.

Allen's has traded on or near this site for over 150 years.

James Purdey and Sons Limited

On the corner of Mount Street and South Audley Street is Audley House, the headquarters of Purdey, Gun and Rifle Makers. Stop awhile to admire the beautifully crafted weapons in the windows, and to gasp at the prices thereof. Purdey's do not sell the sort of shotgun that you would take on a bank raid – though you might have to rob a bank to be able to meet their prices. A high-quality gun here can cost upwards of £20,000.

For these pieces are tailormade to fit the shoulder, the eye, the arm and even the disposition of individual customers. Anyone buying a Purdey gun and subsequently unable to bring down grouse or pheasant, partridge or ptarmigan, cannot blame the weapon. The fault must lie with the sportsman or sportswoman. If the guns sold here were good enough for George V – allegedly and obsequiously regarded as the finest shot in the country back in the 1920s – then they should be good enough for lesser mortals, modern Frank Bucks and Annie Oakleys.

Purdey's sell everything to do with the sport of shooting. Here you can buy gun stocks and gun barrels; game books, in which to record your slaughter; ready-made cartridges and hand-loading cartridge machines to make your own; rolls of what the army used to call "regulation flannelette", a soft fabric that you tear into small pieces about the size of a business card and use to clean the inside of your gun barrel. The only shooting accessory that they don't sell are Labrador dogs, to retrieve whatever you bring down.

Henry Maxwell and Company Limited

If the blood lust is really on you, then you might like to visit Henry Maxwell's, just a few doors down South

Audley Street and on the other side of the road. Here you can buy hunting pink, the bright red jackets beloved of those who follow hounds in pursuit of the fox. They're very smart, and if fox-hunting might be abolished in Britain, there's no reason why gentlemen shouldn't wear them to parties.

Maxwell's was founded in 1750, and they proudly display in their window that they were boot- and shoemakers by appointment to Don Alfonso XIII, King of Spain. He may well have found their excellent footwear useful and comfortable when he fled from Madrid on a warm spring night in April 1931.

top:
What the well dressed huntsman is wearing – the interior of Holland and Holland.

One of the gunsmiths at Holland and Holland hand crafts part of a twelve bore shotgun.

The Joys of St James's

One of the pleasantest shopping areas in the West End of London is St James's Street, a wide avenue that sweeps down from the Ritz in Piccadilly to Pall Mall and St James's Palace. This is the heart of London's clubland, but that is a private world, and a more accessible way of passing the time is to visit one, or all, of the old shops. There's D.R. Harris, a chemist's which has been in the same premises since 1790; James J. Fox, the cigar merchants; and Justerini and Brooks, wine merchants for some 200 years.

The richest gems in the St James's Street collection are to be found clustered together at the bottom end of the street, on the east side. Here, in 1698, the Widow Bourne opened a grocer's where, among other goods, she sold coffee – you can see the sign hanging outside No. 3 St James's Street today. Her daughter married a painter-stainer called William Pickering, after whom Pickering Place (to the rear of No. 3) was named. It's a delightful little square, the smallest in London.

And today, the most famous shops in St James's Street are to be found at No. 3, No. 6 and No. 9.

far right:
For centuries the feet of ladies and gentlemen have beaten a path to this door – Lock and Company of St James's Street…
below:
… while a few doors away lie the alcoholic wonders of Berry Brothers.

No. 3: Berry Brothers and Rudd

Towards the end of the 18th century, John Berry came to London from Exeter, where he had been a wine merchant. He took over the shop at No. 3 when St James's was the centre of the *beau monde* – powerful politicians, witty writers, elegant women and stiff-necked nobility. Berry built up an impressive list of clients: Byron, Beau Brummell, Pitt, Peel, Charles Lamb, Charles James Fox, Nelson, the Duke of Wellington and many others. They came to buy his wonderful clarets, and to be weighed on a set of scales that is still in use today, for the famous watched their weight with just as much concern then as they do now.

In the shop you can see the beautiful leatherbound books in which customers' weights have been recorded for over 200 years. There are eight volumes for male customers, but only one for females.

For some 50 years Berry and his family also sold tea and coffee, but from around 1850 they concentrated on wine. The cellars grew, and now stretch right under St James's Street and Pickering Place down as far as Pall Mall itself, housing some 216,000 bottles of wine, brandy and port. In the late 1830s, Prince Louis Napoleon, later the Emperor Napoleon III, plotted his political coups and stored hundreds of proclamations in these cellars.

There are still thousands of bottles of the finest wines imaginable in the cellars – and they're quite happy to sell you just one. Go there, and indulge yourself.

No. 6: Lock and Company

James Lock came from a family of tobacco and coffee importers who settled in St James's to escape the City after the horrors of the Great Plague of 1665 and the fire of 1666. In 1759, Lock inherited a hatter's shop which

had been established in 1676, and the business has been there ever since.

Over the years, Lock's have sold all manner of hats – livery hats for servants, riding hats for ladies, Blenheims (first worn by the Duke of Marlborough), "Anthony Edens", "Rex Harrisons", and the redoubtable bowler. The original bowler was a domed hat, hardened by shellac, created by a progressive farmer named Coke of Holkham to protect the heads of his gamekeepers from overhanging branches on his estate. The prototype hat was made by Thomas and William Bowler in their workshop at Southwark, and then brought to Lock's to be tested by Coke himself. There is no record of which tree provided the overhanging bough.

The rich and famous have all bought their headgear at Lock's. Lord Nelson ordered a special cocked hat with a fitted eyeshade here, and took it with him to Trafalgar. You can see it today on his effigy in Westminster Abbey. The Duke of Wellington wore a cocked hat supplied by Lock's at the battle of Waterloo.

Today the hats are more peaceful, but the shop is much as it has been since the 17th century.

No. 9: John Lobb

John Lobb, Bootmaker, has been described as "the most beautiful shop in the world". The business was established in Victorian times by John Lobb, ironically a lame

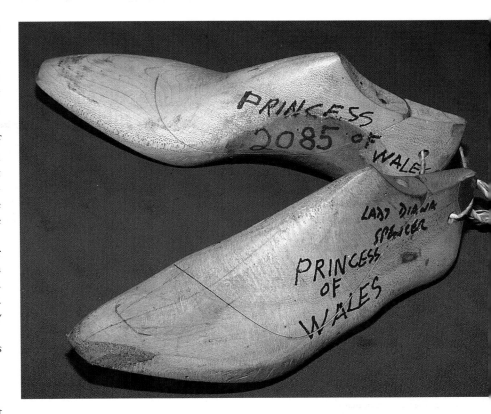

Cornish farm boy who became bootmaker to Edward, Prince of Wales. From that moment, the rich and famous queued to be shod: Caruso, Andrew Carnegie, Marconi, George Bernard Shaw, Cole Porter, Groucho Marx, Frank Sinatra, the Duke of Windsor and thousands more.

Buying a pair of shoes at Lobb's is an experience. It begins when a fitter notes the exact dimensions of both your feet, and makes detailed tracings of them for the last-maker. The last-maker fashions complete models of your feet in maple, beech or hornbeam wood. A clicker then selects and cuts the leather for the shoes, and hands this over to the closer, who stitches the uppers together. The maker fits the uppers to soles of best English tanned oak-bark leather. Finally the polisher buffs the shoes until they dazzle the eye.

The shoes will cost a considerable amount of money. They will last a very long time.

To fit the feet of a modern Cinderella. The shoemaker's lasts for Diana, Princess of Wales – one of the hundreds of pairs of lasts for famous former customers of John Lobb.
below:
Guiseppi has been hand making shoes at Lobbs for over thirty years.

left:
Made to order for a discerning clientele – the hands of a hat-maker at Lock and Company.

One of the World's Greatest Booksellers

It is said that you are never more than 30 feet from a rat in London – which is not a great advertisement for the penthouse suites in expensive hotels. Certainly you're rarely more than 30 feet from a bookseller. You can buy books from railway station kiosks, department stores, trestle tables under the arches of Waterloo bridge, stalls in Portobello Road or Clerkenwell Market, almost every shop in Charing Cross Road, libraries, supermarkets, gift and souvenir shops, museums and galleries, churches and garages, and the Stationery Office in Kingsway.

Hatchard's in Piccadilly isn't the biggest bookstore in London – that honour belongs to Foyles in Charing Cross Road – but it is the oldest, and, to many, the best.

Every good bookshop has its own powers of seduction, slowing your gait as you walk by, until you are compelled to stop and look at the window. And then you begin to search your mind – wasn't there a book recently published that you had been meaning to buy. Hatchard's will have that book, and the staff will know about it. One of them will have read it, or read of it. Or maybe there

was a book published years ago, possibly still in print. Hatchard's will find that book, and quickly. It's a bookshop with the stock of a supermarket, but the service of an enthusiast.

It was founded by John Hatchard in 1797, five doors away from its present position. On 30 June he wrote in his journal: "This day by the Grace of God, the Goodwill of my Friends and £5 in my pocket I have opened my shop in Piccadilly." He had started life as an apprentice to Mr Ginger, a publisher who sold books from a coffee shop on the site of the National Gallery in Trafalgar Square. Some 15 years later, Hatchard believed he had learnt all he needed to know about selling books.

From the very beginning, the shop established a reputation as booksellers to the rich and royal, though Hatchard subsidized his business by writing and selling pamphlets. Piccadilly was a smart and fashionable area. You can still get some idea of what it must have looked like if you go there very early on a summer's morning, before the traffic begins to get snarled up along it. Stop by Burlington House, once one of several large private houses in the street. Look across the road at Hatchard's and at Fortnum's. They were both there 200 years ago.

In 1810, the wit and writer Sydney Smith recorded: "There is a sort of well-dressed prosperous gentleman who assembles daily at Mr Hatchard's shop, clean, civil personages well in with people in power."

Today you may well see more women than men buying books there – and you don't have to be prosperous to go in and browse. Like any good bookshop, it has always been a civilized place. Here many British prime ministers have shopped for books. The Duke of Wellington used to ride his horse down Piccadilly from Apsley House, dismount, stride through the shop to the back room, bark out his orders for books, and stride out again. William Wilberforce used the shop for meetings of the Anti-Slavery Society. Among regular customers have been Macaulay, Byron, Thackeray and George Bernard Shaw. Cecil Rhodes was a difficult customer, who demanded that Hatchard's translate all the Roman authors used by Edward Gibbon as sources for *Decline and Fall of the Roman Empire*. It took the staff six years to comply. Oscar Wilde and Lord Alfred Douglas were frequent visitors, as were Kipling, Chesterton and Virginia Woolf – and almost all leading British writers today.

Signing Sessions

Crowds gather in and around Hatchard's when authors and celebrities arrive to sign copies of their books. A queue stretched down the entire length of Piccadilly while Bette Davis chain-smoked her way through a signing session of her autobiography, and her fans grabbed the cigarette stubs as souvenirs. Ginger Rogers brought traffic to a halt. Twiggy attracted a crowd that pressed so eagerly upon her, she fled.

Margaret Thatcher, General Colin Powell and Oliver North brought vast numbers of admirers, critics, and the curious. The followers of Arthur Miller, Salman Rushdie and Umberto Eco were of a more literary and discreet nature. The record for the most books signed in a day at Hatchard's is held by Sir Alec Rose, the yachtsman. He signed 1250 copies in a single session.

Books and Flowers

On 7 March 1804, seven men gathered in the back room at Hatchard's. Among their number were John Wedgwood, of the famous pottery family, and Sir Joseph Banks, President of the Royal Society and the man who had sailed as botanist to Captain Cook's Australian expedition. The seven shared an interest in plants, and that spring day they founded the Royal Horticultural

Society. And that is why, each year, two centuries later, visitors to the Chelsea Flower Show will find Hatchard's in attendance, with a vast display of books on gardening.

Young legs have to find their way to the top floor for the children's book department at Hatchard's. Older legs may prefer the lift.

Two London Grocers

Fortnum and Mason have been selling fine things to eat and drink for over 200 years. The store was opened in 1770, on a site very near the present one at 181 Piccadilly. The founders were Mr Fortnum and Mr Mason, and every hour on the hour you can see their likenesses parade above the main entrance to the store. All you have to do is look up at the clock, and they emerge, circling round and bowing politely to each other.

The Founders

Charles Fortnum was originally a footman in service to George III. One of his duties was to place new candles in the numerous royal candelabras, and, being a resourceful man, he decided to augment his wages by selling the old candle-ends to Queen Charlotte's Ladies-in-Waiting. Fortnum learnt a great deal about the tastes of the royal household, and when he retired, he made good use of his palace connections.

John Mason was a friend and an astute businessman. He realized that the rich and idle would prefer to have their purchases delivered to them, so he set up a stables nearby, housing horses and wagons. Mason's Yard – just behind the store – was named after him.

Supply and Demand

Two hundred years ago Fortnum's sold "Hart's Horn", "Gable Worm Seed", or "Dirty White Candy", and a fine sweetened cocoa powder – Sir Edward Parry took 220 pounds (100 kg) of it with him when he set out to discover the Northwest Passage in 1819. Army officers took special hampers of Fortnum's delicacies when they were posted overseas. An entire department of the store was engaged in attending to the needs of the many gentlemen's clubs to be found in nearby St James's. Queen Victoria commanded Fortnum's to send a vast consignment of beef tea to Florence Nightingale in the Crimea, during the war with Russia in the 1850s. A generation later, Mr Heinz entered the store and bought the entire stock of his own, newly invented, tinned goods.

The Store

It is best to go to Fortnum's early in the morning, before it becomes crowded. In the restful green and white environment, you can saunter from counter to counter, selecting a packet of Bath Oliver biscuits, some Gentlemen's Relish, a packet of the best Earl Grey tea, an extravagantly priced bottle of Armagnac. Sadly, you can no longer buy chocolate-covered ants, or jars of locusts in honey – these delicacies have been swept aside by the blunter tastes of the late 20th century. Then visit one of the three eating places in the store, where you will see children tucking into monster ices in large chunky glass dishes, or elderly folk scoffing sandwiches that look as though they've been designed rather than made. You may even see women using powder compacts.

The staff are still dressed as though for a funeral.

Martyn's of Muswell Hill

Just a few miles north of Fortnum's, in Muswell Hill Broadway, is W. Martyn. It's a small grocer's shop, roughly five yards wide and ten deep, that could easily fit into a single corner of Fortnum's. Martyn's is very special, because its interior has hardly changed at all since it opened in 1897.

The windows are stuffed with baskets of golden sultanas, cashews, walnuts, dates, figs, and packets of cranberry and orange stuffing. There are jars of apricots in Amaretto, lemon and coriander sauce, green peppercorn sauce, malt whisky mustard and lime curd. There are bottles of hazelnut oil, fish marinade and Staffordshire sludge salad dressing. As you walk in you are greeted by the smell of roasting coffee, the sound of your steps on plain wooden floorboards, and the sight of dark wood shelves stocked from floor to ceiling with the splendours of past and present grocery.

A photograph of the founder, William Martyn, gazes down on a beautiful set of scales that has weighed coffee, rice, sugar, flour and a thousand delights since the 1930s. In one corner sacks of green coffee beans snuggle together: Santos, Mysore, Java, Colombia, Kenya. Fat little jars tempt you with sweets – acid drops, brown humbugs, traditional Black Bullets. There are bigger jars of mandarins in Grand Marnier, pickled walnuts with port, Bramley apple sauce. Next to the tins of Highlander's Broth, pheasant consommé and Royal Windsor soup, there are packets of lemon biscuits, Wilson's shortbread and English spice biscuits.

The lower shelves are propped up on ancient biscuit tins that look as though they have been there since Queen Victoria's Diamond Jubilee. Along the top shelves there are large storage tins, numbered from 1 to 24. Once upon a time these contained all the bulk items – sugar, flour, rice and tea. Look carefully along the shelves towards the rear of the shop and you will see the ridges worn in the wood by the sliding of these tins off and on to the shelves over 60 or more years.

It's a long way to Muswell Hill from the West End, but the journey is well worth the effort.

opposite:
The finest of provisions in the finest of settings – inside Fortnum and Mason's.

Piccadilly Circus

All sorts of places used to lay claim to being the Heart of the British Empire. To most Londoners, the only Empire left is the one in Leicester Square, but many tourists and all ex-patriot members of the civil and military services accept that Piccadilly Circus was the centre-point of the empire on which the sun never set, in other words "The Centre of the World". Less romantically, Paul Morand, a French visitor in the 1930s, called it "the navel of London".

Piccadilly is a strange name. If you know what it means and its origin, then you are ahead of 99% of Londoners. In the early 17th century, a tailor named Robert Baker worked in The Strand. He designed a stiff collar, called a "picadil", which became the height of fashion in the reign of James I. Having made his fortune, Baker bought land to the north of what is now Piccadilly Circus, and built a house there which those resentful of his success called Piccadilly House. The name became applied to the area in general in the 18th century.

The original Circus was designed by John Nash in 1819. Formerly it had been a simple crossroads, but Nash brought the sweep of Regent Street round to make a complete circle. The Circus was then wider and grander than it is now, but the Metropolitan Board of Works made a mess of it in the 1880s when they knocked down the buildings in the northeast segment of the Circus to make way for Shaftesbury Avenue. They also granted to the new buildings leases which had no restrictions on advertising, unlike the original Crown leases.

And so, in 1910, the happy landlords allowed the firms of Bovril and Schweppes to erect the first of the giant electric signs for which Piccadilly Circus became famous. Before the Second World War, Piccadilly Circus was a colourful mixture of cafés and oyster bars, theatres, shops and flower-sellers, and what many regarded as the loveliest statue in the capital. It was that mixture of toffs and their working-class skivvies that nostalgia freaks adore.

But, with the exception of the southern edge, the Circus has steadily slipped down-market. The western side used to be the home of the St James's Hall, where Wagner once conducted and where Dickens gave his last public reading in 1870. Then it became Swan and Edgar's, a fine department store. Now it's Tower Records: the façade is much the same, but inside horrible

A meeting place for visitors to London for over a hundred years – Piccadilly Circus.

half-floors and mezzanines have been created, so that you feel you're on a strange cargo ship loaded with CDs.

Eros

The statue in the middle of Piccadilly Circus is one of London's oddities. It was erected "by public donations" in memory of the reputedly kind old seventh Earl of Shaftesbury – a man who did much for the health and well-being of many. It was the first London statue to be cast in aluminium, but it was supposed to be of the Christian Spirit of Charity, not the heathen God of Love. It was also supposed to have a large fountain coming out of it, but it was placed in a tub so small that the water from the fountain splashed all the passers-by.

While the Duke of Westminster was unveiling Eros in 1893, the Duchess sipped water from one of the metal drinking cups, until it was snatched by a thief who ran off with it. *Punch* magazine hated it, and called it "A London Pest": "Some have called it a girl, some have called it a boy; many of the public, no doubt, regard it as a mythological bird...".

In the 1920s the statue was moved to Embankment Gardens while Piccadilly tube station was excavated and built. Poor Eros then spent all the Second World War in Egham, Surrey, and many years after it lying on a mattress in a dark little room in County Hall.

When Eros was finally replaced in position, he ended up facing the wrong way. Eros and his bow are supposed to point to the northeast, up Shaftesbury Avenue, in memory of the dear old Earl, not southwestwards in a slightly cockeyed manner down Lower Regent Street.

Albany

Situated between the north side of Piccadilly and Vigo Street where it joins Burlington Gardens is Albany, a set of bachelor chambers – unless you want to appear a complete duffer, you must call it simply "Albany", not "The Albany". It was originally the home of Lord Melbourne, but in 1802 it was sold to a young builder named Alexander Copland, who converted it into some 60 separate establishments.

It has always been a fashionable address. Residents have included Palmerston, Gladstone, Sir Thomas Beecham, Henry Fox Talbot (the pioneer of photography), Dame Edith Evans (women were admitted after the First World War), Edward Heath and Lord Macaulay. Byron also lived here, his table piled high with books, a macaw and a crucifix, while he nibbled biscuits and Lady Caroline Lamb's ear. She used to visit him disguised as a manservant, which probably added a lot to the fun they had together.

The floodlit statue of Eros. The wary or the hopeful will note that he has already loosed his arrow.

Early Morning London

A spring morning, 5 am

The sky is still grey, and the early commuters have their car headlights on. Milkmen are stooping to leave milk, juice, yoghurt and eggs on a million doorsteps in the suburbs. The first buses, trains and tubes rumble in and out of town. Office cleaners, who have already finished their day's work, are sleeping their way home. There's birdsong in the leafy avenues of suburbia, but silence in the centre of the city.

6 am

A steady trickle of workers seeps into London. Lights are on in newspaper offices, but the shops are shuttered, empty and dark. Delivery vans have the streets all to themselves. Refuse carts block narrow lanes while their crews collect the plastic sacks of rubbish, and there's no following vehicle to scream its protest at being delayed. The bars and the cafés are closed, chairs stacked on tables, jukeboxes and video consoles silent and powerless. In office windows the hat-stands and coat-stands are naked.

The massive wooden west doors of St Paul's cathedral are shut tight, for Morning Prayers do not start until 7.30. The Central Criminal Court is locked up. Its wrought iron gates make it look like a dark medieval dungeon.

6.15

The busiest places are the wholesale markets of London – they've been working for hours at New Covent Garden, Billingsgate and London Bridge.

In Smithfield, fleets of white vans and refrigerated lorries are loaded with meat. White-coated porters drag trolleys piled high with plastic sacks containing everything from calves' heads to pigs' trotters, from oxtails to turkey gizzards.

Hospitals never sleep, but the outpatients' department in nearby St Bartholomew's Hospital won't be open for another two hours yet.

6.45

Coffee and sandwich bars are opening around Holborn. Floors are swept, water put on to boil, boxes of croissants, rolls and sliced loaves are unpacked. Half the workforce of London will be demanding takeaway cappuccino and toast in the next couple of hours.

Cars speed in, enjoying the clear streets, the prospect of another hour and a half of free parking, and hundreds of empty spaces. The street sleepers who have spent the night in doorways begin to stir, stretch and fold their wafer-thin blankets. Very soon staff and customers will be barging through the doorways where the homeless have spent the night.

7 am

All is still and quiet in the land of the lawyers, the solid grandeur of Bedford Row and Gray's Inn. No one will be required in court until 10 am at the earliest. A large

marmalade cat sleeps in the window of a barber's shop just to the east of Red Lion Square. Pigeons are waddling safely along streets that will be humming with traffic in an hour's time.

7.15

Soho Square is empty, wet from overnight rain. The restaurants of Greek Street and Dean Street look dark, cold and deserted. The Webshack Internet Café is closed, but the mobile phones are out already in Wardour Street.

A young man in turquoise overalls and a pink baseball cap lopes along Broadwick Street, followed by a pinched-faced young woman wrapped in a grubby sleeping bag but still looking frozen. The man stops a hurrying worker and asks if he's interested in classical music. The young man has two cardboard boxes of LPs, that he got from "a mate". The worker isn't interested, but gives the young man £2 anyway. The young man and young woman appear pathetically grateful.

7.30

Just as Smithfield is beginning to pack up, stallholders are setting out their wares in the fruit and vegetable market of Berwick Street. London is like the world – just as one area goes to bed, another is waking up.

One of the staff at "Simply Sausages" fills the shop window with 24 gleaming stainless steel bowls, and then hurls different-flavoured sausages, one by one, into each bowl. Through the plate glass window you can hear the thud of the sausages as they land.

A water cart sprays the pavements of Kemp's Court, and a road sweeper does his best to make Livonia Street clean and tidy.

7.45

A shop assistant arrives for work at J.D. Sports, Oxford Street, on a mountain bike, and cycles straight into the shop. Sales staff who work in the large stores cluster together outside, waiting for the doors to open. To the north of Oxford Street, in the heart of the "rag trade" district, things are much quieter.

And even at this comparatively late hour, men and women are wheeling vacuum cleaners along the pavements, dashing from office to office in a last-minute frenzy of cleaning.

A brimstone butterfly blows along Great Portland Street.

8 am

Crowded trains arrive at the major London stations. Commuters from Brighton and the Cotswolds, from the dormitory towns of Surrey and Essex, from Croydon and Crawley stride to the tube, to the nearest bus stop or out on to the street. Marching feet tramp over London Bridge, along Cannon Street, across Euston Street.

The peace of early morning London gives way to the rush hour.

from left to right:
The first postal delivery of the morning; an early bus collecting members of the workforce; a stallholder heading for his pitch; commuters hurrying to work.

Late Night London

Few trains leave London after midnight or before 5 am, so any late night revellers in the West End must aim to have enough money left in their pockets by the end of the evening to take a taxi home. There are night bus services from central London to most points of the compass, but the service is skeletal and hourly.

Midnight

The rain is falling steadily and vertically. At bus stops and on station concourses couples bid each other hasty and sodden "goodbyes".

In the suburbs, the only commercial premises still lit are minicab offices, Indian takeaways and the occasional fish and chip shop. The pubs are closed. Last orders were taken an hour ago. The pool cues are back in the racks, the glasses are back on the shelves. The City is still and quiet. It was locked up hours ago. The theatregoers in the West End have long since snuggled into coaches that have whisked them back to the Home Counties. Shopfitters are frantically at work – fitting counters and cupboards ready for the morning trade. A bag lady stops and leans on her bulging shopping trolleys to watch them work.

The dossers and the homeless are trying to keep themselves warm and their tobacco dry in doorways along The Strand. A few people are still seeking fun, but the bouncers in suits and bow ties outside Stringfellow's nightclub and the Long Island Iced Tea Shop make sure that they have to look for it elsewhere.

A busker is playing the theme from *The Godfather* on an alto saxophone under a dripping canopy in Charing Cross Road. There's still a little fun to be had in Chinatown and the rest of Soho, though the waiters and chefs in the restaurants that remain open might not agree.

A group of drunks meander their way in a direction that leads nowhere. The quick-sketch artists are folding their easels and stools and creeping away from Leicester Square. But there are crowds outside the Fashion Café and SegaWorld in Coventry Street, and a small knot of youths are craning their necks to see what is happening at Planet Hollywood. In cafés and late-night coffee bars, managers are counting the evening's take.

At Rock Circus, there's still a chance to buy tights and hairbands, CDs and videos, sweets and lollipops – odd fare for after-dinner munching. Most of the customers are young, and happy despite the rain, though they hurriedly get out of the way of a hugely fat older man who has shed his flip-flops (too treacherous on the soaking pavements) and is walking barefoot.

12.15

A workman is welding railings together in Rupert Street. Traffic floods past the twenty-four-hour store in Shaftesbury Avenue. There are no takers for the striptease shows in Brewer Street, and no browsers in the Soho Bookshop. The last of the revellers begin to drift away. It's too wet even for the young.

12.30

In Oxford Street, a cleaner for the Westminster City Council is steaming chewing-gum off the pavements

with a high-pressure jet, which sends a cloud of mist billowing into the street. He's dressed in lime-green waterproof leggings and a yellow sou'wester. As a gust of wind blows the steam away, his figure emerges like something from Close Encounters of the Third Kind. A total stranger in drenched T-shirt and jogging trousers comes up, shakes hands and says: "You're a great man." Then he kneels before the man steaming chewing-gum off the pavement.

12.45

Dust carts are out in Carnaby Street, picking up the plastic sacks that gleam with rainwater and the rapidly disintegrating cardboard boxes full of rubbish. A police car goes flashing and screaming down Regent Street. Somebody, somewhere, has found the energy to do something wrong. The massive bronze doors of the Café Royal are firmly shut.

Someone is moving office in Little Swallow Street. Two giant pantechnicons bar the way to all other traffic.

1 am

Piccadilly Circus. Water, water everywhere. The rain splashes down in the fountains beneath the statue of Eros and in the fountains of the Horses of Helios at the corner of Coventry Street and the Haymarket. More police cars race down Great Windmill Street on their way to the Crime of the Night.

They've blown the final whistle at the Football Football Restaurant, but a few customers remain at the Sports Café a few doors down, and McDonald's is still going strong. The homeless now sleep uneasily in the doorways, and you feel you should tiptoe by.

1.15

At a little stall outside the National Gallery, a hot-dog seller is frying onions and hoping to attract customers. A young man greets the entire queue waiting for a night bus, and insists on shaking hands with everyone – is this a night of international friendship? Charing Cross Station is shut, so it's time to join another queue for another night bus, in Trafalgar Square. Eventually the bus arrives, and its sleepy contingent shuffle aboard. One or two are eating hot dogs – the stallholder's patience has been rewarded. There's a smell of beer, sweat, disappointment and tiredness, and the windows of the bus steam up as it belts across the river.

Halfway down the Old Kent Road, a young man is throwing pebbles at an upstairs window. But it is not, and never has been, a night for love.

from left to right:
Savile Row Police Station; The Empire, Leicester Square; Tower Records, Piccadilly Circus; and a late night busker.

Down and Out in London

As with most old cities, while the well-to-do developed the commercial and residential heart of London, the poor arrived in increasing numbers.

A long time ago, when the nobles and merchants built fine houses, they employed plenty of servants, and the workshops of craftsmen and traders provided homes for apprentices and workers. However, the growing wealth of the capital wasn't meant to attract those without money.

Yet it always has. For hundreds of years those with no money but plenty of hope have made their way to a city whose streets were reputedly paved with gold. In the words of the traditional song:

> Oh, Molly, this London's a wonderful sight
> Where the people are working by day and by night.
> They don't plant potatoes or barley or wheat,
> But there's gangs of them digging for gold in the street...

Such myths have long been exploded, but the penniless still flock to London. At first they seek work, adventure, excitement. After a while they simply blink through bloodshot, rheumy eyes, looking for a vacant doorway or the steps leading down to a church shelter.

There are tens of thousands of homeless people in London. Most of them are young, all are much younger than they look. A visitor could walk through miles of London without coming across any of them, but one evening in the West End is enough to reveal their presence. Turn the corner from, say, a brightly lit film première in Leicester Square, attended by members of the Royal Family, and there they are – grimy blankets thrown over rank sleeping bags, a bundle of rags that houses a human being.

Many of them have thin, whimpering, shivering dogs for company. Some stalk the streets swathed in bundles of rags and scraps of plastic sheeting. There is one particular hero who patrols the South Bank, fatter than the Michelin Man, wild as the Yeti. His home is a windswept corner of concrete halfway between the Festival Hall and the National Theatre. He asks for no money. How he exists is a savage mystery.

For centuries there has been a misconception that many London beggars are in fact making a good living. In 1784, Archenholz, a German traveller, believed they were making up to five shillings a day (almost a month's wages for a servant). One hundred and fifty years later, little seemed to have changed when George Orwell wrote *Down and Out in Paris and London*: "The stories in the Sunday papers about beggars who die with £2000 sewn into their trousers are, of course, lies." In the late 1990s I saw a sign in the entrance to Waterloo Station urging passengers not to give money to beggars: "many of them", it said, "may be earning more than you do." I doubt it.

Cardboard City

The epicentre of vagrancy in London used to be Cardboard City, a ramshackle collection of boxes and pallets, rags and polythene sheets in the Bull Ring at

Waterloo. At night it was always a creepy and slightly sinister place. Commuters and visitors tended to quicken their steps as they walked through it, an irrational fear suggesting that the poorer people are, the more desperate and dangerous they must be. But the inhabitants of Cardboard City were more likely to squabble among themselves than seek confrontation with a stranger.

The Bull Ring has been developed, and a cinema complex now stands where the charity vans drove down bringing soup and bread, the traditional fare of the destitute. The homeless have drifted away, seeking other concrete backwaters of London in which to make their illegal fires of reeking pinewood, to wrap themselves in blankets and curl up on a bed of rags in a cardboard box that holds about a cubic metre of foetid air. And to hope that, this time, development will leave them alone.

Begging

Most London beggars don't have to be on the streets long to know whence help is most likely to come. The smart City gent with his pinstripe suit (worth several hundred pounds) and his shiny shoes (perhaps another hundred) is unlikely to give them anything. Women are more sympathetic than men, and middle-aged, middle-class left-of-centre Guardian readers are probably the best bet for a 50p piece.

Orwell summed up the beggar's role in society with the sort of compassion you don't always expect from an Old Etonian: "People seem to feel that there is some essential difference between beggars and ordinary working men [he was writing in the early 1930s]. They are a race apart – like criminals and prostitutes.... Yet if one looks closely, one sees that there is no essential difference between a beggar's livelihood and that of numerous respectable people... A navvy works by swinging a pick. An accountant works by adding up figures. A beggar works by standing out of doors in all weathers and getting varicose veins, chronic bronchitis, etc." Not many people agreed with Orwell then; not many, I guess, would today. But the beggars do remind us, very graphically, that there is such a thing as abject poverty in our wonderful modern world.

Art and hunger on the South Bank – one of London's homeless shelters by the Royal Festival Hall.
opposite:
Getting the message out on to the streets – one of London's many sellers of *The Big Issue*.

Eating in the West End – Where to Go

The modern trend in London, as in many other cities, is to turn cooking into theatre and chefs into actors. New restaurants are like palaces of food, places where you may catch a glimpse of the kitchen crew sweating away on your behalf, which seems faintly reminiscent of the worst excesses of the Roman Empire. In all these much-vaunted restaurants it is taken for granted that the food will be a delight. What matters, therefore, in these days when up to £3 million is spent on the design of a single restaurant, is the lighting, the staging, the drama.

This is what tempts many of the rich to the Four Seasons, The Ivy, Le Gavroche, Mezzo, the refurbished Quaglino's, Le Caprice and many others. This, and a chance to play "spot the celebrity – or even better, "sit next to the celebrity". New York and Los Angeles house-rules now operate in top-rank London restaurants. There are "A" and "B" lists of customers. The "A" list is of those people the smart restaurant would like to serve. The "B" list is of those people it is prepared to serve. The

top right:
A fish and chip shop in Marylebone.
below:
Fondly nicknamed 'a greasy spoon cafe' – this one is at the Angel, Islington.

rest of us would do better to go to a less pretentious and far cheaper eating place, but perhaps it is thrilling to watch someone spend £10,000 on a dinner for three, of which £5000 alone goes on a bottle of wine.

There is still a good case to be made for dining at one of the grand hotels of London – the Connaught, the Savoy, Claridge's or the Ritz. There are those who say that the most romantic place to eat in London is the Louis XVI room at the Ritz. The River Restaurant at the Savoy has a fine view of the Thames that has been enjoyed by the famous since the great Escoffier first ruled the kitchen there in the 1880s.

If money is no object and you are happy to book months in advance, the best view of the Thames from any restaurant is that from the Oxo Tower, which has a terrace 250 feet (75 metres) long and spectacular designs on its sheet-glass walls.

Old Favourites – New Favourites

Whatever newcomers appear on the scene, there are many West End restaurants which have stood the test of time and are still much loved by diners. Sheekey's is in the heart of theatreland at St Martin's Court. It has fine fish dishes and offers the chance of seeing real actors (as opposed to chefs) feasting and unwinding after their evening performance. Wheeler's in Old Compton Street and in Duke of York Street, Bentley's in Swallow Street and Wilton's in Jermyn Street also have all that could delight those with a taste for fish.

The Criterion in Piccadilly Circus is 125 years old and still manages to convince some restaurant critics that it is the "sexiest room in London". L'Escargot in Greek Street may be less sexy, but the main ingredient of its "snail tart with smoked bacon" was once regarded as an aphrodisiac.

Among newcomers, Mezzo is exciting and huge, but not quite big enough for the number of people who wish to dine there. Other newcomers (such as the Saint in

Great Newport Street) make life difficult for some would-be diners by imposing a dress code that says "No Suits Allowed". L'Oranger in St James's Street has a lovely terrace, and The Avenue, nearby, is said to be good for posing. You may care to try the "salad of pig's trotters and black pudding with a sauce gribiche" at Hollihead in Wigmore Street.

Simpson's-in-the-Strand

If you want to eat traditional British food in a traditional London setting, then there is really only one place to go. Simpson's started life as the Grand Divan Cigar, a "home of chess", opened by Mr Reiss in 1818. Thirty years later, Mr Simpson joined Mr Reiss and they reopened the premises as Simpson's Divan and Tavern.

The first culinary adviser was Alexis Soyer, the most famous chef of the day, who fled to London during the French revolution of 1830. It was Soyer who established the tradition of serving joints of roast beef and saddles of mutton at Simpson's, wheeled in on a dinner wagon.

The old building was knocked down when The Strand was widened in 1900, but re-opened under Savoy Hotel management four years later. The present interior is much as the old building was in 1848. You can still get excellent beef and lamb from the trolleys, and duck if you prefer. The meat will be carved for you at the table, so that you can choose the crispy outside, the rarer inside, or even a little more of the fat if you're not frightened of the deadly cholesterol – *o tempora, o mores.*

It has long been the custom at Simpson's to tip the carver after you have been served. Not everyone does this, but regulars do, and it's a good way to impress, or embarrass, your fellow diners.

top left:
Carving from the joint at Simpson's in The Strand.

above:
One of London's gastronomic delights – a pie and mash shop in Ealing.

Eating in the West End – What you Eat

Victorian Londoners with money in their pockets ate roast beef, steak and oyster pie, fried whitebait, eels, whelks, mutton chops and devilled kidneys. They were hearty eaters, with scant regard for vegetables. Public eating places were chop-houses, the dining rooms of pubs and taverns, street stalls and a handful of restaurants. Eating out was for gentlemen; ladies stayed at home.

By Edwardian times, the fashion among the well-to-do was for French food of the *grande cuisine*. Within a couple of generations other nationalities successfully invaded London from the far-flung reaches of the old British Empire, bringing with them a taste for a variety of spicy eastern food. The staple English diet of baked meat and soggy vegetables was relegated to Sunday lunchtime at home.

Today, there are signs that English food is regaining a little of the ground it has lost to the French, Italians, Japanese, Thais, Koreans, Malaysians and many others. In plenty of smart eating places in the West End, you can now pay up to £40 a head for fish and chips or sausage and mash.

Some examples are The Greenhouse in Hay's Mews where you can get faggots and gravy, or braised oxtail (unless it is currently under a government ban). Kedgeree is part of a much praised Sunday brunch at Le Caprice in Arlington Street. They still serve cabbage at Simpson's-in-the-Strand. Beneath the Dickensian prints at Tiddy Dol's in Mayfair, delighted tourists tuck into fisherman's pie or rack of lamb.

top right:
Fish and chips. Modern hygiene demands that a polystyrene tray separates the food from the newspaper it's wrapped in.
below:
The kitchen of the Gandhi Indian restaurant in Fulham.

The big names, however, are still predominantly those restaurants which serve either international cuisine (whatever that means), or what Londoners not so long ago would have described as "foreign food". And that may be anything from a slice of mass-produced pizza to "terrine of foie gras layered with confit pears, accompanied by a salad of beans, artichoke hearts and tomato with truffle oil" (Chez Nico at Ninety, Park Lane).

Not all the best restaurants in London are in the West End, but you can eat almost any type of cooking there: Lebanese, Irish, Hungarian, Russian, modern eclectic, Polish, Mexican, Belgian and dozens more.

You will eat better and pay less outside the West End for Indian, Caribbean and African food, and not all the best Chinese cooking is to be found in Soho's Chinatown.

Eating Cheaply

The only home-bred convenience food in Britain is the sandwich. It was invented (so they say) by the Earl of Sandwich some 200 years ago. His Grace was obsessed with card playing, and one day, not wanting to leave the game to eat, he ordered his servant to bring him a slice of meat between two slices of bread. That day the sandwich was born.

And that's just about what the British sandwich remains today. What you see is what you get. In the West End there are dozens of places where you can buy sandwiches. A few of them offer little more imaginative than variations on the 'cheese and something" theme. Happily, the situation is constantly improving, and there are now several chains which will tailor your sandwich to your taste.

Eating on the Hoof

Londoners are increasingly eating on foot, even in the West End, so that they can devote their lunch break to shopping or – heaven help us – more work. The British in general have never truly valued enjoying a good and

lengthy midday meal. So they stride to and fro, snatching what food they can from the street.

In the West End, Regent Street offers limited rations, but Oxford Street and Piccadilly both have doorway sellers of pizza by the slice. There are unappetizing hot dogs and burgers to be had from stalls in and around Leicester Square. In winter you can buy roast chestnuts on the street; in summer, caramelized nuts, and there are always fruit barrows and ice-cream stalls. In a little bistro in Vigo Street and in Soho, you will find *croque monsieur* and wonderful patisserie. But you will look in vain for a decent, reasonably priced fish and chip shop in the West End. You would do better to go to one of the many *tapas* bars, or to Gaby's in Charing Cross Road, where you may be a little cramped for space, but you will discover the best falafel in town, great pastrami and huge salt-beef sandwiches.

Going Up-Market

If you are prepared to pay more money, then you can eat anything you desire in the West End. Here are just a few dishes to tempt you – all to be found within walking distance of Piccadilly Circus:

West African groundnut stew or Senegalese chicken

above:
The seafood and whelk stall in Brick Lane market.
left:
London food, Spanish style - from a West End tapas bar.

in lemon sauce; dosai, idlee and uthappam; dim sum, abalone or wind-dried meats; stuffed vine leaves or kebabs; bruschetta, panini, wild mushrooms; miso ramen or okonomiyaki; gefilte fish and latkes; walnut-stuffed baby aubergines or lamb shawama; beef rendang, laksa, achar and char kway teow; caldo verde and bacalhau…

Pubs in and around the West End

It's not possible to list all the good pubs in the West End, but we can start with De Hems in Macclesfield Street. It was named after the Dutch sailor who ran it in the 1920s and was a meeting place for the Dutch Resistance in the Second World War. It's one of the best buildings in Soho, with ground-floor windows that open out to embrace the street on warm days and nights. Nearby is the French House, the local for members of the Free French in the 1940s. It's a friendly place, frequented by boozy celebrities, carrying on a tradition that was forged by the likes of Brendan Behan, Jeffrey Bernard and Dylan Thomas (who once left the only manuscript of *Under Milk Wood* here).

In Panton Street, just off Leicester Square, is the Tom Cribb, whose eponymous owner was a bare-knuckle fighter in the 17th century. The pub still has links with boxing, but the cellar is no longer used for cockfights.

The Marquis of Granby in Chandos Place is a wonderful pub – quiet, cool and dark. Claude Duval, a notorious 18th-century highwayman was captured by the Bow Street Runners in this pub, and legend has it that Ian Fleming was drinking here when he thought of the code name 007 for James Bond. Not far away, in Rose Street, just off Garrick Street, is the Lamb and Flag. It's often crowded, but if you can squeeze inside the darkly painted, polished and stained interior you will find good food and good beer.

There are dozens of Red Lions in London. One of the best is in Crown Passage, just off Pall Mall. It's 400 years old, small, charming, and has the second oldest beer licence in London. On the last Saturday in January, modern cavaliers in 17th-century costume meet here to celebrate the memory of Charles I, King and Martyr. His son, Charles II, also had connections with the pub. A secret staircase and tunnel enabled Nell Gwyn to slip across to her royal lover in St James's Palace.

Although the gin shops have all gone, the area around St Giles still has many fine old pubs, including the Plough in Museum Street, long popular with writers and artists, and the Princess Louise in High Holborn, where even the gents' lavatory is the subject of an architectural preservation order. The White Hart in Drury Lane has been a pub since 1201, though it has been extensively restored over the last 800 years. If you fancy something less ancient, there's the Punch and Judy in Covent Garden. The pub takes its name from the nearby site of the first recorded Punch and Judy show in the 1660s. It's a fine all-weather pub, whose customers spill out into the glass-roofed courtyard. There's even a balcony from which you can watch the street performers below.

At one time Ye Olde Cheshire Cheese in Wine Office Court, off Fleet Street, was the most famous pub in London. It's a remarkably well-preserved 17th-century chop-house, a rambling old pub with small, cosy rooms and sawdust-covered floors. The whole place still creaks atmospherically, though the building was underpinned

right:
The Grapes, Mayfair – all that you need from a London pub.
below:
The interior of the Cittie of Yorke in High Holborn.

in 1990. It reeks of the London of Dickens, indeed – it was mentioned in *A Tale of Two Cities*.

Not as old, but more spectacular, is the Cittie of Yorke in High Holborn, once the site of a medieval inn, and later a 17th-century coffee house. Today it has a soaring roof, huge Gothic windows and one of the longest bars in Britain. Brooding magnificently over the bar are enormous wine butts, each of which used to hold 1000 gallons (5470 litres) of wine. The butts have been empty since the 1940s when it was feared that, if a bomb fell and ruptured the barrels, the customers would be drowned in a flood of Burgundy – a delightful way to go. On a cold day you may warm yourself by the pub's unique triangular coal-burning stove – and if you want to know where the smoke from it goes, you'll have to lift the floorboards.

The Seven Stars in Carey Street is one of the few pubs to have survived the Great Fire. It's one of the smallest pubs in London, crammed with charm, and used to be the first port of call for newly declared bankrupts, who would totter over from the Law Courts to drown their sorrows. Across the road from the Law Courts is the George, named not after a king, but after the George who owned it in the 18th century when it was still a coffee house.

Journalists, too, have taken over some of London's finest pubs. In Fleet Street itself there's the Old Bell Tavern, built by Sir Christopher Wren as a hostel for the workmen rebuilding nearby St Bride's Church after the Great Fire. Other pubs linked with the press include the Printer's Devil in Fetter Lane, the Cartoonist in Shoe Lane, and the White Swan in Tudor Lane, known to its regulars as the "Mucky Duck". *Punch* magazine was conceived in the Punch Tavern, Fleet Street, in 1841.

A warm afternoon, a cool pint of beer, and no work for the rest of the day – bliss outside the Lamb and Flag, Rose Street.

Soho

Many people love Soho.

It's a busy, bustling place, whose working population and residents both seem to enjoy the cosmopolitan atmosphere and the profusion of good things to eat from all over the world. It's made up of a couple of dozen streets, a small square, and a number of narrow courts and alleys. There's a daily fruit, vegetable, music and bits-and-pieces market in Berwick Street. Wardour Street is largely devoted to the film industry, advertising and the media in general, though it does also have its proper Soho quota of coffee bars and pubs. Greek Street is full of restaurants.

It would be impossible to starve in Soho. There are eating places everywhere, some of the best in London. Go to Soho for patisserie, bread, chocolate, good wine, the best pasta. It has one of the best butcher's shops in London (Fenn's) and a wonderful fishmonger in Brewer Street. Above all, it serves the finest cups of coffee. The very gutters run cappuccino in Soho.

And you will come across some intriguing oddities, such as a sweep smelter's in Wardour Street.

Soho's History

Over the centuries Soho has become the centre of bohemian London, but it was not always so. In the Middle Ages, Soho was good farmland belonging to the Convent of Abingdon and the Hospital of Burton St Lazar. Henry VIII purloined the land to make part of a royal park for the Palace of Whitehall. Republicans had their revenge 100 years later, when they cut off the head of Charles I outside that same palace.

Most authorities accept that the name "Soho" has its origins in an old hunting call. It was used by the followers of the Duke of Monmouth at Sedgemoor, the last battle fought on English soil, in 1685. The Duke of Monmouth was a Soho resident who lived in a house on the south side of Soho Square. He was also Charles II's illegitimate son, who foolishly sought to enlist the support of Protestants to overthrow his Catholic half-brother James II before James had had time to make himself thoroughly unpopular.

In the late 17th century, hundreds of Huguenot refugees from France settled in Soho, indelibly stamping

Shady street, shady ways. One of Soho's decreasing number of sex boutiques.

a foreign character on the area. By the mid-19th century it was the most densely populated part of London, a wild and colourful mixture of theatres and music halls, shops, cafés and restaurants. The playwright and novelist John Galsworthy described late-19th-century Soho as "untidy, full of Greeks, Ishmaelites, cats, Italians, tomatoes, restaurants, organs, coloured stuffs, queer names, people looking out of upper windows…".

By the early 20th century, Soho was truly cosmopolitan, with Germans, Russians and Poles joining the French, Greeks and Italians. It had a racy air to it, smacking of garlic and licentiousness. In the 1920s and 1930s, advocates of free love and anarchy sat at tables covered with check cloth, watching candles spluttering in the necks of Chianti bottles, munching pasta and rejoicing in their rejection of British culture. It was *La Vie en Rose* transplanted to central London.

By the late 1950s, Soho had become the sex-spot of London. Young lads paced up and down, keen *voyeurs* – if not of the sexual act, at least of the sexual appetite when displayed by others. In groups of two or three, they would prowl round Soho at night, distressed, excited, fascinated and terrified by the streetwalkers and their plaintive call: "D'you fancy a good time, love?"

The Struggle for Soho's Soul

A few years later, Britain underwent one of its periodic reviews of sexual morals. D.H. Lawrence's *Lady Chatterley's Lover* went on trial in 1962, but was found not guilty. The prosecution case was laughed out of court when leading counsel suggested to the jury at the Old Bailey that it was the sort of book they would not wish their servants to read. The 1957 Wolfenden Report recommended the de-criminalization of homosexuality between consenting male adults, and the Street Offences Act of the same year attempted to drive prostitutes from the streets.

As the doorways emptied, near-beer clubs, striptease parlours and clip joints mushroomed in the sleazy cellars of Soho. Visitors to London were the main targets. Sad men from Newcastle or Nagasaki fluttered like moths to the bright lights and the peroxide hostesses, only to be presented at the end of an unfulfilling evening with monstrous bills for coloured water and archly provocative company. The police did more than turn a blind eye. From the mid-1960s until the early 1970s there was neither the will nor the necessary legislation to curb the growth of Soho's lucrative, expensive but tatty exploitation of vice.

All this meant that Soho lost much of its Bohemian charm and became wretchedly seedy. The problem was

The Good (or Bad) Old Days – a Soho brothel in the mid 1950s.

that Soho had lost more than 80% of its resident population in 80 years. The heart had gone out of the area, and there was, seemingly, no one left to care for what had once been a most attractive part of London. Something had to be done, and London owes a great debt to the few remaining residents who got together in 1972 to form the Soho Society. Their aims were twofold – to curb the proliferation of sex outlets and to thwart other plans for commercial development. It took much hard work and determination to rescue Soho and restore its pride. Today a few of the old-style clubs still exist, and small groups of visiting businessmen are still being presented with bills of up to £185 for a round of drinks. But Westminster Council and the Society have co-managed a remarkably successful clean-up act, and Soho is now both civilized and buzzing with excitement. One of the civilizing influences is the large gay community, which has adopted Soho as its capital.

Wardour Street is the centre of the British film industry.

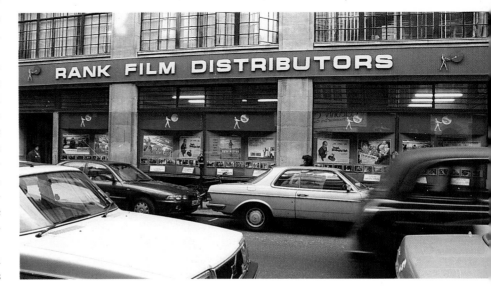

Chinatown

above:
Even the telephone booths have oriental roofs in Chinatown.
below:
Chinese New Year celebrations in Gerrard Street.

In the triangle of land bordered by Coventry Street, Shaftesbury Avenue and Charing Cross Road you will find London's Chinatown. It has never been officially colonized by the Chinese, but eastern infiltration reached such proportions some 25 years ago that even Westminster City Council accepted that there could be no other name for this part of Soho. It was finally and officially designated Chinatown on 29 October 1985. For some unaccountable reason, it was opened by the Duke of Gloucester.

You enter Chinatown as you pass the oriental barrier at the Wardour Street end of Gerrard Street. At once, your nostrils are assailed by the smell of Chinese spices – the air seems full of monosodium glutamate. A few steps along Gerrard Street and you pass under one of the gaudy but impressive archways that mark your entry into Chinatown. They're painted in gold and red, but are best seen at night when they are brightly illuminated. The Chinese characters on all the archways bordering Chinatown were sponsored by the Hong Kong Govern-

ment. The two stone Chinese lions halfway along Gerrard Street were sponsored by the People's Republic of China, but the area seems to owe more to capitalism than communism.

It's a small but busy area, where the street names are all written in Chinese as well as English, and where even the red telephone booths have neo-oriental roofs. There are Chinese pastrycooks, selling steamed cakes, sweet buns, curry beef buns, mixed nut moon cake, coconut and peanut rolls. There are gift shops, displaying on their top shelves mildly pornographic Chinese "girlie" magazines. At the Chinese novelty shops you can buy what look like the worst and cheapest toys in the world.

Eating in Chinatown

The reason why 90% of visitors come to Chinatown is to eat. There are dozens and dozens of restaurants, spilling out of Chinatown proper into Lisle Street, Leicester Square and Upper St Martin's Lane. Steam writhes out of the kitchens with the promise of dim sum. Glazed ducks shine in the windows, some with crispy heads and beaks still attached. The menus outside promise all the Chinese dishes you've ever tried and a great many you probably haven't.

In what was once the house of Paul de Lamarie, the King's silversmith from 1738 to 1751, you can now sample crabmeat with straw mushrooms; mustard greens, shredded pork and egg drop; jellyfish *hors d'oeuvres*; and fresh lobster in black bean sauce. Search further and you will find dishes even more exotic: scallops roll with seaweed and bacon; stir-fried cuttlefish cakes; steamed minced pork with salted duck egg; shark's lips with duck web; fish maw; and fresh dragon whistlers.

If you fancy cooking your own Chinese meal there are supermarkets where you can buy everything from beanshoots to onion flowers, loquat to rice wine, and aniseed by the ton. Go through the barrier at the eastern end of Gerrard Street and you are still in Chinatown. In the centre of Newport Place there is a Chinese fishmonger where you can select your carp from the dozens swimming in large tanks. Opposite is what looks like a tiny Chinese bandstand. It's a very convenient place in which to eat your Chinese takeaway on a warm evening.

If you still haven't found the right Chinese restaurant, you could try Gerrard Place (which used to be called Nassau Street), or Macclesfield Street, or Shaftesbury Avenue itself. And, if you really aren't in the mood for egg foo yong, call in at De Hems, the only Dutch pub in London, where you can get mayonnaise with your chips in the upstairs *t'Oude Trefpunt*.

The Chinese New Year
Every February there are special celebrations in Chinatown for the Chinese New Year. It's usually the coldest month in London, but the bright colours of the prancing dragons or lions and the shimmering costumes of the dancers do much to chase away the winter chill. There are firecrackers, displays, bands of Chinese musicians, acrobats and parades. You don't have to book; in fact it's not easy to discover exactly what will take place. Things simply happen, and crowds gather in an *ad hoc* fashion wherever they want.

The Street of a Thousand Dishes – one of the many Chinese restaurants in Soho.

A Word of Warning
Beware of parking a car in Chinatown late at night. It's a perfectly safe part of London, but the barriers are locked at midnight and not opened again until 6.30 the following morning. You could, therefore, find yourself having to walk home with a stomach full of eel with garlic and chilli, suckling pig, spare ribs and deep-fried wan ton.

left:
Dancing dragons bring in the Chinese New Year in Soho.

Westminster

Who Rules London?

The City of London has been ruled by a succession of Lord Mayors and a Court of Aldermen for centuries. The court meets some 12 to 15 times a year in its own court-room, or sometimes in the Mansion House. The aldermen are elected for life, although since 1977 that has meant until the age of 70. A candidate must already be a Freeman of the City, and, even if elected, he can be rejected by his fellow aldermen. The aldermen are also Justices of the Peace, sitting in judgement in both the Mansion House and the Guildhall. They have always been a proud and powerful group of people – still today, the monarch has to ask permission before he or she can enter the City of London.

Government of the rest of London has had a far more complicated and chequered history. The problem has long been to develop happy working relationships between central government (whether king or parliament) and London government, and between central London government and the separate local boroughs. One of the major causes of the English Civil War of 1642 to 1651 was the enmity that existed between Charles I and London.

For hundreds of years, London was run by "vestries" – small units of householders who met in the vestry of their local parish church. By the mid-19th century, however, it was clear that London needed a more centralized government. The rich vestries of the West End opposed such a move. The poor vestries of the East End supported it, and prevailed.

The Metropolitan Board of Works

The Metropolitan Board of Works was established by the Metropolis Management Act of 1855. It was the first London-wide authority. Although the Board achieved some lasting successes (excavating the vast main drainage system of London; building the Victoria, Albert and Chelsea Embankments; and securing Hampstead Heath as an open space for Londoners), it never had sufficient power to control smaller parish interests.

There were also allegations of widespread corruption among members of the Board, and few people were sorry when it was abolished in 1889 and replaced by the London County Council. And not until that time was the sprawling urban mass officially called London.

The London County Council and the Greater London Council

Surprisingly, it was a Conservative government that set up the London County Council – an act it later deeply regretted, for the LCC was usually run by a Labour majority. The government's hand was partly forced by fear of revolution – there had been riots in London in 1886 and 1887. The LCC became the first London-wide authority to be directly elected by the people of London, and its jurisdiction covered some 117 square miles.

For the 75 years of its existence, the LCC was busy. It cleared vast slum areas and built hundreds of thousands of houses for the poor. It developed Kingsway and the Aldwych, and established the London Passenger Transport Board, co-ordinating most of London's public transport. It built two tunnels under the Thames and rebuilt six bridges. It ran education in the capital. It doubled the area of parks and open spaces in London, and established the Green Belt round the outer suburbs – land which could not be built upon.

The LCC also built County Hall, on the South Bank, diagonally across the Thames from the Palace of Westminster. The Conservatives saw the new building as a monster challenging the power of central government. Ten years after establishing the LCC, they had sought to put a brake on its powers by setting up the London boroughs (Islington, Camden, Stepney, Poplar, Deptford, etc), which they hoped would be large enough to challenge the LCC's authority.

In 1965 a Labour government abolished the LCC and replaced it with the Greater London Council (GLC), a body appointed to run all 610 square miles of Greater London. The rivalry between central government and London government came to a head during the Conservative administration of the 1980s – especially when the GLC erected a large scoreboard on the top of County Hall, publicizing the number of unemployed Londoners. The scoreboard, the GLC and County Hall had to go. London became the only capital in the world without any strategic authority to cover its whole area.

County Hall, once the proud headquarters of the Greater London Council, now the home of the London Aquarium, and soon to be a expensive apartment block.

The New Order

On 7 May 1998, a referendum was held. Londoners were asked, in a single question, if they wanted an elected mayor and an elected assembly. The result was an overwhelming "Yes".

Who Owns London? The Individuals

The Dorchester Hotel, Park Lane – owned by the Sultan of Brunei.

Once you have discovered the amount of London in the possession of institutions such as the Church and Crown, it may seem that there isn't a lot of the city left for individuals to own. In some cases, of course, a landlord may own only a property or two, though they may be choice sites. The Sultan of Brunei owns the Dorchester Hotel in Park Lane, and the Prince of Brunei owns Asprey's, the jewellers in New Bond Street. There are, however, several families with large and valuable estates in London – most, but not all, are aristocratic.

The Grosvenor Estate

The largest and the richest private landlord in London is Gerald Cavendish Grosvenor, Duke of Westminster. The wealth of the Grosvenor family is based upon a marriage in 1677 that brought with it, as dowry, 300 acres (120 ha) of land on what was then the western fringe of London. Now, that same land is the heart of Mayfair. The income is enormous – one estimate is that the Duke's income is some £18,000 an hour and his personal fortune £1500 million.

He is regarded as a strict landlord, discouraging the sale of crisps in pubs on the Grosvenor estate, and the display of satellite dishes on the immaculately painted walls of his properties. In 1993 he resigned from the Conservative Party when the government passed the Leasehold Reform Act. This allowed tenants in England and Wales the right to purchase the freehold of their property under certain conditions, and thereby free themselves from the avaricious grip of their landlord. The Duke is, however, surprisingly unsecretive about the extent of his empire. From the Grosvenor Estate Office in Davies Street, Mayfair, you can obtain a map which clearly delineates the Duke's property.

The estate includes much of Belgravia and the US Embassy in Grosvenor Square – the only American embassy in the world not owned by the United States.

Smaller Noble Estates

The oldest private estate in London is the Portman estate, which has been in the possession of the Portman family for over 450 years. In 1533 Sir William Portman, Lord Chief Justice of England, purchased 270 acres (108 ha) of land in Marylebone. Two hundred years later his descendant added a further 200 acres (80 ha) of neighbouring land. Today the names of streets in the Marylebone area (Dorset, Bryanston, Blandford) echo the names of the county and its villages from which the Portmans came.

To the east of the Portman estate is that of Howard de Walden, on land running down from Marylebone Road towards Oxford Street. The estate passed through the hands of several families until it reached the Portland family in the 1720s. In 1879 the unmarried fifth Duke of Portland died and his sister Lucy, Baroness Howard de Walden, took over the estate.

Much of the land around the British Museum belongs to the Bedford family, including Bedford Square itself. The noble families of England had strong ideas as to how their London properties should be maintained in the 18th and 19th centuries, and were particularly proud of the squares that bore their names. In the 19th century, for example, the Duke of Bedford gave instructions that gates should be erected at the entrances to Bedford Square "to keep out animals, low traffic and undesirables".

Less than Noble

Richer than the Duke of Westminster – by just a few million – is Geoffrey Quinn, better known as Paul Raymond. Once upon a time he was a music-hall artiste who played the drums; now he owns 30 acres (12 ha) of Soho – an empire that includes sex-shops, clubs, restaurants and flats, and the notorious Raymond Revuebar. He's reputedly the third richest man in Britain. Having inherited neither wealth nor title, he can at least claim that he has worked to make his fortune.

The Strange Case of Conduit Mead

Three hundred years ago there was a meadow called Conduit Mead, roughly where the streets of north Mayfair stand today. It was watered by the Tyburn stream, which, alas, no longer exists. The meadow originally belonged to the Crown, but the City held a lease of

it. In 1628 King Charles I, always short of money, sold the meadow to the City.

By the end of the 18th century, almost the entire meadow had been built upon. Its border today is marked by New Bond Street, Brook Street, Conduit Street and South Molton Street – some of the most fashionable and expensive streets in London. But the leases granted by the City of London in the 18th century had to be "perpetually renewable" to attract tenants – in other words, the tenants had to be allowed to renew the leases at the original rents for ever. The City's income from these properties is, therefore, still at 18th-century levels.

In 1925 the Law of Property Act stated that "for ever" meant for a mere 2000 years. So, the City of London will be able to increase the rents of its properties on Conduit Mead, but not until the year 3754.

For more information on who owns London, read Andrew Duncan's excellent *Secret London*, from which much of the above is taken.

Shepherd's Market, Mayfair –
one of the characters in the
Strange Case of Conduit Mead.

Wilton Crescent in Belgravia,
part of the Grosvenor family's
vast estates in central London.

Who Owns London? The Institutions

For hundreds of years property in the heart of London – salubrious or slum – belonged mostly to private landlords. Changes in the laws of inheritance and the imposition of death duties at the beginning of the 20th century have resulted in more and more property passing from the private owner to the hands of institutions.

The Crown

Kings and queens of England have been grabbing as much of London as they can for hundreds of years. It is difficult to know exactly how much the Crown now owns – landlords of all shades and descriptions tend to be extremely secretive about their empires. At a conservative estimate, apart from palaces and parks, the Queen owns property valued at over £1 billion in the City, the West End, Kensington and around Regent's Park. The holding is a mixture of residential land and commercial space (over 250 acres or a million square metres).

The Crown Estate

Most of the above is handled by the Crown Estate, a body that hands over the revenue to the government. The understanding is that the monarch will get most of it back by way of the Civil List – money paid to various members of the Royal Family.

The Crown Estate includes most of Regent Street, Lower Regent Street, The Haymarket, Trafalgar Square, Whitehall, and Piccadilly Circus. Added to this are 23 acres (93,000 sq.m) of offices in Holborn, East Smithfield and Leadenhall in the City, and shops and offices in Kensington High Street. Away from the squalor of such commercial enterprises, the Crown Estate also owns mansions in Kensington Palace Gardens and Palace Green; 1000 acres (400 ha) of houses and golf clubs in south London; Richmond Park, Greenwich Park, Hampton Court Park and dozens more.

The Duchies of Lancaster and Cornwall

Quite apart from the Crown Estate, the sovereign is personally entitled to revenue from the lands that comprise the Duchies of Lancaster and Cornwall. That includes the site of the Savoy Hotel, the Oval cricket ground and housing estates in Kennington.

The Corporation of the City of London

Although the Queen owns much of the City of London, the City Corporation has no need to worry. It still owns roughly a third of the City, and a great deal more besides. Among open spaces, the City Corporation owns Epping Forest, Highgate Wood, Queen's Park and Hampstead Heath (which it snapped up when the Greater London Council, the previous owner, was abolished in 1989). You will see signs on London Bridge, Southwark Bridge, Blackfriars Bridge and Tower Bridge informing you that the City Corporation owns all four, and maintains them from a £300 million Bridge House Fund – a fund that is growing at the rate of £20 million a year. South of the river, the Corporation owns much of Borough High Street and Hays Wharf.

The City Livery Companies

The ancient livery companies own a mixed bag of property. Much of it is in the City, where the Drapers' and

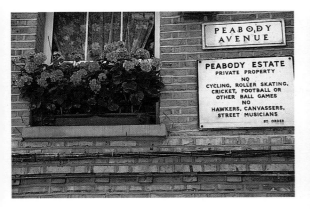

Carpenters' Companies share the ownership of the entire length of Throgmorton Avenue, and the Merchant Taylors' Company owns most of the triangle of land bounded by Finch Street, Cornhill and Bishopsgate. Some of it, however, is in the suburbs – for example, the Leathersellers' and the Merchant Taylors' Companies own almshouses in Lewisham and Barnet, and the Goldsmiths' Company owns 200 acres (80 ha) in Ealing. The Mercers' Company owns a considerable amount of property in the Mercer Street area of Covent Garden.

The Church Commissioners for England

This body was set up in 1948 to look after the assets of the Church of England. It's quite a job, for the Church owns over 150,000 acres (60,000 ha) of agricultural land in Britain, commercial property in the United States, and chunks of London. The biggest chunk is the Hyde Park estate, 90 acres (40 ha) of prime housing to the north of the park in Sussex Gardens, Edgware Road and Bayswater Road. Also on the Church's books are estates in south London, the Royal Lancaster Hotel, and sizeable sections of Victoria Street, Knightsbridge and the King's Road, Chelsea.

The Public Schools

It would take too long to list all the London property owned by these originally charitable, formerly brutal and still exclusive educational establishments. As a sample, suffice it to say that Tonbridge School owns a part of the area around St Pancras Station, and Eton College owns the 60-acre (24 ha) Chalcot Estate north of Primrose Hill. Rugby School owns an impressive piece of WC1, near Great Ormond Street Children's Hospital, as well as the northern part of Lamb's Conduit Street. Christ's Hospital School has land in Soho, Islington and Westminster; the Queen's and the Gielgud theatres in Shaftesbury Avenue; and an industrial estate in the East End.

The biggest school landlord is Dulwich College, which owns most of the village of Dulwich in south London – 1500 acres (600 ha) in all – including London's last surviving toll gate (in College Road) and the Dulwich Picture Gallery. The toll gate brings in about £17,000 a year. Entry to the picture gallery is free.

Walk softly as you stroll about London, for you never know on whose land you are treading.

above:
Part of the Peabody estate in Westminster – housing for the poor in a highly fashionable area.
top left:
Peabody estates are to be found all over London. They were built in the 19th century by George Peabody.
opposite:
The Barbican Centre – the largest residential development in the City of London.

Buckingham Palace

Buckingham Palace is perhaps the most famous building in London – home of the Queen and focal point for any period of national rejoicing. It's the setting for formal diplomatic occasions, state banquets, royal investitures and garden parties. To have been invited to "the Palace" is considered by many the greatest honour possible.

The original palace was built on the site of a monastery – there is said to be a resident ghost – and started life as Buckingham House, home of John Sheffield, first Duke of Buckingham. (Those who wish to appear part of an inner circle of London society still refer to the palace as "Buck House".). The duke died in 1721 and his illegitimate son sold the house to George III in 1762 for £28,000. When George IV came to the throne he announced that his own Carlton House wasn't grand enough for the King of England, so Buckingham House was demolished and Buckingham Palace built in its place. George IV lost interest in the project before it was finished, and spent time and money earmarked for the palace on his preferred Royal Pavilion in Brighton.

By the early 19th century Buckingham Palace was in ill repair. Funds ran out in 1828 and work ceased.

William IV didn't like the place and offered it to the members of the Houses of Parliament, the old Palace of Westminster having recently burned down. They weren't interested and poor William IV lived unhappily in Buckingham Palace until his death in 1837.

Victoria found it uncomfortable. The chimneys smoked, the rooms were cold and dirty. It was badly ventilated , she complained that it smelt. The gardens were full of rubbish. She went off to live in Kensington Palace.

For a while, matters improved. The palace was thoroughly cleaned and made safer and more comfortable. It became Victoria's official London residence, and she and Albert spent a great deal of time there. Once Albert died, however, Victoria took herself off increasingly to Balmoral Castle. Once again, the palace was neglected. When Edward VII took over after Victoria's death, he moodily surveyed it and said: "Get this tomb cleaned up." He also gave orders for some of the hundreds of statues of Victoria's beloved John Brown to be smashed.

The frontage of the palace especially needed attention. The Caen stone facing had weathered badly, and Aston Webb was called in to design a new façade. This is the present east front, dating from 1913. George V took considerable interest in the plans and sent memos and drawings to Webb. "The central balcony should not be

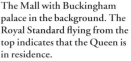

The Mall with Buckingham palace in the background. The Royal Standard flying from the top indicates that the Queen is in residence.

curtailed," he wrote, "as it is used from time to time on occasions when the King and other members of the royal family wish to show themselves to the people." It was first used to acknowledge cheering crowds on 4 August 1914 – the outbreak of the first World War.

Edward VIII loathed Buckingham Palace. When he left it for the last time, after his abdication in 1936, he recorded that a wave of hatred for it swept over him. His mother, Queen Mary, however, loved it. She was the first royal to fill it with flowers and make it a home.

The Palace Today

Since the early 20th century little has changed, inside or out. There are some 600 rooms in the palace, including those used by the Royal Family, by staff and by members of the Royal Household. The Queen has a suite of a dozen or so rooms on the first floor, overlooking Green Park. The palace contains vast state apartments, a magnificent Long Gallery, a covered swimming pool, the Queen's Gallery of paintings, and is surrounded by 45 acres (18 ha) of garden.

Unless you are a hero, a visiting head of state, a leading politician, or a trespasser, you are unlikely ever to see much of the interior. From the mid-1990s, however, the Queen has opened a small section of the palace to the public every summer – mainly to raise money for the rebuilding of those parts of Windsor Castle gutted by fire. The tour of the state rooms costs roughly £30 for a family of four. There's almost always a long queue and you will need a guidebook to identify what you see.

The Boy Cotton

From late 1837 to December 1838, a 12-year-old boy named Edward Cotton lived secretly in Buckingham Palace. How he got in, no one knew, but for over a year he ate and slept in the domestic offices and servants' quarters. Frequent searches for him were made, but Cotton hid in the chimneys – subsequently covering the beds he slept in with soot. He never attempted to break into the apartments inhabited by Queen Victoria, though he did open at least one sealed letter to her – probably hoping that it contained money. While in residence, he helped himself to a sword, two glass inkstands, a pair of trousers and a book. While he stayed in the palace he was safe. It was when he attempted to escape by the equerries' gate that he was spotted, chased and eventually captured on the palace lawn.

The Victoria Memorial

After his mother's death in 1901, Edward VII set about planning a suitable memorial to her. The design was by

Kensington Palace, home of Diana, Princess of Wales after her separation from Prince Charles.

Aston Webb, who used 2300 tons of marble and spent £325,000 and five years building the vast statue at the west end of The Mall. Edward didn't live to see it completed, but when the statue was unveiled by George V in 1911, Aston Webb was knighted on the steps leading up to it.

At times of great rejoicing, crowds climb the statue. At other times such practice is discouraged and you may well be arrested if you try.

The Victoria Memorial – the largest monument to any king or queen in London.

By Appointment

From time to time you may pass shops and stores in London that display royal Coats of Arms (a lion and a unicorn panting at each other beneath a crown, a bunch of feathers and the motto *Ich Dien*, and a strange device depicting a bearded man with a club in a loincloth and the motto "God is my Help"), denoting that they have royal customers. Beneath the Coat of Arms will be words to the effect that "By Appointment to Her Majesty the Queen [or another member of the Royal Family]" Bloggins and Sons are "suppliers of [or purveyors of]" some goods or services. Nobody sells things to the Royal Family – they "purvey" them.

You will see such a sign certainly on Harrods, Fortnum and Mason, Garrard's or Asprey's, but you may also see one on the façade of a small but exclusive gentlemen's hairdresser in Mayfair or St James's Street, or on a florist's shop in Kensington, on the site board of a London development, on a ticket agency, on a car hire firm, on a toy shop, a music shop or a wine merchant's. What all these places have in common is that they have been granted the "Royal Warrant".

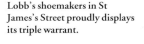

Lobb's shoemakers in St James's Street proudly displays its triple warrant.

The practice began in the Middle Ages, when Henry II granted a Royal Charter to the Weavers' Company in 1155. Astute dealers and suppliers became increasingly eager to be so honoured, and by the reign of Elizabeth I a great many Royal Warrants had been assigned. In the 18th and 19th centuries, a Royale Kalendar was published each year, listing those tradesmen who supplied the Royal Household, including the official Mole Taker and Rat Catcher.

In William IV's reign, these privileged tradespeople first began displaying the royal Coat of Arms, in the hope that the public would believe that what was good enough for the Royal Family was good enough for them, too. William's successor, Queen Victoria, was the first to grant Royal Warrants in their present form – a formal document "appointing" a tradesman as a supplier of goods or services to the Royal Household. Some of the early recipients in her reign were Cadbury's, Schweppes and Twinings. Victoria was also the first monarch to grant a Royal Warrant to a woman. Today some 40 women hold the title.

Only four members of the Royal Family grant warrants: the Queen, the Duke of Edinburgh, the Queen Mother and the Prince of Wales. Each of these four can grant only one warrant per supplier, but a supplier could hold four Royal Warrants, one from each member of the Royal Family. Out of the 925 firms currently holding more than one Royal Warrant, only three hold a complete set: Harrods, the General Trading Company and the Rover Group. Gieves and Hawkes, at No. 1 Savile Row, hold a unique record. They hold three different Royal Warrants to three different members of the Royal Family: to the Queen as "livery and military tailors", to the Duke of Edinburgh as "naval tailors and outfitters", and to the Prince of Wales as "tailors and outfitters".

To qualify for the honour, a firm or shop must simply have provided goods or services to a department of the Royal Household in any of the royal residences – official or private – for at least five years. The odd packet of tea or tin of beans isn't enough. The provision has to have been a reasonable proportion of the total supply of that product to the Household in question over that five-year period. Once granted, the Royal Warrant runs for ten years, after which time it is reviewed by the Lord Chamberlain's Office. Some establishments have held the Royal Warrant through generations of kings and queens. Others have a more ephemeral existence.

Government departments and professionals cannot qualify for a Royal Warrant. Although the Brigade of Guards daily provides a service for the Queen, it cannot boast "By Appointment" on any of its recruiting posters.

BY APPOINTMENT TO
H.R.H THE DUKE OF EDINBURGH
RIFLE MAKERS

left:
The Royal Warrant above the door of Holland and Holland in Bruton Street, Mayfair.
below:
Another of Lobb's satisfied royal customers.

BY APPOINTMENT
TO HIS IMPERIAL MAJESTY
THE EMPEROR OF ETHIOPIA

But it is possible to discover who cares for the Queen's teeth, sorts out her legal problems and prepares the Royal Accounts.

Where to find Warrant Holders

Don't waste any time in the suburbs of London looking for royal Coats of Arms. Most firms and shops with the Royal Warrant are situated in and around Mayfair, Kensington, Knightsbridge and the West End. You will find jewellers in Regent Street, a perfumer's in Jermyn Street, a bookseller's in Piccadilly, a wine merchant's and a tobacconist in St James's Street, a manufacturer of toilet requisites in the Burlington Arcade, a military outfitter's in Sackville Street, a chocolate manufacturer on the corner of the Royal Arcade, New Bond Street, and a rifle-maker in Bruton Street.

The densest concentration of Warrant holders is in Savile Row. Here, apart from Gieves and Hawkes, you will find five other royal tailors or outfitters. Bernard Weatherill Limited are "riding clothes outfitters and livery tailors" to the Queen. H. Huntsman and Sons (incorporating Carpenter and Packer) were appointed tailors to Prince Bernhard of the Netherlands in 1957. Among their earlier royal customers were Queen Victoria, Edward VII, George V and Edward VIII. Pringle of Scotland are "manufacturers of knitted garments" to the Queen. Hardy Amies is "dressmaker" to the Queen. Henry Poole and Company are "livery tailors" to the Queen, and list among their other royal customers the late Emperor Napoleon II and His Imperial Majesty the Emperor Haile Selassie.

The Houses of Parliament

*The Light That
Never Was*

In the summer of 1858, the
House of Commons was forced
to adjourn its sitting because of a
putrid stink coming from the
Thames. Its source was the sewer
of the Westminster Workhouse.
One ingenious citizen produced
a plan to pipe the odious gas
from the sewer to the top of the
Clock Tower, where it could be
used to illuminate Big Ben. The
Commons approved the plan,
which would almost certainly
have resulted in an explosion
that would have destroyed the
entire palace. Happily, last-
minute advice from a professional engineer put an end to the
scheme.

The correct name for what most people call the Houses
of Parliament is the Palace of Westminster, a reminder
that this seat of government began life as a royal residence. Not until the reign of Henry VIII in the early 16th
century did Westminster cease to be the home of kings
and queens.

The wonderful position on the north bank of the
Thames, westward from Westminster Bridge, has been
the site of administrative government for over a thousand years, but the present building is only some 160
years old. The old palace was destroyed by fire in 1834,
ironically as a result of breaking with tradition. It was
decided in October of that year to burn thousands of the
old wooden Exchequer tally-rods – elm sticks with
notches cut in them, used in medieval times for keeping
accounts.

"It would naturally occur to any intelligent person,"
wrote Charles Dickens, "that nothing could be easier
than to allow them to be carried away for firewood by the
miserable people that live in the neighbourhood . . . [but]
the order went out that they should be privately and
confidentially burned." A furnace was stoked beneath
the chamber of the House of Lords to get rid of the rods.
By mid-afternoon there were signs that something was
wrong. The heat in the chamber was so great that the
noble lords could feel it through their boots. The smoke
was so thick that it was impossible to see the walls from
the centre of the room. By the evening, flames were flick-
ering beneath the doors. By the morning almost the
entire palace had been gutted. Only St Mary Underfoot,
the crypt and parliamentary storehouse, Westminster
Hall and the Jewel Tower survived.

Ninety-seven plans were submitted for a new building to house Parliament. The design selected was by
Charles Barry – a vast and ornate example of Gothic
Revival crowned by three towers. The interior of the
palace was the work of Augustus Welby Pugin, from
painted ceilings, tiled floors and stained-glass windows
to wallpapers, clocks, fireplaces and even umbrella stands
and inkwells. It has been said that the design of
Parliament echoes the British Constitution itself – old,

rambling, fussy, hard to follow, and giving the impression that it has been assembled piecemeal.

The atmosphere inside the Palace of Westminster is a cross between a Victorian railway station, a British public school at the time of Dr Arnold and the setting for a Gothic horror story. It is not a welcoming building, though the police officers on duty in and around the palace are usually friendly and informative. It is, however, impressive. The sheer weight, scale and complexity of the decoration take the breath away. Stand in Central Hall, one of the few parts of the palace to which access is easy, and gaze up at the ceiling and the mosaic decoration. Look down at the scarlet and gold of the floor of the Lords' Lobby. Spare a few moments to study the monumental brass doors leading from the same room. Marvel at the intricacies of the mouldings in the Royal Gallery, or of the canopy in the Lords' Chamber, the entrance to the Robing Room and the fireplace therein. You will not see such richness anywhere else in London.

Big Ben

There are three towers in the Palace of Westminster: the Clock Tower (318 feet/100 metres) high, the Middle Tower (300 feet/92 metres) high, and the Victoria Tower (340 feet/105 metres) high. Big Ben is not a tower, nor is it a clock. It's the 16-ton bell housed in the Clock Tower. Thanks to the BBC, however, Big Ben sets the time for the whole of Britain and for much of the rest of the world. Every hour the 16 notes of its melody boom out, followed by the striking of the hour, and the nation checks its own timepieces.

There are two theories as to how Big Ben got its name. One is that the House of Commons was sitting late one night trying to agree a name for the great bell. Members were tired and wanted to go home but could not come to a decision. At last one member called out "Why not Big Ben?", the nickname of the large Chief Commissioner of Works for Westminster, Sir Benjamin Hall. The other theory is that the bell is named after a famous boxer, Benjamin Caunt, landlord of the Coach and Horses in St Martin's Lane.

opposite:
The night before Guy Fawkes Day. Seated from left: Margaret Thatcher, Geoffrey Howe, Keith Joseph, John Nott and Norman Tebbit, 4th November 1981.
right:
The Clock Tower of the Palace of Westminster – home of Big Ben.

Whitehall

Although Whitehall is the name of the imposing avenue that leads from Trafalgar Square down to the Palace of Westminster, the term "Whitehall" is used to cover all central government offices in this part of London. It includes the Foreign Office, the Ministry of Defence, the Treasury and the Parliamentary Counsel Offices. From the outside most of the buildings do little more than impress by their sheer size – inside all is different.

The problem is that access is denied to most people most of the time. Until the 1980s, the public were free to cut through Downing Street to St James's Park, passing the very door of the Prime Minister's residence at No. 10. Because of terrorist threats the government put an end to such liberties, and iron gates and strong police officers now bar the way. As for the government offices themselves, entry is restricted to one or two only over a special weekend each autumn. Should you be lucky enough to be in London at that time, you may well be able to tour the interiors of the Foreign Office and Marlborough House (which is now the home of the Commonwealth Secretariat).

Foreign Office

The FO (as it is familiarly known) is in King Charles Street, near the foot of Whitehall. It's a large grey building whose exterior does little to advertise the lavish joys inside. When Sir George Gilbert Scott designed the building to house the civil servants who administered the then vast British Empire, he described it as "a kind of national palace, a drawing room for the nation".

It is indeed palatial. The Grand Staircase looks like Hollywood at its most ostentatious – beset with richly

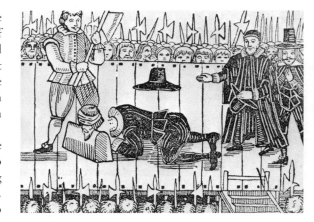

decorated pillars, illuminated by vast and ornate chandeliers as it rises beneath the arched ceiling. In the centre of the building is the Durbar Court, used for state receptions, with a marble floor that simulates the pool of an Indian water garden. Round the walls are busts of all the cowboy adventurers who plundered India on behalf of the British Government, and there are large oil paintings of battle scenes, to remind you that the British Empire was almost entirely created by force.

On the first floor enormous doors, 13 feet (4 metres) high and 15 feet (4.6 metres) across, lead to a series of rooms known as the Locarno Suite. In December 1925 delegates from all over Europe came here for the formal signing of the Locarno Treaties, designed to reduce strife and tension in Europe. They sat beneath coffered ceilings, pilasters crowned with Corinthian capitals and gilded beams in the forlorn hope that they could bring peace to a simmering continent. The Grand Locarno Reception Room has a glorious barrel-vaulted ceiling, beautifully restored, and a breathtaking piano.

Everywhere you go are murals, ormolu and bronze chandeliers, mosaic pavements, magnificent mantelpieces and richly decorated fireplaces. Somewhere in the building is an 18th-century chimneypiece said to have been the one before which Nelson and Wellington warmed themselves on their one and only meeting – which took place by chance.

Marlborough House

Though not in Whitehall itself, Marlborough House has long been a seat of power. It is at the west end of Pall Mall, not far from St James's Palace. It was built in the early 18th century for Sarah, Duchess of Marlborough and bosom friend of Queen Anne. Over the last 200 years it has been the home of many Royals, including Prince Albert, Prince Leopold of the Belgians, and Edward, Prince of Wales. George V was born in

top right:
The execution of Charles I on the balcony outside Westminster Hall, 30th January 1649.
below:
A close-up of the magnificent ceiling of the Banqueting House in Whitehall, painted by Rubens.

Marlborough House and also lived here as Prince of Wales. Among the many improvements made by the Royal residents was the installation of a ceiling stolen from the Queen's House, Greenwich, now in the Blenheim Salon.

The tone is one of sumptuous richness – gold leaf and weighty wallpaper, with satin-covered chairs and marble-topped tables, high moulded ceilings, huge mirrors, extravagant clocks. Scattered throughout are paintings of kings and queens, and in the Green Drawing Room there is a portrait of Sarah, Duchess of Marlborough, herself, looking rather blowsy and showing a lot of cleavage.

The Banqueting House, Whitehall Palace
This is all that remains of the old Whitehall Palace, everything else having been destroyed by a fire in 1698. It was designed by Inigo Jones and was the first Renaissance building in London. Horace Walpole described it as "the model of the most pure and beautiful taste". It is a large, light, airy room, with a ceiling by Rubens, painted as a demonstration of Charles I's wealth and taste, a glorification of the House of Stuart, and a celebration of the divine nature of kingship. The various panels in the ceiling were so placed that the best possible view was that to be obtained from the throne itself, and the least important courtiers had to be content with the poorest view.

After hubris comes nemesis. In 1649 Parliament ordered the erection of a scaffold on the north wall outside the Banqueting Hall, the choice of the site being a public repudiation of Stuart mores and excesses, and a symbolic rejection of the Divine Right of Kings. It was from this room that Charles stepped out on to the scaffold for his execution.

Unlike most of Whitehall, the Banqueting Hall is open to visitors all the year round.

The Ministry of Defence, Whitehall – ugly enough to be bombed, strong enough to withstand the bombing.

Legal London

All over London there are solicitors' offices and magistrates' courts, but if the English legal system has a heart, it beats in a legal powerhouse that is roughly half a square mile between Holborn and the river Thames. Here you will find the Law Courts, the Old Bailey and the four Inns of Court.

There are three types of lawyer in England – judges, barristers and solicitors. JUDGES wear wigs and gowns, have the best seats in court, terrifying power (it is hoped tempered with a sense of justice), and no special training. They are simply barristers who have been promoted. BARRISTERS wear smaller wigs and gowns, have to stand up in court when speaking, and would have preferred to go on the stage. SOLICITORS wear dark suits, sit behind barristers when in court, and do most of their work in offices miles away.

The Royal Courts of Justice in The Strand – the setting for some of the most important, and most boring civil law cases in England and Wales.

The Inns of Court

Barristers and judges have offices in the four Inns of Court: Gray's, Middle Temple, Inner Temple, and Lincoln's Inn. Like most legal institutions in London, the Inns of Court have a Dickensian pall hanging over them. They are quaint, picturesque and totally out of date, but on a sunny day they are well worth a visit. The offices are called "chambers" and the Inns of Court are not courts in the legal sense, but places of congress, gathering places, like royal courts.

One of the prettiest parts of legal London is the King's Bench Walk, where members of legal communities have argued happily with each other for 700 years. Until 1308 it was the site of the headquarters of the Knights Templar in England.

Although most sets of chambers are smartly and comfortably furnished, relics remain – dusty volumes of legal precedents and statutes, and obsequious clerks. Every set of chambers has clerks, whose job it is to prepare their barrister masters for appearances in court. Dickens described the lawyers who occupied chambers as "maggots in nuts", but perhaps that's going a little too far.

Most clerks and barristers are men: the law is a competitive profession which thrives on testosterone. Barristers love the adversarial nature of the English legal process. Where other systems seek to arbitrate or to compromise, litigation in England seeks to establish a clear winner and loser in each case.

Lincoln's Inn fields is the largest square in London. It's a pleasant open space with some fine houses and Sir John Soane's Museum. It was also the setting for Mr Tulkinghorn's home in *Bleak House*. In the grounds of Gray's Inn there's a catalpa tree said to have been planted by Francis Bacon from cuttings brought from America by Sir Walter Raleigh early in the 17th century.

The Royal Courts of Justice or "Law Courts"

The Royal Courts of Justice in The Strand are very different in scale and style from the older Inns of Court. Where the latter are small and cosy, the Royal Courts of Justice are monumental, draughty, cold and forbidding. They were completed in 1882, and the problems involved in their construction killed the architect, G.E. Street. Their style is Disneyland Victorian, a mixture of medieval cathedral, French château and railway terminus.

The public can get into the Law Courts at almost any time between 10 am and 4 pm (the working hours of judges, with an hour off for luncheon), although some cases are heard in camera, when the public are not admitted. You don't have to pay and you don't have to make an appointment. Walk in off the street, have your bag searched and then find your way to any one of dozens of courts. Don't expect to have an entertaining morning or afternoon. This is where civil cases are heard, not criminal. Cases that arrive at the Law Courts involve enormous sums of money – litigation is cripplingly expensive in England and Wales – and are immensely dull.

Bow Street Magistrates' Court

Until 1998 criminal minnows in London, as opposed to criminal sharks, used to be tried at Bow Street, opposite the Royal Opera House. The singing wasn't as good, but the acting was much better. In the old days, proceedings here always began with a parade of drunks and prostitutes, who received summary justice. The drunks were given a small fine or a few days in gaol; the prostitutes were invariably fined £2. Few of the accused were in the dock more than a couple of minutes; some barely had time to focus on where they were and what was happen-

A barrister makes his way to the Royal Courts of Justice, humbly and on foot.

ing before they were on their way back to the street, the pub, or the cells.

A word of warning – whatever court you visit in London, make sure that your conduct is exemplary, and show respect to the pompous and the powerful who run the legal system. Failure to do so may result in your being a participant rather than a mere spectator, for judges take a very severe view of what they regard as contempt of their authority. Prison may well await the cheeky or obstreperous.

The Central Criminal Court or "Old Bailey"

If you want drama, go further east to the Central Criminal Court, with the famous statue of Justice on top. This is where Dr Crippen, Lord Haw-Haw (William Joyce), Christie and the Yorkshire Ripper (Peter Sutcliffe) were tried and condemned.

As in the case of the Law Courts, you don't have to book to visit the Old Bailey, though you probably won't be able to get in to see a trial that has attracted a lot of publicity.

Soldiers of the Queen

above right:
A squadron of the Household Cavalry moves out from Knightsbridge Barracks.
below:
The Horseguards Parade at the east end of the Mall, the venue for the annual Trooping the Colour.

London has always been a garrison city. Roman legions were stationed in Londinium in the first century AD. William the Conqueror built the Tower as his power base when he seized London a thousand years later. Troops were billeted in London in the Civil War of the 17th century, in the Napoleonic Wars of the early 19th century, and increasingly in Victoria's long reign. Still today London has a Garrison Sergeant Major – a tall, smart and impressive man with an office just off Whitehall.

The number of troops in peacetime London has steadily grown. There are barracks in Birdcage Walk, Knightsbridge, Regent's Park, Woolwich, Chelsea, Mill Hill and throughout the outer suburbs. Some of them house troops with specialist functions (the Royal Army Medical Corps, the Army Postal Service). Others are for troops whose duties are largely ceremonial.

But they are all soldiers, there to deal with the citizens of London should they take to the streets in armed or unarmed insurrection. The Queen, the government and the establishment are all well protected. The police may form the front line of this defence, but the army is always waiting in the background.

The Changing of the Guard

Every morning a long and complicated military manoeuvre begins outside Wellington Barracks. One of the four bands of the Brigade of Guards gathers and starts to play. A small group of guardsmen, resplendent in bearskins and ill-fitting scarlet jackets, black trousers and blindingly well-bulled boots, is inspected and prepared for a spell of guard duty at Buckingham Palace or St James's Palace. Orders are shouted. Senior NCOs snarl and make cutting remarks – and all this in public view. The army has never believed in hiding its disciplinary processes – this is where soldiers were publicly flogged until 1868. Two officers appear and march the length of the parade ground, to no apparent purpose. An NCO darts forward and thrusts a stick under the arm of one of the officers. The band breaks into a march. The guard detail strides off and the Changing of the Guard is under way.

At much the same time, a group of soldiers on horseback, members of the Household Cavalry, move from Hyde Park to Whitehall, to relieve the troopers on duty at Horse Guards Parade. They are chaperoned through the traffic by two mounted members of the Metropolitan Police.

It is all very picturesque and very expensive. The annual cost of military bands in Britain exceeds the Arts Council grant for music.

King George V and the Guards Band

While the Guard is changing at Buckingham Palace, whichever of the Guards bands is on duty provides background music from the front of the palace. One day in the 1920s, the Guards' director of music chose to play a selection from a new operetta.

After a minute or two, a royal footman appeared, bearing a message from the King on a silver tray. The director was delighted, until he opened the envelope and read the message within. It said: "His Majesty does not know what the band has just played, but it is never to be played again."

Royal Salutes

Even more expensive, though far less frequent, are the firing of royal salutes. On the Queen's birthday, and other special royal days, the King's Troop of the Royal Horse Artillery race down from St John's Wood on 71 horses, lugging half a dozen 13-pounder guns. In a scene that would do credit to many a Hollywood costume extravaganza, they manhandle their guns into action in Hyde Park and fire a salute of 41 rounds – 21 rounds because it's a royal salute, and another 20 because Hyde Park is a royal park.

At the same time, the Honourable Artillery Company fires a 62-round salute at the Tower of London – 21 rounds because it's a royal salute, 20 rounds because the Tower is a royal palace and fortress, and an extra 21 for the City of London.

Both salutes can be witnessed by members of the public. The Hyde Park salute begins at noon, the Tower salute an hour later. This is because the members of the

Honourable Artillery Company are really civilians, and they dress up to perform in their lunch break. If you like Gilbert and Sullivan, you'll love the royal salutes.

above:
Guardsmen on sentry duty at St James's Palace.
left:
A member of the Blues and Royals, not to be confused with the Life Guards.

Ava Gardner and the Guard at Buckingham Palace

For 150 years, the guardsmen on duty at Buckingham Palace stood outside the palace courtyard. Like the troopers in Whitehall, they were within man- or woman-handling reach of the public. In the early 1950s, the American film star Ava Gardner posed for a photo session with one of the guardsmen. He, poor soul or lucky guy – whichever you prefer – was entirely powerless to prevent this, but the photographs led to a revision of thinking by Buckingham Palace, and the guardsmen have since then been kept safely out of public reach at the back of the courtyard.

London Pageantry and Ceremony – The Magnificent

Many of the displays of pomp and ceremony to be seen in London owe their continued existence to the renaissance of pageantry in late Victorian times. After the death of her beloved Prince Albert, Victoria removed herself from the public gaze. The monarchy, as an institution, became extremely unpopular. There were fears of riots, rebellions, revolutions. Thanks to the cunning of men like Lord Esher, Victoria was persuaded to come out of retirement and to become the figurehead in a whole series of revived ceremonies. In the age of Barnum and Bailey, the Queen of England was the star attraction in the greatest show on earth.

Her own coronation in Westminster Abbey on 28 June 1838 had been a shambles. There was no proper rehearsal and it lasted five gruelling hours. Victoria, who was only 19 years old, had slept badly the night before and had been roused by celebratory gunfire at four in the morning. Once she reached Westminster Abbey, she discovered the orb was too heavy and the throne was too low. There was an unseemly scramble for the commemorative medals hurled by the Lord Chamberlain into the congregation. At the same time, the 82-year-old Lord Rolle, on his way to pay homage, fell down the steps leading to the throne. The clergy didn't know what to do. The Archbishop of Canterbury forced the ring on to the wrong finger, and Victoria almost screamed with pain. The Bishop of Durham – a key player – disappeared at a crucial moment. The Bishop of Bath and Wells, having turned over two pages of the ceremonial book at once, prematurely announced that the service was over. Victoria started to leave and had to be called back.

Things could only get better, and from then on the set-pieces in Victoria's reign (her Silver, Golden and Diamond Jubilees and countless other special occasions) passed off smoothly and magnificently.

Coronations and state funerals are once-in-a-lifetime occasions, but there are other state occasions that take place annually, several times a year, or daily.

The State Opening of Parliament

This takes place in November, at the Palace of Westminster. The Queen rides in the Irish State Coach from Buckingham Palace, along what is known as the Royal Route to Parliament Square. The route is lined with members of the armed forces, military bands play, and even in the late autumn drizzle it's a colourful occasion.

Trooping the Colour

Perhaps the most impressive military parade in the world takes place on the Queen's official birthday. In Victoria's reign it was held on 24 May (Victoria's birthday), a suitably warm time of the year for an outdoor parade. Edward VII's birthday was in murky November, so he decided to give himself (and his successors) a second, official birthday in June.

The Lord Mayor's coach parades through the City of London.

right:
The Band of the Royal Marines takes part in the celebrations marking the Lord Mayor's Show.

left:
The massed bands of the
Brigade of Guards in the Mall
as part of the ceremony of
Trooping the Colour.
below:
An officer inspecting members
of the Coldstream Guards.

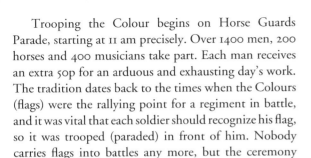

Trooping the Colour begins on Horse Guards Parade, starting at 11 am precisely. Over 1400 men, 200 horses and 400 musicians take part. Each man receives an extra 50p for an arduous and exhausting day's work. The tradition dates back to the times when the Colours (flags) were the rallying point for a regiment in battle, and it was vital that each soldier should recognize his flag, so it was trooped (paraded) in front of him. Nobody carries flags into battles any more, but the ceremony continues.

Beating Retreat

During the first two weeks in June, this ceremony takes place on three or four evenings a week on Horse Guards Parade. It has nothing to do with running away, but originally was a drummed signal to members of a town garrison that the gates were about to close. The Mounted Bands of the Household Cavalry and the Massed Bands of the Foot Guards play, the Parade is floodlit, the setting is dramatic, the ceremony impressive.

The Lord Mayor's Show

This isn't a show at all. It's a procession that takes place annually on the second Saturday in November. From the mid-14th to the early 18th century it was held on the river, but nowadays the Lord Mayor processes by state coach to the Royal Courts of Justice in The Strand, for "approval" by the Queen's Justices. The Lord Mayor's Show keeps growing – with more floats, more bands and more supporters each year, celebrating the riches and financial clout of the City of London.

A Terrier named Caesar

The state funeral of Edward VII in 1910 has been called "The Last Greatest Show on earth". It was attended by the Kings of Portugal, Spain, Denmark, Norway, Bulgaria, the Belgians, the Hellenes, and by Kaiser Wilhelm II of Germany. The procession marched from Westminster Hall, where Edward's body had been lying in state, to Paddington Station, en route to Windsor. Leading the parade of kings were Edward's horse with his master's boots reversed in the saddle, and his pet rough-haired terrier, Caesar. The Kaiser remarked that never before had he yielded precedence to a dog.

left centre:
The Queen makes her way to
Horse Guards Parade for
Trooping the Colour.

London Pageantry and Ceremony – The Modest

Much London ceremonial is relatively small in scale, but every day there is something strange, charming, quaint, or surprising to see, ranging from the nightly Ceremony of the Keys in the Tower of London to the triennial Beating the Bounds in the City.

Changing Guard at Buckingham Palace

This is perhaps the best-known of all London ceremonies – we have already looked at its preparation. It takes place at 11.30 every morning and lasts about 45 minutes. The Old Guard stands in the forecourt of Buckingham Palace, waiting for its replacement to swing through the gates to music from one of the Guards bands. The Captain of the Old Guard hands the keys of Buckingham Palace to the Captain of the New Guard. The band plays again, and the Old Guard marches off. A similar ceremony takes place at St James's Palace, and you can get much closer to it.

Guard Mounting from Horse Guards

This takes place at about 10 am on eight mornings in May, on Horse Guards Parade. It's a ceremony roughly 250 years old, in part a rehearsal for Trooping the Colour, but it doesn't attract as big a crowd, so you get a better view. As the Guards parade, officers take up their position by marching in slow time with drawn swords across the parade ground.

In less polished times this was to check that they were sober enough to fulfil their duties. The best place from which to view Guard Mounting is near the Guards Monument in St James's Park.

The Ceremony of the Keys

Every night, at exactly 9.53 pm, the Chief Yeoman Warder leaves the Byward Tower in the Tower of London carrying a candle lantern and a bunch of keys. These are no ordinary keys, for they represent the Sovereign. He then marches with four members of the Tower Guard to the gates of the Tower, locking each in turn. When the procession reaches the Bloody Tower, it is challenged by a sentry and the following little drama is enacted.

The Ceremony of the Keys –
the Chief Warder of the Tower
is challenged by the Guards.

SENTRY: Halt. Who comes there?
CHIEF WARDER: The Keys.
SENTRY: Whose Keys?
CHIEF WARDER: Queen Elizabeth's Keys.
SENTRY: Pass, Queen Elizabeth's Keys. All's well.

The Chief Warder removes his bonnet and cries "God preserve Queen Elizabeth," and everyone replies "Amen".

This has been going on for over 700 years. If you are lucky, you can get tickets to see it through a travel agent or by applying directly to the Tower of London.

Quit Rents Ceremony
On 26 October every year, the City Solicitor hands a bill-hook, a hatchet, six horseshoes and some nails to a representative of the Queen at the Law Courts in The Strand. The odd collection of ironmongery is the traditional payment of quit rent – rent in lieu of services – for a parcel of land in Shropshire.

Beating the Bounds
Once every three years (1999, 2002, 2005 etc) on Ascension Day, the custom of Beating the Bounds is enacted. It begins with a service at the Chapel of St Peter ad Vincula, Tower Green. This strange ceremony, in which choirboys thrash buildings at certain points along the parish boundary, dates back to times when maps were few and inaccurate. One way of teaching the rising generation where their parish began and ended was to march them round the perimeter, bumping them into walls or whipping them at key places. Today's ceremony is just as colourful, but less brutal.

Sweeping the Road
Each year on the second Wednesday in July, a new Grand Master of the Vintners' Company is installed. The Vintners leave their headquarters in Upper Thames Street at 11.50 am, and march to the church of St James Garlickhythe for the ceremony. The procession is led by the Bargemaster, Beadle, Stavesman and Clerk, but is preceded by the Wine Porter. Dressed in white smock and top hat, the Wine Porter uses an old-fashioned broom to sweep the road clean. The custom dates back to medieval times when the City streets were muddy tracks.

Blue Coat Boys' March
In late September the boys of Christ's Hospital School, Sussex, march in 16th-century dress of long blue coats

and yellow stockings from Newgate to a service at St Sepulchre's, Holborn, and then on to tea at the Mansion House. The march celebrates the founding of the original Christ's Hospital at Newgate by Edward VI, ten days before his death.

Maundy Thursday
There are various celebrations in London on Maundy Thursday. The Queen distributes specially minted money annually, but the practice takes place in London at irregular intervals. Also unreliable is the ceremony of Farthing Bundles at Bromley-by-Bow. This was started in 1907 by Clara Grant, who charged children one farthing (the least valuable coin in existence) for surprise parcels of toys, puzzles, pencils, beads and other "bits of nonsense". To qualify for the gifts, children had to be poor, and small enough to pass under a special arch, across which were painted the words:

Enter All Ye Children Small
None Can Come Who Are Too Tall

Maundy Thursday, April 1935. Two ancient Londoners in jovial mood after receiving their Maundy Money from the Duchess of York and a very young Princess Elizabeth.

Clubland

The area in and around St James's has long been known as "Clubland". It has nothing to do with night-clubs, or sex clubs, or dance clubs, or any such dens of vice, though many of the oldest foundations in Clubland began life as gambling dens. In Clubland you will find "gentlemen's clubs", founded in the 18th and 19th centuries for the sprigs of the aristocracy, for dandies and for sportsmen of all ages.

There are perhaps scarcely more than 20 of these institutions. Each has cultivated its own clientele, with different political views, different interests, and different professions. In their heyday there were clubs for clergymen and soldiers, Tories and Whigs, country gentlemen and travellers, actors and writers. After being elected and paying their subscriptions, members could drink or dine at their club, stay there overnight, enjoy the facilities of the gaming tables, the library, the sitting room. In some cases, confirmed bachelors knew no home other than their club.

To be elected a member was an honour. To be refused amounted to social disgrace. When the playwright Richard Sheridan applied for election to Almack's Club in the late 18th century, he was blackballed three times by George Augustus Selwyn, wit and politician – on the grounds that Sheridan's father had been on the stage. Eventually poor Sheridan was elected when George IV, then Prince of Wales, detained Selwyn

The heart of London's Clubland – Pall Mall, looking east.

in conversation while a new membership ballot was held.

Little has changed. The London club is an astonishingly well-preserved monument to a way of life that has always recognized only the rich, the powerful and the male. It's a secretive world, especially at times when wealth and privilege are under attack. It's almost impossible to infiltrate – you will need to be introduced as a guest by a member. Don't expect to gain entry by ringing the bell and asking nicely if you can come in. It's not easy to spot a London club as you walk past – they do not declare themselves on the door – and it is virtually impossible to discover what goes on inside, but stories of club life from the past are legion.

In the 18th and early 19th centuries, fearsome gambling took place at clubs such as Brooks's, White's and Boodle's. Horace Walpole recorded that "a thousand meadows and cornfields were staked" at every throw of the dice. Charles James Fox lost over £200,000 in a lifetime of card-playing at his club. Edward Gibbon, author of *The Decline and Fall of the Roman Empire*, played cards non-stop for 22 hours and lost £11,000 at one sitting. But there were winners, too. General Thomas Scott, according to a contemporary report, "came to the whist table with a clear head, and, possessing as he did a remarkable memory… he was able honestly to win the enormous sum of £200,000."

Later in the 19th century, Almack's (forerunner of Brooks's) was described as the "seventh heaven of the fashionable world". Women took over the running of the club, and dancing took the place of gambling. The Lady Patronesses – Lady Jersey, Lady Castlereagh and the Princess Esterhazy issued an order "to prevent the admission of gentlemen in *Trowsers* to the balls on Wednesdays – at the same time allowing an exception to those Gentlemen who may be knock-kneed, or otherwise deformed".

But such wise and kindly feminine influence in a man's world was short-lived. True, most clubs now have special areas for lady members, access to which is sometimes by a back staircase, but the heart of a London club is still a smoke-infested male enclave of heavy armchairs, old prints and cartoons, cups and medals in display cases, and some very strange artefacts. The Army and Navy Club has Captain Cook's magnifying glasses, The Athenaeum has Charles Dickens's chair, and members at Brooks's may gaze to their hearts' content at Napoleon's death mask.

The Dreadful Day

Rents in London reached an all-time high in the 1880s. Landlords were greedy even by their own standards, and

workers were crowded into rat-infested rooms, to pay a crippling price for lodgings that were rotting about them. Thousands were unemployed. The red flag flew at meetings. Tempers were short and hope was gone. The President of the English National Revolutionary League urged that kings and priests should be swept away as "emblems of tyranny and force and fraud".

A march by the unemployed through the West End in February 1886 got out of hand. Hundreds of rioters ran through the streets and headed for Pall Mall. Picking their targets carefully, they stoned and smashed the windows of many London clubs, among them The Athenaeum, the Reform, and the Army and Navy. It seemed that a revolution was very near, but, as so often in London's history, the moment passed without further unrest.

The following year Queen Victoria celebrated her Golden Jubilee. There was one further outbreak of violence, when troops savagely attacked a peaceful Socialist demonstration in Trafalgar Square on 13 November 1887, killing two of the demonstrators, but, in the end, the revolutionary ardour of the 1880s came to nothing. The clubs repaired their windows, and the members returned to snoring behind their newspapers.

The interior of the Royal Automobile Club in Pall Mall in Edwardian times.

A Stroll Around London's Clubland

Should you wish to goggle at the outside of London clubs, you will find most of them in St James's Street, St James's Square and Pall Mall.

The Turf Club is at 5 Carlton House Terrace. It's an aristocratic club founded in 1864, which a few years ago had sixteen dukes among its members. The club claims to have codified the rules of whist. Just round the corner, at 107 Pall Mall, is The Athenaeum, founded in 1824 and reckoned the elite of London clubs. It was designed by Decimus Burton and has a drawing room over 30 yards long, where Anthony Trollope, the novelist, used to sit and write. Past members have included prime ministers and archbishops.

Next door to The Athenaeum is the Travellers' Club, unique among London clubs in that it does permit guided tours. Membership was originally confined to those who had travelled at least 500 miles (800 kilometres) from London. Today that would include more than 90% of the population.

Next door is the Reform Club, where the famous 19th-century chef Alexis Soyer presided over the kitchens – a man said by Thackeray to make "a more delicious soup for a halfpenny than an ignorant cook can concoct with pounds of vegetables and meat". The Reform was the setting for the scene in Jules Verne's novel where Phineas Fogg accepted the challenge to go *Around the World in Eighty Days*.

No. 89 Pall Mall is the home of the Royal Automobile Club, a youngster founded in 1897 "for the Protection, Encouragement and Development of Automobilism". It was built on the site of the old War Office, is the largest London club and has a swimming pool in its basement. It was selected by the English spies Guy Burgess and Donald Maclean as the rendezvous for their last lunch together before they fled to the Soviet Union in 1951.

A hundred yards further to the west along Pall Mall, at No. 71, is the United Oxford and Cambridge University Club. As its name suggests, you have to be a graduate of Oxford or Cambridge to be a member, and it helps if you're a man. There are approximately 4000 male members and only 580 female "associates". The club has a vast library with its own full-time librarian. The relief panels along the façade of the club represent (from left to right) Homer, Bacon, Shakespeare, Apollo and Athene with the nine Muses, Milton, Newton and Virgil. Milton and Newton went to Cambridge – the others have no right to be there at all.

Cross the road and retrace your steps eastwards. At No. 36 Pall Mall you will find the Army and Navy Club, founded in 1837 by a group of officers from the East India Company. They returned from service in India and had to wait such a long time to join the United Service Club that they decided to start their own. The club's nickname is "The Rag", coined by Captain Billy Duff, who came into the club late one evening and complained that the menu in the dining room was a mere "rag and famish affair". The Rag and Famish was then a brothel in Cranbourn Street.

Turn left into St James's Square, and at No. 16 you will find four clubs: the East India, the Devonshire, the Sports and the Public Schools. The clubs have amalgamated, or more accurately been swallowed by the East India Club. Until the late 1960s England's rugby and cricket teams were always selected at the Sports Club.

Now make for St James's Street. Here you will find the *crème de la crème* of London clubs: White's, Boodle's, Brooks's, Pratt's and the Carlton.

White's is at the top, very near Piccadilly. It's the father of all London clubs, originally called "The Chocolate House" and opened in 1693 by Francis White. When White died in 1711, the chocolate and coffee house was taken over by his widow. The modern club is very secretive indeed, but it is said to have a membership list that reads like *Burke's Peerage*.

Boodle's is further down, on the same side as White's. Boodle's used to boast a finer service than could be found in any hotel in London – coins were boiled before being passed to members as change, to make sure they were clean and germ-free. It was founded in 1762 by Francis Boodle, the son of a Shropshire innkeeper, and it's still the club favoured by privileged country gentlemen who have come to London to attend to matters of business.

Opposite Boodle's is Brooks's – so exclusive it does not have a street number. Just the other side of Park Place from Brooks's is Pratt's, the original manager being William Nathaniel Pratt, steward to the seventh Duke of Beaufort. Nowadays it's owned by the Duke of Devonshire. There is a tiny basement with a dining room that can accommodate only 14 of the 600 members at any one time. All the staff at Pratt's are called "George" by members. No women are allowed, either as members or as guests.

One block further down is the Carlton. It has been an informal meeting place and headquarters for members of the Conservative Party ever since it was founded in 1832. "The Carlton is a beastly club infected by the worst of the species," wrote Arthur Balfour to Lord Curzon, but that doesn't excuse the IRA bombing of it in 1990.

opposite:
The Royal Automobile Club stands on the site of the old War Office in Pall Mall.

The Stiff Upper Lip

above:
The statue of the Duke of Wellington at Hyde Park Corner.
above right:
Apsley House, home of the Duke of Wellington.
below:
The new gates into Hyde Park, erected in honour of the Queen Mother.

The well-known *Oxford English Dictionary* (sadly, there isn't a *London English Dictionary*) defines "to keep a stiff upper lip" as "to show no sign of weakening, yielding or suffering".

It's a late-19th-century phrase in origin, redolent of the British Empire's finest hours. It's typified by Wilson's Last Stand, when a patrol of 33 men were ambushed by hundreds of Matabele warriors in Rhodesia in 1896. The patrol fought till their ammunition was exhausted, shook hands with one another and then sang "God Save the Queen" before they were slaughtered to a man.

The type still exists. They are gentlemen of the "Old School" – nobody knows which particular school, though Eton College would probably claim to be a strong contender; atavistic survivors of a bygone age. Round their stiff necks there are stiff collars and old school or regimental ties – preferably the Brigade of Guards or the Blues and Royals. They are dressed in impeccably dark suits, immaculate bowler hats and beautifully polished shoes. Each carries a copy of *The Times* ("although it's not what it was, you know, old boy") and a neatly furled umbrella. The rarest of the breed may sport a monocle – extra points if you spot one of these. Their eyes are often watery, though they seldom show any signs of emotion. Their noses are on the large side. Their lips are thin as well as stiff.

Their natural habitat ("stamping ground" is the phrase they would use) is the West End, especially Mayfair or the area to the south of Piccadilly. They are sometimes glimpsed disappearing into the clubs around St James's.

Their politics are about as conservative as possible, though they would regard the modern Tory Party with disdain and disapproval, as a load of get-rich-quick Johnnies with no manners whatsoever. They can be gracious and charming to anyone, regardless of background or nationality, though deep down they still believe that

"wogs begin at Calais". Again and again they have been written off, but somehow they have managed to survive and keep their upper lips stiff.

No. 1 London

At the western end of Piccadilly, near Hyde Park Corner, is Apsley House, otherwise known as No. 1 London. It was the home of Arthur Wellesley, first Duke of Wellington. He had a decidedly large nose – he was nicknamed Old Conky by his soldiers – and his upper lip was as stiff as any man's.

He commanded the British Army at the battle of Waterloo – which he claimed was won on the playing fields of Eton. After defeating Napoleon, he was idolized as the saviour of England, and Apsley House was the gift of the nation to him. Wellington was a popular Prime Minister of Britain from 1828 to 1830. When he opposed the Great Reform Bill of 1832, however, he was regarded as a monster incarnate.

At the time, supporters of reform showed candles in their windows, in celebration of the bill. The duke's windows in Apsley House were conspicuously dark. So the London mob smashed all the plate-glass windows on the ground floor. The duke himself wasn't there, but his servant courageously fired two blunderbusses at the mob, and they retreated. The duke was furious. "The people are rotten to the core," he wrote.

The Duke of Wellington's Duel

In 1829 Wellington (then Prime Minister) challenged George Finch-Hatton, ninth Earl of Winchelsea, to a

duel. The earl had accused Wellington of seeking to establish "Popery" in Britain. They met at 6.45 am on Saturday 21 March on Battersea fields (now Battersea Park). The duke's second paced out positions for the two opponents. "Damn it!" cried Wellington. "Don't stand him up so near the ditch. If I hit him he will tumble in."

When the order was given to fire, Wellington deliberately aimed wide. Winchelsea simply loosed his pistol off into the air. Winchelsea's second then handed Wellington a pencilled note apologizing for the original accusation. Honour was satisfied. It was probably the last duel to take place in London.

Hyde Park Corner

Almost opposite Apsley House is Hyde Park Corner, once the site of the tollgate between London and the villages of Kensington and Knightsbridge. On the island surrounded today by the sea of traffic is a statue of Wellington, mounted on Copenhagen, the horse he rode at Waterloo.

It replaced an earlier statue so hideous that a French survivor of the battle who saw it is said to have exclaimed: "We have been avenged!"

The Hurlingham Club

In Ranelagh Gardens, SW6, is the Hurlingham Club, the last outpost of the British Empire. In the middle of the 19th century it was a pigeon-shooting club – much needed today in London. Later it became the headquarters of the Hurlingham Polo Association, but, dashed unsportingly, the polo grounds were compulsorily purchased by the Labour-run London County Council in 1946.

Nowadays, the club is an oasis of aristocratic calm, though there are signs that change is afoot. It has a cricket ground, tennis courts, a golf course, swimming pool, bowling greens, and, most importantly, several croquet lawns. If you have the right background, you can also indulge in fencing and archery. If you don't have the right background, you'll be lucky if you manage to peer over the hedge.

The memorial to the Duke of Wellington at Hyde Park Corner.

London Style – The Legacy

London is always elegant, sometimes fashionable, seldom chic. London style is traditionally based on wealth – save for the occasional appearance of Cockney cheek, there's rarely any hint of the gamin that Paris so adores, or the street-smartness beloved of New York. It's also essentially traditional, with the weight of centuries of breeding and exclusiveness behind it. The sought-after areas of London are not those most recently developed. Given the choice between a spanking new penthouse apartment in Docklands, or an 18th-century mews cottage behind Harrods, discerning Londoners would always opt for the latter.

Style in London applies to where you live, how you live, how you dress, where and what you eat and drink, where you are seen and what you are seen doing, where you work out, what you drive, the drugs you take, the pets you keep, how you speak, where you shop, where you send you children to school and who attends your parties. There are hostesses in London who go into paroxysms of despair if they cannot persuade a cabinet minister or two to attend their "little bash".

18th-century dukes and viscounts – Mayfair, Belgravia, Kensington and Knightsbridge. No part of London developed in the 19th or 20th century has yet matched their urbane allure. Consequently, almost no part of London south of the Thames has ever been à la mode – with the possible exception of Blackheath and Greenwich, which from time to time have been recognized as having a certain picturesque charm.

Living

There is something grandly, pig-headedly old-fashioned about much of this, a legacy of the days when aristocratic families ruled London society with a rod of iron. The smart addresses in London are still those favoured by

Outfitting

The stylish male Londoner, therefore, does what he has always done, what his father and grandfather did. He gets his shirts in Jermyn Street, his suits in Savile Row, his waterproofs at Aquascutum, his cricket flannels at

Lillywhite's in Piccadilly Circus, his boots at Lobb, his wine at Berry Brothers and Rudd, his game pie at Fortnum's. All this has nothing to do with being "trendy" – upstarts with new-found fortunes can buy £300 trainers, jazzy sports glasses and designer casuals at a dozen hi-tech, "where-it's-at" stores. London style centres on the correct, not the outrageous. Let others roar around town in their Porsches and Ferraris, the stylish Londoner quietly motors by in his Rolls or Bentley.

As for men, so for women, London style is traditional – cashmere twinsets and rows of pearls, well-cut skirts that are neither too long nor too short, "good" shoes, headscarves from Liberty's and smart Jaeger coats, hairstyles that are never out of fashion and never in fashion. The day is a busy round of shopping at Harrods, driving the children to their boarding schools in the country, walking the spaniel or Labrador in the park, drinking just one sherry before dinner, and avoiding the limelight.

Home-Making

Enter the home of a stylish Londoner and you will see little to suggest the coming of the third millennium. The house will smell clean and fresh, with a hint of country blossom and not the slightest whiff of joss-stick. The wallpaper will quietly suggest the 18th or 19th century – perhaps one of the William Morris designs from Sanderson's, or, more daringly, a Zoffany of Mayfair recreation of the great days of the Victorian salon. The furniture will be innocent of chrome or plastic. It won't be modular or post-Bauhaus, or rely for its rigidity on modern adhesives. The dinner (roast lamb and mint sauce, new potatoes and fresh peas, followed by rhubarb crumble and custard) will be cooked on and in an Aga. The whole house will be as up-to-the-minute as it was a hundred years ago.

Eating

Fashionable restaurants may come and go, but they are not stylish in the London sense. If you wish to eat London-style, and you have plenty of money, never mind Le Gavroche, the Ivy or Chez Nico – above all, never mind Mezzo. Go to the Riverside Restaurant at the Savoy, to Bentley's for oysters, to Wheeler's in Old Compton Street for lobster or sole, to Simpson's in the Strand for a cut off the joint, to Rowley's in Jermyn Street or Rule's in Maiden Lane. There will be not a trace of raspberry coulis.

The people who maintain London style are not the people who make the front pages of gossip or scandal magazines. They are not glitzy, showbiz folk. They avoid the limelight whenever and wherever possible – though their photographs may appear in the society pages of *The Tatler*. They are charming, in the sense that they are never abrasively rude. They keep their feelings to themselves. They would describe themselves as "comfortably" well-off, though they would insist that sending the children to private schools is a huge financial sacrifice. Secretly, they are very wealthy indeed. Some of them are among the richest in the country, though you would never get them to admit it – after all, understatement is all part of London style.

above:
A uniformed commissionaire guards the gleaming showroom of Jack Barclay in Berkeley Square.
left:
Keeping it in the family – Robert Gieves, outside Gieves and Hawkes in Savile Row.

London Style – Revolution in the Sixties

The most famous pedestrian crossing in the world – where the Beatles walked in Abbey Road.

In the 1960s strange and exciting events took place in London. Fuelled largely by a revolution in British pop music, London took off like a rocket, and the world followed its lead. There was an enormous growth in the self-confidence of Londoners: they knew they could succeed where they had seldom succeeded before, and let the world know that they were succeeding.

London entrepreneurs, designers, artists and promoters suddenly realized that they were capable of having good ideas and putting them into practice. They opened boutiques where they sold clothes and hats, tights and shoes, lotions and potions that were new, attractive, outrageous. They opened restaurants and bars, cafés and clubs that catered for the tastes and pockets of the young. And the crowds flocked in from all over the world. The most famous of the pioneers became front-page celebrities – the faces of Mary Quant and Vidal Sassoon were as familiar to the public as those of the Beatles.

The heart and hub of it all was Carnaby Street, till then famous only as the home of John Inderwick, who began the fashion for Meerschaum pipes in the 19th century and bought a mine in the Crimea to ensure regular supplies. Now this little road to the east of Regent Street became more popular as a tourist venue than Buckingham Palace or St Paul's. It was the Mecca of style, crammed with what a hit song of the time referred to as "dedicated followers of fashion". A nearby pub in Great Marlborough Street changed its name to the Dog and Trumpet, to mark its connections with a certain well-known record company.

The rocket was still soaring right through the 1970s. Previously, the only claim to fame of the King's Road, Chelsea, had been that No. 120 had once been the home of Thomas Crapper, inventor of the water closet. Now the whole street became the home of punk – gaudy, assertive, confrontational. Tiny dens of design sold chains, studs, nails, leathers and all the accoutrements of that brash vogue. Vivienne Westwood opened a shop selling clothes whose design, she acknowledged, owed much to the world of pornography. She was arrested, and charged with committing a breach of the peace. London was still swinging.

Then came the mean-spirited Eighties, and the rocket ran out of fuel and fell back to earth with a thud. The party was over. Many of the boutiques went out of business or moved to smaller premises. The music lost its charm. Colour drained away from shirts and dresses, socks and boots. Where had all the flowers gone?

Carnaby Street is still swinging, but the swingers are all 30 years older. The Dog and Trumpet was refurbished in 1996 and renamed the Fanfare and Firkin – you may fare better at the Shakespeare's Head across the road. Strolling musicians still play in the pedestrianized street, and the little shops are still busy, though they tend to specialize in shoes, handmade cosmetics, caps and waistcoats, or gifts and souvenirs, rather than the "great gear" of the 1960s.

The Beatles Shop is in Kingly Street, sandwiched between Carnaby Street and Regent Street. Here you will find T-shirts, miniature street signs of Penny Lane and Abbey Road, and a whole host of Beatles memorabilia. Just off Carnaby Street, in Beak Street, is Lonsdale – a boxing shop that sells shorts, robes, punchbags, towels, books on boxing, hand straps, hook and jab pads, ankle weights and callisthenic body suits.

Elsewhere, much has changed. Biba changed hands and style, and is now to be found in Shorts Gardens, to the north of Covent Garden. The Apple Boutique and the Tiger Boutique are no more. Twiggy and the Shrimp have long since departed from the catwalk. Vidal Sassoon styles the hair of the Hollywood *glitterati*. But all bad things must come to an end, and London has recovered from the dark days of the 1980s and early 1990s. The London Fashion Week, held each year in February, rivals those of Paris, Milan, and New York. Vivienne Westwood flourishes in Davies Street, round the corner from South Molton Street, a parade of jewellery and clothes shops.

King's Road

This is an ancient thoroughfare that runs all the way from the World's End Distillery in Fulham to Sloane Square. In its heyday, it vied for glory with Carnaby Street – packed with young hedonists in search of fun, freedom and fashion.

The King's Road proper begins at the Z-bend near the Man in the Moon pub, with a parade of boutiques selling anything from fifties repro shirts to the *avant-garde* outrageous. As it moves eastwards it becomes a happy miscellany of art shops, coffee shops, dumpling and noodle bars, designer shops, galleries – some of which look settled for hundreds of years, others presenting a more fly-by-night appearance. Here and there you get a glimpse of the glories of the Sixties and Seventies. The occasional boutique shouts its individuality from its colour-drenched window.

When you need refreshment, have a drink at the Chelsea Potter (dark and atmospheric), or eat at the Pizza Express in what was once the home of Princess Seraphina Astafieva, the ballerina. Further west than the Z-bend the street is dull and has never been part of the swinging scene – though it does have a very up-market Oxfam charity shop, with a window that contains (at the last count) wine buckets, *Christie's Review of the Year* and a Moschino jacket.

In the heyday of Swinging London – shoppers in the King's Road, Chelsea, in August 1967.

The Suppliers of London Style

London style, like any other, is a mixture of appearance, behaviour and taste. What matters is how you dress, where you shop, what you buy, where you keep your money, and where you spend it. The four institutions detailed below have a combined history of over one thousand years of catering for the upper echelons of London society, of laying the foundations of London style. You are free to walk into each of them, and each is well worth a visit.

Coutts and Company, 440 The Strand

In 1692 John Campbell of Lundie moved to London and set up a bank at "The Sign of the Three Crowns" in The Strand. It was one of the first banks in London. Today, still in The Strand and still a bank, it is known as Coutts and Company. Among its many famous former customers are King George III, William Pitt the Elder and the Younger, King Louis Philippe, the Duke of Wellington, Sir Walter Scott, Chopin and Tennyson.

The old banking hall, built in 1904, was redeveloped in the 1970s. Gone is the Edwardian splendour, but the modern Garden Court is a pleasure dome in which to do business. It's roughly the size of four tennis courts, with a fountain in a carp pool, beds of flowers, trees, marble floors, comfortable settees and a fine statue of Thomas Coutts, who ran the bank for the second half of the 18th century.

Tradition seldom disappears entirely in London. Managers at Coutts still wear frock coats, just as they did 200 years ago, and they still have to be clean-shaven. There are no bearded bankers at "The Sign of the Three Crowns".

Henry Poole and Company, 15 Savile Row

In the Garden Court of Coutts and Company, you will find two display cases with ledgers from the firm of Henry Poole and Company, outfitters. One ledger is open at the page showing the dealings of Winston Churchill with the company, the other those of Benjamin Disraeli.

James Poole started the firm in 1806, after he had made his own uniform as a member of the Volunteer Corps, then being recruited to fight against Napoleon. The original premises were in Brunswick Square, but James's son, Henry, moved to premises in Savile Row, W1, in 1846, and the firm has been there ever since.

Henry also dabbled in politics. He and Baron de Rothschild advanced Prince Louis Napoleon £10,000,

and, not surprisingly, Poole's were subsequently granted a Royal Warrant by Louis when he became Emperor of France. They obtained their first British Warrant after Edward, Prince of Wales (later Edward VII), admired the clothes they made for an actor named Charles Albert Fechter in a performance of *Ruy Blas*.

Justerini and Brooks, 61 St James's Street

Giacomo Justerini, a young Italian, started his wine business in 1749 in what is now Pall Mall. He had come to London from Bologna in pursuit of an opera singer with whom he was in love. The love affair came to nothing. The wine business he founded has lasted 250 years, during which time Justerini and Brooks have been granted Royal Warrants by every successive monarch from George III to Elizabeth II.

Justerini sold the firm to one George Johnson in 1760, and retired to Italy. The Johnson family were in charge for three generations, but in 1830 were bought out by a wealthy young man named Alfred Brooks, one of whose regular bibulous customers was Charles Dickens.

Although the firm has moved a couple of times in its history, it is now happily settled in fine premises near the bottom of St James's Street, SW1. Its vast cellars are at Forest Gate in east London.

Gieves and Hawkes, 1 Savile Row

Gieves and Hawkes made uniforms for the officers in Nelson's navy, and for the great Horatio himself. The company moved to London in 1890, and to Savile Row in 1912. The main salesroom today was originally the Map Room of the Royal Geographical Society – the room in which the body of the explorer David Livingstone (also one of the customer of Gieves and Hawkes) rested prior to burial in Westminster Abbey on 18 April 1874.

At the back of the shop is a small lobby that houses a tiny museum of military uniforms – helmets, epaulettes the size of hams, and dress uniforms that date back to the Peninsular War. The link with the services has been constant. The company sent a yacht equipped as a tailors' workshop to the Crimea in the 1850s. They published a mail order catalogue in the 1880s which featured a vast number of "comforts for the troops" – everything from a cholera belt to a cashmere overcoat.

Mutiny on the Bounty
Gieves and Hawkes even made uniforms for Captain Bligh of HMS *Bounty*. When Charles Laughton was offered the role of Bligh in the film *Mutiny on the Bounty*, he visited Gieves and Hawkes and asked if they could supply him with details of how Bligh dressed. After a few minutes, the salesman returned to Laughton with a ledger that recorded Bligh's measurements and an exact description of the uniform he wore.

above and top:
What the well-dressed racegoer is wearing – and has been for the past fifty years. A herringbone coat with velvet collar from Turnbull and Asser.
left:
Gieves and Hawkes, No. 1, Savile Row.

The London Season

Every year a sequence of sporting and social events makes up what is known as the London Season. It's a social calendar that developed in the 18th and 19th centuries to occupy the upper classes for the spring and early summer, when they left their country estates and took up residence in London.

It began over 250 years ago, once better housing and hygiene had made the annual visit of the plague almost a thing of the past. From spring to the end of July the rich assembled in the capital, opening up their grand houses in Mayfair for weeks of outings, parties and balls.

The Season had, and still has, a series of fixed points: the private view at the Royal Academy; the Royal Military Tournament; the flower show by the Royal Horticultural Society; the Fourth of July celebrations at Eton College; polo at Hurlingham; cricket matches at Lord's between Oxford and Cambridge, and Eton and

Harrow. "How much more tolerable those functions would be without cricket", commented Mlle Sans Sève, a French visitor to the London Season. She enjoyed the bands playing, the carriages parading, the parasols twirling, the outrageous hats bobbing on well-coiffed heads, but couldn't abide what was then England's national game.

Outside London, the Season includes the Henley Regatta, race meetings at Ascot and Epsom, and the week's sailing at Cowes, Isle of Wight. For the poor, the Season used to offer employment and leftovers from the good life. When it ended, servants, flower-girls and dressmakers would say: "We'll have to live off air pie now." For the rich, the Season offered a round of continuous self-indulgence.

Every night there were several parties and at least one ball. Every day the young and beautiful used to saunter between noon and 2 pm along the Knightsbridge side of Hyde Park. Etiquette decreed that the sauntering was not to be too ostentatious and was not to last too long.

A bevy of debutantes descend to the ballroom of the Grosvenor House hotel for Queen Charlotte's Ball, 19th May 1950.

This posed a problem, for the main function of the London Season was to act as a marriage market. Unmarried daughters of the wealthy or aristocratic were launched into society in the hope that they would quickly find suitable husbands. Woe betide any sad girl who was not well suitor-ed by the beginning of August.

These were the débutantes – well-bred, refined, beautifully groomed and dressed young women, brought up to dance gracefully and hold their tongues, to hang on a man's every word, to be modest and available. The highlight of the Season was their formal presentation at court to the King and Queen.

Dressed in white, the debs formed a fluttering line, and one by one curtsied to their sovereigns. One brave soul has gone down in history. When presented to King George V in 1911, the young woman knelt before him, then raised her head – an unheard-of liberty – and said: "Your Majesty, stop forcible feeding!" She was referring to the barbaric practice of forcing soup into the stomachs of imprisoned suffragettes who were on hunger strike. The young woman was hurried away, and a shocked King George wrote in his diary that night: "I don't know what we are coming to."

In the Swinging Sixties, the monarchy decided it had better things to do, and the presentation of débutantes at court ceased. It was replaced by the present highlight of the Season – Queen Charlotte's Ball.

Queen Charlotte's Ball and Hospital

The annual ball was first held in 1922 to raise money for Queen Charlotte's Hospital in west London. The hospital was founded in 1752, but first came under the patronage of Queen Charlotte in 1804, its purpose being "to afford an asylum for indigent females during the awful period of childbirth and also to facilitate the repentance of suffering and contrite sinners". Since 1929 the ball has been held at the Grosvenor House Hotel in Park Lane, home over the years to many an unrepentant sinner.

Debs' Delights

The cast of players rarely changes during the Season. The same young women are accompanied by the same young men night after night. This is because there are two lists. One is of those young women who are "coming out" – having their first formal taste of London social life. The other, prepared with less forethought, is of suitable attendant males. These escorts are known as "Debs' Delights". They are usually lieutenants from the smarter regiments of the British Army or young men carving out successful careers for themselves in the City. Towards the end of the 19th and the beginning of the 20th

centuries, money became more important than breeding for this list.

The Season in Verse

The poet *par excellence* of the Season was John Betjeman, but a hundred years earlier a poet named W.M. Praed wrote some verses to commemorate its heady summer days and nights. Praed called the poem *Good Night to the Season*:

> Good night to the season! – the dances,
> The fillings of little hot rooms,
> The glancings of rapturous glances,
> The fancyings of fancy costumes;
> The pleasures which fashion makes duties,
> The praisings of fiddles and flutes,
> The luxury of looking at Beauties,
> The tedium of talking to mutes;
> The female diplomatists, planners
> Of matches for Laura and Jane;
> The ice of her Ladyship's manners,
> The ice of his Lordship's champagne.

Mrs Vernon Royal and her twin sons, both pupils at Eton College, arrive at Lord's cricket ground for the annual match against Harrow, 11th July 1931.

Auctions

Dotted about the traditionally fashionable areas of London, pre-eminently in Kensington or the West End, are galleries and auction houses belonging to the four leading giants of the gavel – Bonhams, Christie's, Phillips and Sotheby's.

For the last 250 years, these auction houses have between them sold and re-sold treasures from all over the world. Hundreds of the most prized paintings of all time have passed through their hands, to be knocked down to private collectors, museums, banks and insurance companies in every continent. The same is true of beautiful porcelain, rare books, exotic jewellery, and the most exquisite furniture.

Business has been good in the last 50 years. The collectors' universe has expanded at a phenomenal rate. The hammer now falls on film costumes, cartoons, toys, stamps, coins, cards, photographs – anything from a clockwork mouse to a stuffed fish.

Bonhams and Phillips

Bonhams is the fourth largest of the quartet of great London auction houses. The company was founded in 1793 by William Charles Bonham and George Jones in a small gallery in Leicester Square. The firm grew steadily over the next 150 years, moving first to Oxford Street and then to New Burlington Street. Bonhams now have showrooms in Montpelier Street, off the Brompton Road, and in Lots Road, Chelsea.

Phillips is three years younger than Bonhams, the creation of Harry Phillips, former head clerk to James Christie. In 1797 Phillips acquired premises in New Bond Street, and entered London society, then recovering from its post-French Revolutionary paranoia. The firm remained in family hands throughout the 19th century and well into the 20th. Fire destroyed the original office premises in 1939, and the main office and showrooms are now across the road at 101 New Bond Street.

Sotheby's

Sotheby's, found world-wide, is the biggest and oldest of London's fine art auctioneers. It was established in 1744 by Samuel Baker, a London bookseller. Baker held only one sale a year at first, then moved to bigger premises in Covent Garden. The firm was joined in 1776 by John Sotheby, Baker's nephew, who was in turn followed by three more generations of Sotheby's until the family connection was broken in 1861. All this time – indeed, right up to the 1930s – Sotheby's was primarily an auction house for the sale of books.

Since 1917, the firm's headquarters have been in New Bond Street. They began dealing in paintings towards the end of the first World War, since which time the firm has grown enormously, with an annual turnover that runs into billions of pounds. The art side of the business continues to be based in New Bond Street. Sales of books, manuscripts, coins, medals and jewellery are held in part of what was once the Aeolian Hall, in Bloomfield Place, off Bourdon Street, just west of New Bond Street.

Christie's

In 1766 Christie's was founded by James Christie, a former midshipman in the Royal Navy who resigned his commission to become an assistant to a Covent Garden auctioneer. He set up business in Great Castle Street, but moved to Pall Mall in 1770, where he became Gainsborough's neighbour. Christie was also a friend of Sir Joshua Reynolds, David Garrick, Richard Sheridan, and Thomas Chippendale, the great furniture-maker.

The firm prospered, especially after the outbreak of the French Revolution, when many hard-pressed *émigré* nobles wished to sell jewels and paintings from their châteaux to finance their new life in London. In 1823, James Christie's son moved the expanding business to King Street, where it has remained ever since. Though once described as "gentlemen pretending to be auctioneers", Christie's has always prospered, with an annual turnover of hundreds of millions of pounds. The firm was bought by a French businessman and owner of the Château Latour vineyard, François Pinault, for £721 million in 1998.

Playing Leap Frog with Van Gogh

The occasionally bitter rivalry between Christie's and Sotheby's was highlighted in 1987. In March of that year Van Gogh's *Sunflowers* was auctioned at Christie's in London, and sold to a Japanese insurance company for a record £24.75 million. Whether or not the painting is genuine remains the subject of controversy (and a probable lawsuit), but the record was broken just eight months later when Sotheby's New York branch sold Van Gogh's *Irises* for £30 million. In 1990 Christie's again went into the lead when they sold the same artist's *Portrait of Dr Gachet* for £50 million. Sotheby's then achieved a major *coup* by gaining the right to stage "the Biggest Auction of All" – the sale of everything that had belonged to the Duke and Duchess of Windsor, in February 1998. It is said that top executives from both auction houses are not averse to wooing wealthy widows and estate lawyers, in their attempts to get their hands on the few great masterworks of art that still remain in private hands.

Knock-Down Prices

There are other auctions in London. In draughty warehouses or dingy sheds in London's outer suburbs there are car auctions, where ready money can buy a bargain (or a near-wreck) at a very low price. It's best to take a car expert with you, and make a careful inspection of any car you wish to bid for – the cars are sold "as seen", and you are unlikely to get your money back if you change your mind. It's almost as risky as buying a Van Gogh.

opposite:
Old Masters – a fine art sale in progress at Christie's auction rooms in King Street.
below:
Old Bangers – one of London's many car auction sites.

Westminster Abbey

The first poet to be buried in this section of the abbey was Geoffrey Chaucer in 1400. He gained his place not because of his poetry, but because he had been an important 14th-century civil servant. Others have been granted their memorials over the centuries, but not all are buried here. Ben Jonson (incorrectly spelt "Johnson" on his monument) was buried in the Abbey, standing upright to take up less space. James Macpherson, a literary hoaxer of the 18th century, lies next to the great Dr Johnson, a man who hated and despised him. Poets and writers honoured include Milton, Gray, Goldsmith, Dryden, Wordsworth, Browning, Austen, Tennyson, Dickens, Hardy and Kipling. Some have had to wait a long time before successive deans of the abbey have considered them sufficiently respectable to be commemorated. There was no memorial to Shakespeare until 1740, to Burns until 1885, to Blake until 1957, and to D.H. Lawrence until 1985. Poets' Corner has now been declared full. As with the first, so with the last to be included – Laurence Olivier, who was neither poet nor writer but an actor. There is an abbey ghost, which is discussed later in Haunted London.

Westminster Abbey is one of the four buildings that immediately spell London – the others are Buckingham Palace, the Tower and St Paul's Cathedral. It has been the setting for much of the capital's pomp and ceremony for almost a thousand years. In its echoing splendour have been held royal weddings, coronations, memorial services for the great and the good (and others). It's a masterpiece of medieval design that contains more of the nation's history than any other building in Britain. It is also the parish church of the Royal Family when they are in residence at Buckingham Palace, and is known as a Royal Peculiar – unique in that it is a church not under the control of the Archbishop of Canterbury (Leader of the Church of England), but directly under the control of the Queen (Head of the Church of England).

History

The abbey was founded on the site of a seventh-century Saxon church, built on what was then Thorney Island, in the middle of a wide and sluggish Thames. A charter of 785 refers to this "terrible place called Westminster". Edward the Confessor founded the monastery here in 1042, and the present church was consecrated on 28 December 1065, eight days before Edward died. Within a year the Norman Conqueror, William I, was in possession of London, snatching the crown from the Archbishop and crowning himself to hasten proceedings in the abbey when he mistakenly thought the crowd outside was getting out of hand.

Since then every king and queen has been crowned in the abbey save Edward V (one of the two princes murdered in the Tower of London, possibly under orders from Richard III), and Edward VIII (who gave up the throne for love and Fascism before his coronation).

Although venerated today, the abbey has not always been treated with respect. It was the one monastery that Henry VIII felt it would be unwise to pillage, but Cromwell's men had no qualms. They camped in the abbey and "wretchedly profaned the very table (altar) itself by setting about it with their tobacco and all before them". Cromwell himself was originally buried in the abbey, but, when Charles II returned to the throne in 1660, the body was disinterred, hanged at Tyburn and then beheaded.

Henry V is buried here, with the helmet, shield and saddle he used at the battle of Agincourt in 1415. His queen, Catherine de Valois, lay in the abbey in an open tomb for 300 years. On 23 February 1669, as a birthday treat, the diarist Samuel Pepys – never less than bold when it came to approaching a woman – kissed the lips of the long dead queen. "I had the upper part of her body in my hands, and I did kiss her mouth, reflecting upon it that I did kiss a Queen".

Among the famous buried here are several prime ministers, including the Earl of Clarendon, Pitt the Elder, Pitt the Younger, Peel, Palmerston, Gladstone and Spencer Percival. Percival is the only British Prime Minister to have been assassinated, to date – he was shot, just across the road, in the lobby of the House of Commons by one John Bellingham, a bankrupt who had a grievance against the government. The abbey also houses the mortal remains of Thomas "Old" Parr, who was said to have been born in 1483 and died at court in 1635, Isaac Newton, Lord Rutherford, Robert Stephenson, Dr Arnold, David Livingstone and Henry Irving.

The abbey is a vast and awesome place, gleaming white and pink outside, dark and forebidding inside. It is used as a chapel for morning prayers by the pupils of Westminster School, after which time tourists and visitors are admitted – those whose faith in travel brochures has brought them here from all over the world by plane, train, bus, coach and the District and Circle Lines of the London Underground.

The River Thames

Old Father Thames

To poets the river Thames has been an object of great beauty. To Londoners it has been a source of food and water, and stinkingly, a main drain. It has provided a living for thousands of sailors and dockers, wherrymen and ferrymen, and has been the death of millions as, until recently, its water became increasingly putrid and unhealthy.

For 1700 years there was only one way of crossing the Thames dryshod – by London Bridge. In the last 250 years the Thames has been spanned by a further 19 road bridges, several rail bridges, a footbridge or two, and undercut by over 20 tunnels (road, foot, Tube lines, conduits for cables and hydraulic power; a few are disused). It's no longer a major obstacle for those who wish to cross London, except at the morning and evening rush hours.

But the poets were right – the Thames is a beautiful river, well worth exploring, from its sparkling reaches in Kingston, to the west, to its broad industrial basin of motor and sewage works east of London at Dagenham and Thamesmead. John Burns, a man of London and a socialist, called it "liquid history", and indeed a boat trip up or down the Thames reveals much of London's past, as the river brushes past Richmond and Chelsea, the Houses of Parliament and the Tower of London, the docks and wharves of Limehouse and Millwall, and the palace of Greenwich.

It has carried the flotsam and jetsam of London's rubbish, the bodies not just of its own victims, the hopes of its trade. Londoners think of it as their river, but it belongs to the Crown. In 1857 Queen Victoria and the City of London went to law, each protesting they owned the Thames.

For once, the Crown emerged victorious, and was proclaimed owner of the river from Cricklade, 100 miles (160 km) to the west of London, right down to the London Stone at the mouth of Yantlet Creek, where the river is four miles (6 km) wide and the prevailing south-westerlies whip across from the Kent marshes to Southend-on-Sea, a pleasure resort known to some as the Cockney Coney Island.

London has lived in constant fear that the Thames would burst its banks. From time to time it has. In 1099 "the sea flood sprang up to such a height and did so much harm as no man remembered that it ever did before". In 1237 the Great Hall of Westminster, then London's Law Courts, was so deeply flooded that lawyers conducted their business in rowing boats. In 1524 it was predicted that the river would flood the whole of London on 1 February. Thousands of Londoners climbed to the top of Parliament Hill, four miles to the north, to watch. They were disappointed. But 50 years later the Great Hall was flooded again, leaving hundreds of fishes floundering on the floor. In 1663 Pepys recorded in his *Diary* that all Whitehall had been drowned.

The threat was always there. In the 1870s embankments were built on both sides of the river, but the Thames flooded again in 1928, when 14 people died in the basements of Westminster, and in 1953, when 300 people were drowned in the Thames Estuary.

Today London is protected from its river by the Thames Barrier, which stretches 520 yards from Silvertown to Charlton. It looks a bit like a submerged version of the Sydney Opera House, but its massive arches can rise and close within 30 minutes and it has already saved London and its inhabitants several times. It was first planned in 1904 and completed 78 years later. Only when there's money to be made – rather than spent – does London move quickly.

The Thames is nothing like as busy as it used to be. Tugs pull strings of barges full of landfill down to the wastelands of Essex. Speedboats cut through the water rushing City gents to their finance houses. Pleasure boats carry tourists to St Katharine's Dock or Greenwich or Richmond. But the lightermen of the old docks have gone – as have the old docks themselves, to make way for middle-class riverside residences – and you can no longer take the steps down to the riverside and cry "Oars" to summon a waterman who would ferry you across. It's a pity, for the hundreds of London watermen were a rough, witty, bellicose lot, notorious for their foul language. In 1761 an order was issued that watermen should be fined half a crown (12.5 pence) for each verbal

The dome of St Paul's and the Nat West Tower dominate the Thames skyline.

transgression, the money to go to "the poor, aged, decayed, and maimed members of the watermen's Company, their widows and children". The men and women who run trips on the Thames today are far more polite, but just as verbose, and they will expect you to put something in the cap that's passed round to show your appreciation of the commentary they provide.

Upstream you will still recognize the Thames of Jerome K. Jerome's *Three Men in a Boat*, the river of expert sculls and amateur rowers, of noticeboards and "boorish riverside landowners". But in central London the Thames is fairly quiet. No longer do paddle steamers churn their way to Margate or Southend for a day out; the motor car has seen to that. River buses come and go, an obvious answer to London's chronic traffic congestion, but one not generally exploited.

Never mind. Simply stand by the Thames anywhere in London – on bridge or towpath, embankment or pub balcony – and you will see a sight well worth study. At night the Thames sparkles with the reflected lights of the monuments that cluster alongside. On a bright day the sunlight bounces off its surface, giving you a blurred image of its further shore that has all the magic of an Impressionist painting. Even in the grey and cold of a winter's day, the Thames is a delight.

Stand on Tower Bridge and look down to the Pool of London and Old Wapping Stairs, where pirates were hung in chains below the waterline in Execution Dock. Stand on Chelsea Bridge, and look upstream, where the banks of the river are lined with the greenery of Battersea Park to the south and the grounds of the Royal Hospital to the north. Stand on Westminster Bridge – it was good enough for Wordsworth.

Best of all, retrace the footsteps of Caesar's legions, the rebellious peasants of medieval times who followed Wat Tyler and Jack Cade, or today's millions of off-duty Londoners. Simply walk alongside a stretch of water that one Londoner regarded as "the noblest river in Europe".

A fine mix of 18th century houses on the bank of the Thames at Strand on the Green.

The River Thames from Waterloo Bridge

St. Paul's Cathedral

Commercial Union Building

Blackfriars Bridge

NatWest Tower

Lloyd's Building

Oxo Building

IPC Tower

Coin Street housing

London Weekend Television

National Theatre

Pleasure Boats

Guy's Hospital

above:
On the last stretch of the Great River Race – a ten oar crew pull for the line.
right:
Rowers come from all over Europe to take part in the annual Great River Race.

Three Thames Races

Every spring, Oxford and Cambridge – both of which have rivers of their own – compete in the University Boat Race. The course is four and a half miles (7 km), from Putney to Mortlake – four dry minutes in a train, 20 sodden minutes in a coxed eight. The race began in 1829, and originally it took place miles out of London (from Hambledon Lock to Henley), but in 1845 the crews came downstream and they've been there ever since.

The race starts at the Duke's Head pub in Putney, and finishes at the Ship in Mortlake. Although it's lost some of the mass appeal it had in Victorian times, when every towpath and tree along the route was crammed with rival supporters, it's still a major London sporting event – and worth attending, if only to marvel at the old Light and Dark Blues, allegedly mature supporters of Cambridge and Oxford respectively. Boat Race Night (the evening following the race) was traditionally a time when graduates and undergraduates of both universities got drunk and misbehaved in central London – knocking policemen's helmets off and being sick all over the West End.

Every autumn the Great River Race takes place – from Ham House near Richmond to Island Gardens in Docklands, a distance of 22 miles (35 km). It's open to all types of boats powered by oars or paddles: skiffs, whalers, gigs, kayaks, and even dragon boats. Crews come from all over Europe – many from the Netherlands – to take part.

They race as the tide runs out, going at a surprising speed downriver. Between 250 and 300 boats take part, and the race is handicapped so that they arrive at the finish in a remarkably compact flotilla, sometimes with oars clattering together as they race for the line. On a golden afternoon in late September it's a very pretty

The Oxford crew in pursuit of Cambridge in London's most famous boat race.

sight, not unlike a Canaletto painting, best viewed from the north bank, with Greenwich Palace opposite in the background. It also has a wonderfully old-fashioned look about it – a crowded Thames with people lining both banks.

At the end of the race the crews beach their boats and head for the nearest pub, some even rowing over to the Trafalgar Tavern on the south side, where they are given a warm welcome despite their soaking clothes and the mud caking their legs from trudging ashore.

But the river race that really belongs to London is that for Doggett's Coat and Badge. Thomas Doggett was a comedian and manager of the Drury Lane Theatre. When he died in 1715, his will provided for a "Badge of Silver weighing about twelve ounces [340 gm] and representing Liberty . . . and eighteen shillings [90 pence] for Cloath for a livery" for the fastest young waterman on the Thames.

The race is held at the end of July every year, and the course is four and a half miles – exactly the same distance as the University Boat Race – from London Bridge to Cadogan Pier, Chelsea. It's the oldest annual contest in the British sporting calendar. The single scullers take about 30 minutes to cover the course, rowing against the ebb tide – pretty good going when compared with the "eights" of Oxford and Cambridge. It's easier to watch than the University Boat Race, and, although pubs have less to do with it, you can see the sculls that the watermen use chained and padlocked to the wall of a modern pub called Doggett's Coat and Badge on the south side of Blackfriars Bridge.

left:
Alfred Edward Gobbett is congratulated after winning the 1938 Doggett's Coat and Badge race.

Crossing the River

There have been several London bridges, and many had lively histories. The original was built of wood by the Romans. It was deliberately burnt down in 1014 by Ethelred of England and Olaf of Norway to divide the forces of their Danish opponents. The event was celebrated in a Norwegian poem that began: "London Bridge is broken down…".

The next London Bridge was destroyed by a gale 50 years later. It was rebuilt, but burnt down in 1136. Another 40 years on, the first stone London Bridge was built. It lasted for 100 years, though many of the houses erected on it were destroyed by fire in 1213. Then, in 1282, five of the 19 stone arches of the bridge were swept away. Small wonder that for centuries children have sung:

London Bridge is falling down,
Falling down, falling down.
London Bridge is falling down,
My Fair Lady…

In medieval times the parboiled heads of traitors were coated in tar and displayed on the bridge, as a warning to all. There were shops, houses, a chapel and a pumping machine on the Old London Bridge, which was demolished in 1823. A new bridge was then built just upstream, designed by John Rennie. This was the bridge that the Americans bought in 1968, shipped out to Arizona and rebuilt at Lake Havasu City – to the delight of many Londoners, who got the idea that the Americans thought they were buying Tower Bridge. In fact, the citizens of Lake Havasu City got very little even of London Bridge – just the facing stones. Most of Rennie's bridge now lies in a disused quarry in Dorset, in the west of England.

The present bridge was finished in 1972. It is wide, graceful and safe, which is perhaps all one needs of a bridge – especially one that has had such a shaky history.

Lord of the Ford

Occasionally drunken or foolish young men leap from bridges into the Thames, as proof of their manhood. If they're unlucky, they may not surface. If they're lucky, they swim to shore with nothing worse than a stomach full of dirty water. If they're very lucky they get a ride in a police launch – such actions are not approved of by the river police.

Back in March 1952, the river police left Lord Noel-Buxton well alone. He was reputedly the tallest member of the House of Lords (unlikely – most hereditary peers are enormous), standing six feet three inches (1.95 metres) in his baronial socks. The noble Lord believed in the existence of an ancient Roman ford across the Thames from St Thomas's Steps on the South Bank to the Speaker's Stairs at the Palace of Westminster. He

Old London Bridge, complete with houses and shops, from a print of 1787.

reckoned that, at low tide (9 am that day) the river would be only five feet three inches (1.6 metres) deep at its deepest point. So, clad in shirt, pullover, flannel trousers and a pair of rubber-soled shoes, Lord Noel-Buxton waded into the Thames at a few minutes past nine.

Although the theory has subsequently been proved correct, he hadn't taken account of the fact that the modern Thames is narrower and hence deeper than it was 2000 years ago. He had to swim most of the way, and it wasn't until he was only 22 yards from the Speaker's Stairs that he could touch bottom with his foot and keep his head above water. Nevertheless, Lord Noel-Buxton felt he'd proved his theory and claimed that the water had been only a foot (30 cm) too deep to prevent him

wading the whole way across. What the river needed was a lord seven feet three inches (2.2 metres) tall.

The Greenwich Foot Tunnel

A pedestrian tunnel joins the Docklands and Greenwich. It is about 440 yards long, and was built between 1897 and 1902, so that dockers working on the West India Docks but living south of the river could get to work.

It's best to walk the tunnel from south to north, because there are 100 steps at the Greenwich end, but only 69 at the Docklands end. For the less agile, there are lifts at both ends. The tunnel in cross-section is a slightly flattened circle, so walking along it is a bit like walking through a Swiss roll or a *roulade*. It's roughly four yards in diameter, coated with grubby white glazed tiles, and is happily free from advertisements. When it's busy, it's delightful – when almost empty it can be a little eerie for the faint-hearted.

Tightrope over the Thames

People have found a variety of ways of crossing the Thames. As part of the Festival of Britain celebrations in September 1951, Monsieur Charles Elleano, a 43-year-old French tightrope walker, crossed on a cable 1100 feet (340 metres) long, stretched from the Embankment Tube station to the South Bank opposite. It took him 25 minutes, which is quicker than by car during rush hour. Newspaper reports suggest that his passage wasn't easy: "Several times he swayed and sank to one knee as he edged slowly forward." And it was made even more difficult for M. Elleano by a passing tug, whose smoke hid him from the watchers on both banks, and can't have helped him to see where he was going.

As he neared the South Bank, however, he became more confident, taking ten backward steps and sitting down on the cable. And when he finally reached the shore, he was embraced by his wife and children. It was a bold French contribution to a very British festival.

top:
New London Bridge and the Monument, from the south bank of the Thames.
left:
The pedestrian tunnel under the Thames at Greenwich.

Afloat on the Thames

HMS *Belfast*

London is obsessed by memories of the Second World War. It is celebrated in a museum devoted to the Blitz, Churchill's Cabinet War Rooms in King Charles Street near Downing Street, the Imperial War Museum, and in HMS *Belfast*, a relic of the war and the largest cruiser ever built for the Royal Navy.

HMS *Belfast* was launched in March 1938 and took part in the battle of North Cape, the Normandy landings, and the Korean War. She remained in service until 1965, and was saved "for the nation" and became a floating museum six years later.

From the gun turrets in the stern of the ship you get probably the finest view in London of Tower Bridge and the Tower itself – especially Traitors' Gate. The guns have a range of 14 miles (23 km), which means they could hit almost anything within the M25 ring road. There is a notice beside them that says: "Please be careful when elevating or training the guns." Presumably the fear is that a careless visitor might train them on the toffs dancing and dining in the Savoy Hotel (upstream, north) rather than on the Millennium Dome (downstream, south). The lat-

ter has already taken enough punishment from press, public and politicians.

Inside HMS *Belfast* there is an audio re-enactment of the Battle of North Cape, when *Belfast* and several other British ships sank the German *Scharnhorst*. There are sound effects of Morse code messages and shells bursting, and orders are barked out in very upper-class English voices. The overall effect is much more like the soundtrack of a British war film than the real thing. You need to be prepared for encounters with the life-size dummy figures that are scattered throughout the ship, to represent the wartime crew. It's quite unnerving to round a corner and come face to face with a wild-wigged plastic Officer of the Watch.

In the souvenir shop you can buy books, souvenirs, posters, periscopes, binoculars, and an odd assortment of videos – mostly of American war movies (*Run Silent, Run Deep*; *Battle of the Medway*; *Destination Tokyo*), none of which have anything to do with HMS *Belfast*. There are also mugs for sale with jokey slogans on them ("Galley Slave"), packets of NAAFI tea and ginger-snap biscuits. It all smacks a bit of the last days of the British Empire.

HMS Belfast, sole survivor of the Royal Navy in the Second World War, at her permanent berth by Tower Bridge.

The Woolwich Ferry

Crossing the Thames was a problem for East Enders long after the West End was well supplied with bridges. The first recorded ferry at Woolwich was in 1308, when the town was just a little fishing village. It was provided to join two parts of the same parish, one in Essex, one in Kent. And for almost 600 years the ferry was the only way across this stretch of the river. Today there are three tunnels under the Thames in East London, but they weren't built until the late 19th and early 20th centuries.

Since hundreds of dock workers in the early part of the 19th century had to get from their homes south of the river to the West India Docks on the other side, an Act of Parliament of 1811 authorized a "common ferry" at Woolwich. It was a simple horse-powered raft, slow and cumbersome to operate. Passengers wishing to cross had plenty of time to wait, and the waiting rooms on both sides of the river eventually became pubs – the Marquis of Wellington and the Prince Regent, both of which were demolished long ago.

By the 1880s, a faster, bigger ferry was needed to transport passengers and freight across the river. In 1884 the Metropolitan Board of Works (forerunner of the London County Council) agreed to build and run a modern ferry, and five years later services began on the Woolwich Free Ferry. The original paddle steamers that operated have long gone, but the ferry is still there and, wonder of wonders, it's still free. Three boats work the ferry, all named after left-wing politicians: *John Burns*, *Ernest Bevin* and *James Newman*. A single crossing takes eight minutes from the time you step on to the time you

step off, a return trip less than twenty minutes. A great many large trucks from mainland Europe use the ferry, so there's quite an international flavour to it, like a mini-Channel crossing without the duty-frees.

From the ferry there are fine views upstream of the Thames Barrier, and on a bright winter's evening (up to the last crossing at 8.30 pm) you may see the lights of aircraft using the City Airport just a few hundred yards away. Downstream all is wide and flat, as London begins to straggle away.

The ferry has been closed only four times in well over a century – in the General Strike of 1926, once following a collision with an American ship, for three months in 1949 while the terminals were being rebuilt, and for a couple of weeks in 1989 after the *Ernest Bevin* failed to respond to the controls and hit the south terminal with such force that she destroyed half the fendering round it. Like the man she was named after, the ship is clearly a tough customer.

Ernest Bevin, one of the fleet of ships that sail to and fro every day on the Woolwich Free Ferry.

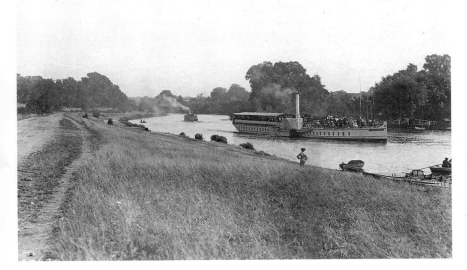

left:
The pleasure steamer Queen Elizabeth sails up river from Kingston Bridge to Hampton Court in the summer of 1907.

The Thames Barrier

London is constantly sinking. There's no need to panic, it's happening very slowly – at the rate of about eight inches (200 mm) every century. But early in the 1970s, planners realized that strong winds and an abnormally high tide could now flood something like 50 square miles (13,000 ha) of the centre of London. There was the risk of a bad flood once every 50 years, and a disastrous one every 200 years. So they built the Thames Barrier.

It's over 1500 feet (520 metres) long, straddling the Thames at Woolwich Reach. Many people wrongly assume that it's a dam. It isn't. It's what it says it is – a barrier, with moveable gates. When the gates are open, they are lying on the river bed, so that ships can pass safely over them. When they're shut, they hold back the waters that would otherwise flood London. Quite what that might do to the inhabitants of Hornchurch and Thamesmead downstream, nobody seems sure. So far all has been well, and the barrier has been closed in earnest a dozen or so times.

The beautiful silver arches, glinting in the sun and reminding all London Aussies of the Sydney Opera House, are covers for the electro-hydraulic machines that open and close the gates. The whole thing cost £500 million, and looks beautiful on a summer's evening. Unfortunately the Visitors' Centre, which is on the south side, shuts at 4 pm.

In October 1997 the strength of the barrier was tested by a 3000-ton freighter, which ran into it early one misty morning. The freighter suffered more than the barrier, but at least attracted more visitors to the site.

The Thames Barrier, with Canary Wharf and Docklands in the background.

Greenwich

In terms of exclusivity and snobbishness, Greenwich is almost on a par with Hampstead. It's an upper-middle-class island in the sea of working-class southeast London, and it's very old. Traces of a Bronze Age settlement have been found in Greenwich Park, just to the west of the Old Observatory. The name "Greenwich" comes from the Anglo-Saxon for "green port".

For 150 years, the heart of Greenwich was a royal palace, the birthplace of Henry VIII, Mary I and Elizabeth I. It was Henry's favourite residence. He hunted in Greenwich Park, then far larger than today. In England's 11-year period as a republic, the palace was converted into a factory to make biscuits for the navy, and then briefly became a gaol for Dutch prisoners of war from 1653 before it was demolished in 1690.

Greenwich Park used to be the setting for royal games – tilting, wrestling, spear- and sword-fighting – and amorous adventures. Henry VIII's second wife, Anne Boleyn, is said to have dropped a handkerchief here during a May Day tournament, as a signal to a lover. Although this was a slur on her character, the next day she was sent as a prisoner to the Tower. Two weeks later she was beheaded.

The park is a much safer place today, full of squirrels and families, amateur footballers and skateboarders.

At the foot of the park, where the land flattens towards the river, is the replacement royal palace, part of which became the Royal Naval Hospital, built 300 years ago by Wren to be the sailors' equivalent of the Chelsea Hospital for soldiers. In 1864 the patients were removed, and the hospital became the Royal Naval College, with its marvellously beautiful Painted Hall and its extremely well-stocked wine cellar. In 1996 the Conservative government decided to sell it, as a means of making cuts in the defence budget. The National Maritime Museum,

above:
The Royal Naval College, Greenwich, originally a hospital for sailors. 'Columns, colonnades and friezes ill accord with bully beef and sour beef mixed with water,' complained one patient.
right:
The old Royal Observatory in Greenwich Park.

embracing the exquisite Queen's House by Inigo Jones and part of Wren's Greenwich Hospital, was until 1934 a home for the orphaned children of sailors; it is well worth a visit.

The *Cutty Sark* and the *Gipsy Moth IV* lie alongside each other in dry docks by Greenwich Pier, where the river buses call. The *Cutty Sark* was a tea clipper, sailing between China and Britain in the 19th century. Francis Chichester sailed single-handed round the world in *Gipsy Moth IV* in the mid-1960s. He was subsequently knighted by the Queen in the Grand Square of Greenwich Palace; she used the same sword with which Francis Drake had been knighted by Elizabeth I nearly 400 years earlier.

The Greenwich Meridian
and the Old Royal Observatory

Until the late 18th century, most countries throughout the world used their capital cities as the zero point from which to measure longitude. But in 1767 the first *British Nautical Almanack* was published, an indispensable handbook for all navigators. The British zero point was established at Greenwich, and the rest of the world followed Britain's lead. At the top of Greenwich Park you can stand astride the meridian line – it's marked by a brass strip on the path – with one foot in the eastern hemisphere, and one in the western.

In 1880 Greenwich Mean Time became the standard time for the whole of Britain except Ireland. Until then, each town had its own time, which made the compilation of railway timetables a nightmare – trains could arrive at a station earlier than the time at which they'd left the last station. In 1924 the Greenwich "pips" were introduced on BBC radio, to identify the precise second at which the hour was reached. At 1 pm every day, a ball rolls down the mast at the Old Observatory, so if you sprint, you've just got time to catch the 1.15 river bus back to Charing Cross Pier.

The Old Royal Observatory used to house mirrors, telescopes and all the instruments of the Astronomer Royal and his colleagues. In the early 1950s the observatory moved to Hurstmonceux in Sussex, some 50 miles away, to escape the London fog and smoke. A couple of years later, Parliament passed the Clean Air Act, which might have made the move unnecessary. Appropriately for Greenwich, it was a masterpiece of British timing.

The Millennium Site

There are mixed views about the wisdom of the Dome, designed by Richard Rogers as the centrepiece of Britain's celebration of the new millennium. The inhabitants of many cities (Birmingham and Manchester first among them) are angry that, once again, to London goes the glory and the attention. There are also many, Londoners included, who wonder whether the billion or so pounds that it is costing wouldn't have been better spent on schools or hospitals.

Whatever the rights and wrongs, the die is now cast, and the Dome sits like a giant yellow turtle on what was once the wastelands of East Greenwich. There is the promise of fun and wonderment for all to see... so long as the Jubilee Line extension is completed in time to bring the millions of visitors. In the words of the Duke of Wellington at the battle of Waterloo, it will be a "damned close-run thing".

Some of the old ships' figure-heads in the Cutty Sark.
above:
The Millennium Dome rises above the wastelands of North Greenwich.

left:
The tea clipper Cutty Sark in her permanent dry dock at Greenwich.

The South Bank

The South Bank was originally the concrete strip of cultural development that lies between Hungerford Bridge and Waterloo Bridge, but it's constantly stretching downstream. Until the Festival of Britain in 1951 the south side of the river was always the poor relation of the north side.

Even now, there are those who believe that culture shouldn't exist south of the river, and that the sooner the Festival Hall is closed down and the National Film Theatre moved north to Islington or Hampstead, the better.

But, for the moment, the South Bank remains, a monument to the traditional London planners' inability to make the most of a prime site. A silly little road snakes round to the river side of the Festival Hall, moving it a heartbreaking 30 or 40 yards away from the Thames. You can sit in the café inside the hall and get a good view of the north bank. What you can't see is the river itself.

Having learnt nothing from the mistakes made in the positioning of the Festival Hall, and, indeed, the Queen Elizabeth Hall (from which you can't see either the river or the north bank), planners and architects made an even greater mess of the National Theatre. They had plenty of time to get it right. The project was first proposed in 1848, but the foundation stone wasn't laid until 1951, and the building wasn't opened until 1976. Like the Queen Elizabeth Hall and the Hayward Gallery and all the labyrinthine walkways around the South Bank, the National Theatre is made of grey concrete. It's very difficult to find a way in, because all the doors are at an angle of 45 to the river, as though shying away from it. And, once inside, it's almost impossible to find a satisfactory view of the river. But the three theatres inside the National (the Lyttelton, the Olivier and the Cottesloe) present an interesting, usually first-rate, mixture of drama, great and good, small and experimental, old and new. And the Mezzanine Restaurant there is the best place to eat on the South Bank.

In the late 1990s there were and are plans for a vast revamping of the South Bank: enclosing the Embankment footpath, building pontoons over the river

from Hungerford Bridge, and giving the site more commercial appeal. If the pace of past development is maintained, we shall be well into the next millennium before anything radical appears.

Gabriel's Wharf

Just downstream from the National Theatre, the large office buildings that line the river give way to a little backwater called Gabriel's Wharf. It's a mixture of independent small shops and modest eating places. There's a tiny bandstand which is sadly under-used, and you can hire bicycles to ride up and down the Embankment.

Next to Gabriel's Wharf is Coin Street, which consists of a row of terraced houses with a community garden. This is one of the few places in London where the less-than-rich have a chance to live by the river, which has made it something of a bone of contention with the more commercially minded.

The Oxo Tower

The tallest building on this stretch of the river is the Oxo Tower. When the Oxo company bought the site from the Post Office in the 1920s, they used it as a warehouse in which to store meat imports from South America.

At that time, the old London County Council banned illuminated signs. So Albert Moore, the designer of the tower, incorporated circles and crosses in stained glass at the top of the tower, spelling out the name "Oxo" on each of the four faces of the building.

The top of the Oxo Tower is now a fashionable and very expensive restaurant, run by Harvey Nichols of Knightsbridge. There are those who love it dearly, and book months in advance and are prepared to pay high prices for fine wine and food, but service that has been described as keen rather than exemplary. But there are many more of us who simply wish to go up in the lifts and enjoy one of the most enchanting views of the stretch of the Thames joining Westminster and the City.

Hayes Galleria

Further downstream is the Hayes Galleria, a covered shopping precinct. It's a busy and rather touristy place, with a modernistic galleon made out of junk metal in the middle of a fountain as its centrepiece. I have no idea why, but there is also a pitch for *boules* or *petanque*, though your boule will land in a pit of gravel instead of on the hard sandy soil of southern France. Consequently, far less skill is required: it's more like bombing than bowling. And the Cottons Centre is worth a visit, if only to enjoy perhaps the best atrium in London.

The Oxo Tower – high life on the South Bank.
bottom:
New life for old warehouses – the Hayes Galleria.

Konditor and Cook

If you're on the South Bank and hungry, go to Konditor and Cook, in Cornwall Road, by Waterloo East station. At the back of the old-fashioned corner shop, you will find wonderful sandwiches, two or three hot dishes (the kedgeree and the cauliflower bake are superb), salads, hot olive bread, cakes and biscuits. And if you don't want a take-away, Konditors have a sit-down restaurant in the Young Vic theatre in The Cut, five minutes' walk away.

The London Dungeon

Tooley Street runs parallel with the railway by London Bridge station. In the last 20 years it has come up in the world, and is now much smarter than it has ever been in its 400-year history. But it is also an area that seems devoted to blood, toil, tears and sweat. It contains the Britain at War Exhibition, and a series of paintings of battles of the Second World War, as well as the London Dungeon.

At the entrance to the London Dungeon there is a notice which says that this "experience" is not for the squeamish. What it doesn't say is that it costs the brave or foolhardy or sadistic £8.95 to get in.

The tone of the "experience" is established at the beginning. The staff of the London Dungeon are clearly encouraged to adopt a jokey impoliteness, from the opening "where do you think you're going?" onwards. But the worst thing about the London Dungeon is that it's a slow-moving experience.

It's a popular venue, and even on a damp autumn afternoon you may have to queue for some time to get to the Gothic-arched ticket window; between each section of your visit you have to wait patiently until the party ahead has been cleared away. Since the whole thing takes place under the arches of London Bridge, in dark caverns, this can build up a sense of stifling frustration.

It claims to be a study of injustice and warfare as they have affected Londoners over the last 2000 years. Odd, then, that the final section is devoted to "The Theatre of

the Guillotine", a five-minute visit to Paris at the time of the French Revolution.

Other sections of the Experience are "Under Siege", "The Age of Reason", "The River of Death" and "Jack the Ripper". There are wall texts which combine historical inaccuracy with colourful writing: "…the poor victim is choked by a rope, disembowelled by the blade, and as his last breath of life escapes from him forced to see his guts roasted in the fire. If not dead by then, the removal of his limbs is the final degradation of his mortal body…".

Under Siege

This is very much the Hollywood school of history, where inconvenient facts are ignored. Resting under a mock stone catafalque is the head of Mary Queen of Scots, who never had anything to do with London and was executed in Fotheringay, 100 miles away. An animatronic Anne Boleyn makes her final speech before her execution (1536) to Latimer and Ridley while they are burnt at the stake 19 years later. There's a lifesize display of the murder of Archbishop Thomas à Becket, who admittedly was born in London but was killed in Canterbury Cathedral.

The Age of Reason

After a prolonged wait and much insulting by a costumed guide, all visitors are sentenced to death in an Old Bailey Judgement. The sentencing judge has a face covered in livid scars and wears a London Dungeon T-shirt and an 18th-century wig, though we are all accused of treason against His Majesty King Charles I, who was beheaded in 1649. It's always good to see actors gainfully employed, but you feel these actors would be much happier doing the warm-up for some television show. And the corrugated iron roof lacks period authenticity.

The River of Death

The "River of Death" takes you to Execution Dock. A notice advises you not to take the ride if you have a heart

top:
Thomas à Becket is murdered everyday at the London Dungeon.
below:
Medieval torture, modern ghoulishness.

condition or suffer from claustrophobia (though what anyone suffering from claustrophobia would be doing in the London Dungeon is hard to imagine). But when you ask one of the bullying guides what you should do to avoid the River of Death, they go all to pieces and don't know what to say.

Jack the Ripper

After more waiting you enter the world of Jack the Ripper. Here at last we are in touch with London, and are given some fairly accurate historical information. But the London Dungeon's strange mixture of gore and flippancy reaches its apogee in Ripperland. For no clear reason, a sheet of flame bursts forth from the wall of the laboratory where two dummies are supposedly carrying out a post-mortem on one of the Ripper's victims. Now that really is a surprise. But it's here that it becomes clear-

est of all that the London Dungeon is not a place for children, and not much of a place for adults.

With the final section devoted to the Reign of Terror in the French Revolution the pretence that we are experiencing London's past disappears completely. There is an anticipated beheading by Madame la Plastique Guillotine and we are mercifully released to the Pizza Hut café and the Souvenir Shop – with its sweets, ice-creams, gew-gaws and Judgement Day T-shirts. Tooley Street seems sweet and clean after all that.

The dark side of London's past – the entrance to the London Dungeon under the arches at London Bridge station.

Tower Bridge

Sir Horace Jones's late Victorian masterpiece – Tower Bridge.

In 1970 the good people of Lake Havasu City, Arizona, bought London Bridge, a pleasant enough construction built in the 1820s. It was then shipped to the States, stone by stone. What they *thought* they were buying was Tower Bridge, which is far more interesting and would have been a much better buy.

Tower Bridge was built in the early 1890s, in response to popular demand. The citizens of London had presented many petitions for a new crossing below London Bridge. Crowds cheered when the bridge was officially opened in 1894, and it was described as "a colossal symbol of the British genius", though critics hated it. H.G. Wells called it a "stockbroker in armour".

In London terms, it's a very special bridge, simply because it has to "open" to allow large ships to pass below. It is a bascule bridge. In style it matches St Pancras station or the Palace of Westminster. Indeed, you could imagine that it broke free from the latter and floated majestically downstream until it ran aground next to the Tower of London.

The Tower Bridge Experience

The tour of Tower Bridge consists of a succession of films about its history and construction. They are all very informative, but nothing like as exciting as the upper walkways or a visit to the engine room.

There are two walkways, originally built to allow pedestrians to cross the bridge when the bascules were raised. Try to visit in autumn or winter, when the air is clear and there's no summer haze, because the views from the walkways are spectacular. Upstream you can see the Tower and Traitors' Gate, the Monument, St Paul's Cathedral and the B.T. Tower. You also get the best view of some of the happier modern design in the City – the buildings cluster together as though covering a small hill, rising up to the Lloyds Building.

The downstream view is even better. You see how the shape of southeast London is formed by the ranges of hills that lie beyond. The panorama stretches from Crystal Palace, eastwards past the Greenwich Observatory, the Harmsworth Quays building, Canary Wharf, and then back up river to St Katharine's Dock. Nestling by St Katharine's Dock is what seems the most desirable residence in the whole City – the Old Dockmaster's House. And all the time pleasure boats, police launches and the occasional barge pass up and down the river, way below.

In the downstream walkway there's also a fine exhibition of old photographs of the bridge and its surroundings over the last 100 years. My own favourite is that of the Horsleydown Steps leading to Dead Man's Hole. The picture was taken a short while before the bridge was opened, in the early summer of 1894. You can see the last ferry operating across the Thames in London – a simple, small, slim boat powered by a single pair of oars. There's the ferryman himself, and you cannot help wondering what became of him.

The Engine Room

Don't miss this. It is the heart of the whole operation and a temple to the splendours of Victorian engineering. As you enter, you are reminded that this is a working bridge.

There's a whiteboard on the wall with details of the days and times that large ships will be coming upstream and the bridge will have to be opened. The old coal-fired boilers are clean and gleaming in their obsolescence, and there's a grim animatronic stoker sitting by a pile of real coal and muttering information about how little coal was needed to keep the engines fuelled. Take little notice, and pass on to the engine room itself.

It is almost a religious experience, though here we are worshipping not God, but power. It's a wonderful mixture of grand and small, of giant machinery and tiny fixtures and fittings. The working engine wheezes and pants away, and each turn of the massive wheel is registered on Harding's Improved Counter. When I was last there, it was registering 1,886,151 turns. There are beautiful brass taps and levers and little curved glass phials of lubricating oil, enormous iron spanners and silkily smooth pistons. Enjoy it all.

below:
Tower Bridge and HMS Belfast. The giant inflatable Mountie rising on the river bank was part of a promotion by the Canada Tourist Board. He never got off the ground.

The Foolish and the Brave

In 1912 Frank McClean became the first person to fly a plane between the walkways and the bascules of Tower Bridge. Since then, five other pilots have repeated this feat, and one has crashed attempting it. In case you wondered, it's illegal.

On the evening of 30 December 1952 there was a misunderstanding between two of the Tower Bridge watchmen. As a result, the bascules began to open and lift while Albert Gunter was driving his Number 76 bus across. Albert saw the danger and accelerated as fast as he could. His bus didn't exactly leap the gap between the bascules, double-decker buses can't leap. But it did cross the gap and skitter safely down the other side. The bus was full of passengers. For his great presence of mind and bravery, Albert received £5, which valued each passenger's life at around 10p in today's money.

If you're ever lucky enough to be at Tower Bridge when the bascules are raised, spare a thought for Albert.

Shakespeare's Globe Theatre

Just upstream from Southwark Bridge, on the south side of the Thames, is the New Globe Theatre, a reconstruction of the Shakespearian theatre built in 1598–9 by Cuthbert Burbage. Cuthbert was the son of James Burbage, the man who built the first ever playhouse in London. Indeed, many of the timbers from Burbage Senior's theatre were used to build the original Globe.

The old theatre had a short and busy life, and was by all accounts a rough place. Shakespeare himself was a "sharer", a man who controlled the business side of the venture and took a share of the profits. He also acted in the Globe company, and many of his plays received their first performance there. But a spark from a theatrical cannon set fire to the thatched roof during a performance of *Henry VIII* in 1613, and the theatre burnt to the ground. Fortunately, all within escaped unhurt save for one of the groundlings who had "his breeches on fire that would perhaps have broyled him if he had not with the benefit of a provident wit put it out with bottle ale". The theatre was rebuilt in 1614, but, like all London theatres, was closed by the Puritans in 1642. It was pulled down two years later to make way for some seedy tenements.

The New Globe was for many years the dream of the American actor Sam Wanamaker. There were those who said that the housing needs of local people should take preference over the reconstruction. There were rows. There were protests. But art must have its way, and work began in the early 1990s. Wanamaker's dream turned out to be an expensive one. The New Globe cost £16 million in all, of which £12.5 million came from the National Lottery. Much of the rest of the money came from all over the world. The United States, Canada, Denmark, Japan, Germany and many other countries contributed. Thousands of people sponsored individual bricks at £2 a time. The idea was to re-create the genuine article, an Elizabethan theatre built by the hand labour of master craftsmen and women, using only British materials – although in the case of the reeds for the thatched roof, French would have been better.

And it was trucks and lorries, not pack mules, that delivered the green oak, willow, bricks, York stone, sand, lime, goat's hair and reeds of which the Globe is made. The main structure of the building is made of oak beams joined together with oak pegs – the only nails in the theatre are in the pine benches. The sand, lime and goat's hair were mixed together to make the plaster for the walls, and then spread over willow laths. The bricks are the same size as 16th-century bricks: shorter, narrower and flatter than modern ones.

When the theatre first opened in 1997, the aim was to recreate the atmosphere of performances in Shakespeare's day. When a play calls for music, it's played on period instruments. There are no microphones, no sound system, no stage lights – although there is back-up lighting if plays over-run in the summer and it starts to get dark. A certain amount of restlessness is encouraged in the audience, and heckling is not unknown, but the authorities don't allow the card-playing and gambling, fighting and foul tobacco smoking of Elizabethan times. The repertoire is limited to the works of Shakespeare, Ben Jonson, Marlowe and their contemporaries.

But there is one sop to modern times: a system of water sprinklers over the thatched roof and fire-proof

The GLOBE on the Banke Side, where Shakspere acted.
From the long Antwerp view of London in the Pepysian Library.

With the drawing from which this Cut was made I was favoured by the Reverend Mr. Henley STEEVENS.

centre:
The old Globe Theatre, Bankside, circa 1600
below:
Queen Elizabeth I attends a performance of The Merry Wives of Windsor at the Globe Theatre, while the author looks proudly on.

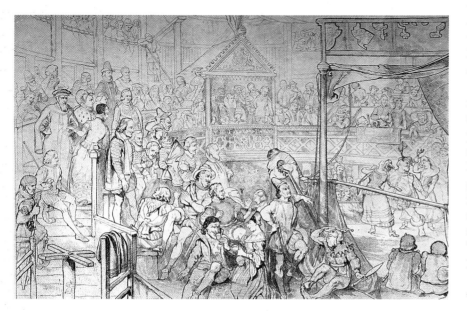

cladding inside the plaster walls. The New Globe is safe from cannon sparks.

Shakespeare in London

Shakespeare made his modest fortune in London, and London has made a considerable fortune out of Shakespeare. In the 18th and early 19th centuries Londoners were treated to bastardized versions of the great tragedies – *Macbeth* was performed with singing and dancing, *King Lear* was rewritten to allow Cordelia to stay alive and marry the Fool, and *Romeo and Juliet* was given a happy ending. But actors such as David Garrick and Edmund Kean did much to restore the Bard's text.

The first regular season of Shakespeare plays was at the Old Vic (originally the Royal Coburg Theatre) in 1914, and the theatre became the only permanent home of Shakespeare in London. In 1960, the Royal Shakespeare Company was formed, with the Aldwych Theatre as its base in the capital. Nowadays the best Shakespeare is probably to be found at the National Theatre or the Barbican; the most authentic at the New Globe; the coldest in Regent's Park Open-Air Theatre; and the keenest at the Vanbrugh Theatre (owned and operated by the Royal Academy of Dramatic Art).

The new Globe Theatre, with the Bankside Power Station looming in the background.

Chelsea

above:
The Chelsea Physic Garden.
below:
Houseboats at Cheyne Walk.
Seals have returned to fish in
this stretch of the Thames.

Chelsea is a very old part of London. There was certainly a Bronze Age settlement here. In the 8th century, King Offa built a palace for himself on the banks of the Thames near Cheyne Walk. At very low tides, ancient timbers are revealed, sticking out of the Thames mud. They are all that remains of a dyke Offa built to protect his palace. In Tudor times Sir Thomas More lived in Chelsea until he made the painful journey downriver to the Tower.

Chelsea has always sought to set itself apart from the rest of London, to be "different", to be Bohemian. It's the sort of place where people prefer living in houseboats to houses. Even Chelsea Football Club was long regarded as something of a joke, until they won the FA Cup in 1970. Back in the Twenties and Thirties the Chelsea Arts Ball was an annual bacchanalia where not-so-poor artists dressed in costume and went wild with excitement. Thirty years later, the King's Road became a fashion centre for those of similarly wayward and mould-breaking dispositions.

Cheyne Row and Cheyne Wharf

Writers and artists are not fools: they know a good place to live when they see it. And Chelsea is a very fine place to live. The main streets are clean and bright and beautiful: the side streets and the mews are delightful. No. 24 Cheyne Row used to be the home of Thomas Carlyle. Those who came to visit included Dickens, Thackeray, Emerson, Mazzini and Chopin, who played on Carlyle's piano. It was here that an over-zealous housemaid set fire to the original manuscript of Carlyle's *The French Revolution*, so that the poor man had to rewrite it from

Chelsea Pensioners

Chelsea is probably most famous for the Chelsea Pensioners. They are the residents of the Chelsea Hospital, founded by King Charles II for veteran soldiers along the lines of the Hôtel des Invalides in Paris. The Hospital is yet another of Sir Christopher Wren's great London triumphs, built round three courtyards – the centre one has a statue of Charles which is wreathed in oak leaves on 29 May (Oak Apple Day) to commemorate his escape from the Battle of Worcester on 3 September 1651. Don't ask why the celebration takes place in May, it just does.

But on the day, the 420 Pensioners (all old soldiers) set aside their everyday uniforms of navy blue, and dress in ceremonial scarlet, with special three-cornered hats. They have long been popular London figures, invited to many sporting events – conspicuously Wimbledon – and much respected by those of us who have mercifully escaped combat. You'll often see them, in their everyday dark blue uniform, walking along the King's Road.

Another Maytime occasion at the Hospital is the annual Chelsea Flower Show, more of which later.

scratch. You can still see the chimney from which the smoke issued on that awful day.

Chelsea Blunderer

Those with a liking for the bizarre may care to visit Tryon Street (fourth turning on the right from Sloane Square as you go along the King's Road). It's a very short street, with a good pub but little else of note in it. It was named after Vice-Admiral Sir George Tryon, a barmy sailor of Victorian times. Tryon gave an absurd order, which resulted in two of his ships colliding off Tripoli in 1893. He was one of the hundreds of sailors that drowned. Quite rightly, there isn't a statue of Tryon anywhere in London, but I cannot understand why a street should have been named after him.

Chelsea Physic Garden

In Royal Hospital Road lies this secret walled garden, founded by the Society of Apothecaries in 1673. Its aim then, and now, was "to promote botany in relation to medicine". In the 17th century the healing arts were known as "Physic". Where the gravel walks meet at the centre of the garden there's a very weatherbeaten statue of Sir Hans Sloane, the natural historian and physician, who bequeathed the garden for public use.

It's a fascinating and beautiful oasis where you'll find trees, plants and shrubs from all over the world. It's also a delightful example of working London, where the studies of the old apothecaries continue, so much of the garden is taken up with beds of herbs, medicinal plants and vegetables. In the special Garden of World Medicine there are healing plants ranging from deadly nightshade (carried by troops as an antidote to nerve gas in the Gulf War) to the Aboriginal mint bush, whose leaves yield an oil used to ease breathing by loosening phlegm.

Even the birds in the Physic Garden seem healthy. The fat, sleek wood pigeons that nest there are far more attractive than their limping, moulting cousins that plague Trafalgar Square.

There is much to see. Some of the most attractive plants are the catalpa and date-plum trees, and the beds of vegetables. One of the finest sights in all London on a bright autumn day is the sun shining through the scarlet stalks and purple foliage of the leaf beet.

top left:
Chelsea Hospital – 'quiet and dignified and the work of a gentleman.'

Kew

below:

The Pagoda and the Palm House at Kew Gardens.

Much of west London is horrendous – flat, windswept suburbs of mass-produced Twenties and Thirties houses, with planes screeching overhead landing or taking off at Heathrow. But there runs, like a silver thread through a piece of old sacking, a line of charming settlements nestling on both banks of the Thames. All of them are worth a visit: Chiswick, Barnes, Strand-on-the-Green, Syon Park, Old Isleworth, Petersham, Kingston.

Kew is one of the finest, with a pretty green, and some fine 18th-century houses. In George III's reign, the green was an overspill area for his many royal children. They couldn't all be accommodated in nearby Richmond Palace, so the Dukes of Cumberland, Sussex, Kent and their sister Elizabeth went to live in Kew. Their mother breathed a sigh of relief and said: "I shall always love little Kew for this." Scantily dressed women used to run "smock races" on the green, and military reviews were held there. Today the most exciting thing you will see is a cricket match.

But the reason why most people go to Kew is to visit the Royal Botanic Gardens.

Kew Gardens

There isn't a "best" time of year to visit Kew Gardens. Every season has its own attractions – spring blossom, summer richness, autumn colours, and the winter warmth of the conservatories. The 300 acres (120 ha) were laid out by Capability Brown, bounded on the west by a broad bend in the river, and on all other sides by a brick wall. There are three entrances: the Lion Gate to the south; the Victoria Gate to the east; and the Main

Gate to the north. The Main Gate is the most impressive – a massive 19th-century wrought iron structure of elaborate design. It is only rarely fully opened.

Once through the gate, all is glorious swathes of lawn, avenues of trees and shrubs, little temples tucked away where you can sit and rest, impressive statues, and stretches of peaceful water. When you need a rest, visit the refreshment pavilion, south of the flagpole. It was built in 1920 to replace one burnt down by the suffragettes.

The most exciting botanical specimens are to be found indoors. The Palm House was built by Decimus Burton and Richard Turner over 150 years ago, to house trees and shrubs from Africa, the Americas and Australasia. Enter, and climb the spiral staircases. Here you find yourself in tropical treetops, the air hot and heavy with moisture, gazing down at the exotic trees. There's the Traveller's Tree from Madagascar, with leaves ten feet (3 metres) long. In the wild travellers used to drink the water that collected in them. There are monstrous bamboo, 50 feet (15 metres) high, and oil palms, banana trees, coconut palms, and the peach palm whose fruits taste like a cross between a potato and a chestnut.

In the Tropical Water Lily House there are rice plants, papyrus plants (no longer to be found in Egypt), and beautiful water lilies. The famous giant water lily (*Victoria amazonica*) is in the Princess of Wales Conservatory. At its biggest, its leaves are six feet (2 metres) across and can support a weight of 100 lb (45 kg). It's the plant that inspired William Paxton's design for the Crystal Palace. There was a specimen of the same lily in one of the greenhouses at Chatsworth House, where Paxton worked for the Duke of Devonshire. One day Paxton saw his young daughter sitting on one of the lily's leaves. He realized how strong the leaf must be, and studied its under-structure, noting the ribbed veins that spread from the central stalk. The columns and arches that he designed to support the roof of the Crystal Palace in 1851 were exact copies.

Maids of Honour

When you have seen all you want of Kew Gardens, leave by the Victoria Gate, turn left and walk some 400 yards along the Kew Road. This will bring you to Newens, the only place where you can still buy a local delicacy known as "Maids of Honour".

Legend has it that Henry VIII invented the name. He came across Anne Boleyn and her maids of honour eating these cakes from a silver dish. Henry, who had an eye for the ladies and a stomach for everything, was delighted by both. It is more likely that the name comes from Maids of Honour Row in Richmond, where the original shop was. Here, one of the Newens family served his apprenticeship. The family moved to Kew, and have been making the cakes on the same site for generations.

The cakes are like a vol-au-vent, though larger in diameter, with a little splodge of what looks like sugary custard at the bottom. Eat the pastry circumference first, and save the sweet centre for the last delicious mouthfuls.

There are more wonders in the Temperate House, such as the dragon tree, originally from the Canary Islands. A long time ago, people believed dragon's blood, obtained from a mystical animal, would give them protection against sorcery. But what they thought was blood was resin from this tree. In parts of Europe it was used to treat ailments ranging from dysentery to loose teeth. The Italians were more sophisticated. They used it as a varnish on their violins. Nearby, the *Encephelatos woodii* is one of the world's rarest plants. Only one specimen has ever been found growing in the wild (in Zululand in 1895), and that's now disappeared. Sadly, the one in Kew has never produced cones. Don't miss the Chinese coffin tree, and the fat-trunked *Jubea gilensis*, which grew too big for its place in the Temperate House, and had to be moved to the highest part of the building, even though it weighed 54 tons.

Richmond

The first thing you should know about Richmond is that a tiny house here will cost £250,000. Once you know that, you can guess much of the rest. Richmond is a most pleasant London town, with clean flagstone pavements and fine trees, antique shops, two theatres, a museum and lots of bookshops. It's inhabited by mildly progressive and cultured people, who live in an extremely pleasant environment which they are determined to take good care of.

It's a cosmopolitan place. You hear French, Spanish, German, Italian and more exotic tongues as you walk about. It's stylish – in an old-fashioned way. The residents exercise their cocker spaniels and Labradors – dogs that lost their city chic 30 or more years ago. In Richmond you see people wearing real leather shoes which have been beautifully polished – not necessarily by the wearers.

And the secret of Richmond's popularity with Londoners is that it's only 17 minutes from Waterloo, on one of the best-served rail tracks in the metropolis.

A Walk around Richmond
Start in the centre, near the railway station, and head for Richmond Hill. As you climb, you come across some stunningly beautiful early 19th-century houses and some quite foul 1960s developments. And, as you climb, you're also aware that to your right, somewhere down there, is the Thames, but it's tantalizingly hidden from view by trees. So a good time to walk round Richmond is in the winter, when there are fewer tourists, fewer cars and fewer leaves.

Near the top of the hill is the Terrace, laid out in the 17th century. Here the trees open out and the view is one that poets have praised for centuries. James Thomson called the scene below "the matchless Vale of Thames". Other enthusiasts included Alexander Pope, Horace Walpole and Lady Mary Wortley Montagu. Away to the left are water meadows, occasionally flooded by the Thames, and beyond them the village of Petersham. On a clear day you can see both Hampton Court and Windsor Castle.

On the Terrace itself, there is a row of some 50 wooden seats, each endowed in memory of some past Richmond resident who enjoyed the view, so there are plenty of places to sit and rest. There's even a small drinking fountain. And after the rest, it's worth climbing

The oldest river crossing in London – Richmond Bridge.

a little more, past Wick House – where Sir Joshua Reynolds lived – to the Royal Star and Garter Home at the very top. Once upon a time an old and very much loved hotel stood on this site. Now there's a neo-Georgian building that houses disabled ex-servicemen. Quite rightly, they have the finest views of all.

Opposite there's a delightful wrought iron edifice on a small roundabout, by the entrance to Richmond Park. It was originally a fountain and drinking trough erected by the Richmond Branch of the RSPCA. Now it's a little land-locked lighthouse, twinkling away as the traffic swirls past.

Leave the Terrace and plunge down the footpath that leads to the river. At the entrance to a public garden, note the confusing sign that simply says: "THESE GATES WILL BE CLOSED HALF AN HOUR BEFORE CLOSING TIME". Food for thought. Then, on to the towpath along the Thames, past real boathouses where boats are still made and mended. Go under Richmond Bridge, built of Portland stone in 1777, and turn right up Friar's Lane. This leads to Richmond Green, a pretty, tree-fringed cricket ground, criss-crossed by footpaths which must make fielding excitingly unpredictable. The houses round the green are a mixture of 17th and 18th-century, all very charming, especially Maids of Honour Row which was named after and inhabited by the women who "attended" upon the Princess of Wales in the 1720s. Turn right again off the green and you are back in the centre of the town.

Richmond Park

Early in his miserable reign, Charles I enclosed 2500 acres (1000 ha) of other people's land to create Richmond Park. His minions built a wall ten miles (16 km) long to keep out the locals and keep in the deer which the king wished to hunt.

This piece of royal greed infuriated the residents of Richmond, but it took over 100 years for them to gain access. In the mid-18th century a Richmond brewer

Richmond from the Thames.

named John Lewis led a campaign that finally opened this beautiful park to all.

In October and November, the deer in the park are culled to manage the herd, and in some cases haunches of venison are presented to the Queen's closest friends and admirers. The venison that is occasionally found on the menus of Richmond restaurants will almost certainly have come from elsewhere. Gone are the days when daring poachers slipped into the park to try their luck with bow and arrow.

Eating in Richmond

Back in the 1950s and 1960s, Richmond was said to be the London district with the highest ratio of eating places to people, and it's still crammed with restaurants, cafés, wine bars, snack bars and fast-food outlets. There are *tapas* bars, Mediterranean restaurants, Italian pizzerias, vegetarian cafés, coffee shops, French bars, *crêperies*, Lebanese restaurants, patisseries, and dozens more places where you can fill your stomach. And if all else fails, you can always buy hot sausages at Lindy's in the town centre.

The one thing to eat that you cannot buy in Richmond are the little cakes that share the name of the row of houses on the Green – Maids of Honour. This local delicacy has almost entirely disappeared, but you can still find them at the café opposite the Victoria Gates, Kew Gardens – just a couple of miles downstream.

far left:
Autumn in Richmond Park – perhaps the best time for a visit.
below:
Boatbuilders take a break from work by the Thames at Richmond.

Hampton Court

above:
Hampton Court's Astronomical Clock, designed by Nicholas Oursian in 1540.

below:
Wren's 'new Versailles' – the rear façade of the Palace.

If you insist on doing things in style, you should arrive at Hampton Court by boat. Hire some watermen to row you there – it won't be easy, as the last of them disappeared early in the 20th century. But that is how Cardinal Wolsey travelled to this beautiful Tudor palace by the Thames.

A much easier way to go is by train from Waterloo to Hampton Court station, and then simply walk over the bridge, but there is little romance in that. So try instead a train to Hampton Wick, and then walk through Hampton Court Park. On a dry autumn morning, the sun sucks up the mist from the grass on which deer are grazing, and then strikes the warm brick of the palace itself. The park is full of trees and birds – woodpeckers, coots, geese, swans, herons, even a flock of the green parrots that are rapidly increasing in numbers all over London.

You approach the palace from the east, along the grass track that runs beside the Long Water, a straight channel of water half a mile long (about 1 km), leading to ancient wrought-iron gates. Go through the gates and into the formal gardens, but watch out for goose droppings on the gravel walks.

Hampton Court Palace

The palace is built around three courtyards: the Base Court, the Clock Court and the Fountain Court (which is the one you come to first when you enter via the park instead of coming in through the main entrance). The Clock Court is the smallest and prettiest, surrounded by the older parts of the palace, and crowned with a huge astronomical clock built in 1540. It incorporates the signs

of the zodiac, the phases of the moon, the months of the year and the days of the month – a kind of Tudor calculator. The Fountain Court is the newest – the centre of the 17th-century extension built by Sir Christopher Wren, who wanted to demolish most of the Tudor palace and build a new Versailles. The Base Court is the plainest and least interesting.

As you edge your way about the palace, through the groups of schoolchildren, you have to keep reminding yourself that Cardinal Wolsey started all this. He was a butcher's son from Ipswich, who made his way up through the Church to become Henry VIII's lord chancellor. When Henry broke with Rome, Wolsey, who failed to support him effectively, was cast aside, and the king grabbed the palace. In other words, like so much of London, Hampton Court was appropriated by a monarch for his or her use. Only in the Georgian Rooms do you come across mention of the Cardinal – in the Wolsey Closet, a small, dark-panelled room with a rich gold, blue and red ceiling, heavily embossed with the Tudor rose.

The King's and Queen's Apartments are also full of wood panelling, and huge tapestries, large paintings and copies of Raphael cartoons – the originals are in the V and A Museum. Most of the palace is red or brown, suitable colours for an autumn visit. In the Georgian Rooms, there's a sumptuous crimson flock wallpaper superior to anything you'll see in an Indian restaurant.

In the cartoon gallery, you can see tiny traces of the damage caused by the fire that devastated the Fountain Court in 1986 – a few scorch marks in the oak of one of the window seats. If you can't find it, ask one of the very helpful guides, who'll be delighted to have someone to talk to. The guides are all dressed in frock coats and top hats and look like the commissionaires that stand outside posh hotels. They are not to be confused with the tour leaders, who dress in Tudor costume, bringing a touch of Disneyland to the palace.

Most of the rooms are bare or sparsely furnished, though the walls are all bright with portraits of kings and queens, royal mistresses and a few surprise guests – Cardinal Richelieu turns up in one of the galleries near the Royal Chapel. The Queen's Rooms, overlooking the Fountain Court, are stuffed with 18th-century bric-à-brac – plates, tureens, spoons, four-poster beds, bed-warmers, etc.

The Tudor kitchens and wine cellars are dark and moody. In the shop you can buy mead, silver birch wine, and packets of mixed spices for making mulled wine.

The Maze

Fifty years ago the maze was a poor, bedraggled specimen. The yew hedge was so ill-nourished that you could almost as easily walk through it as round it. Now it's much healthier, and it's a true maze. You might spend far longer in there than you had intended, though with luck you won't get quite as lost as Harris did in *Three Men in a Boat*.

When you leave the Palace

I don't recommend walking all the way back to Hampton Wick. Better to walk out through the main entrance and over Hampton Court Bridge, perhaps stopping for coffee or something stronger at the Mitre Hotel, by the river's edge. From the bridge you get a fine view of the enormous motor cruisers moored upstream, and of the footpath to Kingston, three and a half miles (about 6 km) downstream.

Take no notice of the commercial parade of shops opposite Hampton Court station. It's a plain 1930s L-shaped development, not even worthy of a scullion or a kitchen boy.

The Royal Tennis Court
For no extra charge, you can visit the Royal (or Real) Tennis Court, and, if you're lucky, have a short knock-up with an expert. The game is older than lawn tennis, more sedate, but far more complicated. It looks fiendishly difficult – a cross between tennis, squash and billiards. Outside the court there's a fine fig tree, but even the guides can't reach the ripe figs.

Windsor

Windsor Castle from the meadows of Eton.

There are those who would argue that Windsor doesn't belong in a book about London – you can't get there on a Travelcard. But Windsor Castle has for centuries been the alternative London home of many kings and queens, and its fortunes have been inextricably linked to those of the capital.

The little town of Windsor is dominated by the castle and the royal connection. The tone of a visit is set within a few paces of the charming riverside station. There's a large monument to George V – first sovereign of the House of Windsor – and a tiny plaque commemorating the deaths in 1543 of three Windsor martyrs: Henry Filmer, Anthony Pierson and Robert Testwood. This is a royal place, where little importance is attached to those who got in the way of kings.

Windsor has a fine theatre ("The Royal", of course), two railway stations, lots of eating places and pubs (most of which carry the obligatory "Ye Olde" as part of their title). The town centre is small and pretty, with cobbled alleyways leading off the road up to the castle itself. It's very royal and loyal. In the local information office, you can buy Charles I mugs, Henry VIII jigsaw puzzles (the ones of Anne Boleyn presumably have the "head" piece missing), Elizabeth I mint chocolates and Windsor baseball caps.

Windsor Castle

At first sight, the castle looks like a fussily restored 19th-century Scottish hotel: large, clean, austere, and not very welcoming. It has none of the warmth and charm of Hampton Court. Once inside, you're confronted with a strange mixture of architecture: medieval fortress, Tudor domestic, Victorian Gothic. It's like a set for an historical film, but without any swashbuckling.

Most of the castle is private. Your ticket will gain you access to the State Apartments, the gallery, Queen Mary's Dolls' House, and to the St George and Albert Chapels.

St George's Chapel is grey, like an engraving, with a flat fan-vaulted ceiling, a dark old organ and lots of tiny side chapels. It's the burial place of lots of kings and queens, as well as royal refugees allowed in by Queen

Victoria (Theodore of Abyssinia, the King of the Belgians, Her Serene Highness Princess Louisa Wilhelmina Adelaide of Saxe-Weimar and others). It's also very much an "in-house" establishment, the last resting place of ancient Windsor clerics, attendants, yeoman warders and royal hangers-on.

The Albert Chapel takes the breath away, built from the same construction kit as the Albert Memorial in Kensington Gardens: marble columns and panels, stained-glass windows, over-ornamented capitals, and over-rich decoration in red, green, gold and blue. It reminds you of the colour illustrations of puddings in Mrs Beeton's *Household Management*. The extraordinary centrepiece is a sarcophagus of Mexican onyx on which reposes a marble effigy of Prince Albert Victor, Duke of Clarence (one of the less likely Jack the Ripper suspects).

From the ramparts you get a fine view of Eton College Chapel and the Slough gas works beyond, and there are a couple of fat artillery pieces which aren't pointing at anything important. Queen Mary's Dolls' House is well worth a visit, and the gallery has regularly changing exhibitions of the highest quality, including drawings (many by Michelangelo and Leonardo), paintings, insignia, fine porcelain and rare photographs – all from the royal collection.

The guardsmen who march about the castle grounds have to stop to unlock little gates as they progress. They look, and march, very much like the Wicked Witch's guards in *The Wizard of Oz*.

Eton

Five minutes' walk downhill from the castle is a footbridge over the Thames – more of that below. Cross the bridge and you're in Eton.

In the autumn, winter and spring Eton is a quiet place with antique shops and bookshops, a very pukka barber's shop, a couple of gentlemen's tailors and more pubs. There's also a restaurant called the Cock Pit that's nearly 600 years old, though the largely Italian menu is considerably more modern.

Eton is famous only for its college, founded by Henry VI in 1440 for "the poor and needy". The Duke of Wellington claimed that the battle of Waterloo was won "on the playing fields of Eton". His contemporary, the poet Southey, called it a "seminary for brutality". For at least 100 years it has been the British elite's top school, with fees that run to £30,000 a year. The college overruns the village of Eton. You can glimpse courtyards and quadrangles through old gateways, and at certain times of the day see the pupils hurrying through the village in Victorian garb. In any other part of London they would almost certainly be jeered or hooted at by some. In Eton they are seen as part of a tradition of which locals are tremendously proud.

above:
Henry VI's Chapel at Eton College.
bottom left:
The entrance to Windsor Royal Station – Queen Victoria disliked the unseemly speed with which trains whisked her from London to Windsor.

The Windsor – Eton Bridge

From the bridge you can see the Thames curving upstream round Brocas meadow, named after a knight beheaded by Henry IV. A few miles upstream is the Queen's Ait, headquarters of the Eton "wet bobs", those who prefer rowing to land-based sports. On a fine summer afternoon you may even see the "whiffs", "perfects", pairs, fours and other rowing boats pulling to and fro.

The bridge itself is where the main highway to London crossed the river some 600 years ago. A strict tariff of unfair tolls was charged for using it until Joseph Taylor took the local corporation to court and freed the bridge from this unjust imposition in 1898.

London Water

London has never been short of water. It has an average annual rainfall of between 20 and 30 inches (500 – 750 mm), and the whole metropolis rests on a vast, natural subterranean reservoir. The problem has always been to get enough usable water to the surface.

For centuries, the Thames was the only source of water for most Londoners, and, at the same time, the main sewage outfall. As the population grew, the Thames became increasingly polluted by human excrement, drugs, minerals, poisons, dead animals, and what the 18th-century novelist Tobias Smollett called "the scourings of all the washtubs, kennels and common sewers". The only creature to thrive on the contaminated water was a boar, which escaped from a butcher's in the City and lived for six months in the common sewer of the fleet Ditch. It quadrupled in weight.

There were tributaries of the Thames that were a little purer, and wells, notably at Hampstead and Islington. Indeed, there's still a well outside the National Gallery in the very heart of London. But these supplies were inadequate for the whole city, and were out of the reach of most citizens.

As early as the 13th century, entrepreneurs started piping water into the centre. The Great Conduit brought water from the Tyburn to the City, along a route that followed modern-day Oxford Street, Holborn and Cheapside. Over the next 500 years lead, stone and wooden pipes were installed, providing Londoners with free water, but even when the City Prison in Cornhill was turned into an underground reservoir, there wasn't enough and it was often contaminated. The fleet river was dammed to make more reservoirs – today's Hampstead and Highgate ponds. Water was pumped out of the Thames near London Bridge at the rate of 216 gallons (980 litres) a minute, using a vast paddle-wheel. The wheel was destroyed by the Great Fire in 1666. A new river, or canal, was built to carry water 30 miles (48 km) from Hertfordshire to Sadler's Wells. All to little avail – London's drinking water was still scarce and deadly.

Two events in the mid-19th century hastened change. The first was a terrifying increase in the number of Londoners dying from cholera – an average of 20,000 each year. The second was the growing stench of the Thames itself – especially during the summer. The point was reached when the House of Commons had to cease sitting one summer afternoon, as members of parliament rushed from the Palace of Westminster clutching handkerchiefs to their faces. At last the government took action. The Metropolis Water Act of 1852 ordered the privately owned water companies to filter all their water through sand beds, and not to take water from the Thames below Teddington Weir, well to the west of the city. Fifty years later, London's water supply was taken into public ownership. In the 1990s it was sold off again.

The Modern Supply

Deep underground there are millions of gallons of water, stored beneath the clay and rock on which London is built. One worry is that the level of the underground water is rising, at the rate of ten feet (3 metres) a year. Nearly nine million gallons (40 million litres) of water a day have to be pumped out of the maze of underground tunnels beneath London.

Below Enfield, in north London, Thames Water (the private company which sells London's water and disposes of its sewage) stores 3 billion gallons (14 billion litres) in a thick layer of chalk – an 80-million-year-old reservoir, four times as big as the biggest surface reservoir. In winter the chalk is saturated. In summer, when supply is low and demand high, the water can be pumped up, purified and distributed through the vast ring main that now encircles London.

Most of London's surface reservoirs are to the west. There are 20 of them altogether, at Staines, Surbiton, Ashford Common, Hampton, Kempton Park and Walton-on-Thames, holding enough supplies for a mere three weeks. The reservoirs themselves are pleasant enough places, with plenty of geese and ducks to be seen, but there are those among us who wish that they were a lot further from Heathrow airport. Concerns are also

Dr. John Snow

Dr. John Snow

In Sackville Street (just off Piccadilly) there is a plaque to the memory of one of London's unsung heroes – Dr John Snow. Investigating the cause of cholera, Snow proved that a single pump in a single East End street had been responsible for many local deaths. He published his findings in a pamphlet entitled The Mode of Communication of Cholera. Within three years the supply of London's water was dramatically improved. Dr Snow deserves a statue. At the very least, his plaque deserves a pilgrimage.

below:
Stain Hill Reservoir at Sunbury-on-Thames.

growing about a modern contamination of London's water. The female hormone oestrogen is accumulating in effluents from sewage treatment works, and reports of "partially feminized and hermaphrodite fish" have increased.

It's a pity. The water in the Thames itself is now far less polluted industrially than it was 50 years ago. Since then, fish have returned to the Thames in central London in ever-increasing numbers. In the good old days, when County Hall was London's headquarters instead of yet another unnecessary hotel, there used to be a vast tank full of all the species of fish that were to be found in the Thames. Now the same building houses an aquarium, full of dolphins. Dolphins don't belong in London.

left:
A horse drinking trough survives in Marylebone.
below:
The Regent's Canal near Little Venice.

The Oldest Police Force in the World

It is a sad fact that the oldest police force in the world was founded, not to protect people, but to protect property. The Marine Police Force was founded on 2 July 1798 by John Harriott and Patrick Colquhoun. London's river had a police force 31 years before the city.

The River Police, as the force came to be called, were established to protect the ships and goods in the London docks. In the late 18th century some 34,000 ships made their way up and down a six-mile (9-km) stretch of the Thames – from Westminster down to the Isle of Dogs – with up to 8000 queueing between London Bridge and Greenwich at any one time. It could take a whole year for a ship to move up-river and discharge her cargo. During that year well over half the cargo would be stolen. Complete wharfside factories sprang up for the specific purpose of converting stolen goods for resale. It was reckoned that a third of the 33,000 dockers working in London were professional thieves – night plunderers or "light horsemen", day plunderers or "heavy horsemen", scuffle hunters and river pirates. Pilfering is too mild a word for what was happening – it was costing the owners of the goods £500,000 a year (about £300 million at today's value). The government refused to take any action, but something had to be done.

Patrick Colquhoun was a successful merchant who wrote a *Treatise on the Police of the Metropolis*. The book was an immediate success, and a group of West India merchants asked Colquhoun to help them deal with dockyard thefts. They were prepared to pay for protection, so Colquhoun and Harriott took their money – about £4500 – and set up the Marine Police Force.

It was extremely tough work. The plunderers were violent and dangerous men. Pitched battles were fought between the police and the dockers. The police were armed with cutlasses, swords, pistols and blunderbusses. Colquhoun had to set up several different forces – guards on the ships, guards on the quays, and guards on the river itself. At the same time, the River Police had to deal with every other crime, from cock-fighting to sheep-stealing,

top right:
One of the River Police inflatables – the fastest boats on the Thames.
below:
The River Police Headquarters at Wapping.

right along the river from London to the Kent and Essex marshes. They were also responsible for recovering the bodies of stillborn and new-born babies, thrown into the Thames by desperate mothers faced with poverty and social disgrace.

Today the River Police are known as the Thames Division of the Metropolitan Police. They patrol the Thames from Staines bridge in the West to Dartford Creek in the east in boats (top speed 26 knots) and inflatables (top speed 40 knots). They also have a van that responds to calls relating to canals, lakes and gravel pits. Their officers receive a year's special training, but it's reckoned that it really takes five years to learn about the ways of the river.

In some ways, their work is like that of the traffic police. There's a speed limit above Wandsworth bridge of eight knots. From Wandsworth bridge down to the sea there's no speed limit at all, so anyone rushing along through the water can be charged only with "dangerous navigation". To the understandable chagrin of the River Police, there's no such thing as a maritime driving test, so absolute beginners can take to the water in the fastest craft there is. Not that the River Police set out to look for trouble. If they come across someone water skiing (illegal on the Thames), they'll probably be content with issuing a friendly warning.

The most gruesome part of their work is recovering bodies from the water. They pick up about 60 a year. London's bridges are still the jumping-off point for several suicides a year – mostly male victims. The river temperature never rises above 10° Celsius, even at the height of summer, and in winter can be as cold as -4°. On a hot July day the average person would be dead from hypothermia after just ten minutes in the water.

Bodies recovered from the river are taken to the landing stage at Wapping Stairs. There they are laid out to be photographed and fingerprinted, if there is enough left – some bodies appear after six months in the water. In the old days, Thames Division were the only police with the authority to pronounce someone dead, a job now done only by doctors and forensic scientists.

The Princess Alice Disaster

On 3 September 1878 the pleasure steamer Princess Alice left Swan Pier on a day trip to Southend. There were some 850 passengers on board. We don't know how many, because in those days nobody kept a check. On her way back, the Princess Alice was struck by an empty collier, the Bywell Castle, and 640 people were drowned, in the biggest maritime disaster ever in British waters.

The River Police could do little to help. They were then equipped only with rowing boats, and it was impossible for them to deal with horror on such a scale. Indeed, it was this tragedy that finally convinced the authorities that the River Police should have steam launches. But rowing patrols didn't end until 1922.

Swans on the Thames

In Britain the swan has always been regarded as a royal bird that you meddled with at your peril. To steal a swan's egg could lead to a year's imprisonment and a hefty royal fine. To snare or steal an actual swan meant even worse punishment. Small wonder that a Swiss visitor to England in Elizabeth I's reign described swans as living "in great security, nobody daring to molest, much less kill, any of them".

You won't see many swans downstream from Putney these days, but any that you do see on the Thames belong to either the Queen, the Dyers' Company or the Vintners' Company. To find out who owns a swan, you have to be bold and get near enough to examine the bird's beak. If there is one notch on it, it belongs to the Dyers, if there are two, it belongs to the Vintners. If there are no notches, the bird belongs to the Queen. This is in accordance with a law passed by Henry VIII, a fat monarch who was very good at appropriating things.

Swans were first brought to Britain in the reign of Richard I, a gift from Queen Beatrice of Cyprus, and ever since then their ownership has been tightly controlled. Apart from the City Livery companies, the only other rightful owner of swans on the Thames has been Eton College. The owners haven't been very successful at protecting their swans. In the 1950s there were over 1000 swans on the river, sadly now there are perhaps only 500 or 600 left.

Swans were valued by royalty for their meat – said to be a great delicacy at royal banquets – and their feathers, which found their way into many a royal pillow. Swan is still served at the annual dinner that marks the end of Swan-Upping (see below). In January 1780 Parson Woodforde recorded in his diary: "We had for dinner a Calf's Head, boiled Fowl and Tongue, a Saddle of Mutton rosted on the Side Table, and a fine Swan rosted with Currant Jelly Sauce for the first Course . . . I never eat a bit of Swan before, and I think it was good eating with sweet sauce. The Swan was killed 3 weeks before it was eat and yet not the lest bad in it."

Swan-Upping

The Queen still has a "Keeper of the Swans in the Thames from the town of Graveshende to Cicester [Cirencester]", who presides at the swan-upping ceremony. Each year in late July or early August, the keeper and the swanherds from the Dyers' and Vintners' companies round up the new cygnets (baby swans) to mark their beaks with the appropriate notch. A small flotilla of boats travels slowly up the Thames, resplendent with banners. The notchers, or "uppers", are dressed in red, green, blue, white and gold. It's a colourful sight, but it's also quite a risky business. Swans can be vicious creatures, and one blow from their powerful wings could break a human arm. And although it may be part of Britain's glorious heritage, to the swans it's a pain in the neck.

Until 1980, the flotilla started "upping" at Southwark Bridge, and made their way steadily upstream to Pangbourne – about 50 miles (80 km) up the river. Now, however, the swan-uppers start at Sudbury, just a few stops from the western end of the Piccadilly Line.

The Dyers' Company

Like the Vintners, the Dyers are one of the 100 or so City Livery companies. These companies, or guilds, of craftsmen started in the 12th century and now cover a wide range of occupations, from air pilots and apothecaries to wheelwrights and woolmen.

The Dyers' Company is one of the oldest, getting its Royal Charter in 1471. They own 30 almhouses for the poor at Crawley in Sussex, and support a school in Norwich and two universities. Because their records were destroyed in the Great Fire of 1666, the Dyers aren't certain when they acquired the right to own swans, but it seems to have been granted by Henry VIII, some time

below:
Adult (with bright beak) and adolescent swan on the Thames.

between 1520 and 1543. A prominent dyer was at that time Henry's chamberlain.

Each year they hold a Swan Dinner. The Dyers say the bird tastes like fishy mutton.

The Vintners' Company

The Vintners are a company of wine importers which received its Charter in 1364, a year after they had entertained the kings of England, France, Scotland, Denmark and Cyprus to a feast. Since then, five has been the Vintners' special number – they even give five cheers instead of the usual three.

Like the Dyers (and many other City companies), the Vintners own almshouses (also in Sussex) and give money to educational causes. They don't know why they have the right to own swans, but it appears to have been granted a little earlier than the Dyers' charter, perhaps as early as 1483.

Each year they hold a Swan Feast. The Vintners say swan tastes like fishy turkey.

above:
The Mute Swan – the commonest species of swan on the river.
top left:
Two young swan-uppers set off for the annual round-up of swans, London Bridge 1950.

River Pubs – West

The bad news is that all the well-known old pubs by the Thames attract a great many customers, especially at weekends, on bank holidays and during the summer. To many Londoners and visitors there's little in life better than sitting by the river, sipping a drink and watching the tide flow in and out. The good news is that not all modern pubs are grim, especially those by the river. Anyway, it's not what they look like, but what the view from them looks like. The important thing is to explore. London is full of wonderful pubs, and not all of them are famous sand known.

A lot of the best Thameside pubs are very old. There have been pubs on the site of the London Apprentice at Isleworth for well over 600 years. The present building is 17th-century with Victorian additions. It looks out over the stretch of the Thames crossed by Caesar in 54 BC and Appius Claudius in AD 43. It has been the haunt of smugglers and highwaymen, artists (including Turner

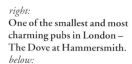

right:
One of the smallest and most charming pubs in London – The Dove at Hammersmith.
below:
A floating pub on the Thames at Battersea.

and Constable) and both industrious and idle apprentices. It changed hands in 1828 when the owner lost a bet on a 37-round bare-fist fight.

A little way downstream, at Hammersmith, is the Dove. It opened as a coffee house in the 17th century and in Victorian times was William Morris's "local". No one is certain, but it is believed that James Thomson wrote *Rule Britannia* in one of the upstairs rooms. Graham Greene and Ernest Hemingway used to be regulars. It's said to have the smallest bar room in the world, just over 32 square feet (3 square metres). Go there in March, on Boat Race Day, to see Oxford and Cambridge flash past – but get there early. If you want to see the finish of the Boat Race, or if you like haggis on Burns Night, go to the Ship on Thames Bank.

Also in Hammersmith is the Black Lion, which became the Black Swan in A.P. Herbert's *The Water Gypsies*. It's a fine 18th-century pub with its own skittle alley and allegedly its own ghost. If you fancy drinking surrounded by Great War artefacts, try the nearby Blue Anchor.

The Bull's Head at Strand on the Green is right on the river. It's a lovely pub, especially if you can get there when it isn't crowded. It's also the place where Oliver Cromwell escaped capture by Royalists when he fled by a secret tunnel to what is now called Oliver's Island, just opposite the pub. And, while you're in Strand on the Green, pop into the Bell and Crown, or

the City Barge, where some of the scenes in The Beatles film *Help!* were shot.

The White Hart near Barnes bridge has tables and seats that go right down to the river's edge. On a fine summer night it's a delight – you can even paddle in the Thames if you feel like it. The beer is good and the view upstream very reassuring. You can even see the lights of the brewery twinkling in the distance.

Don't bother with the Barmy Army at Twickenham unless you are keen to observe the drinking habits of the jolly hopefuls after whom it was named – the English sporting fans who trudge round the globe watching their national team lose.

The White Cross at Richmond is in a pretty position, just by Richmond bridge. It's liable to flooding, but has good food and is a delightful pub. Ignore the Slug and Lettuce, almost next door, not because there's anything wrong with the pub, but as a warning to the brewery giants that chains of pubs with silly names are a bad idea. Similarly, don't bother with Bar M at the Star and Garter, Putney, unless you want to see the stainless steel menus.

The River Rat in Battersea is the place to go if you want peace and quiet while you drink. The landlord wisely threw out all the games machines some years ago. Across the river in Chelsea, the King's Head and Eight Bells used to be two riverside pubs. Naval officers drank at the King's Head: ordinary seamen drank at the Eight Bells. Now it's all one pub, but, sadly, no longer on the riverside. The Thames is a deeper, narrower river than it used to be, and the Chelsea Embankment has come between the pub and the water.

If you want to drink *on* the water, try the Tattershall Castle further downstream on the Victoria Embankment near Waterloo Bridge. It's an old paddle steamer that used to ply the Humber between Hull and New Holland. The choice of beer isn't enormous, but the views are great. In the summer there are barbecues on deck. You might wish to avoid Thursday, Friday, Saturday and Sunday nights, when the on-board night-club operates.

The London Apprentice at Isleworth gets its name from the apprentices who used to row up to the pub from the City on their days off work.

River Pubs – East

There are few riverside pubs of note on either bank of the Thames from the Albert Bridge downstream to Blackfriars Bridge. Those with a scorching thirst may well find what Wodehouse's Bertie Wooster once used to call the occasional watering-hole, but such places are strictly functional.

On the south bank, just upstream and downstream of Blackfriars Bridge, are two modern pubs: the Doggett's Coat and Badge and the Founder's Arms. The views from both these pubs are good, especially in the evening as the lights come on across the river. If you can bear it, it's better to trudge on eastwards in search of somewhere more attractive in itself.

The Anchor at Bankside – a short walk from London Bridge station – is old and charming. It has old oak beams and a minstrels' gallery. There are cubbyholes, which were used to hide felons who'd escaped from the nearby Clink Prison. Pepys probably drank here, Boswell and Dr Johnson certainly did. Try a pint of best bitter and a dish of London Pride (fillets of smoked eel with horseradish sauce).

Further downstream is the Angel at Rotherhithe. Part of this inn is built out over the river, and there are trapdoors in the floor used by local smugglers. Pepys was a regular visitor, and Bloody Judge Jeffreys liked to sit here watching pirates being hanged at Execution Dock across the river. During the Napoleonic Wars, the pub was on the beat of both the press-gangs and doxies, to the terror and delight of sailors respectively.

After the Angel you have a choice. You can go to Rotherhithe station and cross the Thames by the Underground. One stop to the north is Wapping, where you will find the Town of Ramsgate. Colonel Blood was captured here when he stole the crown jewels in 1671. In 1688 the London mob tracked Judge Jeffreys to this pub, and he had to be rescued by the local militia and taken to the Tower for his own safety. When Nelson first went to sea he bought his kit at a shop next door. Convicts awaiting transportation to Australia used to be chained in the pub's cellars.

Alternatively, you can keep to the south side of the river and head for Greenwich. Here you will find the Old Ship and the Trafalgar Tavern, both pubs with honest literary pasts. In the mid-19th century the "gentlemen" of *Punch* magazine used to dine at the Old Ship, making a considerable amount of noise. The Trafalgar Tavern has had a somewhat chequered history. It was first a pub, then a seamen's home, a working men's club and a block

of flats. Happily it reverted to being a pub in 1965 and has been very splendidly restored, with chandeliers, heavy curtains and rich Victorian plaster mouldings. Thackeray, Dickens, Wilkie Collins and other "ichthyophagi" (fish-eaters, to those less pretentious) came here frequently to drink claret, and to eat platefuls of fried whitebait. Thackeray so enjoyed eating these little fish that he wrote an entire magazine article about the experience in 1844.

The Gun, in Cold Harbour, off Preston's Road, is a clapboard waterside tavern that has long been the choice of lightermen, seamen, dockers, customs men and river police. It is small and delightful. You can sit and gaze out across the Thames at the Millennium Dome, while your mind turns, more romantically, to thoughts of Lord Nelson and Lady Hamilton, who once dallied here.

While you're in Greenwich, the Cutty Sark Tavern is well worth a visit, especially in the summer when you can take your drink to the riverside and give thanks that you're not in Docklands, across the river.

If it isn't too late in the evening, now is the time to walk along the pedestrian tunnel under the Thames from Greenwich to the Isle of Dogs. You need to move upstream as quickly as possible. Don't dawdle in Docklands – there aren't any pubs worth drinking in there. Hurry on to Limehouse. There's a fine choice here: the Gun, the Grapes and the Barley Mow. Nelson and Lady Hamilton used to meet at the Gun and fire a few broadsides. Dickens took the Grapes as his model for the Six Jolly Fellowship Porters in *Our Mutual Friend*. The Barley Mow used to be a brewery. It's situated just where Limehouse Cut (London's oldest canal) joins the Thames, and it's a wonderful place from which to watch the sun set on the Thames as you drink.

After all this, we still have to visit one of the most famous pubs in the whole of London: the Prospect of Whitby in Wapping Wall. It was built in 1520, and like so many London riverside pubs it was popular with thieves and smugglers. American tourists "discovered" it in the 1950s, but it survives and prospers. Dickens drank here (is there a pub in London he didn't frequent?), did Whistler and Turner.

There's a nice, and true, story about the Prospect of Whitby. In the 18th century a sailor sold an unknown plant here that he'd collected in his travels to a local market gardener. It was the first fuchsia to come to Britain. We can blame the sailor for every hanging basket of flowers in the land.

The Grapes at Limehouse – one of the finest Victorian pubs in London.

The City of London

Buildings: The Big Four

The square mile of the City is richly sprinkled with interesting and delightful buildings, despite the destruction meted out over the centuries by fire, bombs and developers. There are charming pubs and restaurants, fine churches, and at least one delightful courtyard – that of the Apothecaries' Hall, in Blackfriars Lane.

However, the largest and most important – according to local magnates – are the financial institutions. The City is crowded with banks, insurance companies, finance offices and investment houses.

Gone are the days when gold and banknotes used to be delivered to such places in horse-drawn vehicles, but, if you have a nose for money, you should be able to smell it if you stand on the bustling triangle of land where Cornhill, Cheapside and Lombard Street meet.

Here are gathered the mighty headquarters of the army that once ran the financial heart of the City – the Bank of England, the Mansion House, the Guildhall, and the Royal Exchange. And, lowering over them all, like the Martians in H.G. Wells's *The War of the Worlds*, are the Nat-West Tower and the Lloyd's Building.

The Bank of England, Threadneedle Street

The Bank of England was founded in 1694 to supply William III with the funds he needed for his war against Louis XIV of France. It was largely the brainchild of Charles Montagu, who raised £1.2 million in eleven days from some 1250 people.

By the early 18th century, the Bank had outgrown its premises in Mercers' Hall, Cheapside, and needed a home of its own. This was completed between 1724 and

The Bank of England, Threadneedle Street – bastion of Britain's finances.

1765. During the Gordon Riots of 1780, a mob attacked the Bank but did little damage and was driven away by soldiers. From then until 1973, it was guarded nightly by a small detachment from the Brigade of Guards. Nowadays, sadly, it has its own, less colourful, internal security force.

The commissionaires at the door are more picturesque. In scarlet waistcoats, pink frock coats and black top hats, they will politely stop you entering the building, and will direct you to the Bank of England Museum. Entry is free. The exhibits include plates for printing banknotes, details of where you may find the small box in which the Bank keeps its odd handful of £1 million notes (the highest denomination), and glass cases of gold bars and nuggets.

The Mansion House

To the south of the Bank, across the road, is the Mansion House, the official residence of the Lord Mayor of London. It was designed by George Dance and built between 1739 and 1752. When work began on the building, a complete set of coins (from one farthing up to one guinea) minted in 1739 was sealed within the wall next to the foundation stone. Unfortunately, nobody can now identify where the foundation stone is.

Like the Bank, the Mansion House has had some tricky moments in its history. In 1768 the windows and chandeliers were broken by supporters of John Wilkes, who were disgusted to find the Mansion House unlit. This was interpreted as a sign that the Lord Mayor was not prepared to celebrate the election of Wilkes to Parliament. The windows and chandeliers were mended, but smashed again twelve years later in the Gordon Riots.

The Mansion House is also one of the City's two magistrates' courts. Beneath it are ten little cells for male prisoners, and one cell for females which both resembles and is called the Birdcage. It once housed Emmeline Pankhurst, the Suffragette leader.

The Guildhall

One of the very few continental-style piazzas in London – there's another outside the west front of Westminster Cathedral – is outside the Guildhall. To the south is Wren's gloriously light and brilliant church of St Lawrence Jewry, so called because it stood on the eastern side of the old City, where the Jews lived. To the west is a modern wing of the Guildhall, to the east a compromise between old and new. To the north is the resilient Guildhall itself, whose medieval walls have withstood the Great Fire of 1666 and the incendiary bombs of 1940.

It is the centre of civic government in the City, and the venue for meetings of the Court of Common Council. It is, in many ways, the heart of the City.

The Royal Exchange, Threadneedle Street and Cornhill

The Royal Exchange was for centuries the London equivalent of the Paris Bourse, a meeting place at which merchants transacted business. Until the mid-16th century such deals had to be struck in the open air. "These meetings were unpleasant and troublesome," wrote John Stow, a Tudor chronicler and freeman of the Merchant Taylors' Company, "being constrained to endure all extremes of weather, or else to shelter in shops."

A wealthy London merchant, Sir Thomas Gresham, had been impressed by the Bourse in Antwerp, and campaigned for London to have a similar institution. In 1566, 45 householders were evicted from their homes and work began on the first Exchange. Within a few weeks of its completion it had become a resort for idlers – a species abhorrent to the City. So it was perhaps as well that it was destroyed in the Great Fire.

A second Exchange was completed in 1669. In 1838, this building also burnt to the ground, in a fire that began in rooms occupied by Lloyd's insurance company. The third and present building was opened in 1844 by Queen Victoria. It is now the offices of the Guardian Royal Exchange Assurance Company, but the steps outside are still one of the few places in London from which a new sovereign is proclaimed.

The eight Corinthian columns of Sir William Tite's Royal Exchange.

The City Coat of Arms on a litter box.

Buildings: New Kids on the Block

At the end of the Second World War much of the City lay in ruins. The first priority, in the opinion of the Establishment, was to help the financial life of London return to normal, so rebuilding concentrated on banks and offices. As you walk about the City today, you can see many dull examples of 1950s and 1960s architecture. By the 1970s, some City institutions had grown too big for their premises. It was time to move on, or pull down and rebuild. It was then that plans were made for three key new buildings in the City: the Stock Exchange, the National Westminster Tower and the Lloyd's Building.

The Stock Exchange, Capel Court

The London Stock Exchange has its origins in a phenomenon known as the South Sea Bubble. This was the name given to a period of wild financial speculation in the first two decades of the 18th century. The market climbed rapidly. On paper, fortunes were made. Each day new schemes were floated, many of them initiated by the South Sea Company, the least ridiculous of which was to import thousands of walnut trees into Britain from Virginia. In August 1720, the South Sea Bubble burst and the market crashed.

From the wreckage and misery, some 150 of the more respectable jobbers formed a club, an early forerunner of the Stock Exchange. Their base was Jonathan's Coffee-House in Exchange Alley. Other, less respectable stockbrokers joined them, and the project eventually failed.

The first true Stock Exchange opened in Threadneedle Street in 1773, moving to Capel Court in 1801. The present building is the third on that site. It opened in 1972, designed by Messrs Llewelyn-Davies, Weeks, Forestier-Walker and Bor and Fitzroy Robinson and Partners. There is an old saying, "too many cooks spoil the broth".

The National Westminster Tower, Bishopsgate

It took ten years for the National Westminster Bank to obtain permission to build their tower, 600 feet (184.5 metres) high, on the site of their own old building and the City of London Club. Thanks to a hard-fought conservationist campaign, the club survives. Its Palladian architecture, dating back to the 1830s, sits uncomfortably in the shadow of the Nat-West Tower – a pairing described by Max Gordon, who restored the club, as "architectural schizophrenia".

But the Tower, designed by R. Seifert and Partners, has much to commend it. Until Canary Wharf was built, it was the tallest building in Europe, and it's infinitely superior to anything in Docklands.

From the distance, seen across the Thames, it serves as the focal point for a whole cluster of buildings that give the impression the City is built on a sharp-pointed hill. Close up, you feel you are in *Metropolis* – one of thousands of scurrying extras in the classic German silent film. From a distance it looks smooth. Close up you see the metal battens that run from top to bottom, as though holding the tower together. And, as the light bounces off and echoes round the gleaming chrome and glass, you expect the whole tower to be powered and lit by static electricity. At the very least, it is a far more impressive building than Barclay's Bank in Gracechurch Street, which looks as though it was designed by Aubrey Beardsley on a bad day – it resembles a group of capless mushrooms that have sprouted through the pavement.

Lloyd's of London, Lime Street

Lloyd's has been in business for over 300 years. It originated in the coffee-house kept by Edward Lloyd in Abchurch Lane, on the corner of Lombard Street. The coffee-house became the centre of ship-broking and marine insurance, activities probably introduced to London by the Lombards in the 16th century. Over the years less than honest souls began to muscle in on this reputable business, and in 1769 a New Lloyd's Coffee-House opened in Pope's Head Alley.

By 1774 the business had expanded, and rooms were taken in the second Royal Exchange. When this building was destroyed by fire in 1838, Lloyd's moved to South Sea House, Threadneedle Street, headquarters of the notoriously speculative company that crashed so spectacularly in 1720. Not until 1925 did Lloyd's have a home of its own – a fine building in Leadenhall Street.

In 1986 the company moved to Lime Street, to the building designed by (Lord) Richard Rogers. It rises above the surrounding streets like some vast collection of industrial catering equipment, or as though it had been assembled from the leftovers of an oil refinery construction kit. Looking at the building, you expect it to produce toxic waste rather than insurance policies.

You listen, to see if it clatters in the wind. You feel it is a building that would dent easily.

There it is, this pile of microwave ovens and refrigerators, with hoses from vacuum cleaners connecting one to the other, and with windows that look like meat safes from the 1930s. It's a building that would be a joy to scale from the outside – no need to use the lift. But it is undeniably powerful, and it is wearing well. Inside, there is a visitors' gallery, and it's well worth going.

opposite:
Richard Rogers's Lloyd's Building – becoming less controversial with each passing year.
below:
The Nat-West Tower – 52 storeys and 600 feet (200 metres) high.

City Characters

Few people in London know what goes on in the City, and precisely what bankers, brokers, jobbers and others do. There is a general understanding that the Bank of England is the government's bank, that it prints banknotes and hoards the nation's gold, that Britain's fortunes stand or fall according to how well the bank performs. If pressed, most Londoners could give some account of the work of the Stock Exchange. Other than that, the City's financial life is a mystery.

The City is full of characters – some real, some legendary, some preposterous. Some are to be seen swaggering about the streets. Some are locked away in secret and secure splendour. Some are no longer alive. Some never existed. All combine to produce the strange world of banking, broking, speculating and jiggery-pokery that is the essence of London's financial centre.

Attendants on the Stock Exchange

The London Stock Exchange has some 5000 members, grouped into approximately 400 different firms. The wants of these members are cared for by an army of attendants known as "waiters", in memory of the coffee-house origins of the Exchange. These waiters still wear a livery of blue coats with red collars, and you may see them from the public gallery of the Stock Exchange.

Traders

On weekday mornings and lunchtimes, clustered around City coffee-shops and tobacconists', you will see

young men and women in brightly coloured jackets and striped blazers. They are traders, and there is a fine statue of an archetypal trader, complete with mobile phone, in Cannon Street.

Traders are the vociferous wolves and scavengers of the Stock Exchange, frantically bidding and counter-bidding to buy or sell stock – all desperate to play their part in the making of fortunes for others, and sharing a fat bonus when Christmas comes round.

The Lutine Bell

The *Lutine* was originally a French ship that surrendered to the British at Toulon in 1793. Six years later, renamed HMS *Lutine*, she was carrying gold and silver bullion from England to Germany when she sank with the loss of the entire crew. Later, £100,000-worth of bullion was raised, together with the ship's rudder and bell.

The rudder was made into a chair that is now in the Library at Lloyd's. The bell was used to mark the loss of a ship anywhere in the world. This practice no longer takes place. The bell is now struck on ceremonial occasions, or when the company has particularly good news (two strokes) or bad (one stroke).

right:
A City 'gent' in full regalia – note the assertive tie.
below:
Shoe-shiners at work in Leadenhall Market.

Lloyd's Underwriters

Lloyd's of London is a unique insurance market. It is made up of a group of "underwriters" – men and women who are prepared to take insurance risks for their personal profit, and who have to settle claims, therefore, out of their own pockets. When things go well and there are few claims, Lloyd's underwriters are quietly very happy. When things go badly, they are loudly shocked and (sometimes) financially ruined. You will seldom see Lloyd's underwriters in the City of London. They live in great comfort all over the world, and include in their number writers, politicians, entertainers and sports stars.

Roberto Calvi

On 18 June 1982, the body of a man was found hanging from scaffolding under the northernmost arch of Blackfriars Bridge. Bloodthirsty sensation-seekers may see the exact spot from the Thames Walkway, just upstream of the bridge.

The body was that of Roberto Calvi, chairman of the Italian Banco Ambrosiano. A year earlier, Calvi had been found guilty by an Italian court of illegal dealings that involved billions of *lire* of Banco Ambrosiano money. He was sentenced to four years' imprisonment, but was released pending his appeal. Investigations suggested that the case involved Propaganda 2 (a secret Italian masonic lodge), the Mafia, and some dubious financial dealings on behalf of the Vatican.

When Calvi's body was discovered, his pockets were weighed down with bricks, concrete and a large amount of cash. At first it was said that he had committed suicide, but in 1983 an inquest delivered an open verdict on his death. His family still believe that he was murdered.

The Old Lady of Threadneedle Street

There are three theories as to the origins of the Old Lady. One is that the nickname for the Bank of England was coined by the playwright Sheridan. Another is that the name was first applied by the artist James Gillray, in a cartoon of 1797 entitled *Political Ravishment, or the Old Lady of Threadneedle Street in Danger.*

There is also a theory, however, that there really was an Old Lady. Her name was Sarah Whitehead, and her brother worked in the bank in the early 19th century. Every night Sarah waited for him outside the bank. In 1811 he was convicted of fraud and executed. Poor Sarah became deranged. Dressed in black, she still waited for him to finish work every evening outside the bank. Night after night, until her death, kindly officials escorted her back to her family.

The Town Crier of the City of London rests his legs and throat.

The City Whizz Kid

There are men (and one or two women) employed in the City of London whose salaries are measured in millions of pounds a year. Like the people of power, they are grey, shadowy creatures whose photographs are rarely printed in the newspapers, whose residences are seldom identified, and whose lifestyle – even if it is lavish beyond the wildest dreams of the masses – is discreetly luxurious. These are the men who manoeuvre financial institutions into positions from which they can devour entire chains of hotels, shops, motorway service centres and satellite companies. In City terms, they are senior citizens – almost all in their forties, some into their fifties.

Younger, brasher, noisier and (some would say) nastier are the City Whizz Kids. In the grasping and greedy Eighties they were high-profile – swilling champagne nightly in wine bars, burning rubber between Fulham or Battersea and the City in their Porsches, living and playing hard. In many ways they were reminiscent of the Mohocks of 18th-century London, gangs of wealthy young blades who created mayhem in and around Fleet Street at night, leaving a trail of fear and fury behind them.

On the threshold of the 21st century, the Whizz Kids are more muted. The financial trough at which they feed is no longer full to the brim every day. The Nineties saw terrifying culls. Whizz Kids arrived at their City offices early in the morning, to find notes awaiting them telling them to clear their desks and be gone by noon. This terrifying process was known as "downsizing", and, for many, meant a permanent end to the good life.

City Whizz Kids are identified on the street by what they wear, how they walk, what they drive. Suits are *de rigueur*, and double-breasted suits are in at the moment, so waistcoats are out. They are worn with the jacket unbuttoned, and with the hands thrust deep into the trouser pockets. The true Whizz Kid doesn't wear turn-ups on his trousers, and does not reveal a stretch of shirt cuff below the sleeve of the jacket. The suit is cut with more swagger than style. Shirt and tie fashions change every so often. Currently, shirts are plain, brightly coloured (usually blue), and the striped shirt has temporarily had its day.

Rarely does the Whizz Kid wear a club tie, and never a regimental one – no Whizz Kid has ever been in a regiment. The fashion in ties is for plain coloured one year, the next for geometrically patterned, the next for exotic

Nick Leeson and Barings Bank

It was a City Whizz Kid, Nick Leeson, who brought about the collapse of the oldest merchant bank in London. Barings had been trading since 1762, and had occupied the same headquarters at 8 Bishopsgate since 1805. There had been a small financial hiccough in 1890, when the Bank of England had intervened to rescue them, but in the late 20th century they were still happily engaged in corporate finance and banking, investment management and security trading.

Then along came Nick Leeson. By late February 1995, at the age of 28, he had run up losses of more than $1 billion on the Asian market. Barings said he'd carried out unauthorized transactions. Inspectors in Singapore said he'd been allowed to use highly risky instruments without adequate supervision. Leeson fled to Germany, but was returned to Singapore and sentenced to six and a half years' imprisonment. Back in London, Barings was forced into receivership and then acquired by a Dutch financial group, Internationale Nederlanden Groep NV. Such is the power of the Whizz Kid.

floral designs. Shirts and ties are the only items of apparel that mark the passing of the years. The suit remains much as it has for the last hundred years.

Shoes are leather, but not bulled to a military smartness. Blakeys (small metal tips to the heels) are out of fashion, but could return in a year or two. Golfing umbrellas and mobile phones are obligatory fashion accessories. Briefcases are rigid, the sort that withstand a herd of stampeding elephants. The head is always bare. Overall, the Whizz Kid seeks to look like a cross between an international financier and an Italian footballer.

The walk along the pavements of Gracechurch, Lombard or Gresham Street is purposeful, but there is a great deal of tension in the body and the Whizz Kid seldom looks comfortable. There is an inner conflict between fitness and fatigue. The face has dark circles round the eyes, indicating the price the metabolism is paying for the lifestyle. The pink face gives off a strong scent of Calvin Klein aftershave.

City Whizz Kids still love their motors, but are less dashing in what they choose to drive. The Porsche has been forsaken for Audis and BMWs, cars that have sporty performance but do not carry the aura of bad luck about them – the effects of a market crash last longer than those of a car crash as far as the Whizz Kid is concerned.

Lunch is either a takeaway sandwich (chicken tikka or avocado and mozzarella) eaten in the office, or a couple of pints of Young's or Fuller's drunk standing up in a snug, long-established City pub. Lunchtime conversation is never about business. The Whizz Kid talks about the Arsenal back four and England's chances in the latest international competition.

City Livery Companies

Some of the richest organizations in the City of London are the Livery Companies. The earliest were established in the 12th century and have gradually increased in both scope and number since then, though no new companies were created between 1709 and 1930. In the last 70 years there has been a revival of interest in Livery Companies, and over 20 new ones have come into being, so that such ancient foundations as the Fletchers, Loriners, Cordwainers and Salters have been joined by the Air Pilots' and Air Navigators' Guild, the Solicitors' Company, and the Environmental Cleaners' Company.

The aim of any Livery Company has always been to promote the interests of colleagues within the same trade, though they also endow and support many charities. Traditionally they were called "guilds" or "misteries" (from the Italian *mestiere*, a trade). In medieval times, members of a guild all wore the same uniform or "livery", hence Livery Companies.

Membership of a Livery Company is obtained by one of three methods – patrimony (having a father who was a member of the company), apprenticeship (learning the trade of the company), or redemption (simply buying your way in).

The companies have had stormy histories. Relations between them and the City authorities, though currently extremely cordial, were initially poor, with both sides wrestling for power. The different companies fought each other, sometimes to the death. In 1267 the Goldsmiths and Taylors fought a pitched battle, in which the Clothworkers and Cordwainers joined. In 1340 the Fishmongers and Skinners took up arms against each other.

More peaceful times followed in the 17th and 18th centuries, but the number of members declined alarmingly, and it wasn't until Victorian times that membership of a Livery Company once again became prestigious. The companies no longer have any of their medieval power, but they remain fiercely independent. Since they have no shareholders, they are not obliged to publish accounts, and outsiders are largely ignorant of how they work. The popular conception of a Livery Company is of a group of like-minded and conservative men who meet infrequently at monstrous banquets.

The Top Ten
The top ten Livery Companies, in order of historical precedence, are:

1. Mercers' Company – exporters of wool and woollen goods. Famous past members include William Caxton, Sir Thomas More and Dick Whittington.

2. Grocers' Company – originally the Pepperers' Company, dealing in spices, drugs and tobacco. Famous past members include Sir Philip Sidney, Pitt the Elder, Pitt the Younger.

3. Drapers' Company – dealers in wool and woollen cloth. Over 100 Lord Mayors of the City of London have been members.

4. Fishmongers' Company – in medieval times, both rich and powerful, as fish played an important part in people's diet for religious reasons.

5. Goldsmiths' Company – forerunner of all modern banks.

6. Skinners' Company – controllers of the fur trade. The Skinners have long disputed their position with both the Fishmongers and the Merchant Taylors.

7. Merchant Taylors' Company – originally makers of tents and the padded suits worn under armour. Famous past members include John Stow, John Speed and Sir Christopher Wren.

8. Haberdashers' Company – makers of hats and in early

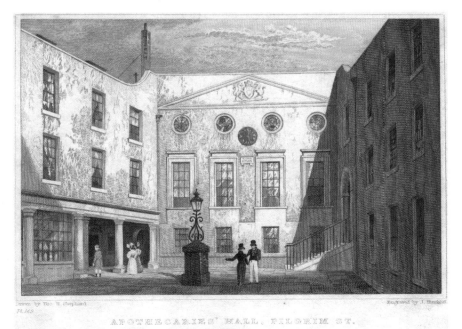

Apothecaries Hall, circa 1800. The old Hall was destroyed in the Great Fire and reconstructed by Thomas Lock in 1688.

times importers of fashion goods from Milan (hence "milliners").

9. Salters' Company – gained their wealth through salt, essential for preserving both fish and meat in medieval times. They also dealt in chemicals.

10. Ironmongers' Company – makers of iron bars, rods, horseshoes and cartwheel rims.

Livery Company Halls

Most Livery Companies had fine halls in medieval times, in which members met and dined together. Sadly, the vast majority of these were destroyed in the Great Fire of 1666. Parts of the Ironmongers' Hall survive, dating back to 1587, and the Merchant Taylors' Hall has a section originally built in the 14th century. One of the finest is that of the Vintners' Company in Upper Thames Street,

with a dining capacity of 140, a tapestry of 1466, and Van Dyck's portrait of St Martin, their patron saint.

There are some charming oddities among the present halls. The Leathersellers' Hall is an almost perfect 38-foot (12-metre) cube, and the Master Mariners' Hall is HMS *Wellington*, a former sloop moored in the Thames. The Fishmongers' Hall still houses the dagger with which Sir William Walworth slew Wat Tyler at Smithfield in 1381, thereby dealing a death blow to the Peasants' Revolt.

All that remains of the original Merchant Taylor's Hall are fragments of the clay floor. The present Hall was built in 1959.

The Great Plague

The first recorded outbreak of the plague in London took place in 664AD. From Saxon times, London was host to the plague almost every summer. Each year the Black Death, and its no less destructive successors, spread rapidly through the fetid and crowded City, carried by fleas on the rats that infested the houses of rich and poor alike. Those citizens who could afford to flee hurried from London to their country estates. Parliament moved to the City, to avoid the "foul air" of Westminster. The Law Courts shut down for three months every summer (they still do). The king and his courtiers departed to Nonesuch in Surrey or to Oxford, Greenwich, or even Southampton. Large parts of London became silent and empty. Sometimes the Law Courts decamped early, and set up shop on Hampstead Heath, where the judges lived under canvas.

Nobody understood what caused the plague. Many believed it was carried by cats or dogs (who were slaughtered in their thousands whenever plague broke out), or that it was borne on the wind, and that victims became infected simply through breathing "foul air". So London went on growing, and Londoners maintained their unhygienic way of life: defecating in the streets, using open drains as sewers, throwing scraps of decomposing food out of their windows and waiting for the "rakers" to take the stinking piles away in their carts. And the rats multiplied and waxed fat – the more so since there were so few cats left.

The plague that broke out in the summer of 1665 was no different from its predecessors save in its appalling virulence. In 1625 an outbreak had killed 40,000 people – one in ten of all Londoners. The first signs of the Great Plague (as it has come to be known) appeared in the parish of St Giles in the Fields, just outside the City walls. In early April, the authorities admitted that 398 people had died of the plague. On 7 June, Samuel Pepys noted in his *Diary*: "This day, much against my will, I did in Drury Lane see two or three houses marked with a red cross upon the doors, and "Lord, have mercy upon us' writ there." Three months later it was raging. The Bill of Mortality (a list of deaths in London) for the week 15 to 22 August recorded 3880 deaths from the plague. A month later 7000 people a week were dying.

By the time it began to abate, three months later, over 100,000 Londoners had died. It was a dreadful time. Sufferers, maddened with the fever, threw themselves into mass graves. Each night carts rumbled over the cobbled streets, their brave drivers exhorting households to "bring out your dead". When the carts were full, they were driven out of the City to plague pits, where their grisly loads were dumped. Some of these pits were only a few hundred yards away – one was uncovered at Green Park Underground Station when the Victoria Line was being built in the 1960s. Other pits were further away, in the marshland of Kent and Essex. Two hundred and fifty years later, there were people who claimed that the very earth in such places had become infected, killing their pets and making their children ill.

Early symptoms of the plague were like those of a cough or cold. Then a rash appeared on the arms or chest, erupting later into horrendous boils or buboes (hence "bubonic plague"). Quacks peddled potions made up of salt, pepper and urine, or made fortunes bleeding or purging sufferers. Herbalists offered rosemary for sale at a monstrous eight shillings (40p) a bunch. Dr Thomas Lodge, the only orthodox physician left in the City, recommended carrying a bundle of arsenic under the armpit, that part of the body where the tell-tale boils often first erupted. Many turned to tobacco: popular belief had it that no London tobacconist died of the plague. There was even a story that one schoolboy at Eton was flogged for not smoking. Though a few victims survived and recovered, the vast majority died.

As the winter of 1665–6 approached, the number of new cases dramatically decreased, to less than 200 a week. "It is a wonder what will be the fashion after the plague is done as to periwigs," wrote Pepys, "for nobody will dare to buy any haire for fear of the infection – that it had been cut off the heads of people dead of the plague."

Ring a Ring of Roses

Ring a-ring a-roses
A pocketful of posies,
A-tishoo, a-tishoo,
We all fall down!

For a long time it was thought that this old nursery rhyme was a kind of macabre song about the Great Plague. The "ring of roses" referred to the rash that broke out on the victims' skin. The "pocketful of posies" were the herbs or nosegays carried in an attempt to ward off the foul air of the plague. "A-tishoo" was a reminder that people with the plague often suffered from severe fits of sneezing. "We all fall down" was a clear reference to dropping down dead.

Children still chant the rhyme in school playgrounds. Sadly, it would seem that its romantic origin has been totally discredited, for the rhyme is much older than the Great Plague of 1665. But then, so is the plague itself.

opposite:
Tipping bodies from a cart into a communal grave during the Great Plague in 1665.

The Great Fire of London

The Golden Boy of Pie Corner

There is another, less well-known monument to the Fire, at the corner of Giltspur Street and Cock Lane, near Smithfield Market. Set up on the wall is a statue of the Golden Boy of Pie Corner. The statue is "in Memmory put up for the late FIRE of London, Occasioned by the Sin of Gluttony". A plaque below the statue explains what is meant by this:

The Boy at Pie Corner was erected to commemorate the staying of the Great Fire, which beginning at Pudding Lane was ascribed to the Sin of Gluttony when not attributed to the Papists as on the Monument and the Boy was made prodigiously fat to enforce the moral.

top centre:
The only wooden house built in London after the Great Fire.
right:
The Great Fire from the Thames, 1666

It began in the early hours of Sunday morning, the Second of September, 1666, in a baker's shop in Pudding Lane, close to London Bridge. The baker's oven had overheated and set fire to his house. He and his family escaped, but his maidservant perished. There was a strong easterly wind, and sparks were blown to the piles of hay and straw in the yard of the Star Inn on Fish Street Hill. The inn itself caught fire.

At first, few people were worried. Sir Thomas Bloodworth, the Lord Mayor, took a look at the fire, remarked "Pish! A woman might piss it out!", and went back to bed. Six hours later, Pepys noted that 300 houses, several churches and half London Bridge had already been destroyed. Most buildings were made of wood and were densely packed together; the dry wind whipped the flames from house to house. An eye-witness recorded: "The bellowing winds drove the flames forward as their noise was like a thousand chariots beating together upon the stones." There were no fire brigades in existence, and, though the Thames was nearby, there was no means of getting sufficient water to the flames quickly enough.

The inhabitants of London were reluctant to leave. Even the pigeons stayed in their customary roosts, until their wings caught fire and they fell to the ground. But by Monday morning panic began to spread. Desperate householders were offering up to £30 for a cart on which to transport their belongings to safety. The Thames was crowded with packed boats as people fled by river. Pepys met a thoroughly alarmed Bloodworth in Canning Street: "He cried like a fainting woman, Lord, what can I do? I am spent! People will not obey me. I have been pulling down houses. But the fire overtakes us faster than we can do it.'"

On Tuesday morning, Queen Catherine set off for Hampton Court. The navy saved the Tower of London by blowing up most of Tower Street with gunpowder. The following day, Pepys took his wife and his gold to Woolwich. On his return to the City he climbed the steeple of All Hallows, Barking: "Everywhere saw great fires, oil cellars and brimstone and other things burning. The wind had dropped but there was still a blaze at the Temple, Holborn and Cripplegate, where the King himself [Charles II] was seen helping the soldiers."

But the worst was over. On Thursday, John Evelyn walked through the smouldering City: "I clambered over mountains of smoking rubbish and the ground under my feet so hot it even burnt the soles of my shoes and put me all over in sweat." Within the City walls 400 acres (160 ha) had been burnt to the ground, outside, another 60 (24 ha). The fire had destroyed 87 churches (including old St Paul's Cathedral), 44 livery halls and over 13,000 houses. Miraculously, only nine people had died – ten, if you count poor Robert Hubert, a Frenchman who falsely confessed to setting fire to the baker's shop and was hanged at Tyburn.

The refugees camped in the fields outside the City, in tents and hovels. The king rode out, promised them bread, and attempted to quell rumours that the fire was

part of a foreign plot for the destruction of England. There was little looting, though some of the fire-fighters took time off to raid beer houses and sugar stores, mixing the two ingredients together to make a heady and sickly brew.

By Friday 7 September, the Great Fire had been extinguished.

The Monument

Not long after the Great Fire, Parliament decided a monument should be raised near the shop where it began. Sir Christopher Wren was commissioned to design and build the Monument – a simple Doric column of Portland stone, the tallest isolated stone column in the world. It is 202 feet (62.15 metres) high – the exact distance from the base to the site of the outbreak in Pudding Lane – with a flaming urn of gilt bronze on the summit. You can still climb the 311 stairs to the top (you receive a certificate acknowledging your achievement as you come out). James Boswell climbed it in 1767. He found the view overwhelming, "horrid to be so monstrous a way up in the air, so far above London and all its spires".

In 1788 a baker, perhaps appropriately, was the first of a series of people who committed suicide by throwing themselves from the top. When a servant-girl did the same in 1842, the Monument was closed for a while, and there is now a secure iron cage round the balcony. Boswell would have been greatly relieved.

top:
One of the many plaques in the City commemorating buildings destroyed by the Great Fire.
right:
The Monument – 'better to preserve the memory of this dreadful visitation.'

Wren and the Rebuilding of London

right:
The interior of St Mary-le-Bow church, Cheapside - home of Bow Bells.
below:
St Clement Danes, Aldwych – central church of the Royal Air Force.

When the smoke cleared from the Great Fire, a new London rose from the ashes. Merchants and traders who had lost almost all they owned in the blaze hit upon the idea of insurance, and a modern monster was born. The need for trained fire brigades was recognized. For a long time, these were operated by insurance companies, and would deal only with fires raging on one of their clients' properties.

A series of Acts of Parliament restricted the materials that could be used in the rebuilding – brick and stone were to replace wood. Instead of an open sewer running down the middle of the street, roads were cambered to each side and drainage was improved.

As far as most wealthy Londoners were concerned, the immediate task was to get back to business – to prove title to whatever patch of rubble had once been their home and shop, and to rebuild as quickly as possible. But within a week of the Fire, the architect Christopher Wren had presented to the King a revolutionary proposal for rebuilding the City.

Sir Christopher Wren

Wren was an extraordinary man. He was a professor of astronomy at the age of 25, a mathematician, a physicist and an anatomist, a surveyor, but above all an architect. At the time of the Fire he was in his mid-thirties, but had already designed the chapel of Pembroke College, in Cambridge, and the Sheldonian Theatre at Oxford, and was currently employed to supervise repairs at old St Paul's Cathedral.

The Fire completely destroyed the old cathedral but made Wren famous. His plan for rebuilding the City included broad avenues, handsome piazzas, embankments and sweeping circuses. The entire river front was to be lined with graceful quays. Streets were to be widened, broad avenues to be created. Where all had been pokey and cramped, there was to be space and symmetry. Wren was not alone in producing such radical plans. The diarist John Evelyn also submitted a scheme for a new London, banishing "tiresome trades" downriver and proposing in their place "such shrubs as yield the most fragrant and odoriferous flowers and aptest to tinge the air upon every gentle emission at a great distance". He was way ahead of his time; he even had plans for an integrated underground sewer system. One Colonel Birch suggested that the state should buy the entire City and then sell it back to its original owners on the understanding that they agreed to his own plans. Sir William Petty, an economist who was a precursor of Adam Smith, proposed a huge city of five million inhabitants, complete in every detail.

There was even a plan to build another bridge across the Thames, at Putney. The City was horrified. Another river crossing would enable trade to bypass London Bridge, and thereby reduce the City's income. They also argued that it would lead to unemployment among the watermen who carried people across the river by ferry. Both arguments have a very modern ring.

But most of these grand plans came to nothing. Vested interests refused to allow such changes. Traders and householders wanted their old alleys and houses to be recreated – which is why driving round the City of London is such a nightmare today. Wren stood his ground, and had his way over Cheapside, Fleet Street, Poultry and Cornhill, all of which were widened. But even then, some citizens slipped out at night and moved the stakes which marked the new limits of their property, despite threats of heavy fines or being "openly whipped… where the offence shall be committed till his body be bloody".

Wren's Successes

All was not lost. Wren was appointed architect for the new cathedral of St Paul's and for 50 other churches, as well as the Royal Exchange, the Custom House, Temple Bar and the College of Physicians.

Wren produced three designs for the new cathedral. When the second, his own favourite, was rejected he burst into tears; but his third scheme was eventually accepted. Daniel Defoe thought the new St Paul's a "most regular Building, Beautiful, Magnificent, and beyond all the Modern Works of its kind in Europe, St Peter's at Rome only excepted". Parliament, however, became impatient with the time it was taking to complete the building, and in 1697 Wren's annual salary of £200 was halved. But he lived to the ripe old age of 91, and successfully petitioned Queen Anne to have his arrears of pay made up to him.

Wren's churches are dotted all over the City and neighbouring parts of London. They are seen as architectural delights by many, but I've always thought they look a bit like emaciated wedding cakes – the towers are tall and thin, and look as though they are made of icing sugar. Some of the most famous are St Clement Dane's, in The Strand ("Oranges and lemons, say the bells of St Clement's"); St Stephen Walbrook; St Mary-le-Bow, Cheapside (home of the famous Bow Bells); St Magnus the Martyr, Lower Thames Street (the interior of which T.S. Eliot described in *The Waste Land* as "inexplicable splendour"); and St Dunstan in the East.

Today little is left of St Dunstan. It was bombed in the Second World War, and only the tower and nave walls have been restored. There is an irony in this, for, when a hurricane swept London in 1703, Wren was told that every steeple in the City had been damaged. "Not St Dunstan's, I am sure," he said. And he was right.

St Magnus the Martyr, Lower Thames Street. The church is dedicated to the saintly Norwegian Earl of the Orkneys.

The Gates of the City

Among other buildings damaged by the Great Fire of 1666 were some of the old gates of London. Aldgate, Aldersgate, Cripplegate, Ludgate, Newgate and Bishopsgate were all built by the Romans, and all but Aldersgate were the original entrances to the Roman fort. They were also the starting point of many of the Roman roads along which the legions marched to keep order throughout the northwestern extremities of their empire. Watling Street led from Aldersgate, Ermine Street from Bishopsgate. Moorgate was of much later origin. It was built in the 15th century, with a much higher arch than the other gates so that the trained bands could march through with their pikes raised.

By the middle of the 18th century the gates of London had become intolerable obstacles to the free flow of traffic. In the three years from 1760 to 1762 every one of them was demolished. Mr Blagden, carpenter, of Coleman Street bought the materials from Cripplegate for £91. The stones from Moorgate were used to stop the piers of old London Bridge being washed away.

St Paul's Cathedral

At first glance, St Paul's may look like the younger brother of St Peter's in Rome, but it has had a far more stormy history. The 300-year-old cathedral is the fourth to have been built on the site, and centuries before the first Christian cathedral the Romans built a temple to Diana where the present St Paul's stands. Its survival as a place of Christian worship owes much to the stubbornness of the faithful over the years.

The first St Paul's was built in AD 604 by St Ethelbert, King of Kent and the first Christian king of England. He installed St Mellitus as the first bishop of London. The church was made of wood, and burnt down some 60 or 70 years later. A new cathedral was built between AD 675 and 685, and lasted almost 300 years before the Vikings destroyed it. The next structure, Old St Paul's, was built by the Normans. This was a mammoth edifice, the largest in England, bigger than the present cathedral, and with the tallest spire in the world until it was sliced off by lightning in 1561. It is possible to get some idea of the size of Old St Paul's by walking the narrow streets that once bordered its precincts – Creed Lane, Ave Maria Lane, Paternoster Row, Old Change and Carter Lane.

After the Reformation, the nave became a shopping mall, where people bought "beer, ale, bread, fish, flesh and fruit", a hiring market for servants, and a meeting place for lawyers and horse-traders. The tombs and the font were used as shop counters. It was here that the standard measurement of "one foot" (30 cm) was established, the length of the foot of the statue of St Algar at the base of one of the pillars. The first-ever lottery in Britain was drawn at the west door of Old St Paul's, and the money raised was used to repair harbours rather than the cathedral.

It was not until the 1630s that anyone paid attention to the much needed repairs of the cathedral. Charles I did what he could, but work ceased once the Civil War broke out. Cromwell used Old St Paul's as a cavalry barracks. The parliamentary army broke the windows, burnt the woodwork and smashed the effigies. Perhaps it didn't really matter, for the entire building was destroyed 20 years later in the Great Fire.

Wren's Masterpiece

Wren began work in 1675, and it took 35 years to build the new cathedral. Work was halted on it in 1696 after an earthquake in Dorset delayed the quarrying of supplies of Portland stone. The greatest feat of construction is the dome, a timber frame covered in lead over a brick-built inner dome. The cross on the top is 365 feet (112 metres) above ground, and the cross and the lantern together weigh some 700 tons.

Wren lived across the river from St Paul's while it was being built – there's a plaque on a modest red brick house almost next to the New Globe Theatre in Southwark. He is one of the few architects of a vast cathedral to have lived to see it completed in his lifetime. He visited the cathedral at least once a week, and, as the building got higher, he was hauled up to the dome and the roof in a basket. His son laid the final stone, and Wren was one of the first people to be buried in the crypt. Although he designed more than 50 churches, the Ashmolean Museum at Oxford, the Chelsea Hospital, Buckingham House and dozens of other famous and beautiful buildings, St Paul's was his masterpiece.

James II described St Paul's as "amusing, awful and artificial" – by which he meant "delightful", "awe-inspiring" and "cunningly contrived", for in modern usage the words have lost their 17th-century meaning.

An alarming crack appeared in the dome in 1925. An appeal fund raised £230,000, including a contribution of one shilling (5p) from "thirteen Scotsmen". The base of the dome is now bound by two steel chains, to prevent it expanding in hot weather.

Ceremonial St Paul's

One of the first great ceremonies to take place in St Paul's was a thanksgiving service to commemorate the Battle of Blenheim in 1704. John Evelyn recorded in his diary that among the celebrants were "the Duchesse of Marlbrow, in a very plain garment" and "the Queen [Anne] full of Jewells". The cathedral was also the setting for Nelson's funeral in 1806 (a monumental affair, with perhaps the biggest funeral carriage ever seen), thanksgiving for peace at the end of the Napoleonic Wars, Wellington's funeral in 1852, and a service to mark the recovery of the Prince of Wales from typhoid in the year 1872 – an event which is said to have put an end to resurgent republicanism at the time.

The most famous of more recent ceremonies at St Paul's was the wedding of Lady Diana Spencer and Prince Charles in 1981. St Paul's is at its best on great occasions, and this was spectacularly stage-managed – we may not see its like again.

The Whispering Gallery

When you visit St Paul's, make sure you climb to the stone gallery at the top. The views of London are glorious. And take a partner to try the extraordinary acoustics of the Whispering Gallery. If you whisper against the wall, you may be heard on the opposite side of the Gallery, 107 of St Algar's feet (33 metres) away. The only trouble is that so many people are whispering at the same time that it's not always easy to discern the particular whisper you are listening for.

opposite:
The central nave of St Paul's Cathedral.

The Tower of London

The Tower of London is one of the finest medieval fortresses in Europe, monstrous and marvellous, chilling and fascinating, groaning with history and bulging with legend and romance.

The Scots poet William Dunbar claimed that the Tower was founded by Julius Caesar. He was almost correct. The massive Norman central keep was built on Roman foundations by Gundulf, Bishop of Rochester,

right:
The Tower of London – palace, prison and place of execution.
below:
The White Tower – the inner citadel of the Tower of London.

for William the Conqueror late in the 11th century. It is still the heart of the Tower, with walls 16 feet (5 metres) thick, whitewashed in 1241, since when it has been known as the White Tower.

Other towers, chapels, domestic buildings, guardrooms, inner and outer walls have been added over the centuries. Today, the Tower of London covers 18 acres (7.2 ha). In its 900-year history it has been fortress, palace, armoury, prison, zoo and jewel house. Kings and queens have died here. Traitors have spent their last hours within its walls. The nation's wealth has been jealously guarded in its precincts. The nation's history has been written in its stone.

The Tower has had to be strong to survive. Only a change of wind saved it from the Great Fire of 1666, at a time when the keep was packed with gunpowder for the war against the Dutch and £1.2 million in gold bullion. In 1820 a group of desperadoes known as the Cato Street Conspirators formed a plan to seize the Tower and the Bank of England. They were betrayed by a government spy, and their leader, Arthur Thistlewood, was subsequently hanged in the Tower he had aimed to capture. On 30 October 1841, fire threatened the Martin Tower where the Crown Jewels lay. With the aid of a dozen crowbars, the grilles guarding the jewels were broken, and the treasures were whisked to safety. In 1885 the

Fenians planted three bombs in the Tower. Little damage was done. Despite the widespread destruction of so much of the City in the Second World War, the Tower was largely unscathed.

Famous Prisoners

To many, the Tower of London is most renowned as a prison, and its list of prisoners includes some of the most resonant names in British history: Richard II, the little Princes, Henry VI, Sir Thomas More, Sir Walter Raleigh, Lady Jane Grey, Anne Boleyn, Elizabeth I, Guy Fawkes, the Duke of Monmouth, John Wilkes, Lord George Gordon, the American Revolutionary leader Henry Laurens (who was greeted by the Yeoman warders singing *Yankee Doodle*), Lord Haw-Haw, and hundreds more.

It was the custom for those entering the Tower as prisoners to hand their cloaks to the porter. What they wore when executed went to the executioner. Poor Catherine Howard, Henry VIII's fifth wife, courageously rehearsed her execution. The Duke of Monmouth's execution was dreadfully bungled by Jack Ketch. It took five blows of the axe and some desperate knifework to sever his head from his body.

Escape from the Tower

Contrary to popular belief, there have been several successful escapes from the Tower. In 1101, the Tower's first prisoner, Bishop Flambard, escaped after making his guards drunk. Two Catholic priests escaped in 1597, lowering themselves to the ground by rope and then rowing up the Thames to Uxbridge. Daniel O'Neill, soldier of fortune, walked out of the Tower dressed as a woman in 1642. Ten years later the Earl of Middleton walked to freedom in his wife's clothes. During the Parliamentary Interregnum, Lord Capel, an exceptionally tall man, let himself down by rope from his chamber, waded through a ditch full of mud and water up to his chin, and got away. He was later betrayed, and taken back to the Tower for execution.

Lord Clancarty, an Irish rebel, dressed a block of wood with his periwig and placed it in his bed, with a note saying "This block must answer for me". The Earl of Nithsdale, a Jacobite leader in 1715, was rescued by his wife, who threw a cloak over him and passed him off as her servant. In 1745 a man named Kelly escaped, after spending 50 years as a prisoner in the Tower for his part

The Tower of London from Tower Bridge – medieval might dwarfed by modern commerce.

in an assassination plot against William III. But the most famous escape attempt was that of Colonel Blood.

Colonel Blood and the Crown Jewels

Blood was a Cromwellian Irish adventurer. In 1671 he formed a cunning plot to steal the Crown Jewels. Disguised as a parson, he made himself known to the Keeper of the Tower. Blood brought with him a woman, whom he referred to as his wife, and said she was most anxious to see the jewels. On being shown the crown, Blood's "wife" pretended to faint and was revived by the keeper. A few days later, Blood returned with a present for the keeper, and the suggestion that his nephew would be a suitable husband for the keeper's daughter.

On the day fixed for the wedding, Blood and his accomplices knocked out the poor keeper with a mallet, and grabbed the orb and the crown. They also tried to saw the sceptre in half, for easier handling, before the alarm was raised. They were all captured. Blood was taken before Charles II, who was totally captivated by the man's Irish charm. The colonel received a complete pardon, and was often subsequently seen at court.

above:
Two Yeoman warders – popularly known as Beefeaters.
left:
The ravens of the Tower – last survivors of the Royal Menagerie.

Eating and Drinking in the City

As in the days of Johnson and Boswell, you will still find plenty of good chops in the City, as well as steak and kidney or steak and oyster pies and puddings and rich game puddings. If you preference is for fish, you may explore Beauchamp's Restaurant and Oyster Bar in Leadenhall Market. Here you can sit in the soft beams of sunshine that strike through the roof of the arcade, and work happily through a meal that starts perhaps with gull's eggs and celery salt, and proceeds to a cold whole lobster salad, or a grilled red snapper with coriander butter and rice.

The City has something to suit almost all gastronomic tastes, though vegetarians fare less well here than in most other parts of central London. The current passion and fashion is for southeast Asian and Japanese food – though what Dr Johnson would have thought of lemongrass and sushi may well be unprintable. Tatsuso in Broadgate Circle caters for those who wish to "power lunch" with both teppanyaki and traditional Japanese styles of dining. Moshi Moshi Sushi at Liverpool Street Station serves its sushi on a conveyor-belt system. You take what you want as the plates pass before you. The various colours of the plates indicate the different prices of the dishes.

Devotees of southeast Asian food will find Thai restaurants all over the City. In Limeburner Lane off Ludgate Hill, there is the handsome Singapura restaurant; in London Wall, the jazzier Sri Siam; and in Bow Lane, Tao. One of the finest Chinese restaurants in all London is Ken Hom's Imperial City, in the Royal Exchange building, Cornhill. It's worth visiting the restaurant simply to get inside the building itself.

The oldest pub still pulling pints in the City is said to be Williamson's Tavern, in Grovelands Court off Bow

right:
The Hope, Smithfield – one of a cluster of excellent pubs.
below:
The fruits of the sea in Leadenhall Market.

The bodies of Cromwell, Ireton and Bradshaw – three of the regicides of Charles I – spent the night here in the Old Red Lion, Holborn, before being taken to Tyburn for a posthumous hanging.

Lane, built in 1666 and once the home of the Lord Mayor of London. It also marks the geographical centre of the City. Other pubs have older origins. The Ship Tavern in Lime Street was built in 1447, but has been much restored. Although the present Tiger Tavern on Tower Hill is merely the ground floor of a characterless concrete block, its first predecessor was established around 1500. When the pub was rebuilt in the 19th century, a mummified cat was discovered in a tunnel leading to the Tower of London. The claim has been made that this was the cat with which Princess Elizabeth (later Elizabeth I) played when she was imprisoned in the Tower by her sister, "Bloody" Mary. The Hoop and Grapes in Aldgate High Street is a restored 13th-century inn, also said to have a tunnel leading to the Tower of London. It's the oldest non-ecclesiastical building in the City, and the only remaining 17th-century timber-framed building. The Great Fire missed the house by only a few yards.

The Hand and Shears is a Victorian pub in Middle Street, a favourite haunt of John Betjeman, that stands on the site of an inn built in 1123. The original inn stood in the grounds of St Bartholomew's Priory, and was frequented by drapers and tailors wishing to attend the nearby medieval Cloth Fair. This was where condemned prisoners were served with their last drink on earth before they were conveyed to the scaffold outside Newgate Prison, just a short distance away. The practice continued until the middle of the 19th century – public executions were still taking place outside Newgate as late as 1849.

Happier drinking is to be found in the pubs around Smithfield. Several of these have early morning licences, to quench the thirsts of the porters from the London Meat Market. The Bishop's Finger (formerly the

Rutland) in West Smithfield, the Smithfield Tavern in Charterhouse Street, and the Hope and Sirloin in Cowcross Street all open from six o'clock onwards, and not all their customers drinking beer (or champagne) at that hour work in Smithfield. The Hope and Sirloin serves vast breakfasts to porters and doctors from nearby St Bartholomew's Hospital. Breakfast consists of two fried eggs, tomatoes, baked beans, liver, kidneys, two fat sausages, bacon, two slices of black pudding and fried bread – enough calories to carry the average person through the week.

Cowcross Street, though barely 200 yards long, is rich in pubs. As well as the Hope, there is the Three Compasses, established in 1723. This is a dark and deep pub, running well back from the street. Across the road from Farringdon Station is the Castle, the only pub in London which holds a pawnbroker's licence. You can see the three golden balls hanging above the door.

Ye Olde Mitre Tavern in Ely Court has one of the most charming situations of any pub in London. A narrow archway leads off Hatton Garden to a tiny, pinched courtyard in the grounds of St Etheldreda's Church. The pub is small and cosy, and genuinely old – the present building dates from 1772.

The Old Doctor Butler's Head in Mason's Avenue, off Coleman Street, celebrates a great London eccentric who fired pistols close to patients' ears to cure epilepsy, and dropped ague victims in the river. Dr Butler attracted the attention of King James I early in the 17th century. He produced an ale which he claimed had medicinal properties. The King endorsed the ale and Dr Butler opened several alehouses in which to sell it. This pub is the last remaining of those alehouses. It's a fine building, well weathered and with a good feel to it. There are restaurants upstairs, doorstep sandwiches in the rear bar, and not a whisper of music.

Inside Sweetings, an historical City eating place.

Non stop service for the hungry commuter – the Moshi Moshi Sushi bar at Liverpool Street Station.

St Mary-le-Bow. Cockneys are those born within the sound of its bells.

the same bells rang the curfew for London, after which time no one was allowed on the streets and all taverns had to close.

The original church and the original six bells were consumed by the Great Fire of 1666. The new church was built by Wren, and a peal of eight bells was installed in the tower, some 200 feet (60 metres) above ground. They were replaced by a set of ten bells in the 18th century, to which two more were added a hundred years later.

In the old days, the sound of Bow Bells might have travelled a mile or more on a still, clear day. Nowadays, with high-rise buildings blocking the sound to the east and north, with motorbike couriers and lorries pounding through the streets, with endless building works, and planes screeching in and out of the City Airport, the only still, clear days are Sundays.

Nevertheless, true Cockneys can be found both north and south of the river. According to their own word-of-mouth publicity machine, they are truculent, independent, proud, sharp-witted, cocky, and aggressively loyal to their kith and kin.

According to J. B. Priestley (himself a Northerner, from Bradford) they adore "oysters, fish and chips, an occasional bottle of stout or glass of port, cheerful gossip, noise, jokes, sales, outings, comic songs . . ." (*Angel Pavement*). Much of this is questionable – they seldom restricted themselves to the "occasional" bottle of stout, and nowadays most Cockneys would prefer Martini, lager or a vodka and tonic. When it comes to food, contrary to the opinion of the English Tourist Board and Walt Disney Pictures, cockneys do not live on a diet of jellied eels, whelks, "Kate and Sidney" (steak and kidney) pie, bangers and mash or boiled beef and carrots. Nor do Cockneys smack their lips at the end of every meal and mutter "lovely grub" or "a right good blow-out".

That is all timewarp stuff, inaccurate hangovers from a never-never age when Cockney women wore shawls and vast hats festooned with feathers, and Cockney men stuck their thumbs in their "westkit" pockets and capered about, *à la* Dick van Dyke, singing "Knees Up, Mother Brown". The fantasy is kept alive only by television variety shows and the occasional revival of 1930s musicals such as *Me and My Gal*.

The modern Cockney may still be proud that he or she was born in the old heart of London. The problem is that so few people now actually live within the sound of Bow Bells. A hundred and fifty years ago it was a working-class residential area; since then it has turned into office land, the haunt of commuters by day, quiet as the grave by night – you don't need a curfew to clear the streets. The nearest flats or maisonettes are at the

Cockneys

To the uninitiated all Londoners are Cockneys, but the true Cockney is someone born "within the sound of Bow Bells" – and that means within the sound of the peal of bells from St Mary-le-Bow, Cheapside, in the City of London. Legend has it that they were the bells that called Dick Whittington back to London in the 14th century, summoning him to fame and fortune. In Tudor times,

Barbican estate, which is for well-to-do folk who would not know a whelk if it bit them.

Origins of the Word "Cockney"

"Cockney" comes from the Middle English "cokeney", meaning a cock's egg. The term was applied to mis-shapen eggs laid by young hens who hadn't quite got the hang of their reproductive process. In human terms, it originally meant a weak or effeminate person, i.e. one who lived in a town and couldn't match the strength of the countryman. In the 17th century it came to mean a Londoner, and at that time almost every Londoner lived within the sound of Bow Bells. Far from still being a term of abuse, there is now considerable *cachet* in being able to prove that you are a genuine Cockney.

Cockney School

This has nothing to do with education, but was simply a term coined by a snooty literary critic named John Gibson Lockhart (1794–1854), the son-in-law of Sir Walter Scott. Lockhart applied the term to such writers

above:
Beach chalets at Southend, the Eastenders' seaside playground.
left:
Young Cockneys dig in on the sands of Southend.

as William Hazlitt, Leigh Hunt, Shelley and Keats, all of whom he accused of using rhymes in their poetry that lacked classical purity. They are all still famous. No one has ever heard of Lockhart.

Cockney Culture

Cockney Language

The Cockneys of fantasy are supposed to speak in rhyming slang. They go "up the apples and pears" instead of "up the stairs". A Cockney bloke speaks of his wife as his "trouble and strife". His feet are his "plates of meat". When they want to have a look at something, they have a "butcher's", short for a "butcher's hook". If someone gets into a state, they are said to be in a "right two and eight". A friend or mate is a "China", short for "China plate". Someone who is odd or queer is a "right Burke", said to be short for "Burke and Hare", notorious grave-robbers of the early 19th century – though there is another, unprintable theory. When Cockneys poke fun at someone, they are "taking the Mick", which is short for "taking the Mickey Bliss", which rhymes with "taking the piss". Cockney money is "tosh", short for "tosheroon", which was the treasure that "toshers" searched for in the sewers of London – a great ball of copper and silver coin fused together.

Few Cockneys would use many of these phrases, though lots of Londoners say "Burke" or talk about "hav-

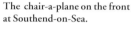

The chair-a-plane on the front at Southend-on-Sea.

ing a butcher's". And there are many words which are particular to Londoners: "boozer" for pub, "kip" for sleep, "the Smoke" for London itself, "knock off" for steal, "doss" for sleep (hostels or lodgings for tramps were called "doss-houses"). Some of these words have been imported into London speech – "kip" is a Danish word, "doss" may well come from the Dutch.

What seems obscure is the reason why Cockneys (and other working-class Londoners) in Dickens's time apparently substituted "v" for "w" (and *vice versa* or *wice wersa*) in their speech. In *The Pickwick Papers*, Sam Weller talks of "vagginers" and "sitivations", of things being "wery excellent" and people being "wery convivial". By the time George Orwell took to the streets of London, nearly a hundred years later, this pattern of speech had almost completely disappeared. There are no traces of it today.

Cockney Humour

G.K. Chesterton thought Cockney humorists the funniest in the world, citing Chaucer, Dickens and W.W.

Jacobs as examples. "London is the largest of the bloated modern cities; London is the smokiest; London is the dirtiest . . . the most sombre . . . the most miserable. But London is certainly the most amusing and the most amused." What Chesterton especially liked was the vulgar quality of Cockney humour.

Many Londoners born before the 1950s have been brought up to see it more as "plucky". And the joke that exemplified this was one first (and mercifully last) heard in the Second World War. It was a joke of the Blitz, a conversation between two Cockneys.

FIRST COCKNEY: I don't care 'ow many bombs that Hitler drops. 'E'll never get me.

SECOND COCKNEY: 'Ow d'you work that out, then?

FIRST COCKNEY: Well, before 'is bombers can get me, they've got to find London, right?

SECOND COCKNEY: Right.

FIRST COCKNEY: And when they've found London, they've got to find the Borough.

SECOND COCKNEY: Right.

FIRST COCKNEY: And when they've found the Borough, they've got to find Tabard Street. And when they've found Tabard Street, they've got to find number 36. And even if they find 36 Tabard Street, they still won't get me, 'cos I'll be round the corner in the pub.

left:
The Pearly King of Wandsworth. His pearly motto reads 'que sera, sera'.
bottom left:
'Oh, I do like to stroll along the prom, prom, prom… ' The esplanade at Southend.

Pearly Kings and Queens

The Cockney community has its own royalty – the Pearly Kings and Queens of London, so named because their clothes are studded with thousands of pearl buttons. In full regalia they are a splendid and shimmering sight – the men in jacket and trousers and flat caps, all weighed down with the decorative buttons, and the women in long coats and flowered bonnets.

The custom of electing "Kings and Queens" began in Victorian times, when they held office to protect fellow costermongers from competitors, and from roughs and toughs generally. This duty is no longer required of them, and most Pearly Kings and Queens devote themselves solely to charitable activities, when not serving the tourist industry. The old East End boroughs (Stepney, Barking, Poplar, Wapping, etc) all have their own Pearly King and Queen, and the titles are largely hereditary. You will see them at the Lord Mayor's Show, the London Marathon and most large ceremonial occasions in East London.

The Cockney Alphabet

There is even a special Cockney alphabet. It doesn't work too well in print, so try reading it aloud:

A for 'orses
B for mutton *[= beef or mutton]*
C for th' Highlanders *[the Seaforth Highlanders were a regiment in the British Army]*
D for mation
E for Adam
F for vescent
G for police
H for a pension
I for Novello
J for oranges
K for restaurant
L for leather *[hell for leather]*
M for sis
N for a penny
O for the wings of a dove *[much loved Victorian song]*
P for relief
Q for a bus
R for mo *[half a mo = half a moment]*
S for you
T for two
U for me
V for "la France"
W for a quid
X for breakfast
Y for crying out loud
Z for breezes *[zephyr breezes]*

It's of no use whatsoever, but people write to the newspapers from time to time, asking for it to be reprinted because they learnt it in their youth – when they thought it was funny – but have now forgotten it.

London Journals:
The Rise and Fall of Fleet Street

In medieval days, Fleet Street was London's religious centre, stuffed with prelates and other holy creatures. The entire length of the street, from the church of St Bride at one end to St Dunstan's at the other, was a path of contrition for the penitent. It was also the place to visit if you wished to see giants, fire-eaters, elephants and freaks. The slide from grace to infamy was completed with the arrival of printers, publishers and newspaper proprietors from Tudor times onwards.

The first Fleet Street paper, the *Daily Courant*, was launched on 11 March 1702, to be followed soon afterwards by the *Morning Chronicle*. Throughout the 18th and 19th centuries the growth in newspaper publishing was steady. *The Times* was first published in 1788, The *Observer* in 1791, and the *Sunday Times* in 1822. The great revolution in Fleet Street came in 1880 with the establishment of the first popular "weekly", *Tit-Bits*, founded by George Newnes, the branch manager of a fancy goods business.

Newnes saw the potential readership that had been created by universal education in England, and designed his magazine for the newly literate working class. Sixteen years later, Alfred Harmsworth (later Lord Northcliffe) launched the *Daily Mail*, at half the price of the other daily papers. During the Boer War, the *Daily Mail* sold a million copies a day, describing itself as "A Penny paper for One Halfpenny". Harmsworth's dictum was "Explain, simplify, clarify". Although Lord Salisbury, the Prime Minister, snootily condemned the paper as written "by office boys for office boys", it was an enormous success. Harmsworth also started the *Daily Mirror*

'All the news that's fit to print…', and then some. Newspapers roll off a printing machine.

in 1903, as a paper for "gentlewomen". The great age of Fleet Street was under way.

It lasted for just a hundred years, to the 1980s. During that time, all the major London-based papers had offices in Fleet Street. The *Daily Express* office was a black and chrome Art Deco monster, the first curtain-wall building constructed in London, with an opulent and impressive entrance hall. It is listed, and is still to be seen at Nos. 121 to 128. Northcliffe's *Daily Mail* was produced from Carmelite House – a building with lifts to rival those of Selfridges department store, and a staircase to rival that at the Foreign and Commonwealth Office. Not until the mid-1920s were newspapers seriously upstaged, first by radio and then by cinema newsreels. Between the wars, leading journalists and columnists were men of enormous prestige, holding court nightly in the Grill Room of the Savoy Hotel (just a short cab ride from Fleet Street), while the presses clattered away, printing their words of wisdom.

It was television, in the 1950s and 1960s, that cut deep into Fleet Street's market. In rapid succession three national dailies, the *Daily Herald*, the *Daily Sketch* and the *News Chronicle*, were forced out of business. New papers came on the scene, but had only a transient existence – the original *Sun*, and Eddie Shah's *Today*, the first newspaper to be set up outside Fleet Street. Then came the second revolution in the history of the Street – as destructive as the first had been regenerative. Rupert Murdoch arrived from Australia and started buying London-based papers. He relaunched the *Sun* and took over *The Times*, but, following Eddie Shah's lead, he also moved papers away from Fleet Street.

Other proprietors followed suit. The *Observer* moved to the southern end of Chelsea Bridge, the *Daily Express* to the southern end of Blackfriars Bridge, and the *Financial Times* to the southern end of Southwark Bridge. *The Times* moved even further – to what became known as Fortress Wapping. The *Daily Telegraph* followed in its wake. Murdoch's great rival, Robert Maxwell, kept his *Daily Mirror* empire in Holborn, arriving by helicopter, landing on the roof, and as he proceeded downwards through the building, sacking any of his staff brave or foolish enough to call into question his vast ego.

The legacy they all left behind in Fleet Street is some of the finest pubs in London. The journalists still go back there – you will find them reminiscing about "the good old days of the Street", coughing on their cigarettes and gulping their gin-and-tonics.

The Story of *The Times*

When *The Times* succeeded the *Daily Universal Register* in 1788, it sold for two and a half pence a copy, roughly the price of a pound (500 grams) of meat. It was not an immediate success in terms of circulation. After 20 years of publication it rarely sold more than 7000 copies a day. It was Thomas Barnes, editor of *The Times* from 1817 to 1841, who freed the paper from its position of subservience to a political party and quadrupled its circulation. Under his leadership it became a radical, campaigning newspaper, critical of government, exposing injustice at home and abroad. While its main rival, the *Morning Chronicle*, became known as the "Grunticle", *The Times* was affectionately nicknamed "The Thunderer".

In 1855 *The Times* (price four pence) was challenged by the arrival of the *Daily Telegraph* (price one penny). Although the *Telegraph* attracted a good many readers, it never had the authority and the influence of *The Times*. Well into the 20th century *The Times* continued to be regarded as *the* British newspaper, the official organ of any right-wing government.

In 1966 it was bought by the Thomson Organization, and sold on to Rupert Murdoch's News International in 1979. Murdoch moved *The Times* from Fleet Street to Wapping in London's Docklands. A massive union rearguard action to save jobs and traditional methods of production failed. The modern paper lacks the prestige of the past, but a price cut has greatly increased its circulation. It now sells for the price of approximately two ounces (60 grams) of meat.

Rolls of newsprint in the vast printing house of a London newspaper.

Newstand selling the London evening paper - *The Standard.*

City Markets – Retail

As well as the famous wholesale markets, the City has many street markets offering an enormous range of goods to locals, tourists and passers-by. The most famous is Petticoat Lane Market, but there are many more, all full of colour, character, bargains, and occasionally pickpockets.

Petticoat Lane

Since 1830 Petticoat Lane has not officially existed. In that year it was renamed Middlesex Street, but the old name has never been allowed to die. People have been selling clothes here for hundreds of years. A map of London of 1608 shows "Peticote Lane", probably named after the old clothes stalls to be found here. In the early 17th century it was a well-to-do area inhabited by Spanish immigrants, but many fled the Great Plague in 1665. It was then taken over by Huguenots and Jews.

There has been a market here for at least 250 years. Sunday is the best and busiest time to visit "The Lane". It takes on the appearance of an entire village given over to market stalls. The whole of Middlesex Street, Wentworth Street, Goulston Street and Toynbee Street is crowded with shoppers and onlookers. Although it's still primarily a clothes market, Petticoat Lane also sells fruit and vegetables, shoes, luggage, watches, batteries, sheets and duvet covers. The stallholders are in full flow, calling their wares and offering homespun wisdom on a woman's place in the world, men's shortcomings, the merits and demerits of children and the state of the world in general.

On weekdays the market is less frantic, and you may have time to savour some of the delights nearby. Artillery Row is a short narrow street and a delight to behold. In Old Castle Street you can still see the old façade of the 1846 wash-houses. The windows have all been boarded up, but there's still enough of the building to give you a very sharp taste of the old East End of London.

Best of all, on a weekday you have the opportunity to visit Dirty Dick's in Bishopsgate, just round the corner from Middlesex Street. The pub takes its name from the sad story of Nathaniel Bentley, an 18th-century merchant. His bride-to-be died on what would have been their wedding day. Bentley locked up the room in which the wedding breakfast had been set, and from that day neither washed nor changed his clothes. He became a celebrity, but his landlord threw him out of his lodgings in Leadenhall Street. Bentley's grubby wardrobe, rotting wedding breakfast and collection of dead cats was then bought by Ye Olde Port Wine House (now Dirty Dick's), and placed on public display in the cellar bar. For health reasons it was thought better to dispose of the mess in the mid-1980s, but you can still see a photograph of it all, and you may be surprised to come across relics of the dead cats. The place is a lovely mixture of pub, restaurant, oyster bar and wine vaults, worth paying a visit.

Leadenhall Market, Whittington Avenue

Strictly speaking, Leadenhall isn't really a market at all – it's simply that some of the shops spill out into the arcade and have stalls selling fish, meat and other goods. The best time to visit is before Christmas, when there are

Bargain hunters jam the pavements of Petticoat lane Market.

staggering displays of poultry, but Leadenhall Market is a beautiful late Victorian glory just a few yards from the Lloyd's Building.

In the 14th century "foreigners" (anyone who lived outside London) were allowed here to sell their poultry, cheese and butter. A hundred years later it became the site of a general market, and in 1881 Sir Horace Jones designed the present arcade, with its richly decorated pink and maroon columns, its high roof and its fascinating mixture of restaurants, pubs, shops and stalls. At the centre of the arcade is the Lamb Tavern, with excellent beer and great showbiz connections. John Wayne spent many days here during the shooting of *Brannigan*, as did Robert Mitchum for *The Winds of War* and Tom Selleck for *Magnum*. It was also the setting for scenes in the BBC TV production of *Bleak House*.

Whitecross Street Market

Whitecross Street, off Old Street, is narrow and quaint. The market is held here every weekday morning, selling essentials or near-essentials at bargain prices to many local residents and one or two passers-by. It is not a collectors' market. Whitecross offers terracotta pots and vases, plants and flowers, teapots and T-shirts, boots and

The ornate gates to Spitalfields Market.

shoes, fruit and vegetables, tapes and batteries, and one or two surprises. There's a stall selling wok sets, and a trailer cooking and selling curries.

Once upon a time there was a Whitbread brewery nearby, and there are plenty of fine Victorian pubs in the neighbourhood. In Whitecross Street itself there are snack bars, or you could try the Cosy Fish Dinner and Supper Bar, whose name keeps alive the working-class tradition of calling the midday meal "dinner". To smart City folk, the midday meal is, of course, "lunch".

Leather Lane Market

Like Whitecross Street, Leather Lane is an old-fashioned street market. You will find very little leather for sale here, but the name probably derives from *leveroun*, the old French word for "greyhound" – perhaps there was once a Greyhound pub. What you will find is an abundance of clothes, drinks, sweets, kitchenware, fruit, cosmetics, towels, plants and flowers, and secondhand books. Appetites can be assuaged by Grodzinski's (baker's), the Traditional Plaice fish restaurant or the Bagel Bakery (sweet and savoury).

Spitalfields

Until 1991, Spitalfields Market was one of London's biggest wholesale fruit and vegetable markets, covering a ten-acre (4-ha) site, with huge heated cellars in which bananas were ripened. Today the market is reduced to five acres, and includes shops and restaurants, as well as food stalls. It's one of the best places in London for organically produced food (bread, fruit, meat, vegetables and eggs) – there are even photographs on the meat counter of the animals that you choose to eat, with their names recorded. The mechanical railway sculpture whirrs into life every 15 minutes.

far left:
Horace Jones's graceful glass and iron roof over Leadenhall Market.

City Markets – Wholesale

above:
The site of the old Billingsgate Fish Market.
below:
The London Central Meat Market at Smithfield.

The City of London has always had a big appetite. Even in Saxon and Norman times, flocks and herds of animals were driven daily from the surrounding countryside to provide the merchants, their families and their servants with meat. Cartloads of vegetables trundled in from the fields of Kent and Essex. Boats tied up at Billingsgate and Queenhithe to unload barrels of fish, harvested from the North Sea and the Channel.

Gradually, the supply of food became centralized in three markets: Smithfield (meat), Billingsgate (fish) and Spitalfields (flesh, fowl and roots). Of these mighty food-stores, only Smithfield remains – Billingsgate moved to the Isle of Dogs in 1982, taking with it the Billingsgate Clock, and Spitalfields moved to Temple Mills in Waltham Forest in 1991. Billingsgate's move had long been expected. In 1883 the market's cramped conditions and poor facilities had been described as "a great scandal to London". But it was full of character and personalities. On the Isle of Dogs today, the fish-porters no longer wear the traditional leather hats modelled on those worn by Henry V's bowmen at the Battle of Agincourt. Nor do they still carry tottering piles of baskets on their heads – the fork-lift truck has done away with all that. But they do still swear and use the language that made old Billingsgate notorious in medieval days.

Smithfield

The name is derived from "smooth field", a large open area where sheep and cattle grazed away their last hours before being slaughtered and sold in the market. This was the site of the annual Bartholomew Fair, a rowdy, bawdy celebration that continued from 1123 until it was suppressed for debauchery in 1855. It was also the place of public executions (hangings and burnings) before those particular attractions moved to Tyburn.

It was always an unruly place. Drovers and herdsmen delighted in letting their animals run amok through the narrow streets round Smithfield – it is even said that this is where the phrase "a bull in a china shop" originated. Dickens captured its hellish squalor in *Oliver Twist*: "The ground was covered, nearly ankle-deep, with filth and mire; a thick steam perpetually rising from the reeking bodies of the cattle… the unwashed, unshaven, squalid and dirty figures constantly running to and fro."

All this has changed. The London Central Meat Market at Smithfield is noisy and busy early in the morning, but the porters that trundle trolleys of pork, lamb and beef are clad in white coats, and look more like doctors than slaughterers. On the whole, they're a friendly lot – as long as you keep out of their way. Nevertheless, a stroll through the colourfully restored market hall is not for the squeamish or the vegetarian. It offers everything a carnivore craves – veal rump, rib-eye and Scotch fillet steaks, fresh shins, oxtails, turkey gizzards, pigs' trotters, shanks, hams, sides of pork, salt silverside and brisket of beef, whole lambs, rabbits (still in their fur), sausages and haggis.

Carnivores and vegetarians alike admire the beautifully restored wrought iron railings, gates and roof supports of the Market – gloriously picked out in stunning pink, green and mauve paint.

Old Billingsgate

The market took its name from Belinus, a Celtic king of the 4th century, who built a wooden quay just to the west of where Tower Bridge stands today. In its heyday it employed 2500 people, including 500 licensed porters. The socialist writer Beatrice Webb went there one May morning in 1925, and found it "crowded with loungers smoking villainous tobacco; coarse talk with the clash of the halfpenny on the pavement… bestial content or hopeless discontent on their faces. The lowest form of leisure… this is 'the chance' the docks offer!"

On a bright morning in spring or summer it was a wonderful sight – for anyone that didn't have to work there. The sun rose behind Tower Bridge, warming the golds and yellows and browns of the wooden boxes of fish from all over the world. All the riches of the oceans were banged down on the quayside: cod, skate, plaice, sole, crab, herring, halibut, turbot, whitebait, and dozens more. In the very early 1980s, it was one of the few riverside sites in London that had preserved its traditional way of working. Now the 19th-century market hall stands quiet and empty, but still, on a May morning, you may fancy you hear the ghostly echo of the obscenities uttered for centuries by the Billingsgate porters.

New Billingsgate

Like New Covent Garden, New Billingsgate Market has lost almost all its colour and glamour. It consists of a low brick warehouse with a modern concrete extension grafted on to it, just across the Thames from the Millennium Dome. On one side is the sluggish water of the West India Dock, on the other the roaring stream of traffic belting along the six-lane A1261. To east and west are large car parks. Like New Covent Garden, it neither attracts nor welcomes customers. This is not the place to visit if all you want is a pair of kippers or half a pint of prawns, but, like Smithfield, it does have interesting goods on display. With a little hunting, you may track down a monster pike, some exotic fish from tropical waters, or a writhing heap of lobsters. Probably the best buy for home consumption is the packets of smoked salmon.

Everything from a haggis to a haunch of venison – inside Smithfield Market.

The coat of arms of the Worshipful Company of Poulterers on the wall of Smithfield Market. Their motto reads 'Remember Your Oath.'

Docks and Docklands

There is a world of difference between the Docks and Docklands. The London Docks have a long history of poverty and prosperity, hard work and enforced idleness, national service and bloody-mindedness. Docklands is new. Much of the Isle of Dogs – the old centre of the West India and Millwall Docks – has been sacrificed to make way for a glass and concrete Gotham City, shining in the sunshine, sulking in the rain, and unredeemed by Batman.

Around what little is left of the old docks, you can still find terraces of Victorian houses, trees, some of London's best and oldest pubs, and old-fashioned Londoners. In Docklands you are surrounded by tower blocks and smart housing units, shopping precincts with delusions of grandeur (where the goods are "purveyed" rather than sold), and "integrated" pubs. This is a land created at a stroke by teams of architects. It is the city of a single concept, and you either like it or loathe it. There are no surprises or sudden revelations, no gems for you to discover. Connecting the two societies is the robot-operated Docklands Light Railway – safe and soulless.

The whole schizophrenic mismatch can be experienced by visiting two pubs. In Ropemakers' Fields, Narrow Street – on the western fringe of the Isle of Dogs – is The House They Left Behind. It's a small, thin build-

ing, standing on its own as its name suggests, a glorious affirmation of its individuality and integrity. On the waterfront of Mackenzie Walk, in the heart of Docklands, is the Henry Addington. It was the first pub to open on Canary Wharf. It consists of one broad sweeping bar overlooking Heron Quay, with good beer and fine (though expensive) sandwiches. But as you sit in it, you feel you are in a room that the landlord has rented in someone else's office. It could never be left behind – it is merely a slice of a monster development.

Those who planned and built Docklands in the early 1980s justifiably argued that something had to be done to the Isle. Modern freighters had outgrown the old Victorian docks. Warehouses were empty, crumbling shells. Dockers had no work. The area was fast becoming an industrial wasteland. Critics of the development argued then, and argue now, that a neighbourhood is not simply a place where people work. It is where they laugh, love, raise families and invest all their hopes and dreams for life on earth. The planners and developers were not in a mood to compromise – they never are. Docklands is a still-growing reality, marching inexorably across the flat landscape.

But the money runs short from time to time, and the earth movers and bulldozers lie idle a while like beached whales in the sticky mud. If the inspiration for the

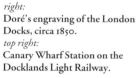

right:
Doré's engraving of the London Docks, circa 1850.
top right:
Canary Wharf Station on the Docklands Light Railway.

prophets of modern Docklands was to regenerate an industrial wasteland, all they have achieved so far is to build a tiny island of prosperity in a sea of poverty. Another couple of pubs serve witness to that. Drive along Manchester Road and you come across two sorry sights within a few yards of each other. On one side of the road is the Cubitt Arms – a simple but attractive, typical Victorian London pub. On the other side is the Dorset Arms, with a signboard that boasts "The Pride of the Isle", and the motto "Who's afear'd?". Both pubs are boarded up. They will never open again. And both pubs are within spitting distance of the sales offices of two new housing developments, offices selling houses priced way beyond the pockets of local families.

A hundred years ago, the entire stretch of the Thames east for five miles from Tower Bridge was crowded with ships. Their cargo filled warehouses to bursting with cotton, meat, wheat, tobacco, cocoa, coffee, tea, sugar, rubber, ostrich feathers and ivory, bales of coir and sacks of cinnamon. As you walk round the Isle of Dogs today, here and there you come across an old barge, an old wherry, an old tug, in the puddles of dock that remain. Amazingly, you still see herons around Heron Quay, and cormorants. But if you stand on Westferry station, and look roughly northeast, across what used to be Chinatown, there is nothing oriental to be seen.

Two fine views and two more pubs to end. The best view of Docklands and Canary Wharf is from the lift bridge where Preston's Road crosses the cut of water leading to West India Docks. Stand there at sunset, and see the tallest building in London (240 metres high) silhouetted against the golden sky. Then turn, and with the sun behind you, look across the Thames to the Millennium Dome. The Grapes in Narrow Street has wonderful views up and down the river, good food and good beer. It has changed little since the time of Charles Dickens, who immortalized it as the "Six Jolly-Fellowship Porters" in *Our Mutual Friend*: "a tavern of

dropsical appearance… long settled down into a state of hale infirmity. In its whole constitution it had not a straight floor and hardly a straight line… It was a bar to soften the human breast." Happily, it has hardly changed in the last 150 years.

above:
Docklands today – it's sobering to compare this picture with Doré's engraving.
left:
A reflective view of the Docklands Light Railway.

The Museum of London

right:
The Museum of London, at London Wall EC2.
below:
One of Cipriani's decorative panels on the Lord Mayor's State Coach.

The Museum of London nestles in the southwestern corner of the Barbican, in London Wall. It was opened in 1976, following the amalgamation of the London Museum and the Guildhall Museum. Like almost any component of the Barbican complex it isn't easy to find, but the effort expended is well worthwhile. If you had only one hour in which to discover the history of London, this would be the best place to spend that precious time. There are always special exhibitions taking

place, but the bulk of the museum is the permanent collection that traces the story of London from distant prehistory to the present day – and all on two floors.

A visit to the museum takes the form of a chronological stroll through a well-marked series of displays, each of which picks out a period in London's history. The displays include artefacts from each period, reconstructions of famous but vanished old buildings, video films and photographs, and printed panels of explanation and information. It's a friendly museum, rightly proud of the city and the people it represents.

Some of the oldest items are flint hand axes from Clapton and Stoke Newington, used to skin and butcher animal carcasses around 20,000 BC. There's a perforated antler-base mattock used for digging 11,000 years ago, found on the site of New Scotland Yard in Westminster. A villainous-looking collection from around 1000 BC includes fish-hooks from Barnes, a flint knife from the Thames, opposite the Tate Gallery, and a slashing sword from Limehouse Reach, Millwall.

Roman London includes a section of pavement unearthed from Bucklersbury in the City of London, many gold coins, carvings, statues, the odd skeleton or two (of a horse), snaffle bits and more sophisticated tools. There are Saxon pots and implements, an iron anchor from Blackfriars, and fine reconstructions of the Tower of London in William the Conqueror's day and Old St Paul's (i.e. before the Great Fire).

As the centuries roll by, the collection becomes richer and more evocative of the times it celebrates. There are Tudor suits of armour from the Greenwich Armouries, weapons of the 16th and 17th centuries, Stuart jewellery and costumes, and reconstructions of Shakespeare's Rose Theatre and of the Whitehall Palace, the stage for both the glory and the ignominy of Charles I. Among items of Stuart furniture, there is the Master's Chair of the Framework Knitters' Company – more magnificent than many a royal throne. A separate display tells the

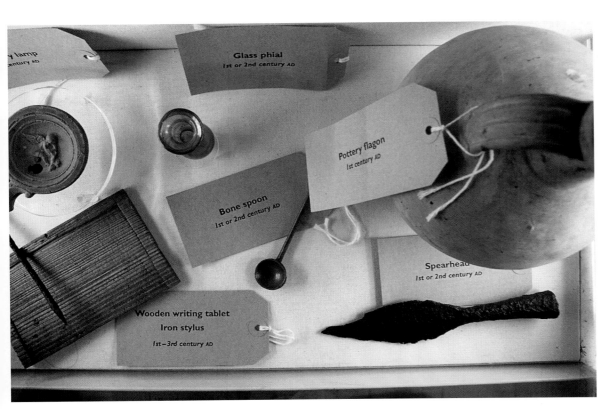

Glass phial
1st or 2nd century AD

Pottery flagon
1st century AD

Bone spoon
1st or 2nd century AD

Spearhead
1st or 2nd century AD

Wooden writing tablet
Iron stylus
1st–3rd century AD

story of the Great Fire of 1666, and of Wren's rebuilding of London. All this is on the ground floor. When you reach the lower level, you need to turn left – turning to the right will take you backwards through the last 300 years of London's history.

A grisly reconstruction of part of Newgate Gaol includes a convincingly heavy iron door and part of the stone façade. The largest, and in many ways the best, section of the museum is that devoted to Victorian London. Here you can study the slums, the early days of the police, and old London theatres. On display are a wooden snuff-taking Highlander typical of those placed outside tobacconists' shops, carriages and wagons, a coster's barrow, an old bread cart, the interiors of a variety of shops, and some of Queen Victoria's dresses.

In the 20th-century section there are displays covering the lives and struggles of the Suffragettes, the early days of radio and television, London cinema and film-making, and the rise of department stores such as Peter Robinson, Debenham and Freebody, and Selfridges in the 1920s. In a corner are the last remaining screen and lift car from Selfridges, designed by a Frenchman, Edgar Brandt, in 1923, and so richly decorated that they look as though they had been plucked from the interior of a medieval cathedral. Visitors can touch a gleaming black Model Y Ford – but the doors are locked.

The Lord Mayor's State Coach

The Museum is also the home of the Lord Mayor's Coach, except on days when the Lord Mayor requires it. Here it stands, glistening in all its scarlet and gold finery, as brilliant as when it was built in 1757. Each alderman contributed £60 to its cost, and the Lord Mayor gave £100. The total cost was £1065. The ornate panels on front, back and sides were painted by Giovanni Battista Cipriani, and depict Faith, Hope and Charity, the Genius and Riches of the City, and the glories of Trade and Commerce.

Every Lord Mayor of London in the last 250 years has ridden in the coach, experiencing particularly bumpy rides in the days when the streets were cobbled, for the coach has no springs, but is slung on leather braces. It weighs almost three tons, but until 1951 had no brakes, which must have added excitement to the descent along Ludgate Hill.

The Villages of London

North v. South: Two Cities

For over 40 years, following the end of the Second World War, Berlin was a divided city. For over 50 years, following the creation of the state of Israel, Jerusalem has been a divided city. For most of the 20th century, after the establishment of the Unionist Movement, Belfast was a divided city. London outstrips them all. North Londoners and south Londoners have waged a war of words (and gestures) against each other for 2000 years.

The Romans sowed the seeds of this conflict when they built their settlement on the north bank of the Thames and refused to have anything to do with the conquered native population dwelling on the south bank. Over the centuries, north London became associated with power, authority and wealth, south London with poverty. Palaces, hotels, galleries, offices, museums and barracks were built in north London. Theatres, bear pits, "stews" and prisons were built in south London. If there was any pleasure to be had in south London, it was always regarded as dubious and/or illicit.

In the 18th century the heart of modern London was established by the development of a number of wealthy estates in such areas as Bloomsbury, Kensington and Marylebone – all north of the river. Dukes and earls sold off their rich pastureland and turned it into much richer squares and avenues. Once these estates had been built, neither residents nor landlords wanted such attractive neighbourhoods invaded by the ugly poor. They erected gates and barriers at the entrances to their lovely parades and piazzas, with guards in attendance, so that the poor should be denied access. And they kept them more permanently at bay by building nothing in the way of cheap housing.

The workers had to find somewhere else to live. So they settled south of the river and did the best they could – in the slums of Waterloo, Lambeth and Southwark, and later in the rows and rows of poorly built houses in the streets and alleys of Plumstead, Woolwich, Deptford and Bermondsey. They were allowed to cross the Thames to run the factories and offices of north London, grudgingly, and at a price. Indeed, the north London rich, out of the kindness of their hearts, built the pedestrian tunnel under the Thames at Greenwich so that the poor dockers of south London could walk to work in the Pool of London and the West India Docks.

Or, at least, that's the north London version of what happened. But it doesn't explain why some of the most beautiful terraces of houses in all London are to be found south of the Thames – in Clapham and Camberwell, in Battersea and Brixton.

(North Londoners will laugh at this sentence, unless they have actually visited Camberwell or Battersea, which is unlikely because the Tube doesn't run there and north Londoners are incapable of visiting any part of London not served by the Tube.)

Lord's and the Oval

The difference (and the antagonism) between north and south London is epitomized in the difference between Lord's Cricket Ground in St John's Wood, NW8, and the Oval in Kennington, SE11. Lord's is cosmopolitan, the headquarters of cricket, the home of the MCC (Marylebone Cricket Club – cricket's governing body) and Middlesex Cricket Club. It is where all the important decisions are taken, where the England team is selected, where the laws are made, where cricketing miscreants are summoned to receive their sentences. To be a member at Lord's costs a great deal of money. You have to put your name down at birth and wait 30 years or so. And if you're a woman, you could not until very recently become a member.

The Oval is the home of Surrey County Cricket Club – metropolitan, vulgar, cheap (relatively) and cheerful (if Surrey are winning). Women have been admitted to full membership at the Oval for decades.

Taking a Taxi South of the River

Whatever the laws governing taxicabs and their drivers may say, you may encounter a problem if you wish to travel from the West End to south London after midnight. There are still many cab-drivers who pretend they're "just about to finish for the night" when hailed and asked to go south of the river. They're not in theory allowed to refuse, but when pressed they do give their reasons for reluctance. It's not that they're frightened of south London, you understand. It's simply that their chances of picking up another fare on the way back from Catford at two in the morning are slight. Mind you, reports suggest that the same sort of thing applies to travellers to Kentish Town, not that far north of the centre. It is said that there is a rule that once you are inside a taxi, the cabbie is obliged by law to accept your fare and (within reason) destination. So, should you wish to go far from the centre of London, late on a wet night, the best thing is to leap into the cab as soon as it stops, and then say where you want to go. The only trouble is, most cabs are now fitted with a locking device operated by the driver, so he can make sure you can't get in until you've told him your destination.

The North and South Circular Roads

Running in a circle round London – some six or seven miles on average from the centre – are the North and South Circular Roads. The North Circular Road was designed and developed as a kind of urban bypass in the 1930s. It runs in a great loop, some 23 miles (37 km) long from Chiswick in the west to Woodford in the east. It's

not a pretty road, flanked by factories and warehouses, and riddled with traffic lights. The South Circular Road wasn't designed at all. It's a maze of two-, three- and occasionally four-lane roads, snaking through seven towns and dozens of shopping centres on its 20-mile (32-km) route from Woolwich in the east to Kew Bridge in the west. Although it isn't flanked by factories, it is riddled with traffic lights, and it's not pretty either.

One final reason for living south of the river. The best vegetarian restaurant in all London is in Deptford. It's in McMillan Street, it's called "Heather's", and the food is superb.

above:
Two faces of south London –
Urban horror at the Elephant
and Castle…
below:
… residential splendour at
Clapham Common, North
Side.

London and Class

Londoners have always fine-tuned the class topography of their metropolis. Some areas are born fashionable, some achieve fashionability, some have it thrust upon them. But for most areas, as for Norma Desmond in *Sunset Boulevard*, there is always the risk that their desirability will fade – to the point where no coats of paint on the front door or wrought-iron railings will restore their faded beauty.

Two hundred years ago London was the playground of the landed gentry, which meant anyone from a royal duke to a rich squire. They had vast estates in the country, where they hunted, raised bloodstock and families, and spent grey English winters. But every spring they came to London, to their houses in Belgravia and Mayfair, bringing with them hordes of servants. Round these wealthy estates were clustered the poor, hoping for crumbs from the rich man's table. They worked as milliners, dressmakers, chimney sweeps, ostlers, crossing sweepers, errand boys.

So the class divide was early established in London. The rich lived in their fine houses. The poor huddled close by. Shops sprang up nearby to provide food, furniture and other necessities. When the Season ended and the rich returned to their country estates, the flower-sellers and knife-sharpeners, the hawkers and street musicians tightened their belts and starved a little through the long winter until the rich rode in again the following spring and business picked up once more.

As the mechanization of farming threw most countrymen out of work, farm labourers trudged to London with their families, desperately seeking employment. To survive they had to learn new skills – to work on building sites, on the roads, in factories and sweatshops. There were plenty of trading houses that needed clerks, and more and more shops that needed sales assistants and "smart lads". This change was registered in new nicknames given to areas of London. A part of Kensal Rise, previously known as "Piggeries and Potteries", became "Soap Suds Island", in recognition of the number of laundries there.

To house the new poor, street upon street of mean terraced houses were built, all within half an hour's brisk walk of elegant squares. The class division of London, based on clear geographical regions, was established. It reached its most nicely defined system in 1900, when Charles Booth published his *Social Map of London*. Booth was a ship-owner and a writer on social issues – he was in fact the man who discovered that footmen in London were paid according to their height. A footman of five feet six inches (1.69 metres) could earn only £20 per annum, while a footman over six feet (1.84 metres) could earn up to twice as much.

Victorian terrace houses built for the artisans of Wandsworth.

The Right Address

Nowadays, southwest London is "better" (meaning classier) than southeast London. Northwest London is similarly "better" than northeast London. West London is OK as far as Kensington and Notting Hill, then becomes unfashionable in Shepherd's Bush and Acton, but fashionable again once you get to Chiswick. East London is a strange mixture – the rich and smart would look down their noses at anyone who lived in Mile End, unless of course they lived in Tredegar Square, Mile End. We are back to the intricacies of Charles Booth's *Social Map*.

South London eccentric – the Acid House in Fulham.

North London is definitely OK – you can't go wrong with an address in Hampstead or Highgate. South London is dodgy – parts of Clapham are acceptable, parts aren't. Dulwich is OK, Tooting isn't. Collier's Wood sounds romantic but isn't. Balham (famed as the "Gateway to the South" on an old Peter Sellers LP) sounds awful but is becoming sufficiently odd to be fashionable.

Who decides these things? Well, tradition dies hard in London, and in many ways it is the traditional factors that decide today whether a district should be fashionable or unfashionable. People still pay high prices and high rents to live in areas that are within easy reach of the wealth of London. All that has changed is that the rich no longer have any use for local flower-sellers or milliners or laundrywomen.

Good and Bad Taste

The self-styled discerning believe that "one instinctively knows when something is in good or bad taste". So, if you need help in deciding, then I'm afraid you haven't got good taste. It is as simple and as final as that.

Nevertheless, a few pointers may be of help. Bad taste is concrete garden gnomes, concrete heraldic lions on brick plinths, signs on houses that say "Beware of the Kids", and plaques with a picture of a pit-bull terrier growling "Go on, make my day". Good taste is stucco on the outside of the house: bad taste is pebbledash. Bad taste is anything made of chipboard or plastic. Good taste is simply framed, original black and white photographs. Bad taste is elaborately framed reproductions of Impressionist paintings.

Finally, it may help to repeat the old joke about the young lad at Eton College writing a story. It was about a family. "They were a very poor family," he wrote. "The father was poor, the mother was poor, the children were poor, the cook was poor, the butler was poor, even the chauffeur was poor." Now, that's class…

Bishops Row, Hampstead – the ghetto of pop stars, property dealers and sundry millionaires.

The Villages of North London

London development north of the Thames is older than that south of the river. Villages close to Westminster and the City lost their separate identity in Tudor and Stuart times. Those a little further afield were swallowed up in the 18th and early 19th centuries, but the two greatest waves of suburban building were those between 1860 and 1900, and between 1920 and 1935. Until the late Victorian age, villages like Edgware, Golders Green, Mill Hill and even Finchley were still rural communities – settlements whose fields and meadows offered a restful, rural day out for those who sweated in the offices and workshops of central London. Foxes were still hunted over fields between Hampstead and Hyde Park until the early 1800s. Many of these villages had long histories – some had been agricultural centres for over 1000 years.

right:
Revellers dancing on Hampstead Heath on a Whitsun Bank Holiday in the 1890s.
below:
Byron's House at Highgate.

Present-day Barnet is made up of three such villages: East Barnet, Friern Barnet and High Barnet. The population of East Barnet rose from 400 to 4000 between 1841 and 1881. By the end of the 19th century it no longer existed as a separate village. Friern Barnet was essentially rural until the coming of the Great Northern Railway in 1851. There were several coaching inns in High Barnet until late in the 19th century, for it was a convenient place for coupling fresh teams of horses to the coaches that rattled into and out of London.

In early Victorian times, the village of Earl's Court was a ramshackle collection of a few houses and cottages, mostly to the east of the present Earl's Court Road. It was surrounded by orchards, farmland and open country. Lanes to the south and east led across fields to Chelsea and Brompton. As late as 1860 Earl's Court Farm stood on the site of the present Underground station. It was a fine farm, with a large wooden barn and an imposing farmhouse.

In the 1870s Kilburn was still a village, and Poplar was a rural community of cottages with cabbage patches and rabbit hutches. Most of these old dwellings were then pulled down to make way for such improvements as the Peabody Buildings. George Peabody was an American philanthropist who gave the enormous sum of £500,000 to provide better housing for working-class Londoners. The apartment blocks that bore (and still bear) his name were healthier and safer, and allowed more Londoners to live in a given area – but they lacked the charm of the old cottages. Although parts of Highbury were developed as early as the 1770s, the area remained largely dairy farms until the 1850s.

There was still plenty of room for gypsies to halt their caravans and camp in the fields of West Hampstead and Chingford in the late 1880s, and as late as 1900 Swiss Cottage stood in the heart of the countryside. The villages of Edgware and Enfield lasted even longer. Edgware remained largely rural until the Northern Line reached it in 1924. Enfield wasn't really developed until the 1930s, when thousands of houses were built on what had been orchards.

Many north Londoners, however, still like to think of Hampstead or Highgate, Islington or Chelsea, Kensington or Camden as "villages". They are proud of independent baker's, draper's, butcher's or grocer's shops. They still refer to the nearest prized pub as their "local". Some even still support their local football or cricket team. The villages may have been swallowed up, but the spirit lives on.

A Hilltop in North London

Islington started life in Saxon times as Gisladune (Gisla's Hill). It was then forest land, owned by the canons of St

Paul's. For hundreds of years the village's main claim to fame was that it was a convenient stopping place for kings and queens on their way to and from the capital. Henry VI was formally arrested here by the Earl of Warwick in 1465.

A hundred years later Islington was noted for its houses, orchards, and its prime hunting land. Henry VIII housed at least some of his mistresses here. In the 18th century it became known as "merry Islington", supplying Londoners with milk from its dairy farms and water from its springs. It was also a place of refuge for many seeking to escape the city's annual visitation of the Plague.

The orchards and farms were broken up into market and nursery gardens, but the builders moved in early in the 19th century, and much of the land became brickfields. It was still a prosperous, salubrious and sought-after part of London, but declined in popularity in the early 20th century.

In the early 1980s, commentators regarded Islington as shabby at best, socially deprived at worst. Then came an influx of professional people, gobbling up the fine but run-down (and therefore cheap) old houses, sending prices soaring and demanding new theatres, restaurants, shops and amenities. By the late 1990s, it was home to dozens of members of the chattering classes, movers and shakers, and even the Prime Minister and his family.

Ealing Studios and Ealing Films

Between 1930 and 1960, what had once been the village of Ealing became famous as the home of Ealing Studios, a film production company that specialized in very British films. These films combined charm and a gentle humour with a constant theme of the victory of the little person over the rich and powerful, or the giant corporation. Although their films were set all over Britain, the real legacy of Ealing's production was a handful of comedies set in London. These contain some the best archive footage of the city 50 or more years ago.

The Lavender Hill Mob has shots of the City of London and parts of west London in the early 1950s. *Hue and Cry* is set almost entirely on the bomb sites of east London, near the docks, in the late 1940s. *The Ladykillers* has wonderful footage of a London cul-de-sac, not far from the studios themselves, with an adjacent railway line that plays a crucial part in the film's *dénouement*. *The Man in the White Suit* is also set in and around Ealing.

The Suburbs of North London

An early 20th century experiment in communal living - Hampstead Garden Suburb.

London began to sprawl beyond the City limits early in its existence. Unlike Paris, and many other European cities, there was no medieval defensive wall to keep out invaders and to restrain development. And so Londoners steadily encroached on the surrounding countryside for centuries. Farms, hayfields and market gardens disappeared, to be replaced at first by single houses, later by rows and rows of houses – for Londoners have long preferred a house to an apartment, and a garden to a shared courtyard. In 1817, a Frenchman remarked on what he regarded as the strange living habits of Londoners, who inhabited "these narrow houses, three or four storeys high… one for eating, one for sleeping, a third for company, a fourth underground for the kitchen, a fifth perhaps at the top for servants". He also likened the families that inhabited such houses to cage birds, hopping up and down the many stairs with remarkable agility.

Today, the suburbs of north London stretch in a vast semicircle from Wembley in the west to Edmonton in the east. The area includes all that is best and worst in suburban London, from the delights of Hampstead and Highgate to the horrors of Colindale. It is a 200-square-mile (52,000-ha) patchwork quilt of old villages that have been gobbled up by streets and avenues, crescents and lanes. Its population is made up of psychiatrists, architects, actors, mechanics, single parents, bus drivers, the unemployed, shop workers, teachers, waiters, musicians, cooks, factory workers, builders and decorators, and a thousand other talents. In bedsits and maisonettes, flats and semis, millions of people live within half an hour's travel of Piccadilly Circus.

London Suburbs of the 18th and early 19th Centuries

The gentry and nobility who owned estates on the fringes of London regarded it as natural that the city should grow outwards. Their main concern was to make sure that such growth should be controlled, should create fashionable new neighbourhoods, and should take place on land that they owned. If it was properly planned and handled, there was a great deal of money to be made, and while they collected the ground rent, it was the speculative builder who put up the houses and took the risks.

The first band of north London suburbs appeared – in Hampstead and Highgate, Islington and Camden. The houses were stylish and large, built on the grand scale. You can see them still today, though many have now slipped into multiple occupation.

With the coming of the railways, and later the London Underground, the whole process speeded up enormously, and the character of the suburb changed. What were needed were homes for the army of clerks and office workers, tradesmen and artisans who could no longer be housed in the old inner city slums. Humbler suburbs appeared, such as Willesden and Neasden, Cricklewood and Hackney.

London Suburbs of the 20th Century

The great change in 20th-century suburban development in north London was the entry of local authori-

ties into the housing market. The London boroughs and the London County Council played a large part in the building of the outer suburbs – Hendon and Edmonton, Tottenham and Leyton. One of the promises made after the First World War was that there should be no lack of "Homes fit for Heroes". Huge "council" estates were built on the fringes of London. The estates were almost entirely semi-detached or terraced houses, with the luxuries of gas, electricity and inside toilets for working-class families.

Even these, however, were beyond the pockets of the very poor, who stayed on in the misery of the inner city slums, around Holborn and Waterloo. The irony is that, of the tiny "two-up, two-down" cottages they were unable to escape, those that still remain are now very much sought-after "bijou" residences. Many a trendy Londoner would give a tidy sum for an ex-slum dwelling in Roupell Street or Theed Street, behind Waterloo Station.

Metroland and John Betjeman

From 1900 to 1938, the extensions to various lines of the London Underground system provided the single greatest factor in the speed and density of the development of the north London suburbs. When the Northern Line reached Golders Green in 1907, it turned a bleak farmland into a thriving community within a few years. This pattern was repeated with the Piccadilly Line at Cockfosters, the Central Line at Ruislip, and the Bakerloo Line at Wembley. Plans to extend the Metropolitan Line from London all the way to Birmingham hastened the creation of what became known as Metroland – the suburbs in northwest London built in the 1920s and 1930s.

Metroland had its own poet laureate in Sir John Betjeman, a man who adored and celebrated trains and train journeys, suburbs and suburban life. Here is the first verse of a poem he wrote about Middlesex, a county that London had almost swallowed whole by the mid-20th century:

> Gaily into Ruislip gardens
> Runs the red electric train,
> With a thousand Ta's and Pardon's
> Daintily alights Elaine;
> Hurries down the concrete station
> With a frown of concentration,
> Out into the outskirt's edges
> Where a few surviving hedges
> Keep alive our lost Elysium – rural Middlesex again.

Hampstead Garden Suburb

In 1907 Mrs (later Dame) Henrietta Barnett conceived the idea of developing 240 acres (96 ha) of land belonging to Eton College as a "garden suburb" where people from many walks of life could live together in artistic and domestic peace. Sir Edwin Lutyens, one of the architects of what came to be known as Hampstead Garden Suburb, described Mrs Barnett as "a nice woman but proud of being a Philistine – has no idea beyond a windowbox full of geraniums, calceolarias and lobelias over which you see a goose on the green".

The Garden Suburb survives today, and is still much sought after despite the restrictions on those fortunate enough to live there. Mrs Barnett's dream of building a suburb where all classes could live amicably together, however, came to nothing. Hampstead Garden Suburb is almost entirely inhabited by middle-class Londoners, usually wealthy.

Hampstead

Hampstead is a London jewel. It has always been beautiful and it has always been loved. There are some who find it a little too precious, a little too lovingly preserved, a little too anchored in its literary and artistic heritage. Most Londoners who have seen Hampstead, however, would be happy to live among its quiet lanes and stately streets.

Hampstead residents pride themselves on being among the most sophisticated and civilized of all Londoners, but once upon a time prehistoric tribes lived here. Queen Boudicca, whose Iceni warriors sacked and destroyed the city in AD 61, is said to have been buried somewhere on Hampstead Heath, though her resting place has never been found. The Romans built a road to St Albans across the vast heathland of Hampstead, though the old village took its name from that of a Saxon farmer. In the 11th century, the Abbot of Westminster hunted here and put up a gallows to frighten the locals, and his successor, 300 years later, came to Hampstead hoping to escape the Black Death. He didn't. He and 26 of his monks died.

On 1 February 1524 a host of Londoners trudged out to the high ground of Hampstead to escape the flood that it was predicted would destroy London. They were more successful, in that London wasn't inundated. Hundreds of Londoners again turned to Hampstead for succour during the Great Plague of 1665. They, too, were spared, and the part of the Heath where they camped was later called the Vale of Health – now one of the most desirable addresses of all.

The Spa at Hampstead

Hampstead's lasting popularity began, however, with the discovery of a mineral spring by a local doctor, late in the 17th century. Where before it had been known as the place where many washerwomen laundered the clothes of City gentry, now, within a short time, the little village became a fashionable resort. The water was sold in flasks, and, although the spring is no longer tapped, the days of Hampstead as a spa are recalled in the names of two of the most charming of the local streets – Well Walk and Flask Walk. There is a memorial in Well Walk recording that the chalybeate well was given by the Hon. Susanna Noel and her infant son (the third Earl of Gainsborough) "to the use and benefit of the poor of Hampstead".

Cynics among Londoners point out that many flasks of Hampstead water were actually sold in London taverns, that the well no longer exists, and that Hampstead is no place for the poor.

Hampstead Heath

One of the chief delights of Hampstead is the vast Heath – 790 acres (316 ha) of sandy hills, hidden valleys, stretches of grass and gorse, secluded ponds and bathing pools, and the remains of the forest that once covered the whole area – much of it was cut down for the timber needed to rebuild the City after the Great Fire of 1666.

Four hundred years ago wolves roamed across the Heath. Today it is the site of annual Bank Holiday Fairs, summer open-air concerts at Kenwood, at the northern end, and two famous London pubs. Jack Straw's Castle was named after one of the leaders of the Peasants' Revolt of 1381. It's a large weatherboarded inn, with mock-medieval battlements and superb views over the Heath. The local fox hunt used to meet here – now it's thronged with coachloads of visitors. In 1780, the landlord played his part in saving London from the worst excesses of the Gordon Riots by liberally distributing ale to many of the would-be rioters. The Spaniard's Inn is a genuine 16th-century weatherboarded inn, with many 18th- and 19th-century literary connections.

Literary Hampstead

The spa at Hampstead had its second flowering in the later part of the 18th century. Among those who gathered there were Dr Johnson, Samuel Richardson, Henry Fielding and Oliver Goldsmith. Other famous literary residents include Leigh Hunt, Wilkie Collins, Gerald Du Maurier, Robert Louis Stevenson, John Masefield and John Galsworthy.

Shelley used to sail paper boats for children on

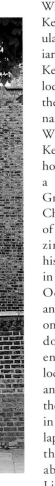

Whitestone Pond, and he, Keats and Byron were regular drinkers at the Spaniard's Inn. In 1817, John Keats and his brother took lodgings in Well Walk, at the house of a postman named Benjamin Bentley. When his brother died, Keats moved to another house in Hampstead (now a museum – in Keats Grove) and lived with Charles Dilke, the editor of *The Athenaeum* magazine. He wrote many of his most beautiful poems in Hampstead, including Ode to a Nightingale, and, when he was ill, lay on a sofa bed near a window in the house. He enjoyed watching the local residents passing to and fro: "I mustn't forget the two old maiden Ladies in Well Walk who have a lap dog between them that they are very anxious about. It is a corpulent Little Beast whom it is necessary to coax along with an ivory-tipp'd cane."

There are still many corpulent little beasts in Hampstead that have to be coaxed along.

John Constable and Hampstead

The painter John Constable was one of many visitors who fell in love with Hampstead, and settled there for part of his life. From 1827 he lived at No. 40 Well Walk, considering the view from his drawing room (it then stretched from Westminster to Gravesend) unsurpassed in Europe.

In the Tate Gallery you can see Constable's painting of the Admiral's House in Admiral's Walk. In Hampstead, you can see the real thing.

The Markets of North London

London north of the Thames is studded with markets. You have to journey well beyond Hampstead and Islington to leave the land of stalls and bargains. But it's not a land for those of delicate shopping sensibilities. Markets can be rough and ready places. If you wish to pick out the particular apples you want, you may well be brusquely directed by the stallholder to "sling yer 'ook" (go away) and try Marks and Spencer instead. And if you take too long making up your mind whether you want a mackerel or a herring, and a queue forms behind you, you may be urged to step aside until you've come to a decision.

For those who like shopping, however, and who like surprises, a trip to a good market can beat a visit to a theatre, cinema or smart restaurant. Certainly markets in north London attract the crowds. Brick Lane Market is almost impassable at times. It's gloriously disordered, with a huge range of goods, and more likely to contain a hidden bargain than almost any other market in London. At the opposite extreme are the Bayswater Road and Piccadilly Markets, open on Sundays only, and selling paintings of dear little doggies, Second World War airplanes, London buses, and other subjects that Rembrandt and company seem to have ignored.

Camden Market

If you want to plunge into north London markets at the deep end, go to Camden. It's a whole collection of separate markets, grouped together along Camden High Street. From Thursday to Sunday there's a market along Inverness Street, selling knick-knacks, souvenirs and socks, fruit and vegetables to a largely middle-class and visiting clientèle.

Opposite is the Buck Street clothes market, a maze of stalls selling boots, trainers, trousers, sweatshirts, children's clothes, combat fatigues, jackets, leather wear, suede coats and some secondhand clothes. When you're tired and thirsty, visit the Buck's Head, the Oxford Arms (across the road) or the Fusilier and Firkin (nearer the canal bridge). But be warned – on National Naturist Day (26 May) the Fusilier and Firkin celebrates nudity with an afternoon of naked drinking. It gets especially crowded then, but it's packed solid most weekends.

At weekends almost the whole of Camden High Street north of the big road junction has a market feel to it, and on a hot humid day the smell of warm leather accompanies you as you walk past the parades of shops on either side. It's worth a trip to Camden just to admire the half-relief decorations on shop fronts like the Tattoo Studio, the Boot Store, Cold Steel and Cerex. The Army and Navy UK shops have a tank seemingly bursting out of one store and a DC3 flying down the wall of another.

There are more stalls in East Yard, up by the canal, which also has a covered market, handy if it starts to rain. Here you can get your name engraved on a grain of rice, and enjoy a fine view of Camden Lock. On Saturdays and Sundays the Camden Lock Market opens on the other side of the lock, and the crowds become enormous, spilling out into the street and stretching up to Dingwall's (by the railway line) and Stables Market (just north of the railway bridge). Dingwall's is a good spot to look for sustenance. There are stalls selling Japanese food, *crêpes*, falafel and Chinese food, as well as the ubiquitous market burgers and hot dogs.

Special Offer – Three More Markets at no Extra Cost!

In a yard just to the east of the junction of Seven Sisters Road and Holloway Road is the Nag's Head Market. It's a compact covered market, with a great deal crowded into it, well patronized by north Londoners and the occasional wayward Scot.

In early summer the trestle tables are weighed down with piles of Galia melons and watermelons, stacked like cannonballs in a gun battery. Alongside them are bright mangoes and gleaming aubergines, peppers and onions, apples and pears, and green vegetables from the exotic to the commonplace. There's an excellent fish stall, selling fresh tuna, black pilapia, snappers, sea bass, yellow crokers, parrot fish, fresh sardines, salt cod, mussels and also prawns.

A gardener's delight – the Columbia Road Flower Market.

There are clothes stalls with jackets and jeans, belts, skirts and trousers, a fine selection of dazzling sequined tops, sandals and flip-flops, sweatshirts and T-shirts. The hardened market customers collect round the stalls selling novelty goods and those indefinable collections of bits and pieces that are irresistible. You can even buy gumshields for just £1 each.

Further to the east, between Stoke Newington and Kingsland, is the Ridley Road Market. This is a true street market, running a couple of hundred yards east of Dalston Kingsland station. It's primarily a food market, though you can also buy sunglasses, perfume, watches, jeans, plates, cups and saucers, hats and bonnets, cushion covers and curtain material.

Feast your eyes on the summer vegetables – broad beans, spring onions, cucumbers, mushrooms, peppers, coriander, tomatoes, chillies, lettuces, watercress, celery, kohl rabi, cauliflowers, ginger, artichokes, okra, sugar snaps, Chinese leaves, bullit (so called because you boil it), white cabbage, obos (aubergines), broccoli and leeks. Five pounds of bananas will cost you £1, and you can fill your basket with peaches, strawberries, melons, lemons, grapes, cherries, papaya, bananas and the humble apples and pears.

If you want plenty of exercise, head north to Walthamstow High Street Market. It's half a mile long, and the best way to patrol it is from the Walthamstow Central end, so that you are walking downhill. The market sells everything from everlasting flowers to short-life batteries, from secondhand clothes to bright new saucepans. You could equip an entire house from this one street, at knockdown prices. This is a real working-class market, well worth a visit. And, if you have the energy, the money and the time left after visiting the market, pop into the excellent sausage shop in Blackhorse Road for a pound of pork and leek, Welsh lamb and mint, or beef with mustard and garlic bangers.

Camden Lock – cafés, canal trips, and a cluster of markets.

Portobello Road

Portobello Road is one of the big London markets, and, like Petticoat Lane, it isn't confined to a single street. It is really a collection of markets in and around Portobello Road, which runs for some three-quarters of a mile (about 1 km) from Ladbroke Grove in the north to Notting Hill Gate in the south. The name derives from the battle of Porto Bello, fought in the Gulf of Mexico in 1739. It's a wonderful market, the sort of place where you end up buying something you never knew you wanted. Purses and wallets empty very quickly here.

If you plan to visit Portobello Market, you have three choices. On weekdays, it is confined to a collection of food stalls between Lonsdale Road and Lancaster Road, well worth patronizing if you are after meat, fruit, fresh herbs or vegetables. Come at lunchtime, and buy some sourdough bread and a dish of takeaway vegetarian food from the mouth-watering selection at the Grain Shop. On Sundays the market is reduced to a few stalls selling junk and bric-à-brac under the Westway arch. Take a deep breath, therefore, gird up your loins and join the shuffling throng on a Saturday, when the market swells to its biggest.

The "world's largest antiques market" operates on Saturdays only, along Chepstow Villas and Lonsdale Road. When it opens at 5.30 am, the only people doing business are the dealers themselves. The majority of the stalls – and there are hundreds of them – are ready for the public by 8.30.

It's impossible to list the range of goods available, but here's a sampler of some of the antique joys in store: handbags, old tins and packaging, bronzes, inkwells, tobacco jars, guns, swords, bayonets, jewellery, books, bottles, boxes, porcelain and pottery, doorstops, candlesticks, cameras, cigar boxes, cigarette cards, clocks and barometers, coins and medals, toy trains, teddy bears, sundials, telescopes, cutlery, fountain pens, photographs, furniture, glass and crystal, lamps, luggage, musical instruments, walking sticks, works of art, prints and posters, sewing machines, typewriters, gold and silver, sports equipment, stained glass, stamps, thimbles, tools.

Just to the south of Cambridge Gardens, the market is crossed by the Westway, one of the eyesores of west London that carries motorway traffic into and out of the capital. It's impossible to pretend that the Westway is anything other than horrendous, but it does at least afford some shelter from the rain if you're visiting the market in bad weather, and it offers a fine acoustic for the Irish fiddler who plays there. It's also a good spot for resting and recovering – in the Sausage and Mash Café, or with a large carton of freshly squeezed fruit or carrot juice. Cambridge Gardens has its own section of the Portobello Market, installed under a large tented roof, which looks a bit like a flying marquee.

Portobello Clothes

A little to the north of the Westway flyover is the Japanese Canteen, another refreshing port of call. This strip of Portobello Road contains three of the most fascinating components of the whole market. The first is RetroFocus, a small stall selling secondhand (and very old) ciné-cameras, projectors, editing equipment and films. Behind the stall is Stuart and Orsini, a shop with a beautiful collection of Victorian, Edwardian and early 20th-century clothes. Here you will find riding habits and cloaks, day dresses and formal dresses, exquisitely decorated blouses – some dating back more than 150 years. Many of the clothes are in astonishingly good condition, but they are not cheap.

Cross the road and plunge into the Antique Clothing Shop, where you will find clothes every bit as beautiful, and not as expensive, though perhaps more in need of a little care and attention. Some of these clothes are not so much secondhand as ninth- or tenth-hand. The shop is crammed with every item of wardrobe, from shoes and slippers to hats and feather boas. There are pullovers and cardigans from the 1920s, Victorian petticoats, flapper dresses, embroidered waistcoats, what would have been described as "thrilling" and "outrageous" hats, and hundreds of dresses to suit every occasion from a tennis party to a funeral.

When you go in and start working your way through the racks of goodies, you may be politely asked what you are looking for, and "is it for a play?" The assumption is that you are in search as much of authenticity as of beauty – and you will find both.

George Orwell and Portobello Road

From 1927 to 1928, George Orwell lodged at No. 10 Portobello Road. Among his fellow lodgers were a Mr and Mrs Craig. Little is known of Mr Craig, but Mrs Craig was a former ladies' maid, and a person of retiring disposition. One night Orwell and the Craigs returned late to No. 10, to find themselves locked out. The neighbours offered to lend them a ladder, so that they could climb in through an upstairs window. Mrs Craig refused to accept the offer. She had lived in the house for 14 years, had never once spoken a single word to her neighbours, and had no intention of opening up friendly relations at that moment – "one could not be too careful in Notting Hill".

So Orwell and the Craigs walked a mile to borrow a ladder from relatives.

left:
Everything including the
kitchen sink – Portobello Road
Market.
below:
A spoon to fit every mouth –
one of the hundreds of stalls in
Portobello Road.

The Pubs of North London

North London has some fine old pubs, many of them rich in decorative detail and with fascinating historical connections – the downfall of Oliver Cromwell is said to have been plotted in the bar of the Holly Bush, off Heath Street, Hampstead. And, because almost all north London pubs are near Underground stations, it is usually possible to find your way safely home after you have drunk, not wisely, but too well, in any one of them.

At the Dover Castle in Weymouth Mews, W1, you can still see the strip mirrors in the ceiling which enabled coachmen, drinking in the public bar, to note when their employers – drinking in the lounge bar – were ready to leave. The George in Great Portland Street, not far away, has a bar nicknamed the "Gluepot" by the conductor Sir Henry Wood, who was frequently exasperated by the time it took members of the Queen's Hall orchestra to make their way back to the platform after the concert interval.

The snug of the Clifton in Clifton Hill, St John's Wood, was often the meeting place for Edward VII and Lillie Langtry. It has been completely restored as an Edwardian pub – just the place to plot a discreet affair. The Ordnance Arms in Ordnance Hill nearby is one of the oldest pubs in north London. It was built 300 years ago, when it stood in the midst of fields and was the headquarters for a private army. Since it is not too far from Lord's the England cricket team have been known

to drink here – rarely celebrating victory, often drowning their sorrows.

In Camden High Street is the Black Cap, so named because, when it was built in 1776, it was originally a courthouse. The judge would don a black cap when sentencing a convicted felon to death. Nowadays it has a mainly gay clientèle, who thrill to drag stand-up comics and singers.

The Warrington Hotel near Maida Vale, W9, was one of the last gin palaces left in London. It still maintains its richly decorated interior, with beautiful lamps, stained glass, chandeliers and a brass footrail. The Albion in Thornhill Road, Islington, was first a dairy and then a coaching inn. It's a handsome building, worth going out of your way to visit. Jack Straw's Castle (mentioned in the section on Hampstead), also a former coaching inn, is in North End Way, on the fringe of Hampstead Heath, with wonderful views away to the south over the city.

The Island Queen in Noel Road, Islington, has perhaps the most eye-catching décor of any pub in London. Giant papier-mâché figures of pirates and politicians hang from the ceiling. Nearby, the King's Head is one of London's best-known theatre pubs. Many productions first staged here have transferred to the West End – one production picked up four TONY awards on Broadway. As late as the 1990s the landlord here refused to accept the notion of a decimalized coinage, and prices were maintained in the old system of pounds, shillings and pence. In 1997 a pint of Guinness cost two pounds four shillings (£2.20).

One of the strangest pubs in north London is Production Village, Cricklewood. It was – and sometimes still is – a film studio, which now houses a pub, a fringe theatre and a restaurant.

The Spaniard's Inn, Spaniards Road, Hampstead Heath

This is perhaps the oldest pub in north London, over four hundred years old, and at one time the residence of the Spanish ambassador to the Court of St James's. The pub has had many literary connections – Shelley, Keats and Byron all drank here. It was also the setting chosen by Charles Dickens for Mrs Bardell's tea-party, shortly before her arrest, in *The Pickwick Papers*:

…The party walked forth, in quest of a Hampstead stage. This was soon found, and in a couple of hours they all arrived safely in the Spaniard's Tea-gardens, where the luckless Mr Raddle's very first act nearly occasioned his good lady a relapse; it being neither more nor less than to order tea for seven, whereas what could have

Jack Straw's castle – named after one of the leaders of the Peasants' Revolt who hid on the site of the present inn.

been easier than for Tommy to have drank out of anybody's cup – when the waiter wasn't looking…

Dick Turpin, the highwayman, stayed at the Spaniard's. His pistols are on display, with a musket ball that he fired at a Royal Mail coach.

The Bull, North Hill, Highgate Wood

The Bull is roughly the same age as the Spaniard's Inn, but its connections are artistic rather than literary. William Hogarth, George Cruikshank (who produced the original illustrations for Oliver Twist), Edwin Landseer and Sir John Everett Millais all took lodgings here. George Morland used to sit outside the pub and sketch passing horses and other animals. There's a picture of him in the bar.

The Flask, Highgate West Hill, N6

The Flask is slightly younger than either the Bull or the Spaniard's, but does also have a connection with Dick Turpin, who once hid in the bar, and William Hogarth, who sketched drunken scenes in the cellars. Karl Marx was a regular here, though history does not record whether he felt the maxim "from each according to his means, to each according to his needs" applied to standing a round of drinks. The pub takes its name from the flasks of water that people drew from Hampstead Wells.

It is also the venue for the annual "Swearing on the Horns", an ancient custom described by Byron in Childe Harold. Male strangers entering any one of Highgate's 20 or so pubs were required to swear an oath on a pair of animal horns, after which they were entitled to kiss the prettiest girl present. The Flask alone maintains this sexist practice.

North London Pubs in Song

Both the Eagle, Islington, and the Old Bull and Bush, North End Road, Highgate, have been immortalized in song. The Eagle is the pub named in *Pop Goes the Weasel*:

Half a pound of tuppenny rice,
half a pound of treacle,
That's the way the money goes,
pop goes the weasel,
Up and down the City Road,
in an' out the Eagle…

It's a very old song, about "popping", or pawning, a "weasel", or cobbler's last. The Old Bull and Bush is the subject of the old music hall song Down at the Old Bull and Bush:

Come, come, come and make eyes at me, down at the Old Bull and Bush,
Come, come, drink some port wine with me, down at the Old Bull and Bush

You may hear either song at their respective pubs, but it's wiser not to request them.

above:
The Spaniard's. In 1780, a group of rioters from the Gordon Riots were kept drinking here until troops arrived to arrest them.
below:
Karl Marx's 'regular' – The Flask at Highgate.

London Cemeteries

Until the arrival of the crematorium, London was in grave danger of running out of space in which to bury its dead. In the days of the Plague, corpses were simply taken in cartloads to hastily dug pits and dumped into quicklime, with no ceremony and no memorial. From time to time, the bulldozers and diggers of modern developers come across such sites, and scoop up a mighty heap of bones. Villains were buried within prison walls, paupers in common graves. In an attempt to save space, some corpses were buried in an upright position. Ancient churchyards were stacked with several layers of bodies, like geological strata. Graves were plundered for booty, or for bodies and skeletons (both of which could be sold to medical students and practitioners). It wasn't difficult, as some bodies were barely covered with earth.

By the 19th century the problem of what to do with the dead was too much for most London parishes. There was a health risk for people living near parish graveyards. In 1824 a journal called *The Penny Magazine* began a campaign to set aside large areas of undeveloped London that could be used as huge cemeteries. It took a while for the campaign to succeed, but by early Victorian times a ring of cemeteries had been established round suburban London.

top right:
Brompton Cemetery – the first London burial ground to come under state control.
below:
Restoration work at Nunhead Cemetery.

Victorian Cemeteries

Some people shirk cemeteries. "Of all the horrible things in the world there is nothing so calmly ghostly as a London cemetery," wrote Richard Jefferies in his novel *Amaryllis at the Fair*. Certainly, if you find yourself hurrying through one towards dusk, with the wind soughing in the ancient trees, darkness closing in around you, and the tips of old headstones poking through the jungle of brambles and undergrowth on either side, they can be creepy places.

But they are also havens for wildlife. At night, when the curious or the respectful have hurried away, they become the moonlit playground of foxes, rats and even badgers. They are also reminders of the countryside that once covered so much of modern, built-up London. They are wooded, rich with mosses and weeds, wild flowers and tangled ivy. They are home to thousands of insects, and dozens of different species of birds.

The most famous is Highgate, simply because that is where Karl Marx is buried. With him in everlasting peace are Michael Faraday, George Eliot and one Tom Sayers – the last bare-knuckle fighter in England. It was said that 100,000 people attended his funeral. If you search hard enough – or ask one of the helpful guides – you will find Tom's grave, and the massive monument to his massive dog. Highgate was the first of several cemeteries to be laid out by the London Cemetery Company in 1839 on a 17.5-acre (7-ha) site.

One of the largest of the Victorian cemeteries is at Kensal Green. Here lie Isambard Kingdom Brunel, engineer of the Great Western Railway, the *Great Eastern* steamship, and the Clifton suspension bridge in Bristol; Sydney Smith, the wit and writer; the novelists Thackeray, Trollope and Wilkie Collins; and Charles Blondin, who crossed Niagara Falls on a tightrope.

In Putney Vale Cemetery are the graves of Lillie Langtry, Edward VII's beloved Jersey Lily; Jacob Epstein; and Clementine Churchill, who was cremated here in 1977. Leopold Stokowski lies in St Marylebone Cemetery. Henry Croft – the first of the Pearly Kings – lies in Islington Cemetery. Mrs Beeton (of the famous Cookbook), Sir Henry Tate (of the famous Gallery), Sir Henry Doulton (of the famous Ware) and Sir Henry Bessemer (of the famous Convertor) lie in West Norwood Cemetery.

Nunhead Cemetery is one of the largest, covering 30 acres (12 ha) in all. By the middle of the 20th century it had become a derelict wasteland, its chapels rotting away, its graves unkempt, the vast bulk of it an impenetrable jungle. Restoration is under way, and it is now possible to find, among thousands of others, the memorial to the five "Scottish martyres" who campaigned for Parliamentary reform and were transported in 1793. There are also memorials to 20 members of the Australian Light Horse killed in the First World War, to 40 members of the New Zealand and Canadian forces, and to nine members of the 2nd Walworth Scout Troop, drowned near Leysdown on 4 August 1912.

Britain's Oldest Pet Cemetery

Locked and hidden away behind the Victoria Gate in Hyde Park are 300 tiny headstones, each commemorating the virtues of a beloved pet. The cemetery was established by the original lodgekeeper at the Gate, Mr Winbridge, in 1881. By 1903 it was full and was officially declared closed. Once a year it is opened to visitors, during London's Heritage Weekend.

Local children brought their dead pets to Mr Winbridge, who buried them in what was really his back garden. Later he donated the plot to anyone who wished to find an appropriate resting-place for any dog, cat, bird or monkey. In most cases the former owners were too upset to attend burials themselves, but took care to compose the inscriptions on the little headstones. "Prince – asked for so little and gave so much", "Jack, a sportsman and a pal", "A dear and lovely kitty who will live in my heart forever", "Chum – so lonely without my doggie". Karl Marx never knew such love.

The grave of Karl Marx in Highgate Cemetery.

The Follies of London

All over London there are follies – buildings that serve no useful purpose, buildings unsuited to the purpose for which they were built, projects that were conceived on a scale too vast to fulfil, bizarre constructions that suggest the designer was possessed of madness and charm in equal proportions.

Some say the first folly ever erected in England was Vanbrugh Castle, on the outskirts of Greenwich. It was Sir John Vanbrugh's home from 1719 until his death seven years later, and remains the only known example of an architect designing an ugly house and then living in it himself. It's dark and angular, with two thin towers, and looks more like a fortified waterworks than an imposing residence.

Follies come in all shapes and sizes. There is the washroom at St Philomena's Convent, Carshalton. Five marble steps lead down to a Roman-style bath, eight by eleven feet (2.5 by 3.4 metres). It was built in 1720, and seems more fitting as a plunge bath for a rugby team than as a place where nuns could perform their ablutions. Out in the wilds of northwest London, beyond the end of the Metropolitan Underground Line, there is a length of rotting and rusting railway track, all that remains of the Manchester to Paris Railway, a grand and foolish scheme hatched by Victorian entrepreneurs. In Aberdeen Place, St John's Wood, stands Crocker's Folly, a fine pub with marble and mahogany fittings. It was originally built as a hotel by Frank Crocker, in the belief that Marylebone Station would be built next door and that he would make his fortune. Marylebone Station was eventually built half a mile away. Frank Crocker made no fortune, and leapt to his death from one of the upstairs windows of his fine hotel.

Not all follies are old. Bourden House, Davies Street, Mayfair, seems a most unlikely place to house a grotto, but there it is, made of shells and erected in 1975. Not far away, in Mallett's of Bond Street, there is an earlier grotto, built in 1968. On the corner of Old Bond Street, opposite Asprey's, there is a bench on which are placed bronze statues of Franklin D. Roosevelt and Winston S. Churchill, apparently sharing a joke. The figures are slightly under lifesize, and there's just room to squeeze between them. There is something sinister-looking about Roosevelt's teeth, and poor Churchill looks more like Bert Lahr as the Cowardly Lion in *The Wizard of Oz*.

Stroll down Glebe Place, Chelsea, and at the end of the street you will come across a house that is beautiful and strange and frightening – like the best fairy tales. It is unique, built in the 1980s, in cream and sienna, with lead drainpipes and lead window-boxes. There is a roof garden and a tower that is straight out of *Puss in Boots*. Inside, the kitchen is prettily tiled, as though it is an outpost of the Food Halls at Harrods.

Well worth inspecting is Inverness Court Hotel, Bayswater, originally built as a love nest for a Victorian businessman and his mistress. Further west there is a folly resembling Wemmick's Castle in Dickens' *Great Expectations*. In east London, in Folgate Street, Spitalfields, an American architect has evoked the spirit of Miss Havisham, from the same novel, by creating a cobweb-encrusted Victorian garret.

Watkin's Folly

In the 1890s, Sir Edward Watkin, then Chairman of the Metropolitan Railway, decided to build a tower to rival and outstrip the Eiffel Tower in Paris. Work started on the site of an amusement park in Wembley, but the enterprise ran out of funds, and building stopped in August 1894 when the first platform had been reached, 155 feet (48 metres) above ground. The stump of the tower was opened to the public on 18 May 1896.

Nothing remains of what became known as Watkin's Folly. It was pulled down to make way for the construction of Wembley Stadium in the 1920s, but its guiding light is commemorated in a little *cul de sac*, opposite Wembley Retail Park – Watkin Road.

British Telecom Tower

Still standing tall and proud is the British Telecom Tower, just off Tottenham Court Road in central London. It was originally built in 1965 as the Post Office Tower, 620 feet (190 metres) high, then one of the tallest buildings in London. Its crowning glory was a revolving restaurant, some 550 feet (170 metres) above street level. Diners were invited to enjoy a meal and gaze at a continually changing London skyline as the restaurant slowly revolved.

The technology never quite managed to match the concept. The restaurant sometimes moved in an upsetting series of jerks. At other times it didn't move at all. Those preparing the food and waiting at table faced the extra challenge of never knowing whether they were on terra firma or not. The restaurant no longer revolves, and is no longer open to the public.

The Millennium Dome

Many Londoners regard the Millennium Dome in Greenwich as the biggest folly of all time. The cost is enormous – some £800 million. The project was

approved before anyone had the slightest idea what it would be used for, and for how long it could be expected to last. While it was already being constructed, Peter Mandelson and other government officials were scouring the theme parks of Europe and America, in the hope of finding some good ideas to pinch. The site chosen – a piece of wasteland to the east of Greenwich – is in the least accessible part of London as far as most inhabitants of the British Isles are concerned, and has necessitated the building of an extension of the Jubilee Underground Line – which is probably unlikely to be ready in time for the New Millennium Eve.

The lyrics of a Noel Coward song come irresistibly to mind:

> Don't make fun of the Festival, don't make fun
>   of the fair,
> We downtrodden British must learn to be
>   skittish,
> And give an impression of devil-may-care…

Franklin Roosevelt and Winston Churchill in bronze immortality, Old Bond Street.

London Irish and London Scottish

An Irish theme pub in Fulham Broadway – note the mock Celtic script.

For more than 200 years Irish men (and to a lesser extent Irish women) have been leaving their homeland and crossing the sea to England, in search of work and food. In the early days they arrived penniless in Liverpool and tramped their way across country to London. Henry Mayhew described the Irish settlements he explored in London in the mid-19th century, off both sides of the Commercial Road in the East End of London: "As you peep through the narrow openings between the houses, the place seems like a huge peep-show, with dark holes of gateways to look through… down the court are seen rough-headed urchins running with their feet bare through the puddles, and bonnetless girls, huddled in shawls, lolling against the door-posts." The yards were full of washing, the houses cramped but well-kept. The people were homesick for Ireland.

But still they came – to dig out tunnels and cuttings for the railways and beds for the canals, and to construct thousands of new houses in London, while they survived in crumbling slums around Drury Lane, Saffron Court, and Market Court, Kensington High Street.

Once the railways had been built, successive waves of Irish immigrants travelled on them from Fishguard or Holyhead to London. It was said that Kilburn became an Irish centre because that was about as far as an Irishman could walk with a suitcase in the rain from Paddington or Euston station.

They brought with them a nostalgic longing for the "auld country", as Mayhew called it, and their own culture in music, dance and the Irish pub. Somehow all three have survived, though the Irish pubs that mushroomed all over London in the late 1990s owe more to the creative genius of marketing gurus than to the Irish themselves.

Scottish immigration to London goes back further. When James VI of Scotland succeeded Elizabeth I in 1603 and became James I of England, he journeyed down from Edinburgh with a host of Scottish attendants. Scottish adventurers, doctors and engineers followed throughout the 17th century. In December 1745 Bonnie Prince Charlie's Jacobite Highlanders marched to within 110 miles of London, throwing George II, his followers and the Bank of England into an almighty panic.

The Jacobite leaders were brought to London, some to be beheaded on Tower Hill, others to be hanged on Kennington Common, just down the road from the Oval. This did little to deter the Scots, who have continued to arrive at King's Cross or Euston ever since. Like the Irish they have brought with them elements of their culture – bagpipes, whisky, haggis and golf.

The Royal Blackheath Golf Club, the first in England, was founded five years after the arrival of James I, on ground adjacent to Greenwich Palace. The Royal Wimbledon Golf Club was founded much later (1882), for Scottish members only. Students of Roman history may wish to dally over the 7th, 10th and 11th holes, which lie over ground where Caesar's legions are said to have camped. The London Scottish Rugby Football Club was formed at Richmond in 1878. Twenty years later the London Irish RFC was established a couple of miles upstream at Sunbury-on-Thames.

Scotland Yard does have a Scottish connection. It was originally part of Whitehall Palace, at the foot of Whitehall, used as lodgings for the kings of Scotland.

Irish Pubs in London

The most famous Irish pub in London is Biddy Mulligan's in Kilburn High Road, NW6. There's Irish cooking and live Irish music every night, and it's right in the heart of London's biggest Irish community. The most spectacular is Waxy O'Connor's in Rupert Street, Soho. It, too, has Irish food and music, and is well worth exploring – it's a large, rambling place. The most authentic Irish pub is O'Hanlon's in Tysoe Street, EC1. This is a real Irish pub with a real Irish landlord who brews his own beer. Here you will find home-baked soda bread, and an Irish ale brewed with bog myrtle and honey.

One of the most popular Irish pubs in London is Brendan O'Grady's in Kennington Road, opposite the Imperial War Museum. In the old days it was called the Three Stags, and used to be Charlie Chaplin's local. In the even older days, Captain Bligh (of *Bounty* fame) lived two doors away. It was never a genuine Cockney pub, though tourists went there in droves hoping to find the entire clientèle doing the Lambeth Walk. It's now very

Irish. The Enterprise in Haverstock Hill, Hampstead, is an Irish literary themed pub, also worth a visit, but Bootsy Brogan's in Fulham Broadway, the Dublin Castle in Parkway near Camden Lock (where the band "Madness" first made their mark), and Filthy McNasty's and the Whiskey Café, despite their names, are not particularly Irish.

There are at least three chains of Irish pubs in London: Finnegan's Wakes, Scruffy Murphy's and O'Neill's. The best and the biggest of them (with 30 branches) is O'Neill's, which sells Cork dry gin, Bushmills whiskey, Ballygowan mineral water, Major and Carroll's cigarettes, and Tayto crisps. Don't bother with the others.

Burns Night in London

There are at least three occasions on which the streets (and sometimes the police cells) of London are filled with Scots – when England play Scotland at Wembley, at Hogmanay (New Year's Eve), and on Burns Night (25 January). Tartan hordes fill Trafalgar Square, stagger along the railway lines at Euston (as though they are setting off to walk back to Scotland), and a pall of whisky fumes hangs over much of the West End. One of the best places to visit on Burns Night is the Clachan, in Kingly Street, near Carnaby Street, W1. In this small pub that used to belong to Liberty's, the haggis is piped in, as tradition dictates. It gets very crowded, but is worth visiting at other times.

top centre:
Robert Burns writing 'The Cotter's Saturday Night', 1785.
below:
Inside a London Irish pub.

London's Football Clubs

Londoners have always liked their football. Today there are a dozen professional London clubs in the various divisions of the English Football League. The oldest established is Fulham, founded in 1879, whose single claim to fame is that they once reached the final of the Football Association Cup. Their ground is one of the prettiest in London, at Craven Cottage, right by the Thames in west London. Since they are now owned by Mohammed Al Fayed, the boss of Harrods, their future may be greater than their past.

The most famous and most successful London clubs are Arsenal, Chelsea, Tottenham Hotspurs and West Ham United – all north of the river, though Arsenal started life as Woolwich Arsenal, with a home ground south of the river. Arsenal's ground at Highbury, N1, was the scene of the first live radio commentary on a football match, on 22 January 1927. To help listeners keep abreast of the game against Sheffield United, the Radio Times magazine printed a plan of the pitch divided into eight sections. While one commentator described the play, the other called out in which section the action was taking place: "Oh, pretty work, very pretty (section 5)... now up the field (7)... a pretty (5, 8) pass... Come on, Mercer... Now then, Mercer; hello! Noble's got it (1, 2)..."

Arsenal's heyday was in the 1930s, when they won the League Championship five times and the FA Cup twice. In 1934, when England played Italy at Wembley, Arsenal supplied seven of the England eleven. Football writers had forecast an England victory by ten goals to nil, but England scraped through by three goals to two after a tough game. The injury list read like a bulletin from the First World War: "Hapgood, broken nose; Bowden, injured ankle; Drake, leg cut; Copping, bandaged from thigh to knee."

Fans of Brentford, Charlton Athletic, Crystal Palace, Leyton Orient, Millwall, Queen's Park Rangers and Wimbledon would almost certainly claim that their teams were every bit as important as the above. Passions run high among London clubs, and there have been times when their supporters have been branded "violent". West Ham fans went through a period of unpopularity in the 1980s. Wimbledon fans have been out of favour from time to time in the 1990s. Millwall fans are always suspect, but cultivate their unpopularity: "Everybody hates us, we don't care!" Most football regu-

Chelea Football Club supporters en route for Stamford Bridge.

Wembley Stadium

Wembley is the Mecca of the English football fan. It is the venue for England's home internationals, and the finals of the FA and League Cups. It was built in 1922–3 as a multi-purpose athletics and entertainments centre for the British Empire Exhibition. In fact, it is all that is left of what Gavin Weightman has dubbed the "Imperial Disneyland" that covered a 216-acre (85-ha) site.

The stadium had a capacity of 120,000, later reduced to 100,000. It has staged hockey matches, greyhound racing, speedway racing, Rugby League finals and the 1948 Olympic Games, but to most Londoners it is the home of football. It has also been the home of controversy. After the 1932 Cup Final between Newcastle United and Arsenal, a British Movietone News film proved that Newcastle's winning goal should have been disallowed. Since 1966 arguments have raged over whether or not one of England's goals crossed the line in the World Cup Final against West Germany.

left:
The road to glory – the approach to Wembley Stadium.

lars, however, are sober and peaceful enough – on the way to a match. Join any District Line train heading for Fulham Broadway on an autumn, winter or spring Saturday when Chelsea are playing at home, and you will travel with hundreds of enthusiasts wearing blue strip, sitting in total silence, ignoring each other. After the match, the atmosphere may well be different. When Chelsea won the European Cup in May 1998, Fulham Broadway was closed to traffic for several hours, and delighted fans lay in the streets, boozily chanting the praises of their heroes.

The White Horse of Wembley

Before Wembley, most FA Cup Finals had been staged at Crystal Palace, where the open parkland setting accommodated crowds of up to 120,000. The first ever Cup Final in the enclosed stadium at Wembley, on 28 April 1923, almost resulted in disaster before the match started. Optimists had put the capacity of the ground at 127,000. No one had expected over 300,000 fans to arrive. They climbed over the walls, swarmed over the turnstiles and battered down the gates leading into the ground. Police and gatekeepers were "swept aside like twigs", according to one newspaper report. Tens of thousands of spectators occupied the pitch for an hour – there was nowhere else for them to go. The players appeared but retreated back to their dressing rooms. George V watched helplessly from the Royal Box.

Legend has it that order was restored by a lone policeman on a white horse. "Energetic, undaunted, resourceful, at once decisive and good-tempered, he dominated the crowd by the sheer force of his personality, and wherever he appeared he received willing obedience and made a little oasis of order in the general chaos," reported the Daily Mirror. The crowds moved back to the touchlines, and the match started at 4.17 pm. Bolton Wanderers beat West Ham by two goals to nil in a scrappy game. The more famous struggle had taken place before the kick-off.

The Suburbs of South London

South London is considerably smaller than north London. It is also much younger. Although many south London suburbs (Lambeth, Dulwich, Camberwell, Sydenham, Streatham) started life as Saxon or medieval villages, much of the capital south of the Thames is of later origin than the main north London suburbs. As you travel through south London you see either the front (by road) or the back (by rail) of vast estates of late Victorian houses, or of the mock Tudor "semis" of the 1920s and 1930s – a style of architecture that the cartoonist Osbert Lancaster christened "By-Pass Variegated".

The Kingston bypass, ten miles (16 km) long, typifies south London suburbia. It was opened in 1927, and during the next 12 years thousands of three-bedroom houses were built along its flanks and around the new light industry factories that it was built to serve. These are the classic London suburban houses – the background illustrations to reading schemes used in English schools from the late 1940s to the early 1980s. Even today, the much maligned suburban attitude is to be found stolidly maintained by the two-children, two-parent families that inhabit houses identical in style and furnishing, and dis-

The spire of St Dunstan's Church rises above Cheam.

tinguishable one from another only by their light-hearted nameplates: "Dunroamin" or "Mon Repos".

These are the suburbs that form a broad semicircle round south London, from Thames Ditton in the west to Thamesmead in the east. On the outside of that semicircle are the suburbs that sprang up in the first half of the 20th century – Morden, Rosehill, Stoneleigh, Cheam, Raynes Park, Colliers Wood and a dozen others. On the inside are the older, Victorian suburbs – Wandsworth, Tooting, Streatham, West Norwood, Catford, Eltham and Charlton. The closer you get to inner London, the older the suburb.

This is the land of privet hedge and laburnum tree, of dogs that are licensed and well cared for, of family saloon cars and a commuter workforce. These are the areas of London that have seldom known real want or deprivation, that escaped the worst of the depression, and that find it difficult to shrug off the optimism that preceding generations have handed down to them. They have better air than the rest of London, lower levels of unemployment, and, of course, the quickest exit to the surrounding countryside.

To the Danish architect Steen Eiler Rasmussen, these are the centres of the "one-family house, open-air life and all that we others admire and are fain to imitate… inseparable from the English mode of thought and life". To Angus Calder outer suburbs like Richmond and Wimbledon, Croydon and Bromley have for decades been the heartland of the English middle class, "zones of tidy gardens, extensive green playing fields, quiet and propriety".

The Villains of South London

South London has long been seen as the home of villains, mobsters, and bad lads generally. Plays, books, films and television programmes have all done their bit to reinforce this notion. In a Victorian melodrama called *The Silver King*, the evil criminal lives in a villa in Bromley. In the most successful television sitcom of the 1990s, the decidedly "dodgy" central characters operate from their home in Peckham.

It used to be said that south London (especially southeast London) was the safest place to live. With so many villains crowded into the neighbourhood, burglars would be afraid to break into a south London house in case they were robbing one of their own.

A friend, who was employed as a pianist in a Catford nightclub, swore that when he took his break, the talk at the bar centred around forthcoming "jobs", with discussion concerning who was to bring the "sawn-off" (shotgun), and who was to supply the "wheels" (get-away car). The club had a short life. It was closed by the authorities following a problem the proprietor had with some Spanish bullion.

Cheam – the Doyen of South London Suburbs

Cheam lies on the fringe of south London. It was a tiny settlement in the 6th century, and for the next 1400 years only one thing happened here. In the 1690s a large hare warren was built, covering 50 acres (20 ha). Everything else remained farmland until the coming of the Southern Electric Railway in the 1920s.

Modern Cheam dates almost entirely from the Twenties and Thirties. It is the epitome of the dormitory suburb, a commuter community. There is no local industry, no farming, no college or university, no cinema, no spa, no hotel, no tourist trade – nothing to tempt anyone to visit. It is quiet, peaceful, tree-lined, well-groomed, highly respectable. Cheam doesn't have anything as common as "streets", but its well ordered avenues, lanes and closes are free from both litter and parked cars. It is one of the few areas of London where every dwelling has a garage.

To a slum-dweller it could represent paradise. To anyone with artistic or Bohemian inclinations, it could represent hell on earth.

above:
By-pass variegated architecture at Morden.
bottom left:
1930s semi-detached grandeur at Wandsworth.

Brixton

Electric Avenue, the heartland of Brixton Market.

The first thing that strikes you when you visit Brixton is that it smells different from other London neighbourhoods. It's not just the sweet smell of ganja that floats up the stairs leading down from the platform of Brixton Station. There's a scent of spice in the air – intoxicating, alluring and almost unnerving in its heady tropical flavour.

The source of it is soon discovered – the piles of Afro-Caribbean vegetation on sale in the shops and stalls around Brixton Market. Here are crates of green bananas, cassava leaves, bitter leaves and dozens of other plants and fruits that Londoners knew nothing of until the arrival of the first wave of West Indian immigrants on the SS Empire *Windrush* in 1948.

They were greeted with suspicion by locals and officials alike. Initially they were housed in the huge Second World War shelters under Clapham Common, but after a while they were pushed out into the open air. Their options were few. They had a suitcase each of clothes, little money and less knowledge of London. They set off to find that paradise on earth, a place with low rents and unprejudiced landlords. They found Brixton.

The centre of Brixton is the junction of Brixton Road and Coldharbour Lane. On one corner stands the neo-Georgian Lambeth Town Hall, a den of red-hot socialism in the 1960s and 1970s. Across Brixton Road, hidden by trees, is the Ritzy Cinema. On the third corner is a large McDonald's, and on the fourth a branch of Pizza Hut. In all of this there is little to distinguish Brixton from dozens of other parts of London. Brixton Road runs north to south, with the usual mixture of high-street chain stores – Marks and Spencer, Woolworth's, Boots, Our Price, the Body Shop.

Step off the main street into Reliance Arcade, and you are in a different world. The arcade is dark and narrow, selling wigs and watches, African crafts and jewellery, cameras, West Indian takeaway food, religious cards and devotional items. Here you begin to see the incredible mix and wealth of cultures in Brixton: Irish, Turkish, African, Portuguese (there's a Portuguese supermarket in Atlantic Road) and Caribbean. This is where you can buy a tin of Guinness and a Jamaican bammy (a flat, round cake of cassava) in the same shop.

There are four clock towers in Brixton, all with working clocks. The prettiest is on the top of Brady's, the large drinking palace near the railway arches. The tallest is on the top of Lambeth Town Hall. The smallest is above McDonald's. The oldest stands immediately under the tiny bell steeple of St Matthew's parish church. So it is difficult not to be aware of time here. But Brixton wakes slowly. There's a sleepy start to most mornings, especially Monday mornings, after the joys of celebrating the weekend. By 10 am, although Brixton Road is crammed with traffic and the pavements are crowded with shoppers, many of the tiny shops in the covered market or in Station Arcade are still locked up tight.

And all is quiet in the handsome residential streets nearby. In 1990 Hanif Kureishi described "the slums of Brixton", with "rows of disintegrating Victorian houses". Things have changed. In the aftermath of the Brixton Riots of 1981 much is being done to improve

Brixton's image. Crucially, property prices have risen alarmingly. There is danger that Brixton will once again become fashionable, no place for the poor. Kellett Road contains several handsome terraces of three-storey houses, richly decorated with plaster mouldings round the porches and bay windows. The same is true of tree-lined streets like Chaucer Road, Shakespeare Road, Spencer Road and Dulwich Road. Such "desirable" properties seem a far cry from Railton Road, the front line during the riots.

A Few Brixton Surprises

Queen Elizabeth I had a house on Brixton Hill, in the days when it was a hill, and not a road. John Major (remembered by a dwindling number of people as the Prime Minister of Great Britain from 1992 to 1997) lived as a boy in a flat in Coldharbour Lane. His father, a music-hall artist, had moved the family there as it was easy to get theatrical lodgings. Brixton has a strong connection with the old music hall. Two of its greatest stars lived here – Dan Leno in Akerman Road, and Fred Karno in Southwold Road.

Effra Road contains the first synagogue to be opened in London south of the Thames. It is now the Eurolink Business Centre, but its fine white façade remains, a pro-

tected building. The strangest building in Brixton is the Old Windmill. It was London's last tower-windmill, built in 1816, and used by locals to grind the gleanings that they collected from the surrounding wheatfields. In 1941 a bomb exploded near the windmill, hurling a pig through the roof. The dazed creature got up, staggered down Blenheim Gardens to a butcher's shop, and then into the Salvation Army hall, where it spent the rest of the night.

In Josephine Avenue there used to be an ancient elm tree, beneath whose branches Sir Walter Raleigh sat smoking a pipe of the first tobacco brought from America. A servant thought his master was on fire, and threw a bucket of water over him.

above:
The Ritzy Cinema in Brixton – independent and eclectic in the choice of films it shows.
left:
The Old Windmill in Windmill Gardens, Brixton.

Dulwich

Dulwich is one of south London's three trump cards when it comes to dealing with the superiority complex of those who live north of the Thames (the other two are Blackheath and Greenwich). But, whereas Hampstead is bosky and hilly, Dulwich is bosky and flat. In Saxon times it lay on the very edge of what was known as the Great North Wood (now "Norwood"), a tiny hamlet called Dilwihs or Dilewic. In medieval times it belonged to the Abbey of Bermondsey, and was called Dilwysshe, Dilewysshe, Dylways and Dullag – all of which must have been extremely annoying for medieval postmen. The probable meaning of "Dulwich" is "meadow where the dill grew", though you may find it difficult to find dill anywhere other than the high-class grocer's in Dulwich Village today.

Dulwich has always been a quiet, peaceful and orderly place. Few roads of any importance passed through the village until the 19th century, and life was pleasant. There was a little straying of cattle, and unauthorized tree-felling, but for hundreds of years nothing more serious than the events of 1334, when William Hosewode was accused by Richard Relf of "…carrying off his wife Edith, one cow worth ten shillings, clothes, jewels and other goods and chattels".

Modern Dulwich owes much of its character and desirability to Edward Alleyn, who bought much of the Manor of Dulwich for £5000 in 1605. Alleyn was an actor, who had made a considerable amount of money from his shares in the Rose and Fortune theatres, and as part-owner of the bull- and bear-baiting house in Paris Garden, Southwark. Judging by contemporary accounts, Paris Garden was as frightening as it was profitable. It was said to be the rendezvous of "the swaggering Roarer, the cunning Cheater, the rotten bawd and the bloudy Butcher".

In the 18th century Dulwich was for a while a fashionable spa, whose waters were carried to London to be sold. The roads were still bad, and smugglers, highway-

men and gypsies dwelt in the woods that surrounded the village. A hermit called Samuel Matthews, grief-stricken after the death of his wife, lived for many years in a cave in Dulwich Woods until he was murdered in 1802.

Byron was educated at a school on the site of the present Grove Tavern. John Ruskin lived for many years in Dulwich, and George Eliot loved its chestnut trees. The most famous resident of recent times has been Margaret Thatcher, who lived for a short while in an expensive and unattractive house on a fortress-like estate off the South Circular Road.

Dulwich College

Edward Alleyn had no children of his own. In 1613 he authorized the building of a schoolhouse for poor boys, on much the same lines as Westminster School and the Merchant Taylors' School. It was opened five years later, and Alleyn spent much of his time there. Over the next 25 years the school grew in size, but suffered during the Civil War, when Roundhead troops melted down the organ pipes and lead coffins to make bullets for their muskets.

The present college really dates back to 1842, when Charles Barry (architect of the Palace of Westminster)

Dulwich Toll Gate

College Road contains the last operative toll gate in London – a nuisance to motorists (especially those who don't expect it), but a joy to lovers of anachronisms. It was set up in 1789 by John Morgan of Penge, but was taken over by the college in 1809 to provide an income for the up-keep of the road itself. A notice by the toll gate informs you of the fees payable. Should you wish to drive "Sheep, lambs or hogs" through the gate, it will cost you twopence halfpenny "per score".

right:
The toll collectors booth in College Road, Dulwich.
top right:
The chapel of Dulwich College – red brick grandeur in south east London.

designed a small grammar school, to be built alongside Alleyn's original foundation, the whole project to be financed from the enormous rents collected from Alleyn's estates in Dulwich. Over the next 30 years or so, new buildings were added in "North Italian of the 13th century" style. Places at the college were increasingly taken up by the sons of middle-class families, and in 1882 permission was granted, by Act of Parliament, to build two new schools for poorer pupils – Alleyn's School and James Allen's Girls' School. In the 20th century, places at both these schools have also been taken up more and more by the children of middle-class families. It seems time for a new Act of Parliament.

Dulwich Picture Gallery

The Picture Gallery in College Road has two major claims to fame. It is England's oldest public picture gallery, and it has an unenviable record of losing pictures to thieves. At times during the 1970s and 1980s, it seemed that any passing nocturnal felons had only to pop into the gallery to find a Rembrandt or a Poussin ready to fall into their hands.

The prime mover behind the establishment of the collection of pictures was Edward Alleyn. In 1811 his endowment was considerably increased by the gift from Sir Francis Bourgeois, court painter to King Stanislaus of Poland, of 371 paintings, most of which had been intended for a national gallery in Warsaw. The gallery was built to the designs of Sir John Sloane, and it's pleasantly old-

fashioned – the walls are covered in paintings, from ceiling to below eye-level. Entrance is free on Fridays, and the permanent collection includes, as well as those mentioned, works by Van Dyck, Murillo and Gainsborough.

bottom:
The façade of the Dulwich Picture Gallery. In the summer, tea is served on the lawn.
below:
A party of schoolchildren studying one of the exhibits in the Dulwich Picture Gallery.

Blackheath

The Elastic Suburb

As in Hampstead, Richmond, Islington and other highly desirable areas of London, property prices are high in Blackheath. A house that is valued at £200,000 in neighbouring Lewisham will cost half as much again in Blackheath. This is why, over the last 20 or so years, local estate agents have fallen into the habit of extending the boundaries of Blackheath, pushing it a little further to the south, east and west. There's no need to push it further north, because that way lies Greenwich – every bit as desirable and expensive as Blackheath.

A Victorian atmosphere surrounds Blackheath. When you go there, you expect to see ladies in crinolines and gentlemen in frock coats and top hats sauntering down Montpelier Row or Tranquil Vale. You feel there should be a military band on the Heath itself, playing selections from Gilbert and Sullivan, with children bowling hoops and queuing for donkey rides nearby.

Nowhere else in London is this feeling so strong. As you walk about, you note the Blackheath Conservatoire of Music, and the concert halls, and wonder if there is any chance that M. Chopin or M. Liszt is visiting to give a recital.

Historically, Blackheath is a far older and grimmer place. It takes its name from the colour of the soil of the Heath, now criss-crossed by many roads, the worst of which is the thundering A2 (Watling Street). Over the ages many men of violence have trudged along this track. In 1011 invading Danes dragged poor Alfege, Archbishop of Canterbury, to Blackheath, and then took him down to Greenwich and murdered him. During the Peasants' Revolt of 1381, Wat Tyler's rebels camped on Blackheath, and John Ball preached his famous sermon that included the lines:

When Adam delved and Eve span,
Who was then a gentleman?

The rebels marched on to the Tower and to Smithfield, where Tyler was murdered by William Walworth. Sixty-nine years later, Jack Cade led another army of malcontents to Blackheath. They were protesting against the high-handedness of Henry VI's officials. Cade was killed and the rebellion subsided. In 1497 a battle was fought on Blackheath, when Henry VII with 25,000 troops defeated an army of Cornishmen who were incensed by a tax imposed to finance a war against the Scots.

In happier times, Blackheath was the site of Henry V's welcome home after his triumph at Agincourt in 1415, and Charles II's welcome at his Restoration in 1660. It was also where Henry VIII met, and had to be persuaded not to reject, Anne of Cleves, his fourth wife (the one who he later divorced, luckily for her). Throughout the 17th and 18th centuries the Heath was a wild and also dangerous place, infested by rogues and highwaymen, who took rich pickings from travellers on the main Dover road.

Blackheath Village

Until the early 19th century, the village didn't even have a church. It consisted of a few cottages and one small public house. The railway arrived in the late 1840s, and triggered the first major development of Blackheath. It was, for a while, famous for its schools. The very young Disraeli was educated here, at the Rev. John Potticary's establishment. Elizabeth Garrett Anderson, the first woman doctor in England, was a pupil at a school run by Miss Louisa Browning (Robert Browning's aunt). Charles Dickens modelled the appalling Salem House in *David Copperfield* on a school in Blackheath.

Some of the glories of old Blackheath have gone. The Green Man, once the meeting-place of local residents, is now remembered solely as a bus stop. The Rink and Rink Hall, built in the heyday of skating, are no more, and the Post Office stands where once Paderewski played the piano and the explorer Stanley lectured to an audience of over 1000 people. Lloyd's Bank now occupies the site of another of Blackheath's former glories – the Alexandra Hall. The Art School, which had 300 pupils in 1896, closed 20 years later. The School for the Sons and Orphans of Missionaries moved to Eltham in 1912 and became Eltham College. But you can still see where John Stuart Mill lived (113 Blackheath Park), where Donald McGill drew some of his saucy seaside postcards (5 Bennett Park), where Nathaniel Hawthorne spent much of 1856 (4 Pond Road), and where Gounod stayed in 1870 (15 Morden Road).

The Ranger's House

Facing Blackheath from the southeast corner of Greenwich Park is the Ranger's House. It was built in 1700 for Admiral Francis Hosier, who fought in the war of the Spanish Succession. It's a beautiful house, inside and out, with a finely proportioned façade of warm red brick. The walls of the gallery, 60 feet (20 metres) long, are covered with paintings of early 17th-century beauties of both sexes, and there are some exquisite pieces of furniture. The most famous occupants of the house have been Philip, fourth Earl of Chesterfield, author of the celebrated 18th-century letters; the Duchess of Brunswick, mother of Caroline, George IV's disliked queen, and grandmother of Charlotte, the Princess of Wales (herself commemorated in one of Blackheath's best pubs); Sir Garnet Wolseley, who set out to rescue Gordon at Khartoum.

Blackheath and Golf

The first English golf club opened on Blackheath in 1608. It was largely the creation of some of those who had accompanied James VI of Scotland to London when he became James I of England in 1603. It cannot have been much fun trying to blast your way out of a bunker or to putt well surrounded by highwaymen, so, understandably, the golf course on the Heath was abandoned. The Royal Blackheath Golf Club is now to be found at the end of a narrow track leading off Court Road, Eltham.

opposite:
Blackheath High Street – all the charm of a village, less than six miles from the heart of London.
below:
The Paragon, Blackheath. The original leases banned residents who practised the 'art, mystery or trade' of fishmonger or schoolteacher.

A New Home for Crystal Palace

When the Great Exhibition closed in October 1851, most people wondered what to do with Paxton's vast Crystal Palace. Paxton wanted it to stay where it was, to provide a Winter Garden with "the climate of Southern Italy where multitudes might ride, walk or recline amidst groves of fragrant trees". Failing that, he would have been happy to see it rebuilt in Kew Gardens or Battersea Park.

Fortunately, the method of construction meant that it could be taken to pieces and rebuilt if a new site could be found. And in 1852 it was transferred at a cost of £500,000 to a 200-acre (80-ha) estate in Sydenham, on a hilltop looking out towards Kent and Surrey. Paxton even enlarged it, and in the landscaped grounds to the south, Isambard Kingdon Brunel installed fountains 300 feet (90 metres) high, with 12,000 jets using seven million gallons of water per hour. For the first 30 years of its existence in south London, the Crystal Palace attracted two million visitors a year.

They came for a ride on the Topsy Turvy; to go boating on the lake; to thrill at Monsieur Blondin's daring as he cooked an omelette on the high wire; to sit in the Great Hall and watch Ransley's Aerial Bicycle Ride and Dive from the Roof into Water; to ascend into the skies above southeast London by balloon; to get lost in the maze; and to goggle at the aquarium.

In the late 19th century and into the 20th century, the park around the Crystal Palace became the most versatile sporting arena in the whole of London. It was the cricket ground for W.G. Grace's London County XI, and from 1895 to 1914 the English FA Cup Final was played there. Motor-cycle racing started in 1927, and was an immediate and huge success – 20,000 spectators turned up for the Saturday afternoon meetings. There were also novelty sports and entertainments – sidecar polo; outdoor boxing matches; dog, cat and cage-bird shows; midget car racing.

The Crystal Palace Pneumatic Railway

One of the reasons why the Crystal Palace was such a success in its early days at Sydenham was that it was well served by public transport. Buses and trams passed along Crystal Palace Parade (buses still do), and there were two railway stations within strolling distance of the park – Crystal Palace Upper and Lower.

But the greatest novelty was the Crystal Palace Pneumatic Railway. This ran along a short tunnel from the Upper Station to the very palace itself, so that visitors who had travelled from Victoria had no need to exert themselves until they were inside the exhibition halls. It was worked by pneumatic power, and there were two single coaches, that would whizz repeatedly to and fro, passing each other in a whoosh of air. Modern public transport can't hold a candle to that.

The Crystal Palace Fire

Nobody knows who or what was responsible for the fire that broke out on the night of 30 November 1936. The

The Crystal Palace ablaze early on the morning of 1st December 1936.

most likely explanation seems to be that a workman failed to extinguish a cigarette he had smoked in one of the paint storerooms.

The fire spread rapidly. The temperature was intense, melting the glass, which flowed down the roads around the park, solidifying in the tram lines as it cooled and bringing all traffic to a halt. The flames could be seen 45 miles (72 km) away in Brighton. Local people wept as the building warped and twisted in the heat, and began to collapse. One enterprising chemist got out his ciné camera, filmed the blaze, hurried home to his darkroom, processed the film and had it showing at a cinema in Orpington while the fire was still raging.

Little remains today, save the 29 brick, iron and stucco dinosaurs that you will find modestly hiding in the park. The outlines of the terraces where the palace stood are still clearly visible today, and if you search among the overgrown shrubs on the eastern edges of the park you may still come across a rusted turnstile. There is a bust of Paxton at the entrance to the National and Youth Sports Centre.

The name lives on, however, for Crystal Palace became the name given to that area of southeast London where it once so proudly stood. There is also the Crystal Palace Football Club, whose fortunes wax and wane from season to season. In the park you will also find the Tea Maze, originally built in 1872 and now fully restored. It's the largest maze in London.

The Concert Bowl

There are other delights. On Sunday nights during the summer, concerts are held in the Concert Bowl, a natural amphitheatre at the southern end of the park. The staple fare is light classical – two regular favourites are Handel's evergreen *Music for the Royal Fireworks* and Tchaikovsky's *1812 Overture* (with cannon and mortar effects). On fine nights south Londoners miles away can both see and hear these grand finales.

The National and Youth Sports Centre

Crystal Palace is still a great sports centre for Londoners. There is a dry-ski slope (not very long, but safe for beginners), an Olympic-size swimming pool, and the headquarters and home ground of one of London's very few Rugby League clubs, the London Broncos.

More importantly, there is the National and Youth Sports Centre itself, opened in 1964 on the site of the old football ground. The stadium seats 17,000 spectators, and the multi-purpose Sports Hall has room for another 2000 visitors.

On the site of the Crystal Palace – the Italian Terrace still survives.

Wimbledon and the All England Lawn Tennis Club

One of the highlights of the London Summer – The All England Tennis Championships in July 1997.

Wimbledon is a pleasant middle-class suburb in south-west London with a 17th-century inn (the Rose and Crown), a vast common that used to be the venue for army reviews and the National Rifle Championships, and a scattering of fine old buildings. William Wilberforce lived there in the 18th century, Sir William Bazalgette a hundred years later. The world would not have heard of Wimbledon were it not for one thing – the All England Tennis Championships.

Wimbledon is tennis. For two weeks every year, at the end of June and the beginning of July, the greatest tennis players in the world and their entourages descend upon the quiet suburb for one of the premier Grand Prix tournaments. Every respectable house in Wimbledon (and most of them are eminently respectable) is rented to players or fans for a small fortune. Special trains and buses rush to the club ground. Taxis hired in central London crowd the roads leading to it. Parking is a nightmare. Food and drink become almost prohibitively expensive, and ticket touts patrol the pavements offering seats in the Centre Court at ludicrously inflated prices.

The All England Club

Although it is known around the world as a tennis club, the proper name for it is the All England Lawn Tennis and Croquet Club. Croquet is still played there, but it has yet to capture the attention of the world's media. What matters is tennis. The club's headquarters were originally in Worple Road, but they moved to the present Church Road site in 1922.

It is almost impossible to join the All England Club. Tennis fans (and players) live to a ripe old age and there are seldom any vacancies. Perhaps the easiest way to join is to win the Men's or Women's Singles, for each year the champions are awarded honorary membership. Other than that, you need to be extremely well connected, preferably through the British armed forces.

For the All England Club is run by retired military officers along military lines. Discipline has loosened a little, but the mixture of volatile professional tennis players and stiff-necked committee members still leads to some thrilling clashes. It's no wonder that John McEnroe found woe in Wimbledon.

The Wimbledon Championships

The Club was founded in 1869, and tennis championships have been played at Wimbledon for well over 100 years. For a long time they were open to amateur players only, but in the late 1960s they were thrown open to all. British players fared much better in the old amateur days. Hugh Lawrence Doherty won the Men's Singles five times in a row from 1902, and Fred Perry three times in the 1930s. The two most successful Wimbledon players of all time have been Helen Wills Moody of the United States, who won the Women's title eight times between 1927 and 1938, and more recently the Czech-born American Martina Navratilova.

The championships are played on grass courts, 16 of them, tended with loving care by a vast staff of groundsmen and -women. The Centre Court is the holy of holies, used only during the championship fortnight, though a few members of the All England Club are allowed to play a test game in the week before, to make sure that all is well. The flawless condition of the grass on the first day of the tournament is something of a British obsession – if scuff marks were to appear before play started, it could well mean the end of All England, if not all England.

left:
A glass of champagne, a tankard of Pimms, strawberries and cream, and… love.
bottom left:
The Wimbledon Championships – Miss Black of Zimbabwe serves.

How to Get a Ticket

If you are in the right place at the right time, it is possible to buy tickets to the Centre Court or Court Number 1. Members of the All England Club have preference, of course, but tickets are advertised in *The Times* newspaper – no prices are ever quoted. Demand is, of course, highest for the later stages of the tournament, and it's almost impossible to pick up tickets for the finals.

Play sometimes continues until 8 pm, later if the light allows and the tournament is behind schedule because of bad weather. By tradition, those waiting at the entrance towards the end of the playing day used to be handed tickets by those leaving before play finished, so it was possible to get in free of charge on a warm summer evening. It was one of the best perks of living in London.

The practice seems to be dying out. Ticket holders have often arranged to hand their tickets to friends, and tennis fans have more stamina these days, staying till the bitter end.

Strawberries and Cream

The culinary delights of the Wimbledon fortnight are strawberries and cream, and Pimms No.1. No visit to the All England Club is complete without a dish of strawberries and a glass of Pimms. The strawberries are large, ripe and luscious, the finest fruit that can be found. The price is monstrous. In a year when strawberries are in short supply they can cost up to £1 each at the refreshment tents. But then, you can always tell your grandchildren that you once ate strawberries and cream at Wimbledon, so perhaps it's worth the financial sacrifice.

Pimms No.1 is a fine summer drink. It's a mixture of wines and herbs on a gin base, drunk in a long tumbler, with lemonade or tonic water or soda water (according to preference), lots of ice, slices of orange, lemon and cucumber, the odd cherry, and a sprig of borage (mint is very much a second-rate substitute). It is sipped.

The Markets of South London

To the southeast of London lies the county of Kent, the "Garden of England". "Everyone knows Kent," wrote Dickens in *The Pickwick Papers*, "hops, cherries and women." For hundreds of years cartloads of fruit and vegetables trundled their way from the orchards and fields of Kent to south London markets. In modern times, when freighters are too big for the London Docks, produce from all over the world has entered London, via the southeast, from the Channel ports.

So it is hardly surprising that many of the best markets in south London specialize in fruit and vegetables. Lewisham Market is at its most glorious in high summer, its stalls piled high with cherries and strawberries (from Kent), raspberries, mangoes, peaches and nectarines, pineapples, melons, bananas and largely home-grown vegetables. The market at Balham also has plenty of good

fresh produce, as do those at Greenwich (which has a fine display of organic fruit and vegetables on Saturdays), East Street, Lower Marsh Street (just south of Waterloo Station), and Woolwich.

Upper Tooting Road has two indoor markets. Broadway Market has a pet stall with an impressive display of tropical fish – all longing for a good home and more space. The women's clothes stall in Tooting Market is run by Jackie Brafman, and is decorated with dozens of photographs of the stallholder rubbing shoulders with showbiz personalities and sports stars. Jackie Brafman is a modest man who prefers not to explain how he knows such famous people. The simple explanation is that he meets them in the course of the work he does for many charities.

Greenwich Market is one of the most popular and crowded in the whole of London. Like the one at Camden, it's really a collection of several markets all within a short distance of each other. Bosun's Yard is open only at weekends. It's an indoor market specializing in craft goods – anything from a paperweight to

featherlight artificial flowers, or from gemstones to glass and china. A short stroll from Bosun's Yard is a fruit and vegetable market, with a stall that sells excellent organic bread of all sorts and sizes. There are also several take-away food stalls to feed the appetite on a hungry day.

Greenwich Antique Market has few antiques, and caters more for those who are interested in secondhand books and clothes, CDs and old toys. The most interesting market in Greenwich is in Thames Street, a little way from the centre and the crowds. The goods for sale are displayed in steel containers once used to house the cargoes of ships – the usual mixture of clothes, books, and bric-à-brac.

The Oldest Market in London

Borough Market claims to be the oldest in London, the natural successor to that market roundly condemned by the authorities in 1276 for spilling on to the southern end of London Bridge. In 1851 the modern market settled in a triangle of old Victorian development created by the railways as they steamed into London from London Bridge Station to Waterloo East and Cannon Street. Here the bricks are still coated with the soot and grime of centuries, and there's an ancient feel to the place. It's the only London market to have a cathedral close by (Southwark), which gives it the atmosphere of a provincial town.

The market is small and covered, quietly busy except when trains rattle overhead. It's a very scented market, full of the smell of produce. If you stand in the middle of the market and shut your eyes, admittedly there's a sporting chance you'll be knocked down by one of the scurrying forklift trucks, but before that happens, you may well catch the aroma of tropical fruits and the riches of summer, blended with the tangier odours of lemons and onions, and the perfume of ripening melons.

Like Smithfield, two or three pubs dotted round Borough Market cater for those who work in the market nearby and are open early in the morning. The Market Porter is a lovely pub, festooned with flowers overflowing from window-boxes and hanging baskets. The Southwark Tavern in Southwark Street and the Globe Tavern in Green Dragon Court open a little later (at 6.30 am), but be warned, they are open "for the accommodation of persons following their lawful trade or calling of Salesmen, Buyers, Assistants, Carmen and Porters attending a public market holden at the Boro Southwark".

Brixton Market

Of all the markets in London this is the most exciting and the most exotic. It is settled under the lee of the rail-

way arches around Brixton Station, mainly in Market Row, Electric Avenue (so called because it was one of the first streets in London to be lit by electric light), and Atlantic Road.

It's primarily a food market. Butcher's shops and stalls sell every bit of the animal fit to eat, and some that look as though they couldn't possibly be – salted pigtails, salted pig snout, pig's heads, fresh small trotters. Fish stalls gleam with sea jack, flying fish, snapper, St Peter's fish, tilapia, kutafish, kinnfish, catfish. African food stalls offer the unpronounceable – ewdeu, sokoyokoto, sawasawa, ousisa, oha, chwo-chwo. There are Halal butchers, pizza outlets, pet stalls, clothes stalls, CD shops (Blacker Dread's Music Store is especially worth a visit), and several cafés.

It's the most colourful and the most cosmopolitan market in the whole of London.

Nine Elms Sunday Market

If you think that Sundays in London are still too quiet, then take a trip to Nine Elms Lane. Here, next to New Covent Garden Market, you will find this lively market every Sunday. This is not the place to come if you are fussy or particular. Nine Elms is not a centre of good taste. But it's worth a visit if you are interested in cheap rucksacks, cheap DMs, pet food, videos, shoes and DIY equipment.

The vegetables of Europe and the fruits of the Caribbean fill the stalls of Brixton Market.

The Pubs of South London

It has to be said that, in general, drinkers south of the Thames are not as sophisticated as those to the north. And because south London is smaller than north London, there are fewer pubs so good that they demand a visit. Nevertheless, there are plenty of gems hidden away, and at least one truly unique pub.

In most south London pubs, drink is more important than decoration and atmosphere, fun more important than history. South London pubs tend to be spacious, with enormous bars. The Falcon, in St John's Hill near Clapham Junction Station, boasts the longest bar in England – a bit of a cheat because it's circular.

Like many pubs to the north and in the West End, south London pubs are often "themed", but whereas the themes of north London pubs tend to be "literature" or "the theatre", the themes of south London pubs are more likely to be the "Wild West" or "boxing". The Ring at Blackfriars used to be the venue for fights (legitimate ones). It was described in the 1930s as a "turbulent centre of boxing". The present-day Ring, like several of the many pubs in the Old Kent Road, doesn't stage fights but has a gymnasium and training facilities for professional boxers. The Henry Cooper in the Old Kent Road

was named after a British heavyweight whose main claim to fame was knocking Muhammed Ali down when the latter was at the height of his powers.

The George Inn, just off Borough High Street, not far from London Bridge, is the only galleried coaching inn to remain intact in London. It was mentioned in John Stow's *History of London* written in 1590, and although damaged during the Great Fire, it was rebuilt in 1676 to the original plans. Shakespeare and Dickens were both regulars here, and Dickens used it as a setting for chapters in two of his novels. It has appeared in countless films and television dramas, but remains a wonderful old pub.

above:
Young's horse-drawn drays outside the Old Spotted Horse, Putney.
right:
Inside The Wellington in Fulham.

The Pubs of Clapham

The Windmill on the Common (on the south side of Clapham Common) is a former coaching inn that dates back to 1665, and was originally kept by the local miller. It was rebuilt in the 19th century and is now a classic Victorian pub. Monday nights are opera nights, when professional singers warble their way through arias and duets. Nearby is the Alexandra, a vast barn of a place with beamed ceilings and wooden floors. Also on the South Side is Oblivion, a modern pub with a large terrace, good food and a barman who is said to make a highly effective Bloody Mary.

The Prince of Wales in Clapham Old Town is a good place to visit, but in many ways the most interesting pub in Clapham is Bread and Roses, in Clapham Manor Street. This is a Workers' Beer Company pub owned by the Battersea and Wandsworth Trade Union Council. It takes its name from a song written during a strike by women textile workers in the USA in 1912:

> Our lives shall not be sweated from birth until
> life closes,
> Hearts starve as well as bodies, give us bread but
> give us roses!

The walls are purple and green (the colours of the Suffragette movement), and there are free coffee mornings for mothers with toddlers and for pensioners. It's a novel and effective way of opposing capitalism. Not far away, in Lavender Hill, is London's finest reggae pub – the Beaufoy Arms.

The Pubs of Wimbledon

There are two charming pubs in a little lane called Crooked Billet, just to the south of Wimbledon Common. One is the Crooked Billet itself, at its best on a warm summer day when you can sit outside and enjoy what seems a country setting less than 15 minutes from the heart of London. The other is the Hand in Hand, four old cottages knocked together in the shade of a spreading chestnut tree. The pub has a south-facing courtyard, a vine-covered wall, and a wooden porch.

Five minutes' walk away, across the other side of the Royal Wimbledon Golf Course, is Camp Road – so named because Julius Caesar made camp here. That was 2000 years ago, too early for the Fox and Grapes, which is only 300 years old. It's a large rambling pub, popular with families, who don't seem to mind the Dickensian characters that decorate the walls. The Rose and Crown in Wimbledon High Street also has literary connections. The poet Swinburne used to drink here.

Vintage car and veteran pub – The Rambler's Rest at Chislehurst.

Sinister Events at the Bedford

The Bedford is an old pub in Bedford Hill, Balham. Like so many London pubs it has served another purpose in its time – it used to be a coroner's court. In 1876 it was the scene of a sensational inquest following a murder at the local priory. The accused was Dr James Gully, who was subsequently convicted and executed, but was probably innocent of the crime. It is said that his ghost still haunts the lounge bar. You may feel happier visiting the Banana Cabaret upstairs, which has comedy nights on Fridays and Saturdays.

The London to Brighton Veteran Car Run

The first thing to note is that this annual event is not a race – racing is not permitted on British roads and only a suicidal maniac would try to race from London to Brighton. It is a celebration of the freedom granted to motorists in 1896. Until 14 November of that year, by virtue of the Locomotives on Highways Acts of 1865 and 1878, the law required that any motor vehicle should be preceded along the road by a person carrying a red flag – as a warning to others that one of these terrifying juggernauts was approaching. The speed of the car was therefore limited to walking speed – 4 mph (6.5 kph) in the country, 2 mph (3 kph) in towns. But in 1896 the old acts were abolished, and the red flag disappeared. At the same time, the speed limit was raised to 12 mph (19 kph).

The man responsible for this great liberation was Harry J. Lawson, "the father of the British motor industry". Lawson was a man of monopolistic ambition, who blocked the granting of many patents and franchises in the early days of motoring, but at least he had vision.

The First Run

At the time there were few motorists in London. Motoring was thought to be a temporary fad of the rich which would soon die out. But when the Act of Parliament abolishing the red flag received the Royal Assent, many London motorists leapt into their de Dion Boutons, Benz three-wheelers, Panhards and Darracqs, and drove down to Brighton to celebrate. The first car to reach Brighton was a Duryea – America's first production car and proudly advertised as "a carriage, not a machine". There were two Duryeas in the first London to Brighton run, but the company folded two years later. The event was received with enthusiasm, even though

The cavalcade of veteran cars crossing Westminster Bridge, November 1997.

some owners cheated. They actually travelled to Brighton by train, unloaded their machines from the wagons, and then smeared them with mud to make it appear that they had driven down. The run was declared an enormous success, however, and was repeated the following year.

The Run Revived

For the next 30 years there were no London to Brighton runs. Then, in

left:
One mile covered, fifty five to go – an early breakdown on Westminster Bridge.
bottom:
Any colour as long as it's black – an early Model T Ford in the Veteran Car Run.

1927, two London newspapers (the Daily Sketch and the Sunday Graphic) revived the idea, restricting it to cars that were at least 21 years old. The cars started from Victoria Embankment, near Scotland Yard, and, as far as possible, followed the original route taken in 1896.

Fifty-one cars entered. The oldest was an 1893 Panhard and Levassor. The youngest was a 1906 Renault belonging to King George V. There were 26 different makes of car, including the familiar (a Fiat, a Mercedes, a Rolls Royce, four Daimlers, two Cadillacs and three Rovers), and the unfamiliar (an Argyll, a Clement Talbot, a Stephens, a Star and a Lanchester). Two cars were driven by women, an 1897 Benz and a 1905 Rover.

Once again there was a certain amount of cheating. Some owners sought to impress by adding a few years to the age of their cars. One enthusiast claimed to have an 1895 Renault – the firm didn't come into existence until 1898. Such boasting was unnecessary, for the cars were rightly regarded as objects of beauty and wonder. Four out of the five de Dion Boutons entered were in daily use, and an 1896 Daimler Phaeton was the second Daimler built.

Several of the vehicles that competed in that run are still making the pilgrimage. Forty-four of the 51 entries made it to the starting line, 37 of them reached Brighton, and 21 managed the journey non-stop. The following year organization of the run was taken over by *The Autocar* magazine, and it was decided that entry should be limited to cars that were over 25 years old. So, in 1928 entries were limited to cars built before 1904, and in 1929 to cars built before 1905. When the Royal Automobile Club took over in 1930, they kept to the same age limit, and still today only cars built before 1905 can take part in the "Old Crocks Race".

The Modern Run

Every year, usually on the first Sunday in November, owners of ancient cars gather at Hyde Park Corner early in the morning. Because of the popularity of the run, and the growing interest in veteran cars, the number of entries is restricted to 300. The cars are inspected by enthusiasts and other owners, who delight in the shining brass lamps and accessories, the immaculate tyres and the well-polished paintwork. The cost – in time and money – of maintaining these vehicles is enormous, but many of the owners are true eccentrics for whom the car is an obsession. On the day of the rally, they are worthy of as much study as the cars themselves – not quite so well preserved, perhaps, but often attired in smart contemporary costume. In the early days, the rally began at the Metropole Hotel, London, and ended at the Metropole Hotel, Brighton – alas, neither still exists. The destination is now Madeira Drive, on the sea front, and the entire route is lined by millions of spectators.

The Heart of London

MTL LONDON

Monopoly

After chess and draughts, Monopoly is probably the most famous and ubiquitous board game in the world. It is not, however, a London game in origin. It was invented in the years of the Depression by an unemployed American, who took his prototype board to Parker Brothers, manufacturers of toys and games.

The English version was produced a little later, with all the sites on the board set in London. Although London has changed considerably since the 1930s, the board is still exactly as it was nearly 70 years ago.

Around the Monopoly Board

The game starts at the cheapest properties – Old Kent Road and Whitechapel Road. The Old Kent Road follows the line of the medieval extension of the Roman Watling Street from New Cross in southeast London to the Elephant and Castle. It has never been a fashionable area – full of rowdy pubs and costermongers' barrows in Victorian times, full of rowdy pubs and traffic today. Whitechapel Road runs eastwards from Aldgate East towards Stepney Green. five hundred years ago it was described as "no small blemish to so great a city", and few people can ever have wanted to erect an hotel on the real Whitechapel Road.

Both Euston Road and the Angel, Islington, however, have moved upmarket since the days when Monopoly was first sold. The Angel was originally a Jacobean coaching inn, the first staging post on the journey north from London. In the 19th century it became a hotel; now it has been restored as a bank. The whole area around the Angel has become more prosperous and more trendy – property worth buying.

right:
A hotel in Mayfair – the entrance to Claridges in Brook Street.
below:
Marylebone Street Station – the last main line terminus to be built in London.

Swiftly passing Jail (or "Just Visiting"), the Monopoly player moves on to Whitehall, Pall Mall and Northumberland Avenue. The first two are dealt with elsewhere in this book, so we shall consider only the third. Northumberland Avenue is a relatively new street in central London. It was opened in 1876 to connect Charing Cross and the then new Victoria Embankment. In its early days it was the site of many hotels; today it is almost entirely offices. In autumn starlings gather in the trees and make an ear-splitting noise.

The next three linked properties are Bow Street, Vine Street and Marlborough Street, all of which have a law-enforcing connection. Bow Street (home of the original Bow Street Runners) and Marlborough Street were long famous for their Magistrates' Courts; Vine Street still has one of the principal police stations in the West End. Bow Street is so called simply because it was built in the shape of a bow. Marlborough Street (really Great Marlborough Street) was built 300 years ago and named after John Churchill, first Duke of Marlborough. In its early days it was the subject of considerable dispute – there were those who declared it "magnificent" and "of prime quality", and those who called it "trifling and inconsiderable". Its position halfway round the board would seem to be something of a compromise. Enough has been said already about Fleet Street, The Strand, Trafalgar Square, Piccadilly and Leicester Square. Coventry Street has moved downmarket since the early days of Monopoly. It used to be a handsome though short street leading from Piccadilly to Leicester Square, with several fine restaurants, among them Scott's, just a few doors down from the London Pavilion. The management of the London Pavilion – then a music hall – opened Scott's as an oyster warehouse in 1872. It grew into one of the best fish restaurants in Europe and was known as Scott's Oyster and Supper Rooms. The restaurant moved to Mount Street in Mayfair in 1967.

Regent Street and Bond Street have kept their charm and their air of fashionable grace, but the commercial success of Oxford Street has done little for its looks. Mayfair and Park Lane remain ridiculously expensive areas of London, and whoever owns property in both has a stranglehold on life just as he or she would have a stranglehold on the game.

Of the four railway stations on the board (Fenchurch Street, Marylebone Street, Broad Street and Liverpool Street) three are still operating. Broad Street closed in the 1980s, a victim of rival forms of transport – especially the tube. Marylebone Street is one of the smallest and prettiest of London termini, but hardly the most exciting as trains from there venture less than 100 miles (160 km) from London.

A Hotel in Mayfair

In early Victorian times, William Claridge was a butler who saved enough money to buy a small hotel in Brook Street and christen it Claridge's. A few years later he bought a neighbouring hotel, and today Claridge's has 189 bedrooms and occupies a large site at the corner of Brook Street and Davies Street. It is generally regarded as the appropriate hotel in London for the rich and the royal – though the Savoy, the Dorchester and others may well disagree.

As you sweep in off the street and enter Claridge's, the revolving door is as smooth as the commissionaire outside. Cross the marble-floored hall and proceed to the lounge – unless, of course, you are rich or royal enough to be staying here. The carpets are soft and yielding. The staircases are wide and curved. The Art Deco lamps are beautiful. In the lounge, a pianist in a white tuxedo plays the songs of Gershwin, Porter, and, as befits this part of London, of Eric Maschwitz (discussed later in this chapter under "London in Song").

The colours are gentle, restful to the eye. The hotel is spacious and quiet. The gentlemen's cloakroom (and the

Two properties in one picture – Trafalgar Square from the Strand

ladies', too, it appears) is impeccable. There can never have been, nor ever will be, any graffiti on these gleaming walls, and there are real linen towels – no traces of roller towels or hand-drying machines.

As for the service – even old William himself would be proud.

A Rainy Day in London

It rains in London. The old pea-souper fogs of the 19th and early 20th centuries have gone – no longer do menacing figures in ulster and muffler, armed with clubs or knives, emerge from the choking mists – but it does rain. Admittedly, London is on the eastern, drier side of England, but it does still rain. Unless the sky is cloudless, you would have to be a bold and optimistic soul to set out for a day in London without an umbrella. Rain, however, need not spoil your day out. Viewed as a challenge, it can be the spur to some pleasant and surprising discoveries. And, in central London, there is always a shop, a café, a pub, a cinema or simply a doorway in which to escape from the rain.

If the rain is heavy, or appears to be determined to persist, those of a more inquisitive nature may care to take the Underground to Sloane Square station. Avoid the rush-hour, and wait on the western end of either platform (near the escalators) until all is as quiet as an Underground station can ever be. Now listen carefully. Above you is a huge pipe, a conduit that carries almost all that is left of the River Westbourne, a stream that once

flowed from West Hampstead to Hyde Park, where it was joined by the Tyburn Brook to continue under Knightsbridge and through the grounds of the Chelsea Hospital to the Thames. In 1730 Queen Caroline of Anspach decided that the Westbourne should be dammed to form the Serpentine lake in Hyde Park. But on a rainy day you may hear its phantom waters sluicing over Sloane Square Station.

Free Shelter from the Rain

When it starts to rain in the West End, you may make for the nearest arcade. There is a small network of arcades that allows you to travel dryshod for much of the way from Trafalgar Square to Carnaby Street. The Royal Opera Arcade leads from Pall Mall to Charles II Street. It's the oldest shopping arcade in the West End, designed by John Nash and G.S. Repton, and has beautiful Regency shop-fronts. It was so named because it ran at the back of the old Haymarket Opera House (now Her Majesty's Theatre). Turn left along Charles II Street, and then right up Lower Regent Street. Hurry

Waiting for the rain to stop – outside a London supermarket.

through the rain to Jermyn Street, and then linger in the shelter of Princes Arcade, which leads to Piccadilly. You could then take a stroll through Fortnum and Mason, taking care not to buy anything as this is supposed to be a free trip. Cross Piccadilly and head north along Burlington Arcade to Burlington Gardens, where you could spend some time in the Museum of Mankind. Now turn right and head for the Quadrant Arcade in Regent Street. Work your way northwards to Oxford Circus, using Dickins and Jones or Liberty's if you need to keep under cover. Three hundred yards north of Oxford Circus is Broadcasting House, headquarters of the BBC.

You cannot roam at will in Broadcasting House (not even the staff can do that), but if you have had the foresight to book free tickets to attend the recording of a radio programme, you will be able to sit down in the warmth of the BBC Concert Hall. Alternatively, you may prefer to go east from Oxford Circus and a little to the north, to the British Museum. Entry is free and there is plenty to see – enough for a month or more of rain.

At the time of writing there are over 70 museums and galleries in London open to the public without charge or

prior application. They range from the huge British Museum to single houses or even single rooms. You will find them, rain or shine, all over London. They range from the Iveagh Bequest at Kenwood and Keats House, Hampstead, in the north, to the Horniman Museum and the Museum of Artillery, Woolwich, in the south; from the Gunnersbury Park Museum, home of the Rothschild family from 1835 to 1925, in the west, to the North Woolwich Station Museum in the east.

The range is vast. There are museums devoted to Chinese art, childhood, pilgrim badges from Chaucer's time, Karl Marx, the Masons, prints, Pavlova, Japanese writing and the Great Eastern Railway. Many of the museums are old houses that have been preserved, along with their contents, to give an idea of what living in London was like at various times in the past. There's Burgh House in Hampstead, Church Farm House in Hendon (which has a fine pub called the Greyhound next door), Forty Hall in Enfield, Hogarth's House in the Great West Road, Leighton House in Holland Park Road (a wonderful purpose-built Victorian artist's studio), Pitshanger Manor and many more.

But with a Little Money to Spend...

One of the greatest pleasures of a rainy day in London is to take tea in one of the city's grand hotels. It doesn't really matter which you choose – tea in any great hotel is unflustered, enjoyable, and comparatively inexpensive. Sit in the lounge of the Dorchester, the Westbury, Grosvenor House, Claridge's or the Ritz, sip your Earl Grey, nibble your scone with clotted cream and strawberry preserve, or your hot buttered toast, listen to a pianist or a string trio, and let the rain fall on others, less fortunate, outside. It may not be good for the conscience, but it is highly therapeutic to the rest of you.

top:
The cup that cheers – tea at Brown's Hotel, Dover Street.
left:
Rain almost inevitably means traffic jams in London, but the couriers thunder on.

London's Lungs – Fresh Air and Fun

Fogs and Smogs

For at least 500 years London has been plagued by problems of air quality. Shakespeare refers to "drooping fogge as blacke as Acheron", and the dampness of the atmosphere in the lower Thames Valley, combined with the smoke from wood and coal fires, often brought thick, choking fogs to the city. By the time of Charles Dickens, fogs posed a real threat to people's health, as the opening of *Bleak House* so graphically describes:

Fog everywhere. Fog up the river, where it flows among green aits and meadows; fog down the river, where it rolls defiled among the tiers of shipping, and the waterside pollutions of a great (and dirty) city… Fog in the eyes and throats of ancient Greenwich pensioners, wheezing by the firesides of their wards; fog in the stem and bowl of the afternoon pipe of the wrathful skipper… fog cruelly pinching the toes and fingers of his shivering little 'prentice boy on deck…

As the number of houses and fires and smoking chimneys grew, fog was superseded by smog, a hideous cocktail of mist, soot and smoke. By the 1950s London was subjected almost every autumn and winter to a series of yellow "pea-soupers" that killed up to 4000 people at a time. In 1956 the Clean Air Act was passed by Parliament, strictly controlling the emissions that businesses and households could pump into the air. It took a while for the Act to bite – in December 1956 there was another bad London smog in which a wild rabbit was found hopping along Knightsbridge and a duck waddling down Liverpool Street, both hopelessly lost. Since December 1962, however, London has been free from bad fogs and smogs.

And it is thanks to some good-hearted souls and determined action on the part of local pressure groups that London is so well provided with open spaces. Indeed, in central London you are never more than half a mile (800 metres) from a playing field, a park, the gardens of a square, or some other greenery.

Wide Open Spaces

For a breath of fresh air Londoners in their thousands take to the large open areas in and around their city. The biggest is Epping Forest, where 6000 acres (2400 ha) of

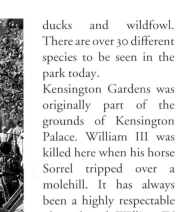

Soaking up the sun – the lunch hour in Hyde Park.

ducks and wildfowl. There are over 30 different species to be seen in the park today.

Kensington Gardens was originally part of the grounds of Kensington Palace. William III was killed here when his horse Sorrel tripped over a molehill. It has always been a highly respectable place, though William IV was once robbed here of his money, watch and shoe-buckles by a man who leapt over the wall and politely accosted him. When William said that there was a seal of sentimental value on the watch, the man promised to have the seal removed and returned to the king at the same time and place the next day. Both kept the appointment.

The Parks Police

A special force known as the Parks Police is responsible for law and order within the royal parks of London. They have a strange area of jurisdiction, for they may also deal with any wrongdoers "within a deer's leap of the boundaries" of any royal park. Their work is seldom arduous. Apart from keeping a watchful eye on Speakers' Corner in Hyde Park, and making sure bicycles are not ridden on path or grass, most of their time is spent dealing with itinerant hot-dog and ice-cream sellers.

the primeval forest that once covered the whole of eastern England from the Thames to the Wash still remain. This is where Queen Boudicca committed suicide as the Roman armies drew nearer. This is where kings have hunted and highwaymen have lain in wait for vulnerable travellers.

The next largest is Richmond Park, 2470 acres (1000 hectares) of open grassland. Some 350 fallow deer and 250 red deer graze here, and you may fish for pike, bream, carp, roach or eels in Pen Ponds. Adam's Pond is reserved for small boys of all ages who wish to play with their model boats.

Hyde Park is the largest of central London's open spaces – 340 acres (136 hectares). It was once home to deer, boar and wild bulls, and was always a dangerous place. Rotten Row (derived from *route des rois*), on the south side of the park, was the first London thoroughfare to be lit at night, after a highwayman murdered a woman who had swallowed her wedding ring to prevent him taking it. It was also where Lord Mohun and the Duke of Hamilton killed each other in a duel in 1712. Their dispute was over a bequest that they could have shared. Apart from being a pleasant place to stroll and relax in, the park, with its Serpentine lake where you can swim or go boating on hot days, and a reasonably good restaurant, is now used for both pop and classical concerts, and for demonstrations.

St James's Park lies south of The Mall. Elizabeth I used to hunt here. Accompanied by his dog, Rogue, Charles I took his last walk across the park on his way to his execution. Charles II swam in the lake, watched by his admiring mistresses. William III built a hide on the island in the lake so that he could watch the visiting

oposite top:
The statue of Peter Pan in Kensington Gardens.
opposite bottom:
A brisk stroll through Hyde Park…
below:
… messing about in boats on the Serpentine.

Chelsea Flower Show

right:
London in bloom – a profusion of roses at the Chelsea Flower Show…
below:
… and a cluster of irises.

The Chelsea flower Show is held for five days in late May in the large open space between the Thames and the Chelsea Royal Hospital, home of the Chelsea Pensioners. It has traditionally marked the beginning of the London Season, and has been patronized by members of the royal family for generations. It is always crowded, and access is strictly limited. Special guests of the Royal Horticultural Society go on the first day, members of the RHS on the second and third days. The public is admitted on the last two days only.

It's a middle-class jamboree, with perhaps the best-behaved crowd in London. Gardeners are not revolutionaries, nor prone to riot. On the other hand, it has perhaps the worst-dressed crowd in London – gardeners tend to be drab folk, better at growing beautiful things than wearing beautiful things. The three rules for attending the show are to wear comfortable shoes (you will be doing a lot of slow walking), allow plenty of time (this is not a one- or two-hour visit) and make sure you have a ticket. If you cannot get in, don't despair. The show is televised every day.

The Chelsea Flower Show is much more than a mere flower show. There are some 20 gardens, created espe-

cially for Chelsea. There are stalls and booths selling plants and gardening implements – the 1998 show revealed a grass-cutting go-cart. There are all the accessories you could possibly need for garden ponds, bog gardens, hothouses and cold frames, orchards, herbaceous borders and rockeries. There is the Great Marquee – the biggest tent in the world – and the entire show is constructed in just five weeks. In mid-April, the site is a bare patch of grass. Just over 30 days later the complete show is ready, though many of the exhibitors work through the night by car headlights on the eve of the opening.

For many visitors, the most fascinating feature of the show is the avenue of gardens designed, built and planted for the show. The entries come from colleges, local authorities, newspapers and magazines, nurserymen, landscape gardeners, garden suppliers and seed firms from many parts of the world.

Most of the entries have been a year in planning and preparing, but only a few days in construction. There are water gardens, cottage gardens, gardens of sculpture, courtyard gardens, Japanese and African gardens, gardens where the accent is on ecology and the environment, gardens which are concerned only with beauty. In just two weeks gardens arise complete with walls, fountains, streams, ponds, mill wheels, pergolas, plants, shrubs and even mature trees.

Plants for these gardens, and for the displays in the Great Marquee, are specially forced or held back so that they reach Chelsea in prime condition. There are plants from China and the Far East, India, South America, the Middle East, Australia, the United States, South Africa and the Caribbean, as well as the finest of home-grown specimens. Every conceivable type and species of flower is to be seen. There are alpines and ferns, ornamental grasses, roses by the thousand, tulips and daffodils, annuals and perennials, old favourites and new discoveries.

On the final afternoon, a great bell tolls to signal the end of the show and the beginning of the great sell-off, when everything is dismantled or dug up and sold to the public. You can buy clumps of award-winning delphiniums for a pound, rose bushes for not much more, fully mature bedding plants at knock-down prices, herbs and vegetables, plants you've always wanted and plants you've never heard of. As the sun begins to set over the Lots Road Power Station, you see people walking along the Embankment with their arms full of foxgloves and hollyhocks, or driving off in taxis with flowering cherry trees and rambling roses sticking out of the windows.

It is one of the greatest joys and beauties of London.

The Royal Horticultural Society

The Chelsea flower Show is organized and run by the Royal Horticultural Society, which was founded in 1804 in a room at Hatchard's Bookshop in Piccadilly. It was largely the brainchild of John Wedgwood, eldest son of the potter Josiah Wedgwood. In 1818 the Society established an experimental garden in Edwardes Square (just south of Kensington High Street at the Olympia end). Three years later it took a lease on 33 acres (12.5 hectares) in Chiswick, where the young Joseph Paxton went to work, and where he was spotted by the Duke of Devonshire.

The first fête – a forerunner of the Flower Show – was held at Chiswick in 1827, and the first floral exhibition of the Society was held in Lower Regent Street four years later. In 1858, thanks to Prince Albert, the Society's President, the commissioners of the Great Exhibition granted a lease of part of their South Kensington estate to the Society, on condition that it laid out gardens and built a conservatory there. The lease terminated in 1882, but eventually the Royal Hospital grounds were offered to the Society. The Chelsea Flower Show, inaugurated in 1913, has blossomed ever since.

One of London's most knowledgeable crowds – visitors to Chelsea.

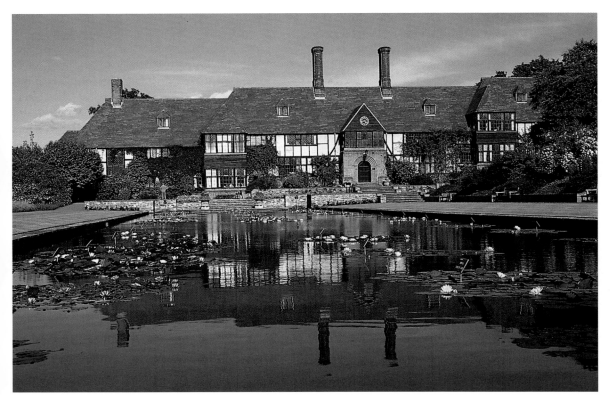

The Royal Horticultural Society's Headquarters at Wisley in Surrey.

Regent's Park Zoo

As you approach the Zoological Gardens in Regent's Park, you hear the whoops, shrieks and whistles of the parrots, cockatoos and macaws. Just for a moment, if you close your eyes and tune out the human hubbub around, you could almost be in some tropical forest.

The advantages of going to the London Zoo (as it's popularly known) in winter are that there are far fewer visitors and you can get much nearer to the exhibits – especially the outdoor ones. The only disadvantage is that the animals are sleepier or lazier in winter and some of them are disinclined to venture out. The advantage of going in summer is that there is more to see and do, though you may have to queue. The Zoo is popular with Londoners and visitors alike. In June and July it's thronged with school parties, in August with families. May and September are perhaps the best times to go.

History

The Zoological Society of London was founded in 1826, and a collection of animals was opened in Regent's Park two years later. Over 1000 visitors a week came to see monkeys, bears, emus, kangaroos, llamas, zebras and turtles. Gentlemen had to leave their whips at the gate, but ladies were allowed to keep their parasols, with which they poked the animals, more out of curiosity than cruelty. The collection was greatly enlarged in the 1830s with the addition of the royal menagerie from Windsor and the animals from the Tower of London – including over 100 rattlesnakes. The Tsar of Russia presented two bison in 1850. The first baby hippopotamus was reared in 1874. The first koala bear to live outside Australia arrived in 1880. In Edwardian times, camels were used to pull mowers to cut the grass.

Since then the Zoo has constantly expanded. The Mappin Terraces for bears were built in 1913, the aquarium and reptile house in the 1920s, the penguin pool in 1936. At the outbreak of the Second World War, many of the dangerous animals were killed, though a few were evacuated to Ireland. The fish were eaten. Since the war, there have been many additions: the Snowdon Aviary (1963), the Elephant and Rhino Pavilion (1965), a new Primate House (1972), the new Lion Terraces (1976), and a new aviary (1990).

A Walk Round the Zoo

Access to most of the terraces, pools and compounds is good, without invading the animals' privacy. The lion enclosure is surrounded by a moat, with a great many notices warning that it is not a good idea to enter the enclosure. One look at the great beasts prowling around is worth more than all these notices together, to most people anyway. The elephant house is fine, though the inhabitants seem bored – perhaps a better state than that of one of the first elephants in the Zoo, the tip of whose trunk was mysteriously cut off by a visitor one Bank Holiday afternoon in the 1870s. The pelicans appear to have a jolly time, chasing off invading seagulls – London Zoo teems with non-resident interlopers.

When the original reptile house opened in 1843, the keeper tried to charm a cobra but was bitten between the eyes and died within a few hours. The present Reptile House is famous in fiction (and slightly less so in fact) as the meeting place for spies and secret agents. This is where confidential documents affecting the nation's security are regularly exchanged. The whole Zoo is also the most popular place in London for divorced and separated fathers who have an afternoon's access to their children.

The Aquarium is full of surprises. After discovering that some piranha fish are vegetarian – a bit like finding out that Dracula preferred tomato juice to blood – it's reassuring to learn that electric eels can generate up to 500 volts of electricity. Spend a while admiring the horseshoe crabs. These are living fossils that have remained unchanged for over 300 million years. They're related to spiders and are not true crabs at all, and they look like alien fighting machines from some old black-and-white movie.

Watching us, watching them – a pelican resident of London Zoo.

The most appealing inhabitants are the giraffes. The first giraffes arrived in 1836, and the pattern of their skin provoked a flutter in the world of ladies' fashion – it was the thing to have a giraffe-patterned dress. You can view today's giraffes from inside or out, admiring these 16-feet (5-metre) tall creatures with beautiful eyes as they gaze with an appropriately aloof air at the visitors goggling up at them.

The Human Species

Students of human rather than animal behaviour will be fascinated by the noises made by visitors to the Zoo to attract residents' attention. It seems that up to 90% of visitors believe that by whistling, making clucking noises with the tongue, or uttering strange squeaks, they can make elephants, rabbits, snakes or spiders approach them. It doesn't matter where these noises are made. Even if two inches (50 mm) of toughened glass separates clucker from creature, the noise will still attract fish or reptiles. And, if all else fails, a tap on the glass is guaranteed to reassure even the most timid resident – so that anything from a mongoose to a stick insect will scurry across and press itself against the glass, right opposite the tapping digit.

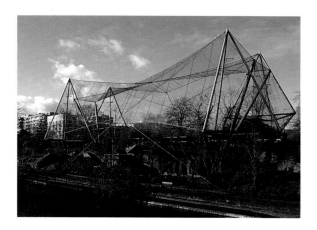

above:
Part of the lion compound at the Zoo.
left:
The Snowdon Aviary was completed in 1964.

Department Stores

The London department store was a late 19th-century invention. The first to be opened was the Bon Marché in 1877. It was established by a printer from Tooting named James Smith, with his winnings from the Newmarket races a year earlier. He changed his name to Rosebery Smith, but with the change of name came a change of luck and the store went bankrupt. The most revolutionary of London's department stores, discussed earlier in the West End chapter, was Selfridges, which opened in Oxford Street on 15 March 1909. The most famous is Harrods, destroyed by fire in 1883, but re-opened in its present splendour the following year.

Many of the stores started life as small shops (Whiteley's, Peter Robinson, John Lewis, Harvey Nichols, Harrods itself). What was new about the stores was not simply that they sold a wide range of goods, but that they dealt on a "cash only" basis. In the past, the upper classes had strolled from shop to shop, ordering their ribbons here, their hats there, their gowns somewhere else, and running up monthly or quarterly bills which they subsequently (perhaps "eventually" is a more appropriate word) settled. The new department stores politely but firmly insisted on cash at the time of purchase. This of course has now changed, and account customers are treated with reverence.

The stores became immensely popular, and there was a time when central London was peppered with them. Many were owned by partnerships: Dickins and Jones, Debenham and Freebody, Swan and Edgar, Marshall and Snelgrove, Derry and Toms, and the Army and Navy. Many have gone. Swan and Edgar is now Tower

Records in Piccadilly Circus. Debenham and Freebody (which used to have the telephone number "Mayfair 1") closed in 1981, only to rise phoenix-like as part of the Debenhams chain a few years later. Many that remain have been swallowed up by the retailing giants that operate chains of stores all over Britain.

The heyday of the department store was in the 1920s and 1930s. The new ring of middle-class suburbs round London provided plenty of customers, who were whisked into the West End by the greatly improved public transport system of buses, tubes and Green Line coaches. Most of the customers were women – there were those who said that London's department stores were the female equivalent of the gentlemen's clubs of Pall Mall. The stores held fashion shows and concerts. Radio programmes were transmitted from Selfridges, which, like Derry and Toms, had a wonderful roof garden where it was possible to take afternoon tea amidst flower beds and shrubs, with the song of birds nearby and the muted roar of the traffic far below.

The Modern Store

The London department store is still alive and well – typified by John Lewis, Selfridges and D.H. Evans in

Oxford Street; Liberty's and Dickins and Jones in Regent Street; and Peter Jones in Sloane Square.

Step inside – but don't inhale too deeply, for you have almost certainly entered the perfume department. The scent of Balenciaga, Dior, Guerlain and Estée Lauder is heavy in the air. Bottles, jars, tubes and sachets of every possible skin preparation surround you. A thousand different shades of lipstick smile at you from shiny glass counters. To one side is "Ladies' Handbags", to the other "Hats" (which probably also contains scarves and "accessories"). Ahead are "Watches" and "Costume Jewellery". In the far corner are lifts and stairs to the Lower Ground floor ("Kitchen Equipment", "China and Glass", "Men's Wear"), and to the upper floors ("Furnishing Fabrics", "Beds and Bedding", "Bridal Wear", "Carpets", "Ladies' Fashions", "Shoes", "Furniture", "Sports Goods", "TV and Hi Fi", and, on the highest floors of all, "Accounts" and "The Place to Eat").

The John Lewis Partnership

In 1864, John Lewis took a small shop in Oxford Street. By 1892 the shop had grown considerably, but not enough for John Lewis. Five years later, in defiance of a ban, he extended his shop into Cavendish Square. The authorities declared he had ruined the Square (they may have been right), and he was thrown into Brixton Jail for three weeks for defying their ban.

In the 1900s, Spendan Lewis (the founder's son) decided that it was wrong that the three heads of the company should receive more money than the rest of the staff put together, and the John Lewis Partnership was born. It runs well over 20 stores and the chain of Waitrose supermarkets. Every one of the 35,000 workers in the enterprise is a partner, and receives a yearly bonus which is a fixed percentage of their year's pay. Today, the head of the partnership receives £300,000, the poorest paid staff get about £6000. The Partnership is run by over 400 elected councils and committees, but is said not to be a Communist Utopia.

The founder also presented his estate – largely consisting of 4000 acres (2400 hectares) in Hampshire – to the Partnership to be shared by all for "their greater happiness". This has caused some problems, for part of the estate is a grouse moor, and there are those among the partners who do not favour the slaughtering of game birds. Nevertheless, the Partnership has been highly successful.

Inside Whiteley's, Queensway, Bayswater.

The Knightsbridge façade of
Harrods at night.

Harrods

Harrods is a long terracotta building, crowned with a cupola and bedecked at all times with the flags of the nations. It is like a museum where you can buy the exhibits, which range from the quaint and the curious through the grotesque to the gaspingly wonderful.

The central spine of Harrods is the Egyptian Escalator, a kind of DNA molecule that climbs through the store and is almost the only means of access to all floors. It is truly Egyptian in style, with fat pillars and

friezes that give Hollywood-like glimpses of the lives of the Pharaohs. It's also quite noisy – music pervades Harrods in a way that would have appalled customers of former times. If you wish to proceed quietly from floor to floor, there is a silent old staircase that leads from a corner of one of the ground-floor Food Halls, just opposite the Herbal and Fruit Tea counter.

Harrods' Banking Hall must be the only place in London where you can handle your financial transactions to piano accompaniment. It used to be the place for meeting one's friends, but that was in the days when the clientèle was comparatively small, and when most shoppers in the store probably knew each other personally. Harrods is now big business. It is on the international stage. And, although shorts, rucksacks, smoking and the use of mobile phones are forbidden, to the Old Guard, Harrods is not what it was. It is still, however, the most impressive of London's department stores.

In 1849 Henry Charles Harrod, a tea merchant of Eastcheap, bought a small grocer's shop in the village of Knightsbridge. Twelve years later, his son Charles Digby Harrod bought the business from him in instalments. By 1867 Harrods had an annual turnover of more than £1000. In 1985 it was bought by the Al Fayed brothers for £615 million. In a corner of the Banking Hall you will find a silver model of the store. It commemorates a wager made in 1917 between Gordon Selfridge and Sir Woodman Burbidge (of Harrods). The stake was to be a model of the store, and the wager was that within six years of the end of the first World War, Selfridge's returns would have overtaken those of Harrods. In 1927, Burbidge wrote to Selfridge, reminding him of the wager and pointing out in a gentlemanly way that Selfridge had lost. So Gordon Selfridge presented Burbidge with the model of Harrods.

There is much to see and buy in Harrods – everything from a golf tee to a grand piano. You can look at clothes, browse in the bookshop, hunt for a puppy or a kitten in the Pet Department, spend £3500 on a candle (should you so wish – it will last 11 months) or £1649 on a statuette of Charles I, complete with head and priced by someone with a sense of history and humour. There are at least a dozen places to eat, though the prices are high and there is a touch of the "only what you see here" about what you may eat in the Dress Circle Bar.

The Food Halls

Harrods' Food Halls are on the ground floor. They are an interconnecting suite of marble-floored and tiled galleries with large displays of everything from jelly beans to langoustines. Some of the Food Halls have eating counters – a Sushi Bar, a Fromage Bar, an Oyster Bar, a Sea Grill Bar. The Halls also contain a Delicatessen (for your foie gras, caviar and truffles), a fromagerie, a charcuterie, a pâtisserie and everything else that the stomach may crave.

The chief glory of the Food Halls is that devoted to meat, poultry and fish. It's the grandest of all the halls, with tiled floor, tiled walls, tiled arches and a tiled ceiling. Around the walls there are coloured mosaics of huntsmen and stags, dogs and ducks, shepherds and sheep, wild boar and tame goats. There are separate counters for veal and beef, lamb and pork. On the poul-

try and game island you can choose from venison, quail, guinea fowl, French squab roasting pigeons, duck sausage and a hundred more delights. In the corner of the fish section there is an ice grotto in praise of the wonders of the sea, with statues of mermaids, trickling fountains, cockleshells and a centrepiece of kippers, herrings and red and grey mullet – which looks far more attractive than it sounds.

The fish counters themselves glow with crabs, New Zealand mussels, crevettes, lobsters, monkfish, wild salmon, swordfish, turbot, tuna, grouper, octopus, Dover sole, pomfret, skate wings, whiting and sleek whole plaice. None of Harrods' food is cheap – you could almost certainly find any of it cheaper elsewhere in London, but not under one roof, not such fine quality, and not so enticingly displayed.

Montpelier Street

Across the road from Harrods and a little to the west is Montpelier Street. It was built on fields owned by the Moreaus, a rich Huguenot family, in the 18th century. In the street there is a fine-looking pub called the Tea Clipper (you will search in vain for a tea shop called the Brewer's Arms), a Mary Quant shop, the Montpeliano Restaurant, and Bonhams Auction Rooms – an ugly blue building that looks as if no architectural style wanted anything to do with it. And, on the eastern side of the street, is what used to be the Montpelier Mineral Water Works.

The meat and poultry halls in Harrods in the 1920s.

The BBC

The British Broadcasting Corporation was first established as the British Broadcasting Company in 1922, and began transmitting radio programmes of a highly respectable nature from Marconi House in The Strand on 14 November. The following year the BBC moved to larger premises in Savoy Hill, a narrow street that leads down to the Embankment, where it stayed for nearly ten years. It was not the obvious site from which to broadcast. Lord Reith wrote of it: "We went to inspect sundry possible sites... finally, as dusk was falling, we came to Savoy Hill. What a depressing place it was. It had been used for some mysterious LCC medical activities, and much dirt and depression had accumulated...."

From the very beginning the BBC sought not to be solely a London-based organization – within 24 hours of the first broadcast from London it was also broadcasting from Manchester – but the headquarters of all BBC activities has always been in the capital. Once established in Savoy Hill, the BBC built several studios along the street, and by the early 1930s the output of programmes was far broader than it had been in the pioneer days. Radio was fast becoming the most popular and successful of all media, however, and was outgrowing Savoy Hill. In 1928 the search began for a suitable site for brand-new purpose-built premises.

The site chosen was at the corner of Portland Place and Langham Street, just north of Oxford Circus, where an 18th-century house built by James Wyatt had recently been demolished. Many of the fittings of the house are now in the Victoria and Albert Museum.

The new BBC headquarters was designed to look a little like the prow of a great ship, ploughing its way down the yeasty waters of Portland Place – the relevance of this being a little hard to fathom. It cost £350,000 to build, and by 1932 Broadcasting House was ready to open its doors and go on the air. It was immediately found to be too small, and extra studio space was bought in St George's Hall, just the other side of All Souls' Church

Broadcasting House, Portland Place – home and headquarters of the British Broadcasting Corporation.

from Broadcasting House, and in Maida Vale, where the BBC still has its major music recording studios.

Broadcasting House

As you approach Broadcasting House (known to BBC staff as "BH") from Oxford Circus, pause a while to admire the sculptures by Eric Gill on the façade of the building. Now continue through what may well be the heaviest doors in London. The centre doors operate automatically, opening as you approach, but the strain on the mechanism is so great that every few weeks they need a rest and are put out of action.

Once through the doors you are in the vestibule – large, light and very much a product of the 1930s. High on the wall facing you is the Latin inscription placed there by order of the BBC's first Director-General, John Reith. Reith was a puritanical Scot who forged the independence and personality of the BBC, and the inscription contains the core of his beliefs. About one person in 10,000 might be able to translate it, so here it is in English:

This Temple of the Arts and Muses is dedicated to Almighty God by the first Governors of Broadcasting in the year 1931, Sir John Reith being Director-General. It is their prayer that good seed sown may bring forth a good harvest, that all things hostile to peace or purity may be banished from this house, and that the people, inclining their ear to whatsoever things are beautiful and honest and of good report, may tread the path of wisdom and uprightness.

Reith was a staunch believer in purity and uprightness. It is said that, in the early days of the BBC, he once entered a conference room, only to find one of his chief announcers and another member of staff in flagrante on the table. He wished to sack both of them, but others argued that the announcer was so popular with the public and the woman so good at her job that they should be allowed to stay. Reluctantly, Reith accepted this advice, but insisted that the table should be burnt.

Once in the vestibule, you can go no further without a pass, though you can walk round into Portland Place and to the entrance of the "BBC Experience". This is a museum of broadcasting where you can try your hand (or voice) at being a sports commentator, a celebrity being interviewed, a newsreader and many other radio roles. There is also a fascinating collection of early microphones, crystal sets, radiograms and other receivers.

BBC Television

BBC TV started life at Alexandra Palace (Ally Pally), north London's 1873 rival to Crystal Palace. The first palace lasted only 16 days before it was burnt to the ground. It was immediately rebuilt and ran a mixed programme of events similar to its south London predecessor. The BBC bought it, converted it into television studios and began transmissions on 26 August 1936. In 1949, the Corporation bought 13.5 acres (5.5 ha) of what had been the site of the Franco-British exhibition of 1908 at Shepherd's Bush.

This is still Television Centre, a bewildering maze of corridors in a building that curves round a central circular courtyard. It is very easy to get lost in Television Centre, and even easier to set off for a room next door to the one you have left, turn the wrong way and have to complete a lap of the building before you realize your mistake. But don't worry, without a pass you won't even get past the gate in Wood Lane.

The Albert Hall and the Proms

A hundred years ago the Crystal Palace and the Queen's Hall in Langham Place were the premier London concert venues, and the only ones with resident orchestras. The Queen's Hall was a classical building with a gold, red and grey interior. The architect, T.E. Knightley, insisted that the grey should be the same as that of the belly of a London mouse, and a string of dead rodents was kept in his workshop to serve as a colour chart.

In October 1895 Sir Henry Wood, a young and very able conductor, inaugurated the first season of Promenade Concerts in the Queen's Hall, though others had been held in Vauxhall and Ranelagh Gardens in the 18th century and at Covent Garden earlier in the 19th century. The concerts were an immediate and overwhelming success – to the extent that there was very little room for actual promenading. They were first sponsored by Chappell's of Bond Street, and from 1927 onwards by the BBC. The Queen's Hall was destroyed in 1941, and the Proms (as they have long been known) transferred to the Royal Albert Hall in 1944, the year of Sir Henry's death.

Every year, from mid-July until mid-September, concerts are held every night at the Albert Hall, with additional concerts in other venues (churches and other halls, even Hyde Park). The festival is still sponsored by the BBC, who broadcast every concert live on radio, and televise a dozen or so. The concerts are a showcase for the BBC orchestras, with guest orchestras from around the world invited to take part. The music is a mixture of the great and loved with the new and unknown. It is rare to find a concert that doesn't contain at least one contemporary "difficult" work, for it has long been the BBC's policy to promote new music. The concerts are, almost without exception, sold out, but the unseated arena directly in front of the platform is reserved for the Promenaders. These are usually young music-lovers and students, who are prepared to queue all day and stand all night to hear fine music, and to roar their approval at the end of every piece.

The Last Night of the Proms

The last Promenade Concert of each season has traditionally been one that celebrates English songs and music, and that veers towards extreme patriotism. The Promenaders dress in bowler or top hats, Union Jack boaters, Union Jack T-shirts, and wild wigs. They carry Union Jack umbrellas. They hurl paper streamers at the conductor and the orchestra. They demand many encores. They sing their hearts out, reserving their most fervent performance for Elgar's Land of Hope and Glory, an unofficial national anthem, and Rule, Britannia. It has to be accepted in the spirit of good, clean fun. Any other interpretation of what goes on can only lead to high anxiety or low depression.

The Royal Albert Hall

In 1852 Prince Albert suggested that part of the profits from the Great Exhibition of the previous year should be spent on a new concert hall in Kensington. He asked Gottfried Semper, who had designed the Dresden Opera House, to draw up plans for a hall, which were later modified by Captain Francis Fowke of the Royal Engineers. The design was grand, but there was insufficient money to finance its construction. Henry Cole, Chairman of the Society of Arts and one of the prime movers of the 1851 Exhibition, suggested that the leasehold of some of the Hall's seats could be sold to the public. One thousand three hundred seats were sold at £100 each on a 999-year lease. The descendants and beneficiaries of the original buyers still can attend almost every concert in the Albert Hall free of charge. It was planned as a Hall of Arts and Sciences, roughly oval in shape, 135 feet (40 metres) high, with external measurements of 272 by 238 feet (65 by 80 metres) and a seating capacity of 8000. Queen Victoria, however, had other ideas. When she laid the foundation stone in 1867, six years after Albert's death, she surprised everyone by naming it the "Royal Albert Hall". The famous echo was discovered at the opening ceremony in 1871. When the congregation joined in the Bishop of London's "Amen", the noise reverberated round and round the building. For over 100 years engineers worked to get rid of the echo, with almost complete success.

Sir Malcolm Sargent conducts the Last Night of the Proms in the 1960s.

The Royal Albert Hall is a superb auditorium (echo excepted). It is rich in scarlet and gold seats, plasterwork, columns, boxes, staircases, galleries and decoration. The atmosphere is heavy with Victorian wealth and splendour. The sheer size is breath-taking, and as a showcase for spectacle it is the finest in London.

Avoid the Last Night of the Proms (you probably won't be able to get in, anyway), but find an excuse to go on another night.

The Albert Memorial

Just across Kensington Gore (which takes its name from the Old English gara – a triangular piece of land left when ploughing an irregularly shaped field) is the Albert Memorial. When Prince Albert died in 1861, designs were sought for a suitable memorial. The one chosen was that of George Gilbert Scott, who wished to create the Victorian equivalent of a medieval shrine. It was derided by many in the early 20th century, and wind, rain and sun played havoc with its colour and detail. Now it has been lovingly, expensively and brilliantly restored, using a mixture of the highest technology, tuning forks, stethoscopes and cat litter. It is worth making a long detour to see.

above:
The Royal Albert Hall – everything from boxing matches to Handel's Messiah.
below:
The main entrance to the Royal Albert Hall during the annual summer season of Promenade concerts.

The British Museum

The main entrance to the British Museum

If there was a little room somewhere in the British Museum that contained only about twenty exhibits and good lighting, easy chairs, and a notice imploring you to smoke, I believe I should become a museum man.

J. B. Priestley, *In the British Museum*

There isn't.

London has Sir Hans Sloane (physician, collector and Lord of the Manor of Chelsea in the 18th century) to thank for the existence of the British Museum. Sloane's name lives on in Sloane Square and Sloane Street, but his greatest achievement was the founding of the collection of books and works of art that formed the original nucleus of the Museum. He suggested in his will that Parliament might like to buy this collection (worth £50,000) for £20,000. Parliament accepted the offer, and in 1753 the Foundation Act was passed authorizing the purchase of Sloane's collection and that of Robert Harley, first Earl of Oxford.

A public lottery then raised £300,000 to pay for the erection of a building in which to house these two collections. Some of this money was used to buy Montagu House, Bloomsbury. It was first opened to the public in 1753, with strict rules of admittance. No more than ten people were allowed in at a time; they had to apply in writing days in advance; their application had to be approved by the curator. In 1757, the collection was further enlarged when George II gave his royal library of over 10,000 volumes to the Museum. Forty-four years later, various items of plunder acquired following the war against Napoleon in Egypt were added, including the famous Rosetta Stone.

Another royal library, 120,000 books belonging to George III, was presented to the Museum in 1823. There was now insufficient room in Montagu House for the whole collection, and in the same year work began on a new building on the same site. It took 24 years to complete, and included the famous circular Reading Room, built on what had been a courtyard to the rear of Montagu House. Ironically, a few years later, much of the British Museum's natural history collection was rehoused in the new museums built in South Kensington.

The Collection

The British Museum has been called "a noble and magnificent cabinet", "the world's greatest storehouse of priceless treasures", "a labyrinthine lumber room", "an interesting monster", and "history's great treasure trove". It is all of these things and much more. It contains, among its millions of items, cuneiform tablets and Assyrian reliefs, the oldest Christian silver yet found in the Roman Empire, the Anglo-Saxon Sutton Hoo treasure, the Portland Vase, the 4th-century Payava Tomb from Greece, 67 ivory chessmen made in Scandinavia in the 12th century, the royal gold cup of the kings of France and England (made in 1380), 3000 clocks and watches, half a million coins, and two and a half million prints.

It has Arabic and Hindustani manuscripts, Egyptian mummies, a Greek Bible dating back to the 4th century, the log book of the Victory, Shakespeare's first folio of 1623 and Captain Scott's diary. It has paintings, pottery, tiles, vases, tombs, sculpture and sarcophagi, jewellery, lamps, papyri, skulls and skeletons, silver bowls and drinking horns, the oldest surviving British musical instrument (13th-century), enamels, Venetian glass, Japanese jars and the Elgin Marbles.

The British Museum Great Court

As part of London's Millennium programme and in celebration of the British Museum's 250th anniversary, the courtyard of the Museum is being restored to its former glory in a "spectacular" development designed by Foster and Partners. The old courtyard has been hidden for 150 years, buried beneath and behind the stacks of shelves that housed books for the Reading Room. The restoration includes an ambitious plan to cover the entire courtyard with a two-acre (0.8 hectare) glass roof, and make it

an education centre and exhibition space. It will also have the obligatory restaurant that accompanies every major London development.

The Reading Room

The Reading Room will remain, in much of its former glory, as a reference library. The original concept for this wonderful circular room was that of Sir Anthony Panizzi, Principal Librarian of the Museum from 1856 to 1866. It was designed by Sydney Smirke and built between 1854 and 1857. The first visit to the old room was always overwhelming, and the restored room should take the breath away. It will be decorated with the original azure-blue, cream and gold colours, and for the first time in its history it will be open to all members of the public.

Karl Marx would certainly have approved.

The Elgin Marbles

From 1799 to 1803, Thomas Bruce, seventh Earl of Elgin, was ambassador to the Ottoman Sultan. He became interested in the ruins of the Parthenon in Athens, the Temple of Athena on the Acropolis. Much of the Parthenon had been destroyed by Venetian bombardment in 1687, and what was left was in danger of succumbing to nature and vandalism. Elgin arranged for some of the figures from the temple to be brought to England.

They were purchased by the British Government for the nation in 1816 and handed to the British Museum. Since then, there have been many and frequent attempts by Greece to get back what she considers rightfully hers. The problem (some would say, the excuse made by Britain) is that under its 1753 charter the British Museum is not allowed to return anything to anybody. Whatever the rights or wrongs, it's worth visiting the Museum just to see the marbles – horses with flaring nostrils, herds of cattle and their human attendants and statues of Athena herself (Room 8).

top:
A detail of the Elgin Marbles.
left:
The gallery that houses the Elgin Marbles.

The British Library

From the peace and quiet of its old surroundings in Bloomsbury, the British Library has been rehoused just to the west of St Pancras Station, on the noisy and noisome Euston Road. Happily, there is a large piazza of bright red brick and white stone that separates the new building from the street itself. You leave the street, cross the piazza, descending gently, and arrive at the main entrance to the Library.

The building looks a little like the marriage of a supermarket with a multiplex cinema. It was opened by Her Majesty The Queen on 25 June 1998. In the large and airy entrance hall, a statue of Shakespeare and a couple of informative video screens gaze down at you, and a thick, glazed and softly lit column of beautiful leather-bound, gold-embossed books rises before you: the spine of the building. It is all very grand, though the colourful mural looks as though its subject matter is derived more from the works of Gilbert and Sullivan than from great literature. At present, entry is free, though there are clear signs that any shade of British government would like to impose admission charges, the cost of the building having been grossly underestimated.

The staff are dressed in a more relaxed style than their comrades at the British Museum. Whereas the old British Library staff used to dress like policemen and women of the 1930s, the staff of the new Library dress like entertainments officers from holiday camps of the 1960s. Nevertheless, a more officious air pervades the wonderful new building, and security is much tighter. There is a problem about bags. In the old days at the British Museum, your bag was searched on entry and examined on the way out of the Reading Room – to make sure you weren't stealing books. At the new Library, your bag won't be allowed in if it is larger than a piece of A4 paper (though it can be thicker, of course). If your bag is bigger, then you have to go down to the lockers on the lower ground floor.

All this means that getting into the new Library and into one of the reading rooms is a much slower process than at the British Museum. There it was possible to get from street to desk in under two minutes. Here it takes at least four times as long, for, having deposited your bag in the locker room, you have to take a lift to whichever reading room you wish to use.

Once settled at your desk, however, everything is a vast improvement. The seats are more comfortable. Every desk has a power point for lap-top computers. The lighting is far better – though you do miss the glorious sunbeams that occasionally broke through the London gloom to light up Smirke's grand dome at the old Reading Room. In the new Library, the desks are bigger

– it's easier to spread out your papers and belongings and the books you have requested from the library. The book service is faster. There are banks of computers at which you can sit and scan the Library's vast catalogue. The acoustics are suitably muted for a reading and working room. The issue desks are near to hand – in the old Reading Room you had to walk through a maze of bookcases to reach them.

The cafés and the restaurant are a great improvement – more spacious, a better selection of teas and coffees, and with access to daylight. The lavatories, too, are vastly superior to the old "facilities" at the British Museum – sparkling clean, tiled from floor to ceiling and, as at 11 August 1998, free of graffiti.

The Collection

Even before the British Library moved to its new home in St Pancras, its statistics were breath-taking: 376 miles (600 kilometres) of shelving, 20 million books, 1.6 mil-

lion music scores, 29 million patent specifications, a million discs of recorded sound and 50,000 hours of tapes. It remains one of the richest collections of books in the world. Prized possessions include the Lindisfarne Gospels; the oldest printed document in the world, found in a cave in northern China; two copies of the Magna Carta; the Bedford Book of Hours; the Luttrell Psalter; a Gutenberg Bible; the letter Columbus wrote on "discovering" the New World; and magnificent collections of manuscripts, music and stamps.

There is a large exhibition room on the lower ground floor, with displays of printing and bookbinding, as well as cases of rare and beautiful books. There's a linotype hot-metal composing machine of the 1880s, a common wooden printing press of the early 19th century, and a whole range of bookbinder's tools.

In the display cases you can see a Book of Hours of King Francis I, John Lydgate's The Life of St Edmund, the Theodore Psalter, an Aubrey Beardsley edition of Ben Jonson's Volpone, an 18th-century printing of the fables of Jean de la Fontaine, and a 1931 edition of Ovid's love poems illustrated by Picasso. There are also beautiful books of the 15th and 16th centuries from China and Asia, and a copy of John Ogilby's Britannia (an early road atlas of Britain).

And all, so far, free of charge. To get into this room you don't even need a reader's ticket. But don't delay your visit for too long. There are ugly rumours that it is only a matter of time before an annual fee is charged for the reader's ticket required for the Library, and £300 has been mentioned as a possible rate. It seems a high price to pay for scholarship.

The new home for the British Library in St Pancras – over budget and behind schedule, but decidedly user-friendly

The National Gallery

The National Gallery had its origins in a house in Pall Mall. It was the home of a Russian-born merchant and philanthropist named John Julius Angerstein, who died in 1824. On Angerstein's death, the British government were persuaded by Sir George Beaumont to buy 38 of his collection of paintings – including works by Raphael, Rembrandt and Van Dyck – for £57,000. Beaumont then donated another 16 paintings – more Rembrandts, and works by Claude, Wilkie and Rubens as well as Richard Wilson.

A new building was needed to house this collection, and a site was selected on the north side of Trafalgar Square. In 1838, the young Queen Victoria opened the National Gallery. Since then, the façade has remained much the same, but the gallery has grown considerably in size. It's a fine building, grand and spacious, consisting of some 50 rooms open to the public, and many offices and workshops hidden away, where paintings are cleaned and restored, and where scholars are given the chance to study great works of art at enviably close quarters. The Department of Conservation is divided into two sections – Upper and Lower. This is partly because the department is on two floors, and also because one department deals with the structure and support of paintings (frame and canvas), and the other with the grounds and paint layers. Although there is open access to the galleries, members of the public are not allowed to enter any of the workshops.

The Collection

There are well over 2000 pictures in the National Gallery, and the vast majority of them are on show at any one time. Paintings are lent to other galleries (and borrowed from other galleries), and occasionally a picture

Grace and beauty on the north side of Trafalgar Square – the National Gallery.

requires attention – otherwise, your own particular favourite is bound to be there.

The collection includes works by most of the great masters of Western art from the 12th to the 19th century. There are paintings by Leonardo, Titian, Velásquez, Goya, Constable, Turner, Monet, Van Gogh and Picasso – though lovers of Turner would do better to go to the Tate Gallery. Among dozens of gems are Van Eyck's The Arnolfini Marriage, Raphael's Pope Julius II, Holbein's The Ambassadors, any of the 22 Rembrandts, Caravaggio's Supper at Emmaus, Van Gogh's Sunflowers, Seurat's Bathers at Asnières, and works by Manet and Degas. More modern paintings are generally to be found in the Tate.

Paintings have come from a number of sources. Some have been purchased by public subscription (Titian's Death of Actaeon), some have been gifts, many have been purchased by government grant. The gallery's first director, Sir Charles Eastlake, visited Italy more than a dozen times between 1854 and 1865, buying 139 pictures, "many of them of the greatest interest and value", and all at bargain prices.

Wartime Recitals

During the Second World War, the National Gallery became the venue for an extraordinary programme of music concerts every day. The most famous of these were the piano recitals given by Dame Myra Hess, attended by workers and members of the armed forces, occasionally to the accompaniment of bombs exploding nearby. The propaganda value of these events was exploited to the full by the government.

The Sainsbury Wing

In April 1985, the National Gallery accepted an offer from two members of the Sainsbury family to finance an extension wing to the west of the principal building. There was much heated discussion about the designs that were submitted for this wing. Prince Charles was foremost among the critics: "I would understand better this type of high-tech approach if you demolished the whole of Trafalgar Square and started again… but what is proposed is like a monstrous carbuncle on the face of a much-loved and elegant friend." The "carbuncle" analogy was probably borrowed from Countess Spencer, who had used it a year earlier.

The wing was completed (not to the carbuncle design) in the late 1980s, and now houses the Early Renaissance collection, galleries for temporary exhibitions, conference rooms, a shop and a better restaurant than the one in the Gallery proper.

Beatrix Potter and the National Gallery

The creator of Peter Rabbit and Squirrel Nutkin visited the Gallery on 26 November 1884, when she was 18 years old. Then, as now, there were many students making copies of the great paintings. She recorded her impressions that night in her Journal:

Went to the National Gallery and enjoyed myself exceedingly. How large it is!... Swarms of young ladies painting, frightfully for the most part, O dear, if I was a boy and had courage! We did not see a single really good copy. They are as flat and smooth as ditch-water. The drawing as a rule seems pretty good, but they cannot have the slightest eye for colour. I always think I do not manage my paint in that respect, but what I have seen today gives me courage, in spite of depression caused by the sight of the wonderful pictures.

A student at work in the National Gallery in November 1933. Students are still allowed to use the Gallery.

The Tate Gallery

On the north bank of the Thames, a little to the east of Vauxhall Bridge, is the Tate Gallery – popularly known as simply "the Tate". It was built in the 1890s, on the site of the old Millbank Penitentiary. Although the Penitentiary was Jeremy Bentham's attempt to reform the British prison service, it was a gloomy building erected on low-lying marshy ground. The experiment failed, and the British government was happy to donate the site to Sir Henry Tate, a millionaire sugar refiner. The Gallery opened in 1897 and cost £80,000 to build. Originally it housed Tate's own collection of paintings and sculpture, of which the most famous item was John Everett Millais' *Ophelia* – still on show today, drifting down the stream in her pre-Raphaelite glory.

The Gallery grew. Sir Joseph Duveen, a Victorian art dealer and benefactor, paid for the building of a new wing to house the Turner collection of 300 paintings and 19,000 drawings bequeathed by the artist to the British nation. In 1926, Duveen's son paid for a further extension to the Tate, and it was enlarged again in 1937 and 1979. Finally, in 1987 the Clore Gallery – financed by the property tycoon Charles Clore – was added to house the Turner Collection. Designed by the firm of James Stirling, architect of the Staatsgalerie in Stuttgart, this section of the Tate is one of the most technically advanced galleries in the world, with superb rooms for study and research.

right:
The front entrance to the Tate Gallery, designed by Sidney R J Smith in 1897.
below:
Young visitors admire a Degas ballerina.

The Tate is a lovely gallery, grand yet not oppressive, large enough to house a comprehensive collection, small enough for most of it to be viewed in just a couple of visits – though fans of Turner will need to come many more times. Go early to the Tate, for it attracts 2.5 million visitors a year, and entry is free. Queues often form for special exhibitions long before the doors open at 10 o'clock in the morning. Don't miss the restaurant, which has walls decorated by Rex Whistler illustrating a story entitled *In Pursuit of Rare Meats*.

At first, the Tate was the London home of British works of art, but now it also houses 20th-century works from all over the world – paintings, sculpture, prints and drawings. There is a wonderful Hogarth self-portrait with his pug dog, the 17th-century painting of the Cholmondeley (pronounced "Chumley") Sisters, Stubbs's *Horse Attacked by a Lion*, several fine paintings by Gainsborough, and Constable's *Flatford Mill*. From the late 19th century there are paintings by Cézanne, Gauguin, many of the pre-Raphaelites, and Whistler *(Nocturne in Blue and Gold: Old Battersea Bridge)*. From the early 20th century there are paintings by Picasso (including *The Three Dancers, Nude Woman in a Red Armchair* and *Weeping Woman)*, Matisse, Dalí

(Metamorphosis of Narcissus), Malevich (the Russian pioneer of abstract art), Munch, Beckmann and Max Ernst. Later 20th-century paintings include those of Rothko, Bacon, Jackson Pollock, Blake, Hockney, Lichtenstein and Warhol. There is also an outstanding collection of modern sculpture, with works by Hepworth, Moore, Caro, Brancusi, Giacometti, Anish Kapoor, and many others.

During its long involvement with contemporary art, the Tate has often been at the centre of controversy. The tabloid press regularly sets up a howl of disapproval whenever the gallery buys a work of art that owes perhaps more to concept than to content. There were strong condemnations of what were regarded as a waste of public money when the Tate purchased a pile of old tyres (arranged to form a submarine) in the 1970s, a pile of new bricks (arranged to form a pile of bricks) in the 1980s, and a brick wall in the 1990s. The most savage criticism, however, was reserved for what London's Evening Standard newspaper referred to as Damien Hirst's "pickled cattle" – properly known as *Mother and Child Divided* – the bisected halves of a cow and a calf displayed in two tanks of formaldehyde.

The Tate at Bankside

Proudly trailed as the London equivalent of the Pompidou Centre in Paris, the Tate at Bankside opens at the very end of the 1990s. It looks nothing like the Pompidou Centre, for it occupies the shell of the old Bankside Power Station. The Power Station was built on the site of the Great Pike Gardens in Southwark, which used to supply fish to local religious houses in the 14th century.

The site is one of the finest in London, hard by the river on the south bank of the Thames, just a couple of minutes' walk from the New Globe Theatre. Since the Festival of Britain in 1951 and the arrival of the Royal Festival Hall, culture has been steadily creeping along the south of the Thames for half a century now, to the occasional dismay of those who believe it should all be housed in Islington

This is a grand scheme. The Tate at Bankside will include sculpture courts, gardens, a rooftop restaurant, a covered street, and an observation tower 300 feet (70 metres) high, housed in what was the central tower of the old Power Station.

The unofficial meeting place for visitors to the Tate.

London in Song

Many cities have songs written about them. The Big Apple is celebrated more than most other cities, with hits such as New York, New York, Manhattan, The Sidewalks of New York and Autumn in New York. Paris has had more than its share of songs and musical tributes, by both French and American songwriters – I Love Paris, Les Toits de Paris, April in Paris and Bonjour Paris.

Songs in praise of London have a rich and varied background. Many of them were written by Londoners, or by people living in London, and for a variety of reasons. Noël Coward wrote London Pride as part of a morale-raising exercise during the Second World War. Twenty years earlier he had written an entire musical revue entitled London Calling, which contained a song called Parisian Pierrot, thus paying homage to two cities at once. George and Ira Gershwin wrote A Foggy Day in London Town for perhaps the worst musical film Fred Astaire made with RKO – A Damsel in Distress. The song contains only one reference to a specific part of London:

> I viewed the morning with alarm,
> The British Museum had lost its charm…

Hubert Gregg probably wrote Maybe It's Because I'm a Londoner because he genuinely liked the city. Gus Elan wrote If It Wasn't for the 'Ouses In Between because he

was a true Londoner who earned his living in the many music halls of the city. It's another song that includes specific references to parts of London, though with perhaps less of the Gershwin style:

> Oh, it reely was a wery pretty garden
> And Chingford to the eastward could be seen,
> Wiv a ladder an' some glarses, you could see the 'Ackney Marshes
> If it wasn't for the 'ouses in between…

In general, it's the less salubrious parts of London that have been celebrated in song. There are no songs about Harrods or the Savoy Hotel or Fortnum and Mason.

There's one song about Buckingham Palace ("They're changing guard at Buckingham Palace, Christopher Robin went down with Alice") and one about part of the Tower of London ("…with 'er 'ead tucked underneath 'er arm, she walks the Bloody Tower…"). But by and large it's the poorer areas of London that have been immortalized in music, with merry tributes to The Strand ("Let's all go down The Strand"), the Old Kent Road ("…laugh? I thought I should have died, knocked 'em in the Old Kent Road…"), and Paddington Green ("…she was as beautiful as a butterfly and as proud as a queen, was pretty little Polly Perkins of Paddington Green…"). Let's All Go Down The Strand was a Victorian song that celebrated the music halls, smoking saloons, shops and arcades of a golden era. The song about Polly Perkins is more in praise of London buses than Paddington Green, and the Old Kent Road has yet to have a golden era.

Even in the Swinging Sixties, when there were some dreadful musical films and shows set in London (*Three Hats for Lisa* and *Expresso Bongo*, among others), the songs tended to feature areas of London off the tourist trail, like Paddy Roberts' *The Ballad of Bethnal Green*.

A mural celebrating the dance on a wall in the Lambeth Walk.

A Nightingale Sang in Berkeley Square

There is a story about Eric Maschwitz, who wrote the song *A Nightingale Sang in Berkeley Square* and the operetta *Goodnight Vienna*. One night in the early 1950s, he and a friend were driving through Lewisham in south-east London. At the time, there was still a theatre in Lewisham (it's now a bingo hall), and a production of *Goodnight Vienna* was in progress. Maschwitz stopped the car and crossed the street to the theatre. The front-of-house manager was standing in the foyer, and Maschwitz, with the curiosity of the work's creator, asked him how the show was doing. The manager looked at him for a moment and said: "It's doing about as well as you'd expect *Goodnight Lewisham* to do in Vienna."

A Nightingale Sang in Berkeley Square is, however, one of the most beautiful London songs. It's full of gentle sentiment, delicate love and the sweetest of romance. It is a song of magic and moonlight, of "angels dining at the Ritz", the "tap-dancing feet of Astaire", and the echo of the nightingale. The lyric has a simplicity that can be quite overwhelming:

> When dawn came stealing up all gold and blue
> To interrupt our rendezvous,
> I still remember how you smiled and said,
> "Was that a dream, or was it true?"

Mussolini and the Lambeth Walk

One of the frequently revived songs about London is The Lambeth Walk, from a 1930s musical show called Me and My Gal. It's a jaunty, jolly neo-Cockney song, the lyric of which is interspersed with cried of "Oi!", and which was made into a highly successful dance number, full of thumbwork (jerking over the shoulder, tucked into the armholes of waistcoats and so on).

The show, the song and the dance became enormously popular. It clearly appealed to Benito Mussolini, ex-professional dancer but by then dictator of Italy. He paid for a dance teacher to be flown out to Italy in 1937 to teach him the steps. Presumably it made a change from the goose-step.

The Strand – one of many London roads commemorated in song.

The London Comedian

A lively night at one of the chain of Jongleur's Comedy Clubs.

Comedians who learned and honed their craft in the old variety halls, in concert parties at the end of the pier, or in the tough clubs of northern England and Scotland, will tell you that many of the best jokes stem from adversity. There are always arguments as to which part of Britain has suffered the most and has, therefore, produced the best comedians and the best jokes – except in Liverpool, where there is certainty. But London and Londoners have had enough hardship and adversity to establish a strong comic tradition.

In the heyday of the old music halls, many of the top comedians came from London. Dan Leno was born in the slums of Agar Town, just to the north of the site of Euston Station. His real name was George Galvin, and he began his career singing and dancing in London pubs when he was four years old. By the time he was 18 he was a champion clog dancer, but he is best remembered as a Cockney comedian and a fine pantomime dame. Leno was a small man; his partner, Herbert Campbell, was a huge man. The two were extremely fond of each other, to the extent that when Campbell died in 1904, Leno pined away and died within six months.

A couple of generations later, the London music halls had a new hero – Max Miller, the "Cheeky Chappie". Miller wasn't born in London, but he was at his best and funniest when he strutted across the stage of one of his favourite London venues – the Holborn Empire, the Metropolitan in Edgware Road, or the Finsbury Park Empire. His humour and delivery reeked of London – brash, vulgar, bristling with innuendo, but often with a self-deprecatory twist that left his audiences laughing at him while loving him at the same time.

One of Miller's oft-repeated lines, as the laughter of the audience subsided, was "there'll never be another, will there…" There hasn't been, but 50 years on from the peak of Miller's career, a new generation of comedians found inspiration in Ben Elton, born and bred in Catford (which was also the home of Spike Milligan for many years). Elton arrived too late for the music halls or variety stages, but served his apprenticeship on the alternative comedy circuit before making his name on television. Like Miller, Elton's comedy relies on observation of the petty tragedies, irritations and insanities of life, and on a quickfire delivery.

In the last 20 years, comedy has become big business in London. There are hundreds of venues where established comedians and nervous beginners can be seen – in rooms over pubs, in clubs and theatres, in converted churches, in the open air. On 27 March 1998, eight comedians went to a supermarket in Ealing to try out new jokes for Christmas crackers. The staff were given monitoring machines to see which jokes got the biggest laughs. There are comedy clubs in Deptford (Up the Creek), in Ealing (at the Drayton Court pub, The Avenue), in a large room above the East Dulwich Tavern, in The Hobgoblin (Effra Road, Brixton), at the Black Cap in Camden High Street (a gay and lesbian comedy pub), at various branches of Jongleurs, and even on the PS Tattershall Castle (moored by the Victoria Embankment).

The Comedy Store

The most famous and the most central of London's comedy clubs is the Comedy Store in Leicester Square. It's a low-ceilinged, underground room, dark and stuffy. The audience is a mixture of first-time visitors (looking more for the curiosity than the comedy), regulars, and those who make heckling their premier hobby. Every night the

bill of fare is a mixture of hopefuls and established comedians. Some hopefuls survive, a few even flourish, most retire with dented egos. As the night wears on, the heckling becomes rougher – alcohol is not a warm-hearted drug when taken underground. When you pay your entrance fee, you take a gamble. Ahead of you may be a night of much laughter and merriment, but it also could be a night of embarrassment and carnage. Either way, it's an experience.

London Heckling

Sometimes a heckler reveals a great sense of humour. When that happens, the comedian is left gasping for breath, wishing he or she had thought of anything half as funny, and sadly contemplating how to get the audience back on track for the rest of the set. The scene is a comedy club in London. A struggling comedian begins his act:

COMEDIAN: Good evening, ladies and gentlemen. What a day I've had. Now, my wife…
HECKLER: (*interrupting with a loud shout*) Sexist!
COMEDIAN: (*hastily changing joke*) There was this Indian…
HECKLER: Racist!
COMEDIAN: (*one last desperate try*) I went to Spain last month…
HECKLER: Tourist!

above:
Graveyard of many aspiring comedians – outside the Comedy Store, Leicester Square.
bottom:
On stage at Jongleur's, Clapham.

A typical London taxi rank – cabbies waiting for fares at King's Cross.

The London Taxi

There are 18,000 black taxi cabs in London, and 22,000 licensed cab drivers. Not all the cabs are out on the street at any one time, but you may consider yourself unlucky if you don't see one every few seconds in the West End and Central London during most of the day. The further you move from the centre, the rarer they become. If it's raining late at night, especially south of the river, taxis can disappear altogether.

Many of the cabs are owned by companies and leased out to drivers, but there are still plenty of owner-driver-operated cabs. Both vehicle and driver are icons of London.

The cab is tall, sturdy, square-looking, with large doors that make leaping in and out easy, and with a very tight turning circle. The driver is usually chatty, affable, politically leans to the Right (or is at least a traditionalist), and really does say: "You'll never guess who I had in the back of this cab the other day…."

Licensed London cab drivers can ply the streets looking for custom. When they don't have a fare, the yellow FOR HIRE sign above the cab is illuminated. Advanced hirers and commissionaires outside posh hotels attract the cab driver's attention by inserting two fingers into the mouth and giving a piercing whistle. Smart City types brandish their rolled umbrellas. For the humble among us, it's sufficient to raise an arm in the air and wave it gently. The cab then stops as near you as possible – it will even use its tight turning circle to perform a U-turn, if necessary. The driver winds down the cab window, and you simply tell him where you wish to go. If you get in first and then tell him, provided the yellow light was switched on he is obliged to take you – whether or not he's "just going off-duty". But it takes some nerve to insist in the teeth of his unwillingness. There should be no need to explain how to get to your destination, because all London black cab drivers have to pass a very special examination before they're allowed out on the streets. It's called the Knowledge.

The Knowledge

Those who want to be London cabbies have to apply to the Metropolitan Police Licensing Authority at the

The cabbie's refreshment hut at Knightsbridge.

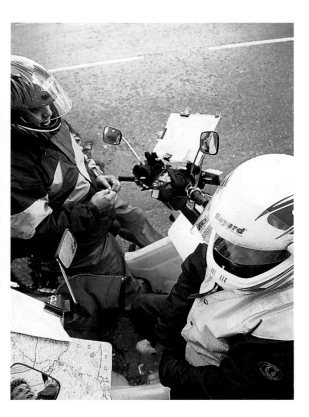

Public Carriage Office in Penton Street. They must produce a medical certificate from their GP declaring that they are physically fit for the job, which can often be hard and stressful. Then they have to prepare themselves for the Knowledge.

The Knowledge is a series of nine interviews or tests, on a viva voce basis. The would-be cabbie has to wear a suit, and has to remain calm, no matter how provocative the examiner may be. The test is not just about knowledge of London, but about personality – can you keep your temper when someone is constantly changing his or her mind, voicing racist opinions, being offensive?

The tests take place in a small room, and are confrontational. At each one you are tested on 90 different routes across London, making 450 routes in all. You are given a pick-up point and a destination, and have to say how you would drive from one to the other. You have to pass every test before you are granted a licence.

Most candidates learn the runs by covering them on scooters or bicycles. They make their way slowly across London, one eye on the traffic, the other on a clipboard mounted on the handlebars of the scooter, both eyes occasionally darting to left or right trying to discern the names of the streets and alleys as they pass.

The licence costs £87 and lasts three years. There's also the cost of a special driving test, the cab licence and the medical certificate – in all some £250. Those who succeed reckon it's worth it, and although the Knowledge is extremely hard work, it does ensure that 99 times out of 100, when you hail a London cab, you will be taken safely and directly to your destination, with no questions asked.

H.G. Wells and the London Taxi

Kipps knew that wherever you were, so soon as you were thoroughly lost, you said "Hi!" to a cab, and then "Royal Grand Hotel". Day and night these trusty conveyances are returning the strayed Londoner back to his point of departure, and were it not for their activity, in a very little while the whole population, so vast and incomprehensible is the intricate complexity of this great city, would be hopelessly lost for ever.
H.G. Wells, *Kipps*, 1905

A True Story
A taxi driver picked up a fare in London, drove a little way, then said to his passenger: "You'll never guess who I had in the back of this cab the other day. Bertrand Russell! Got to be the greatest brain in the world, right? So I said to him, 'Bertie, what's it all about? What are we here for? What's the meaning of life?' And, tell you what, the silly so-and-so didn't know… where did you say you wanted to go?"

left:
Would-be cabbies. Students of The Knowledge find their way about London.
below:
"Where to, Guv?" – King of the Streets, the London cabbie.

Underground Railways

The emblem of the London Underground.

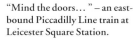

The first underground railway in London opened in 1863, and ran for four miles (6.5 km) from Paddington to Farringdon Street. It was built by the "cut and cover" method (digging a trench, laying the track, and then building a roof or cover over the line), and the trains were hauled by steam locomotives. It was an immediate success. Within a year there were 259 proposals for more underground railways in London. The first true "tube" line (created by boring a tunnel underground) opened in 1870, running under the Thames to connect the Tower with Bermondsey. It was the work of James Greathead, but it ran for only a few months. The oldest existing tube line in London is a section of the Northern Line, running from the City to the Oval and allowing cricket fans of the 1890s to leave their desks and nip across to see the heroes of the Surrey County Cricket Club, at that time the finest team in the land.

Today there are 82 miles of tube tunnel on the Underground system, with over 100 stations, 46 of which are listed buildings. This is good news for lovers of fine architecture, but bad news for the companies that own and maintain the stations. Many of the finest stations are on the Piccadilly Line, but the Northern Line, though otherwise ill-kept and generally grubby, has the best platform surfaces – gleaming, polished slabs of stone. Over 130 giant ventilation fans keep the air reasonably fresh in the Underground, and the temperature is a constant 73° F (23° C).

The two men most responsible for the development of the Underground were an American, Charles Tyson Yerkes, and Henry Stanley, later Lord Ashfield. Yerkes built his own power station at Lots Road, bought up all the rights he could find, electrified the District Line and took over every other section of the Underground system, save the original Metropolitan Line. When he died in 1905 (in the Waldorf Astoria – he was a man who did everything in style), his London railway empire passed to Henry Stanley.

Stanley pushed the system out to the suburbs of London, most of it not as underground but as surface track. He was attacked for extending the Northern Line beneath Hampstead Heath. It was claimed that the line would act as a drain, depriving grass, bushes and trees of the water they needed to survive. But there were those who admired Stanley. The mother of a baby girl born on the Bakerloo Line asked Stanley to be godfather to the child, whom she christened Thelma Ursula Beatrice Eleanor – so that her initials would always remind her of her subterranean origins.

"Mind the doors… " – an eastbound Piccadilly Line train at Leicester Square Station.

The Post Office Underground Railway

In 1913 work started on an ambitious underground railway to connect the main sorting offices of the London General Post Office with several major railway stations. The line was to run from Whitechapel Road, under Liverpool Street Station, and then on under the City to the General Post Office headquarters a little to the north of St Paul's Cathedral. Work stopped on the outbreak of the first World War, and a section of the tunnel was used to store the Elgin Marbles from the British Museum.

When the line finally opened, just in time to deal with the Christmas rush of 1927, it was a network that joined Paddington, Euston, St Pancras, King's Cross, Liverpool Street, London Bridge, Waterloo and Victoria stations, and several major sorting offices – the most famous being at Mount Pleasant. It still carries up to 30,000 bags of mail every day, in some 30 electric trains, along its 6.5 miles (10.5 km) of track. At peak periods the driverless trains run every five minutes.

The Tube in Wartime

The Government had made no plans to use Underground stations as shelters for Londoners when the Blitz began in 1940. London Underground put up notices forbidding the public to enter, and, later, trying to restrict the use of the stations to passengers only. It was direct action by determined and frightened citizens that led to 117,000 people a night sleeping on the platforms of many London Underground stations. Altogether 79 stations were used as shelters.

Once the pattern had been established, a great London resourcefulness was revealed. Citizens organized themselves into station committees, with their own lending libraries, canteens and first-aid posts. Those who sheltered at Swiss Cottage Station produced their own newsletter, The Swiss Cottager, two copies of which are now in the British Museum. The Swiss Cottagers were, however, less happy about the lack of amenities at their station and the sweaty smells. There was no lavatory, and, rather than use the buckets provided, many locals took the train to Finchley Road.

The phenomenon became world-famous largely through the drawings of Henry Moore. Before the Blitz, Moore seldom went into the Underground. Now he rediscovered it:

One evening after dinner in a restaurant with some friends we returned home by Underground taking the Northern Line to Belsize Park... I saw people lying on the platforms at all the stations we stopped at... I had never seen so many reclining figures and even the train tunnels seemed to be like the holes in my sculpture. And amid the grim tension, I noticed groups of strangers formed together in intimate groups and children asleep within feet of the passing trains. After this evening I travelled all over London by Underground...

The Underground over ground at Fulham Broadway Station on the District Line.

Sewers and Shelters

Beneath the streets and buildings of London there is an extraordinary world of pipes and tunnels, passages and railways, cables and bunkers, wine cellars and charnel houses, sewers and shelters. It is a world that is constantly being enlarged. The latest grand addition is the Ring Water Main that encircles London, supplying the city with its clean water. When dry it's possible to cycle through the pipe from Hampton Court to Hampstead, without ever seeing daylight. The journey takes about one and a half hours.

Beneath the Ministry of Defence building in Whitehall there is a large 400-year-old wine cellar that used to belong to Cardinal Wolsey – it was moved 43.5 feet (14 metres) in 1947 while subterranean extensions were added to the Ministry, and then moved 43.5 feet back. Under St Stephen's Walbrook there is a crypt, hidden for centuries, rediscovered in 1960 by the Reverend Chad Varah, and now used as one of the Samaritans' telephone operations rooms. Deep below Chancery Lane is the Chancery Lane Safe Deposit – 5000 safes full of secrets and treasures that may well never be revealed, though we do know that Lloyd George's private papers are there, and that when a section of the depository was flooded in the war, one safe was opened and found to contain a pair of frilly Edwardian knickers with a label which read "My life's undoing".

There is plenty of animal life to be found underground – rats, eels and mice; many fungi and 100 different plants. There was an 18th-century London myth that the underground fleet river in the City was home to an entire species of subterranean pigs. Most London rats live under Westminster, scuttling out at night to feed from the litter bins of West End restaurants. In all there may well be over 10 million rats prospering under London, immune to most poisons and cunning enough to take only a little of any one item of food in case it has any ill effects.

Shelters

Londoners first became conscious of the need for shelters during the first World War. In May 1915 a ton of bombs was dropped on London from a Zeppelin, causing considerable panic. King George V was bundled on to a royal train and shunted into a tunnel, bringing the rest of the railway service to a grinding halt. The Cabinet fled to Holborn and Aldwych Underground stations.

When Winston Churchill became Prime Minister during the Second World War, he was able to indulge his mania for burrowing. An underground office block had already been built in 1933 under the Treasury building at Storey's Gate. Churchill added bunkers in Curzon Street, under the Geological Museum and Faraday House, and at Dollis Hill, where the Cabinet reluctantly met. Churchill even designed a tunnelling machine – a six-foot (2-metre) turretless tank, with a steel plough on the front and a conveyer belt at the back.

There were plans to build ten deep-level shelters beneath London, but only eight were completed – at Chancery Lane and Clapham Common (emergency shelters from V1 and V2 rockets); Stockwell (a hostel for American troops); Goodge Street (Eisenhower's headquarters); and at Clapham South, Clapham North, Camden Town and Belsize Park (which the public were graciously permitted to use). The shelters were furnished with iron-frame bedsteads. You can still see some of these, converted into fencing, outside the flats opposite the Oval Underground station.

In King Charles Street you may still visit the Cabinet War Rooms, where Churchill pored over maps of the military campaigns, planned his strategies, and spoke on the telephone to President Roosevelt. He phoned Roosevelt from a small broom cupboard which was fitted with a toilet lock, so that when the PM and the President were conversing, the sign on the cupboard door showed ENGAGED.

The emergency shelters in Clapham Common serve as a temporary hostel for newly arrived West Indians, July 1948.

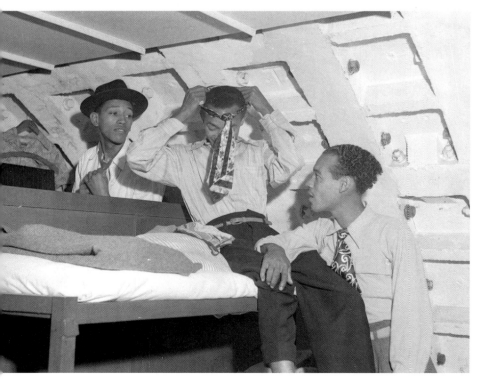

A few miles to the south are Chislehurst Caves, believed to be old Roman chalk mines. During the Second World War these were used to store many of the capital's treasures and works of art, and as a shelter for the public – a church was built underground to minister to their spiritual needs. The caves are still open to the public.

Sewers

Londoners owe a huge debt to Sir Joseph Bazalgette who saved them from floods and fever in the middle of the 19th century. In the 1850s the "Great Stink" from the Thames made it impossible for Parliament to continue its work, and the sewage and rubbish floating in the river threatened to poison or infect the entire population. As paddle steamers plied along the river, they churned up the sewage-laden silt from the river bed, exacerbating the problem. Plans were made for Parliament to move to Hampton Court and the Law Courts to Oxford or St Albans.

London was saved by Bazalgette, who designed and built the system of sewers that still removes London's waste products. It took six years to complete, serving London from Kentish Town in the north to Dulwich in the south, from Acton in the west, all leading to the main outfall at Barking in east London. It's a labyrinth of beautifully engineered tunnels of different sizes that uses gravity to shift the tons of sewage that London produces each day.

Bazalgette also supervised the construction of the Victoria, Albert and Chelsea Embankments – 3.5 miles (5.5 km) of granite protection from the danger of a rising Thames. Although few remember this son of a naval officer of French extraction, Bazalgette is one of the great heroes of London.

Londoners sheltering in the Tube during an air raid in October 1940.

Pubs at the Heart of London

Endless, and pointless, debates could be staged to define the Heart of London. To the miserly, it is the City. To the hedonist, it is the West End. Royal lobbyists would decree it is Buckingham Palace. Parliamentarians would vote for the Palace of Westminster.

To the bibulous, London's pubs are at the Heart of London, pumping a frothy life force through the veins and arteries of the capital for hundreds of years. Even those who are only occasional drinkers see their local pub as the heart of their community. Many London pubs still run their own darts teams, soccer teams, cricket teams and, increasingly, quiz teams.

There are pubs all over London which have played their own small part in its thousands of years of history. The Allsop Arms in Gloucester Place was built on the site of the entrance to the first Lord's Cricket Ground. The Baker and Oven in Paddington Street uses baking ovens that are over 100 years old. In Ladbroke Grove, the Ladbroke Arms is an 18th-century pub given to Lord Ladbroke to settle a gambling debt. Here, in more detail, are some others.

The Ship Tavern, Little Turnstile

The inside of this charming small pub near Lincoln's Inn fields is usually crammed with lawyers, but it's still worth entering to admire the heavily embossed ceiling with its patina of smoke and ale fumes. Outside there is a notice that reads:

This tavern was established in the year 1549. During the proscription of the Roman Catholic religion, it was used as a shelter for priests and services were held here secretly. The neighbourhood was once notorious for the gambling houses of Whetstone Park. Famous visitors here have been Richard Penderell, who aided King Charles's escape*; Bayford, shoemaker and antiquarian; the woman, Chevalier d'Eon, who lived as a man; and Smeaton, the builder of the first Eddystone Lighthouse. It was a centre of Freemasonry, and a lodge with the number 234 was consecrated here by the Grand Master, the Earl of Antrim, in 1786.

(*This was the escape of King Charles II after the Battle of Worcester in 1651.)

Just round the corner from the Ship is a Polish Bar, which looks very much as you would expect a Polish bar to look.

Calthorpe Arms, Gray's Inn Road

This is another small pub near the legal part of London.

Apart from being friendly and pleasant, it has two major claims to fame. It was here that the first murder of a London policeman took place. It was in 1831, a time when the police were almost universally loathed, and the coroner's jury brought in a verdict of "justifiable homicide". Over 150 years later, the Brinks Mat Robbery of 1984 was planned here.

The Silver Cross and the Clarence

Both these pubs are in Whitehall. The oldest sections of the Silver Cross date back to the 13th century and there is a preservation order on its wonderful Tudor waggon-vaulted ceiling. It was licensed as a brothel by Charles I – no doubt its occupants turned out sorrowfully on that January morning in 1649 to watch his execution just up the road. No one seems certain, but it would appear that the brothel licence has never been revoked.

The Clarence caters for a different sort of harlot. It is popular with civil servants from all the nearby government buildings. Much of the pub dates from the 18th century, and it, too, is the subject of a preservation order. Unhappily, this didn't save the gaslights – both inside and out – which disappeared when the pub was refurbished in the 1990s.

The Albert, Victoria Street

Stroll down Whitehall, round Parliament Square and into Victoria Street, and you will find the Albert, sufficiently near the Houses of Parliament to be much frequented by MPs. The upstairs restaurant has a division bell that rings whenever it's time for them to hurry back to vote. The Albert is a handsome Victorian pub that has managed to preserve its gaslights.

The Blackfriar, Queen Victoria Street

A couple of miles away to the east, just opposite Blackfriars Station, is the Blackfriar, built on the site of a Dominican monastery – you can still see a fragment of the monastery wall in Ireland Yard. The interior of this strange, wedge-shaped pub has a medieval air, though it was actually built in 1875. There are ecclesiastical columns, side chapels and friezes, but the chief glory of the Blackfriar is its wonderful Art Nouveau decoration.

Further to the east, in Boundary Street, is the Ship and Blue Ball – another pub with a criminal history. The Great Train Robbery of 1969 was planned here. A gang stopped the Glasgow-to-London mail train and stole £2.5 million. In the upstairs games room of the pub is a false wall, behind which the loot was allegedly stashed. In the 1880s, one of Jack the Ripper's victims was found on the pavement outside.

opposite:
Thank God, it's Friday. The week's work is over, and Londoners cram the local boozer.

The Origins of London

Nobody knows how old London is. There is a fable that it was founded by one Brute, a descendant of Jupiter, about a thousand years before the birth of Christ. Like all fables, it is totally untrue. Through the mists of myth other figures appear. King Lud is said to have rebuilt London long before the arrival of the Romans, making it a beautiful city called "Claire-Lud" or "Lud's Town". Hence its present name.

What we do know is that there was an Iron Age settlement near the Thames, and that the Romans established a military camp. A few years later, the fledgling Roman settlement of Londinium (on the site of the present City of London) was burnt to the ground in AD 60 by Queen Boudicca and the Iceni, in savage revenge for Roman cruelty. The excavations for the Jubilee Line extension in the late 1990s revealed Roman oil lamps and jewellery, and the scorched floors of buildings razed by Boudicca and her followers. The city was rebuilt almost immediately and became an important business and commercial centre, clustered around what is now Cornhill. Londinium was destroyed by fire in AD 125–30, but had sufficiently recovered once again by the end of the 2nd century to become the capital of Britannia Superior (southern Britain). At the height of the city's prosperity, the Roman waterfront in Londinium stretched for roughly half a mile (a kilometre) eastwards from Blackfriars, though it has to be remembered that the water level of the Thames at that time was about four yards lower than that at high tide today.

Beneath the streets, pavements and offices of the modern City lie the remains of many great Roman buildings – temples to Mithras and Isis, at least one monumental arch, the walls and mosaic floors of rich villas, the governor's palace (near modern London Wall), a Roman amphitheatre (near the Guildhall), and Roman baths in Upper Thames Street and Cheapside. Take a walk along The Strand and you are walking along the Roman road that led westwards out of Londinium. Archaeological evidence suggests that Ludgate Hill has been a place of business for 2000 years.

There is also what is known as a "Roman Bath" in Strand Lane, just to the east of Somerset House. Nobody knows whether or not this is a genuine Roman relic. It is a plunge bath of red brick, some five by two yards. It *looks* Roman, and it's certainly old, but it isn't mentioned in any history of London until 1784.

At the beginning of the 5th century AD Rome was in trouble, and the Roman garrison was withdrawn from London. The *Anglo-Saxon Chronicle* records that the army of Hengist, a Jutish freebooter and the first Saxon leader to invade Kent, slew 4000 Britons when it invaded in 457. Those Britons that survived fled in their thousands to London. Though the walls of the Roman city remained, they were ultimately no protection against barbarian invasions. By the 9th century some 3000 to 4000 Saxons were living in "Ludenwic" and the surrounding countryside – Saxon cemeteries have been discovered east of Tilbury, Essex, and in Orpington, Kent. In 842, however, the Saxons were attacked and slaugh-

left:
View from the Museum of
London of part of the old
London walls at the Barbican.
opposite:
The statue of Boudicca, Queen
of the Iceni, on the Embank-
ment at Westminster.

tered in the next wave of foreigners to hit London – the Vikings. For the next 200 years the Saxon hold on London was rarely secure, and it ended with the invasion of William of Normandy, the Conqueror, in 1066. William seized London by force and crowned himself King of England in the Abbey at Westminster. Since then, London has been lucky. It has never been captured by a foreign army, and there has been no revolution to clatter through its streets and splatter its walls with blood. Trouble and strife there have been in plenty, but almost all of it home-made.

In 1180 a monk named William Fitzstephen wrote a flattering description of London and Londoners:

> The citizens of London are universally held up for admiration and renown for the elegance of their manners and dress, and the delights of their tables… I can think of no other city with customs more admirable, in the visiting of churches, ordaining of festivals to God's honour and their due celebration, in almsgiving, in receiving guests, in concluding betrothals, contracting marriages, celebrating weddings, laying on ornate feasts and joyful occasions, and also in caring for the dead and burying them. The only plagues of London are the immoderate drinking of fools and the frequency of fires.

A fellow monk, Richard of Devizes, disagreed:

> I do not at all like that city… No one lives in it without falling into some sort of crimes. Every quarter of it abounds in great obscenities… Whatever evil or malicious thing that can be found in any part of the world, you will find in that one city… Avoid the dice and gambling, the theatre and the tavern… You will meet with more braggarts there than in all France.

Richard of Devizes (itself a pretty little town, though hardly Xanadu, and not without its own dark secrets) went on to warn his readers against the pimps, jesters, smooth-skinned lads, flatterers, pretty boys, effeminates, pederasts, singing and dancing girls, extortioners, quacks, belly-dancers, sorceresses, night-wanderers, magicians and mimes, beggars and buffoons that filled the streets of 12th-century London.

That was nearly a thousand years ago. Since then, London has been the centre of pomp and poverty, pageantry and power for the whole of Britain. It has exerted a two-way force – sucking in the hungry, ambitious, errant, greedy, talented and desperate, and throwing out great swathes of buildings and people from its hub, which occupies the same sticky clay that the Romans first built on.

Life in Shakespeare's London

above:
Edward Alleyn, actor and contemporary of Shakespeare. Later in his life, Alleyn founded Dulwich College.

In 1599 a Swiss citizen named Thomas Platter visited London, and was delighted with all he saw in this city "60,000 paces from the sea". He praised London Bridge, the ships and wherries moored at St Katharine's Dock, the salmon and sturgeon leaping in the Thames, and the buildings filling the tiny streets. It is hardly surprising that much of Platter's enthusiasm was for the river. The Thames was the principal highway of London. Its crowded wharves gave the appearance of a "wooded grove". Its banks were lined with palaces and grand houses. From the Tower to Hampton Court, the Thames was the heart of London.

But there was also much to be seen in the streets of the city. There was Goldsmith's Row, with its glittering tower and continuously playing fountain. In Fleet Street there was a dead Indian on display for any that had ten doits to spare. The Tower housed a menagerie of wild animals – as well as rebels and traitors awaiting execution. Along the middle aisle of St Paul's Cathedral, you could see the gallants and idlers meeting "in a house of talking, of brawling, of minstrelsy, of hawks, and of dogs". On the tombs and monuments, shopkeepers set out piles of goods for sale. For a penny, you could climb to the top of the cathedral tower, and see the finest view of London obtainable. Outside, in the churchyard, was London's book market, where you could buy the "merry books" of Italy.

This was the town that attracted a young man from Stratford-on-Avon. Shakespeare came to London in 1585 and got a job at either the Curtain or the Theatre. By 1592, Shakespeare was both a playwright and a member of the Lord Chamberlain's Company of actors, though the year itself was a lean one as all the theatres were closed by an outbreak of the plague. Six years later, Shakespeare was rich enough to become a partner in the new Globe Theatre, then being built on Bankside. In 1608 he also bought a share in the Blackfriars Theatre. He spent most of the rest of his life in London.

It was a city bustling with life. One of Shakespeare's contemporaries was John Stow, whose great *Survey of London* was published in 1598. In his long life, Stow had seen the population of London more than treble, from 75,000 to 250,000. He had seen plague, pestilence, Protestant martyrs burnt by a Catholic queen and Catholic martyrs burnt by a Protestant queen, beggars and knaves, constables and watchmen, bull-baiting and cock-fighting. He had walked through streets jammed with drays, carts and coaches, bringing to the city apples and cabbages, barley and timber, salt, bricks, cloth, rushes and a hundred other essentials of life.

> In every street, carts and coaches make such a thundering as if the world ran upon wheels: at every corner, men, women and children meet in such shoals, that posts are set up of purpose to strengthen the houses, lest with jostling one another they should shoulder them down. Besides, hammers are beating in one place, tubs hooping in another, pots clinking in a third, water-tankards running at tilt in a fourth. Here are porters sweating under burdens, there merchant's men bearing bags of money. Chapmen* (as if they were at leap frog) skip out of one shop into another. Tradesmen (as if they were dancing galliards**) are lusty at legs and never stand still. All are as busy as country attorneys at an assizes…
>
> **Thomas Dekker**, *The Seven Deadly Sins of London*, c.1600

*Chapmen were hawkers and pedlars
**A galliard was a lively dance in triple time

Bear-Baiting and Cock-Fighting

The national sport of England in Shakespeare's time was bear-baiting. Queen Elizabeth herself much enjoyed this "sweet and comfortable recreation". On Sundays and holidays, crowds forsook the dicing-houses, theatres and brothels of Southwark to gather at the Paris Gardens.

Here, at the bear garden, they witnessed a spectacle that betrays much of the roistering brutality of the age. A bear was chained to a post, and a pack of mastiffs was urged to attack it. The nimbleness of the dogs, but much more the "biting, clawing, roaring, tugging, grasping, tossing and tumbling of the bear" delighted the crowds. The suffering of the animals was appalling.

For the poor, cock-fighting was more accessible and more popular. Everyone knew the outcome of bear-baiting – the bear was eventually killed. No one could tell which cock would win a fight, so there was ample opportunity for wagering. The most famous cockpits were to be found in Lewin Street or at St Giles-in-the-Fields, just beyond the City walls, but Shakespeare is more likely to have visited the Cock Pit on St Andrew's Hill, near Puddle Dock. There is still a pub called the Cockpit on the site.

A Shakespearian Setting

Middle Temple Hall is worth a visit in its own right, to see its wonderful oak double-hammerbeam roof. But it has a special place in Shakespeare's London as the setting for the first ever performance of *Twelfth Night*.

above:
Middle Temple Hall.
opposite bottom:
Bear baiting in London, circa 1600. The bear has just broken its chain, thereby causing panic.

The London of Samuel Pepys

Samuel Pepys was born in 1633 at Salisbury Court, off Fleet Street, the son of a City tailor. He went to St Paul's School and lived almost all the 70 years of his life in London. His ambition was to be a lawyer, but he became a civil servant whose fortunes rose and fell with changes of government and monarch. In 1655 he married Elizabeth St Michel, the 15-year-old daughter of a Huguenot refugee. The marriage was not a happy one. Elizabeth was upset by his philandering, Pepys was infuriated by her untidiness and mismanagement of money. The couple parted more than once. Elizabeth died, childless, in 1669.

In 1679 Pepys fell from grace professionally when he was accused of involvement in the Popish Plot, which supposedly aimed to murder Charles II and place his Catholic brother James on the throne. For six weeks Pepys was locked up in the Tower, accused of treason. He was released and went to live in Buckingham Street, to the east of Charing Cross. Here he amassed a library of 3000 books and spent much of his time conversing with a circle of friends that included John Evelyn, Isaac Newton and Christopher Wren. In 1701 he moved to rural Clapham, where he died on 26 May 1703.

Pepys's Diary

From 1660 to 1669, Pepys kept a journal of everyday life and the dramas of London. He wrote in shorthand, filling six large leather-covered volumes. The diary is a vivid portrait of mid 17th-century London – life at Court, debates in Parliament, visits to the theatre and concerts, outings on the river, the weathering of the body of a highwayman on a gibbet at Shooters Hill, troubles with servants, encounters with harlots, meals and shopping expeditions. The details and the variety of events recorded by Pepys are the diary's greatest strengths.

Pepys and his wife in the 1660s. 'My wife this day put on her first French gown, called a sac...'

We learn that Charles II was a keen tennis player (who weighed himself after each game to see how much weight he had lost) and an amateur scientist, that the Duke of York (later James II) had much to say on the subject of cooking sauces, and that the Lord Chancellor frequently snored during meetings of the Privy Council. Pepys gives the menu for a "very fine dinner" provided by his wife: "A dish of marrow bones; a leg of mutton; a loin of veal; a dish of fowls; three pullets and two dozen of larks, all in a dish; a great tart; a neat's tongue; a dish of anchovies; a dish of prawns, and cheese." He describes the horrors of the Plague and the Great Fire. He records an outing to the Tower to see the lions there, and another to Charing Cross to see Major-General Harrison hanged, drawn and quartered for his part in the execution of Charles I – "he looking as cheerful as any man could do in that condition". The diary's last entry is for 31 May 1669:

> And thus ends all that I doubt I shall ever be able to do with my own eyes in the keeping of my journall, I being not able to do it any longer, having done now so long as to undo my eyes almost every time that I take a pen in my hand... for the discomforts that will accompany my being blind, the good God prepare me.

John Evelyn

Evelyn was born in Dorking, Surrey, in 1620, and first came to London in 1640 to study law at Middle Temple. On the outbreak of the Civil War, he joined the King's army, but after three days left for Paris where he married Mary Browne, daughter of the British ambassador. He returned to London after the war and settled at Sayes Court, Deptford, near the Royal Naval Dockyard. Here he lived for 42 years, before moving back to Surrey and letting Sayes Court to Peter the Great, who "wantonly desecrated" the fine house before moving to Westminster and living two doors away from Pepys. Evelyn died in 1706.

Evelyn's Diary

Evelyn kept a journal from 1641 to his death. Like Pepys, Evelyn witnessed many extraordinary events, from Cromwell's funeral and the Restoration of Charles II to the freezing of the river in January 1684 and the death of a whale that had blundered up the Thames in June 1658:

> It appeared first below Greenwich at low water, for at high water it would have destroyed all the boats, but lying now in shallow water encom-

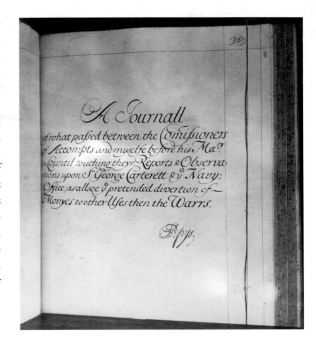

The title page of one of Pepys's Journals. It was discovered in 1935 at Magdalene College, Cambridge.

passed with boats, after a long conflict it was killed with a harping iron struck in the head, out of which spouted blood and water by two tunnels, and after an horrid groan it ran quite on shore and died.

They were exciting days. Evelyn saw the remains of Cromwell, Ireton and Bradshaw dragged from their tombs in Westminster Abbey and taken to Tyburn to be hanged – "fear God and honour the King; but meddle not with those who are given to change!" was the moral he drew from this bizarre spectacle. Evelyn had a wonderful eye for detail – meetings of the Royal Society, a visit to the Savoy Hospital, an outing to a bear garden "to see cock-fighting, dog-fighting, beare and bull-baiting, it being a famous day for all these butcherly sports". He added that he was "heartily weary of the rude and dirty pastime".

The diary was a private journal, and Evelyn made no attempt to publish it during his lifetime. No one knew of its existence until the diary was found in a laundry-basket in Evelyn's Surrey home in 1818, well over 100 years after his death.

The Golden Age of London

Lovers of London pluck a host of golden ages from the city's history. To some the finest hour was Elizabethan London – the glories of the court at Richmond or Nonesuch, the Queen knighting Francis Drake at Tilbury after his voyage round the world, Shakespeare scribbling away while his brand-new dramas were performed at the Bear or the Rose, the stately procession of barges and a thousand other boats up and down the Thames.

To others, London was at its best in the mid-18th century – the London of beautiful houses, of science and art, when the wealth of the rapidly expanding empire poured in from India and North America, when the countryside was still a short walk from the very heart of the city, and the air around was pure and clean.

There are even those for whom the 1930s represent a golden age – the last fling of the old-established families before income tax and death duties ate into their fortunes. The West End was at its most magnificent. In the evening the lights blazed, offering the choice of opera, ballet, theatres, cinemas, music halls, concerts, palaces of variety. Through the night, right up to the dawn, there were clubs where you could foxtrot to the best dance bands Britain has ever produced – Roy Fox, Lew Stone, Harry Roy, Bert Firman and dozens more. At the holy of holies, the Embassy Club in Old Bond Street, you could dance to the music of Ambrose, and possibly bump into the Prince of Wales, or at least someone who had danced with him.

Some of us find it difficult to visualize any Golden Age that includes capital punishment and doesn't include modern dentistry. Nevertheless, here are two glimpses of London's past glories – one from the 19th and one from the 20th century.

Regency London

For most of the period called "Regency", 1800 to 1820, England was at war with Napoleon, not that the hostilities did anything to weaken the delights of London. If anything, life there seemed more brilliant than ever, with gentlemen riding and marching about town in gorgeous

above:
Early 19th century fun, fat and frivolity in Covent Garden.
right:
Flappers and cocktails at the bar of Isa Lanchester's night club, 1925.

uniforms. And they did so against the backdrop of some of the finest architecture ever seen – the new buildings and developments of Regent Street, Piccadilly Circus, Waterloo Place and Regent's Park. Behind the elegant façades of these handsome houses were rooms furnished to perfection, and tables laid with the finest Regency silverware. It was the age when liveried footmen opened doors, waited at table, fetched and carried.

It was also a time when London's literary life was at its richest. On the shelves of Lackington Allen and Co., Booksellers of Finsbury Square, were to be found the latest writings of Keats, Scott, Lamb, de Quincy, Byron, Shelley and Coleridge. It was at Regency London that Wordsworth gazed when he composed his Sonnet upon Westminster Bridge in "the beauty of the morning" of 3 September 1802.

A dozen famous painters of fashionable portraits were ready with brush and canvas to do more than justice to the rich and famous. You had merely to choose amongst names such as Lawrence, Wilkie, Etty, Haydon, Phillips or one of their protégés. Once it was completed, society would flock to see your likeness on display in the Exhibition Room at Somerset House, or in the Royal Academy in Piccadilly. And, once in Piccadilly, it was but a step to Mr Bullock's Museum, a collection of weapons and armour, stuffed animals, curiosities and antiquities described as "one of the most refined, rational and interesting exhibitions the metropolis ever witnessed".

There were such novelties to be seen – the Elgin Marbles at the British Museum, the Chinese Pagoda in St James's Park, the Regent's Canal, the three new bridges over the Thames (at Vauxhall, Waterloo and Southwark), the Conservatory at Carlton House (newly opened to the public), and the magnificently rebuilt Covent Garden Theatre.

Small wonder that Sydney Smith wrote of Regency London: "I believe the parallelogram between Oxford Street, Piccadilly, Regent Street and Hyde Park, encloses more intelligence and human ability, to say nothing of wealth and beauty, than the world has ever collected in such a space before."

Edwardian London

It was nicknamed "Cockaigne", the legendary abode of luxury and idleness, and it lasted from 1901 to the outbreak of war – or, strictly, to 1910 when Edward VII died. It was a London of splendour and jollity, capital of what was still the greatest empire the world had ever known, 11.5 million square miles. It was the city of Kipling and Elgar, John Singer Sargent and George Bernard Shaw,

WATERLOO PLACE, & PART OF REGENT STREET.

All part of John Nash's design to make London the capital of Europe – Waterloo Place, circa 1820.

the London Symphony Orchestra and the Olympic Games. It was the biggest city in the world, with a population of 4.5 million.

The buildings of Edwardian London were huge, monumental, the last to suggest the power and solidity of traditional values. They encircled Trafalgar Square, stamped all the way down Whitehall, covered acres of the West End and Kingsway, and lined the route from Hyde Park Corner to Victoria. They were offices, houses, department stores, the meeting-places of government ministers, the settings for fancy-dress balls.

Never before such joys and delights – cigarettes, horseless carriages, frivolous theatrical performances, knighthoods and peerages for sale, and a king who set a disgraceful example when it came to morality. Edward had a whole string of mistresses, dubbed by Queen Alexandra "his toys". And, again, there were such fascinating novelties – the Franco-British Exhibition at Shepherd's Bush, balloon races at Hurlingham, the new Gaiety Theatre, the Waldorf Hotel with its amazing electric lights and modern bathrooms, the London Opera House in Kingsway.

Silks rustled, top hats gleamed, the Docks burst with the fruit of lands far away, the summers were hot and lengthy. The sense of duty that had stifled much of life in Victorian London had lifted. Many shared Winston Churchill's glee at Edward's accession to the throne in 1901, after more than 60 years of his mother's reign: "Gadzooks, I am glad he has got his innings."

The London of Charles Dickens

Dickens had a love-hate affair with London. It certainly supplied him with a wealth of material: "What inexhaustible food for speculation do the streets of London afford!" he wrote as a young man. His most memorable characters were drawn from London life – potmen, ostlers, servants, pickpockets, lawyers, doctors, ne'er-do-wells, vagabonds. And the majority of the most memorable scenes in Dickens's novels are set in London – the Fleet Prison, the railway excavations at Camden Town, the George and Vulture in Southwark, Jacob's Island, the Old Curiosity Shop and a hundred more.

But it's arguable that he didn't really like London, which he once described as "shabby by daylight and shabbier by gaslight". Several of his early experiences in the city were unpleasant. He got lost as a child in The Strand. His father was imprisoned in the Marshalsea. He was sent to work in a blacking factory at Hungerford Stairs (on the site of Charing Cross station). Overall, his childhood in London seems to have been every bit as bad as that of David Copperfield.

In his novels, Dickens gives London and Londoners a highly dramatic colouring – the Saffron Hill of *Oliver Twist*, Salem House in *Nicholas Nickleby*, the fogs creeping up from the river in *Bleak House*, the London traders in *David Copperfield*, the too delightful Weller family in *The Pickwick Papers*. The pictures he paints are unforgettable, but they are often exaggerated. A more balanced account of London is to be found in his journalistic works, in his articles for *Household Words* and *The Morning Chronicle*, in *The Uncommercial Traveller* and *All the Year Round*.

Here he records everyday life as he saw it, roaming the streets of London by day and night, notebook at the ready, eyes missing little, the mind constantly alive. Dickens was a bold reporter, prepared to visit the most unsavoury parts of a city that was then a frightening and uncomfortable place to live in for the majority of its inhabitants. He describes everything from Scotland Yard to Newgate Prison, from Astley's Amphitheatre ("delightful, splendid and surprising") to the Wapping Workhouse ("a building most monstrously behind the time"). He went to Greenwich Fair ("a three days' fever which cools the blood for six months afterwards") and the gin-shops of St Giles, Holborn and Covent Garden ("there is more filth and squalid misery near those great thoroughfares than in any part of this mighty city").

He met footmen, criminals, the Lumpers who unloaded ships' cargoes in the river, fishmongers, chimney sweeps, turncocks (officials from the waterworks who turned on the water supply), beadles and the landladies of commercial lodging houses ("bed and breakfast, with meat, two and ninepence [13p] per day, including servants"). He went on night patrol with Inspector Field, to an inquest in a parish workhouse, to the cheapest theatres, where he sat in the cheapest seats. He saw "miserable children in rags… like young rats, slunk and hid, fed on offal, huddled together for warmth." London may have frightened him, but it certainly fascinated him.

What Remains of Dickens's London

Much of the city that Dickens knew has disappeared, but a surprising amount remains. The Dickens House Museum is at 48 Doughty Street, a step or two from Gray's Inn Road. Dickens moved to this house with his wife and young baby in 1837, and wrote part of *The Pickwick Papers* and *Nicholas Nickleby* and all of *Oliver Twist* here. In those days it was "a genteel private street with a lodge at each end and gates that were closed at night by a porter in a gold-laced hat and a mulberry-coloured coat with the Doughty arms on its buttons". The Museum contains many Dickens relics – letters, first editions, furniture, personal belongings, and illustrations from his novels. Not far away, near the bottom of Gray's Inn Road, is No. 1 South Square, where the 15-year-old Dickens worked as a clerk to the solicitors Ellis and Blackmore. No. 2 – which has been demolished and rebuilt – was the home of Tommy Traddles in *Nicholas Nickleby*.

The Strand and Fleet Street are rich in associations with Dickens. While David Copperfield was living in Buckingham Street, south of The Strand, he met Peggotty anxiously searching for Little Em'ly on the steps of St Martin's Church, Trafalgar Square. To the north of The Strand is Maiden Lane, where you will find Rules Restaurant, patronized by Dickens. Further along The Strand is Somerset House, where Dickens's father worked as a Navy pay clerk. A little to the east you come across Strand Lane and the Roman Baths where David Copperfield bathed. Just to the south of Fleet Street is Hanging Sword Alley, home of Jerry Cruncher in *A Tale of Two Cities*. On the north side of Fleet Street is St Dunstan's Church, whose clock fascinated Dickens as a child, and not far away is the Cheshire Cheese, described but not named in *A Tale of Two Cities*.

If you are prepared to do a little searching, you can still find the iron-barred windows at the back of the Mansion House in the City, where a very young Dickens peered in, only to be told by one of the cooks "Cut away, you sir!" Across the river, in Angel Court off the Borough High Street, are all that remains of the old Marshalsea Prison – the paving slabs. In Greenwich you can still eat whitebait dinners at the Trafalgar, as Dickens did, and in Limehouse you can drink at the Grapes, known as the Six Jolly Porters in *Our Mutual Friend*. At Wapping there is the headquarters of the river police, where Dickens came ashore after spending a night in a patrol boat on the river that to Dickens seemed "such an image of death in the midst of a great city's life". Some of Dickens's old haunts remain, but not in a guise that he would recognize. It's difficult to associate today's Brick Lane with the Reverend Stiggins, friend and minister to Mrs Weller in *The Pickwick Papers*. You need the imagination of Dickens himself to make that mental leap.

left:
Nicholas Hawksmoor's beautiful church of St Anne, Limehouse.
below:
Limehouse Cut, opened in September 1770.

The Great Exhibition of 1851

London in 1851

It was one of the most optimistic times in London's history. The young Queen Victoria was popular. The London mob was quiet. England was in the first phase of a period of immense prosperity. Income tax was 3d (1.25p) in the pound, God was in his heaven, and all seemed right with those bits of the world that mattered (the British Empire). So it was reckoned the right time to stage the Great Exhibition of the Works of Industry of All Nations – primarily to show that Britain led the rest of the world in all things.

Plans for the Great Exhibition

The three men most credited with both the idea and its success of the exhibition are Prince Albert, Joseph Paxton and Henry Cole.

Cole was a man of many interests. He helped establish the Penny Post, published the first-ever Christmas card, reformed the Patent Laws, wrote children's books, and was a music critic, painter and etcher.

Prince Albert was the Queen's Consort, a person of wide learning, an "ideas man". The Queen adored him. The public had grudgingly come round to admiring him. *The Times* was more reserved, warning Londoners that "the whole of Hyde Park and of Kensington Gardens will be turned into a bivouac of all the vagabonds in London".

Joseph Paxton had started life as a gardener at Chats-

worth, working for the Duke of Devonshire. The Duke had taken a liking to him and had steadily promoted Paxton to the position of estate manager. Paxton built a Great Conservatory in the grounds of Chatsworth, covering an acre of ground, and a Lily House, which was to become the inspiration for the Crystal Palace.

In the Lily House, Paxton planted a seedling of Victoria regia – its leaves then only six inches (15 cm) in diameter. Three months later they were four feet (1.20 metres) across. Paxton noticed that the skeleton of each leaf was strong enough to bear the weight of his seven-year-old daughter Anna.

He came to London, walked round the exhibition site in Hyde Park, and within a week had produced a full set of plans for the Crystal Palace.

Building the Exhibition

During August and September 1850, gangs of workmen levelled the site and laid the concrete foundations. Progress was astoundingly swift. All the components were pre-fabricated, standardized, and in many cases interchangeable. Without scaffolding, the average gang of workers could raise three columns and bolt them together with girders in just 16 minutes. Eighty glaziers fitted 18,000 panes of glass a week, and sealed them in position with putty.

Once the 18 acres (7.28 ha) of roof was fixed, work started on the interior. "All manner of operations seemed going on at once; sawing, planing, glazing, painting, hammering, boarding… machines guiding gutters through a trough of paint… and then through an aperture with brushes, which turned them out at the other side all trimly coated."

And all was ready and prepared for the Royal Opening on 1 May 1851.

The Exhibition through Contemporary Eyes

The Queen spent hours at the exhibition on Opening Day, and wrote pages and pages in her journal about it:

> We saw printing machines, by which numbers of sheets are printed in a second… machines for purifying sugar… a very curious machine for making chocolate; a very ingenious one for making cigarettes and wrapping them in paper… a most ingenious contrivance for transferring mailbags on railways… a very clever patent soda-water machine by which soda water can be made in incredibly short time merely with gas…

The *Giornale di Roma* was much impressed by one particular machine

You stop before a small brass machine… you fancy it is a meat roaster: not at all. Ha! Ha! It is a tailor… Present a piece of cloth to it… it twists about, screams audibly – a pair of scissors are projected forth – the cloth is cut; a needle sets to work, and lo and behold, the process of sewing goes on with a feverish activity, and before you have taken three steps, a pair of *inexpressibles* are thrown down at your feet…

Other visitors were fascinated by the Koh-i-Noor diamond, by a fountain of *Eau de Cologne*, by a collapsible piano for gentlemen's yachts, an expanding hearse, a six-pounder gun from Krupps of Essen, a single lump of gold from Chile weighing three hundredweight (153 kilos), and by Count Dunin's "Man of Steel" – a manikin made of 7000 pieces that could expand from the size of a dwarf to that of a giant, though no one had the slightest idea what use could be made of it.

The Exhibition closed on 15 October. It had been open for just five and a half months and 6,201,856 visitors had between them paid £356,000 in entrance money. Prince Albert was already planning what to do with the profit it had made.

The Kensington Complex

The Exhibition had made £186,000. Prince Albert and the Commissioners used the bulk of this money to buy 87 acres (35 ha) of land to the south of Kensington Road. Here they built a unique complex of buildings devoted to science and the arts.

There were those who scoffed and christened the area "Albertopolis", but a century and a half later this campus of culture still stands. Along with various seats of learning and, of course, the Royal Albert Hall, there are three outstanding museums: the Natural History, the Science, and the Victoria and Albert.

The Crystal Palace in all its glory during the Great Exhibition of 1851.

The Natural History Museum

The Natural History Museum is a glorious terracotta and pale blue building in Cromwell Road. It is one of several places of learning and study in South Kensington, built from the profits of the Great Exhibition of 1851. The design of the new museum was thrown open to public competition, which was won by Captain Francis Fowke. But Captain Fowke died before he could complete his drawings, and the commission was then offered to Alfred Waterhouse. It's his building, completed in 1881, that we see today. From the outside, it looks like a cross between a warm-hearted Victorian public school (if such a thing could ever have existed) and a Byzantine railway station. It's huge, stretching for some 300 yards along the front, with a main entrance that can gobble up visitors by the coachload.

The moment you enter, you realize you are in a cathedral of learning and excitement. Before you have even paid your entrance fee, the skeleton of *Diplodocus* is hanging over you, bidding you a cadaverous welcome. Ahead lies the vast Central Hall, with side galleries devoted to more dinosaurs, human biology, mammals, snakes and other reptiles, and the giants of the oceans. It's worth a visit simply to goggle at the reconstruction of a blue whale, the Boeing 707 of the deep, dwarfing the

above:
One of the delights of Albertopolis – the Natural History Museum, South Kensington.
right:
One of the many dinosaur fossils at the Museum.

stuffed hippopotamus that stands beneath it, and making the human visitors seem mere scurrying ants.

There are cases of butterflies, pieces of extinct sloth, a half skeleton of *Baryonyx* that roamed Surrey 125 million years ago, stuffed crocodiles and alligators, sabre-toothed tigers, polar and grizzly bears, giant pandas, cats and dogs of all shapes and sizes. The Human Biology section is very much a hands-on exhibition, and you can recoup a little of the entrance fee by weighing yourself without charge. Here you can spend a great deal of time discovering yourself, and being alternately delighted and a little worried at what you find.

Upstairs there is a permanent exhibition in celebration of the work of Charles Darwin. This includes some surprises – a display of leeks, onions, mushrooms and toadstools, as well as the better-known inhabitants of the Galapagos Islands. There's also a charming small display to commemorate the surprising morning in 1741 when Peter Collinson discovered a rogue nectarine growing on a peach tree in his London garden.

It's a busy, bustling museum, full of children in both holiday and term-time. But you should pause awhile to admire the interior of the building itself, every bit as impressive as the exhibits. The entrance hall soars up to a magnificent ceiling, with splendid Romanesque arches on either side, and wide, smooth, stately staircases. There are statues of famous naturalists dotted about the museum – of Joseph Banks (who accompanied Captain Cook as ship's botanist on his voyage round the world), of Richard Owen (first director of the museum, in the days when it was just a part of the British Museum), and of Captain Frederick C. Selous. Selous was a hunter, explorer and naturalist who was born in the year of the Great Exhibition, and who was killed in action at Beho-Beho in German East Africa on 4 January 1917.

On the first floor there are displays of fossils, gems, elements, meteorites. There are specimens from the frozen Antarctic and the burning African deserts. And at

to pay more than one visit. But even a complete tour encompasses only a small proportion of its work. The Natural History Museum is a vast data-bank of information on Zoology, Entomology, Palaeontology, Botany and Mineralogy. Behind the doors labelled "Staff Only" there are scientists working away to preserve, protect and explore every aspect of the natural world – from awesome chunks of meteorite to the tiniest bird. It is as much research institution as popular showplace, with specialist libraries of maps, reference works, manuscripts and drawings.

The variety of the exhibits is staggering. In one of the museum's galleries there is a beautiful, glass-fronted wooden cabinet filled with stuffed birds. They are all on display with their feathers puffed out and their beaks thrust forward, so that they look like a mighty thorn bush. There is a very popular section that deals with Myths and Monsters, where you can discover the origins of our ancestors' belief in the existence

above:
Beasts of past, present and mythology decorate the Museum.
left:
The skeleton of diplodocus in the entrance hall.

One of the decorative friezes round the arches of the Alfred Waterhouse's beautiful building.

the top of the stairs leading to the second floor, there is a monstrous slice of a giant sequoia from the Sierra Nevada, California. The tree from which it was taken started life as a sapling in AD 557, when St Columba founded his mission on Iona, and was felled 1335 years later for the 1892 World's Fair in Chicago. It took nine men 12 days to fell it. The death of such a tree is a sad event, but the trophy in the Natural History Museum takes the breath away.

It's a large museum, over 24,000 square yards (20,000 square metres), so to do it justice you will need

of dragons. And leading to the Exhibition Road exit, there are the Earth Galleries – echoing halls with crystalline hemispheres surmounted by statues of the giants and monsters of mythology. Here, while the sound of thunder rolls around you, you will see Cyclops, Atlas and the Medusa.

A Bank of Knowledge – the Science Museum, Exhibition Road, SW7.

The Science Museum

Like its neighbours, the Victoria and Albert and the Natural History Museum, the Science Museum in Exhibition Road, South Kensington, was created out of the profits that accrued from the Great Exhibition of 1851. It's a solid, imposing building – grand, columned, heavy, seemingly indestructible, a little like the New York Post Office. It is a monumental piece of London's Imperial Age architecture, opened by George V in 1929.

When you enter, you find yourself immediately in a hall devoted to the vast engines of power of the late 18th and early 19th centuries. These are the steam-operated monsters that pumped the mines dry, turned huge driving wheels, breathed life into the factories of the new Industrial Revolution. And here they are, still alive and gently hissing. There's Old Bess, a single-action pumping machine of Boulton and Watt from 1777; a mill engine from the Burnley Ironworks of 1903 in beautiful scarlet and silver, black and brass; and a bright green triple-expansion marine engine that used to power the SY *Glen Strathallan*, made in Hull in 1928.

Move on into the next gallery and you plunge into the Space Age. It's a large room devoted to rocket propulsion from Congreve's Rocket to the present day.

Congreve designed a military rocket that it was hoped would strike fear into the hearts of the armies of Napoleon. It didn't, but from such tiny beginnings grew the exploration of space. In the museum you will find the Command Module from Apollo 10, and a replica of Apollo 11's Lunar Excursion Module (all wrapped up in silver foil and looking as though it's ready for a couple of hours in the oven). There's also the Black Arrow – Britain's first and only satellite launch vehicle – and a tiny British message-carrying rocket of 1920. It was used to send express mail, but was not a commercial success.

Pass the Benz motor-car of 1888, the cutaway 1959 Mini, and the Panhard et Lavasseur of 1895 (a survivor of the first-ever London to Brighton Old Crocks run), and you come to the Science of Sport Hall.

This is a hands-on (and feet-on) exhibition, where you can work the different parts of your body and see what happens when you do. You may discover whether your muscles are creaky, stretchy or rubbery. You can test how quickly you react to protect your head, your eyes, your whole body. There are machines that test your skill at tennis, athletics, golf, basketball. There is a simulator that assesses how good you would be as a Grand Prix driver. One lap of the Sports Hall and you will know better than ever before what sport you have a natural aptitude for.

In the basement there is a comprehensive and fascinating display of hundreds of items of domestic equipment: radios, tape recorders, TV sets – there's a Baird 1929 set that looks more like something James Watt might have engineered. There are power tools, vacuum cleaners, switches and plugs, lights and fans, locks and bolts, lavatory pans and cisterns. There are cookers and washing machines, fridges and gas fires, hair-dryers that look like blow-torches and wonderful gas ovens from the 1920s that look as though they were creations of Georges Meliès. Imagine the joys and terrors of the gas-heated bath tub of 1871, the dangers of the electric fires from before the First World War.

Take the space-age lifts to the first floor. Here you will find all manner of measuring instruments – barometers and anemometers, early radar machines, telescopes and pedometers, water clocks and thermometers, Chinese clock towers and sundials from Saxon times, astronomical clocks and the ancient clock from Wells Cathedral – it looks more like a threshing machine.

There's also a static exhibition showing the amount of food eaten by a woman in her twenties and a teenage boy in a month. A chart shows what that intake pro-

duced by way of growth in the body, including hair and nails. Then, by the side, there are four large plastic containers to show what the body produced during that month in the way of sweat, water from the lungs, faeces and urine – and all sponsored by Sainsbury's plc.

This is not a silent place, though there is a quiet section devoted to the typewriter, the talking clock and the microphone. Back in the main galleries, however, you come across the excitement and furore of a collection of machines where children are encouraged to experiment with friction, balancing blocks, pumps, two-way mirrors and much more. It's a weird and wonderful museum because what you are really seeing is the guts of machines old and new – what it is that enables a machine to do its job. You are face to face with those parts of machines that only the expert, the bold or the careless normally invade.

A special section on this floor is devoted to the work of Charles Babbage, who spent much of his life pioneering the first calculating machine. It was hard work, and at one point, in 1821, Babbage cried out "I wish to God these calculations had been executed by steam." But steam was of little help to him, and the exhibition shows how close Babbage came to making his dream come true.

If you have time, make sure you visit a little side room on the second floor to admire the presentation clock and barometer made by Elkington of Birmingham for the Buenos Aires Western Railway Company in 1906. Nearby is the gallery devoted to the production of petroleum – all you need to make petrol and the infamous Ford Edsel.

For those who seek the romance of the early days of flight, there is a wonderful gallery on the third floor, full of tri-planes, bi-planes and the brave little beasts that first flew the skies of the world. Here are flying machines from Lilienthal's moth-like glider to the vertical take-off jets of the 1970s. There's a Spitfire and a Hurricane from the 1940s, a tiny Messerschmidt 163 B-1 Comet of 1944 (the only rocket-propelled fighter to have been used in operational service). You can see the Vickers Vimy in which Alcock and Brown made the first non-stop flight across the Atlantic in 1919, and the de Havilland Moth "Jason" of 1928 in which Amy Johnson flew from England to Australia. The whole gallery is the perfect mixture of dreams and science.

Children at work in the user-friendly galleries of the Museum.

The Victoria and Albert Museum

Popularly known as the V and A, the Victoria and Albert Museum is in Cromwell Road, at the heart of Albertopolis in South Kensington. The original V and A was an ugly building of corrugated sheet-iron, cast-iron and glass, erected in 1857 and christened the "Brompton Boilers". In the 1870s this monstrosity was moved to the East End, where it is now the Bethnal Green Museum of Childhood – thus do the rich hand their unwanted items in charitable benevolence to the poor.

Start your visit to the V and A in the central courtyard garden. Wear sunglasses if the day is bright, or your eyes will have difficulty adjusting to the darkness of the interior. Here, in the courtyard, you may sip your coffee and take stock of your surroundings – the coffee comes in polystyrene cups but there is excellent organic ice cream and sorbets. This perspective will allow you to admire the architecture of Alfred Waterhouse's fine building. It is the exhibition house of the Albert Hall – the same brick, the same decoration, the same ornate and charming rag-bag of architecture. This is late-flowering Victorian London at its most assured.

It's a large museum. It's quite impossible to see even a quarter of what the V and A has to offer on a single visit. You will have your own favourites – from the Italian Renaissance, from China, from the medieval Treasury, from 18th-century Europe. There are galleries devoted to stained glass, costume jewellery, textiles, tapestries, sculpture, carvings and paintings.

But, whatever your predilections, that are some galleries that all should visit. On the same level as the courtyard is the Dress Gallery, with a beautiful range of fashion from a woman's embroidered jacket of the early 16th century to Dior's New Look of the late 1940s. There are beautiful evening and day dresses from Victorian and Edwardian times, a staggering Worth tea gown, dresses and gowns from the 1930s that look as though they are waiting for Ginger Rogers to slip into them and hit some ghostly dance floor. There are the outrageous eccentricities from the 18th century – dresses which made women look as though they were emerging, Venus-like, from giant tea-cosies. There are cabinets of bustles and crinolines, Regency dresses and mantles and a plethora of hats.

Pass through the Dress Gallery and into the long corridor that leads to the treasures of Asia. If the carvings and carpets from India are not to your taste, don't despair. In a corner of the largest gallery of the India section, you will find "Tippoo's Tiger" – a life-size automaton of carved and painted wood depicting a tiger devouring a prostrate European. The operator turned a handle which brought the toy to life and worked a small organ – the keyboard is visible in the tiger's flank. The automaton was built in Mysore in 1790, and fell into British hands after the defeat of Tipu Sultan at the battle of Seringapatam.

On through the Chinese, Korean and Japanese galleries to the wonderful Cast Courts – collections of plaster casts of tomb effigies, statues, altarpieces, monuments, the pulpit of Pisa Cathedral, the central doorway of the church of San Petronio, Bologna, and, most splendid of all, Trajan's Column of AD 123 from Rome. In many cases these plaster casts are in finer condition than the originals. The actual Trajan's Column, for example, has been dreadfully corroded by exhaust fumes since the cast was made in the 1870s. There is also a plaster cast of Michelangelo's David, and you can search for the fig-leaf (exhibited separately) which a Victorian custodian insisted should protect David's modesty.

Behind the Cast Courts is the Canon Photographic Gallery, a collection that starts with early Victorian albumen prints, including one of Henry Cole – first director of the V and A – in the garden of Gore House in 1854. Next to it is a delicately beautiful daguerreotype of Parliament Street from Trafalgar Square in 1839. There are also examples of Eadweard Muybridge's *Animal Locomotion* of 1887, of the work of Man Ray, Bill Brandt, David Bailey and other famous photographers, and there is Helen Chadwick's *The Oval Court* of 1986.

Back through the Dress Gallery and up a level to the Musical Instruments Gallery – you will see a large double bass over the staircase. Here you will find recorders and oboes, natural horns, harps and lyres, barytons and hurdy-gurdys, barrel organs and bird organs, viols and violins, guitars, citterns, lutes and mandores. The bulk of the collection, however, is of very early keyboard instruments – harpsichords, spinets, virginals, positive organs, dulcimers, clavichords, square pianos and chitarrones.

Up just another 14 steps and you come to the gallery devoted to ironwork – lampholders and firebacks, forks and smoothing irons, brackets and candlesticks, balusters and table-legs, railings and gates, tradesmen's signs, fire-dogs and fire surrounds. It's a swirling, scrolling celebration of the metal that the Victorians knew how to use better than any of us.

Gothic London

A masterpiece of Victorian Gothic – St Luke's Church, Sydney Street, Chelsea.

bottom right:
The Prudential Insurance building, Holborn.
below:
Detail from the front of St Pancras Station.

The older suburbs of London are full of dark corners. On nights when the moon is obscured by cloud or the mist rises from the ground, there are places that strike a chill to the heart – cemeteries, churchyards, derelict old houses, abandoned wharves and warehouses, ill-lit alleys. This is Gothic London, the London that is often neglected and seldom appreciated. For well over 100 years the Victorian attempts to revive Gothic architecture have been derided, sneered at and aesthetically condemned. Those with an open mind and open eyes, however, will find much of beauty in the churches, offices and railway stations of the Gothic Revival.

One of the earliest examples of Gothic revival is St Luke's Church, Sydney Street, Chelsea. It has the largest private garden in central London. It's an attractive, honey-stoned building which has weathered charmingly, and it was where Charles Dickens married Catherine Hogarth in 1836. It has a slender, graceful tower and an attractive interior, well worth a visit. It also has a tunnel leading from the church to the Builder's Arms, a nearby pub where the men who built the church used to quench their thirsts.

When the church of St James the Less was built in Thorndike Street, off Vauxhall Bridge Road, in 1861, the *Illustrated London News* described it as rising "as a lily among weeds", for Vauxhall was at that time a desperately poor neighbourhood. It is rich in ornamental brickwork, marble bosses, decorated arches and pillars, one of G.F. Street's masterpieces. Sir Charles Lock Eastlake, who was president of the Royal Academy at the time, wrote of it: "If Mr Street had never designed anything but the campanile of this church it would be sufficient to proclaim him an artist." The interior presents a feast of gilding, brick, tile and marble, glowing with warmth and colour. Even the most devout atheist could scarce forbear to cheer.

Not that all is well with ecclesiastical Gothic Revival architecture. London is riddled with 19th-century churches, and many of them are very bad indeed.

Perhaps the ugliest building in West London is the Westbourne Grove Church Centre, a church of the Charismatic Fellowship, at the corner of Ledbury Road and Westbourne Grove, Notting Hill. It's a really foul stone building with counterfeit medieval leaded windows. The whole structure is picked out in heavy pointing that makes it look like a distraught jigsaw puzzle. You can tell at a glance that it sprang originally from all that was worst in Victorian Christianity – cruelty, oppression, humbug, cant and hypocrisy. Avoid it.

Go instead to All Saints, Margaret Street, Westminster, described by Ruskin as "the first piece of architecture I have seen built in modern days which is free from all signs of timidity and incapacity"; St Mary Magdalen, Bermondsey, for the pews and the chandeliers; Holy Trinity, Sloane Street, for the windows; the Catholic Apostolic Church, Gordon Square, Bloomsbury, where the original congregation used to stand and "utter", a practice much frowned upon; Holy Trinity, Marylebone, where Gladstone and florence Nightingale used to worship; or St Augustine, Kilburn.

There are also secular gems of the Gothic Revival – the Prudential Building in Holborn; villas in Wimbledon and Norwood, Hampstead and St John's Wood; the Tower House in Melbury Road, Kensington, designed as a "model residence of the 15th century" by William Burges, but built in 1881; and the Woronzow Almshouses in St John's Wood Terrace. Finally, heave a sigh for the demolition of the Columbia Market, Bethnal Green. When it was built in 1869 it had the style and grandeur of a flemish cloth hall, with a mass of piers, vaults, tracery and carving, and clocks that played different hymn tunes every quarter of an hour. It was hoped that costermongers would use it for their market, but they preferred the freedom of the streets and this unique building was demolished in 1958.

St Pancras Station and the Midland Grand Hotel

In 1863, the Midland Railway Company began building their London terminus and headquarters on Euston Road, on the site recently cleared of the slums of Agar Town. The old shanties had been described by Charles Dickens as "English suburban Connemara", where "the stench of a rainy morning is enough to knock down a bullock". The new development was one of the marvels of Victorian engineering – a glass and iron shed with a height of 100 feet (30 metres) and a span of 240 feet (73.5 metres).

It is one of the greatest glories of Gothic Revival and one of the finest buildings in London. Under its roof you are in the Age of Iron and Steam. On a wet autumn after-

noon, the concourse has an almost candlelit appearance, with pools of light around the Upper Crust and Whistle Stop snack bars that would have delighted Rembrandt. It's a monument to Victorian decorated solidity – marble columns threading their way through ornate arched windows, walls of heavy wood panelling in a shell of deep red Midland brick. The ticket hall is so dark it puts you in mind of Dracula's Castle, and you almost feel constrained to ask for a Supersaver ticket to Transylvania.

'It has often been spoken of to me as one of the finest buildings in London,' wrote Sir George Gilbert Scott of his masterpiece, St Pancras Station.

The London of Sherlock Holmes

Despite what a great many people think, the great detective Sherlock Holmes is, and always has been, a purely fictional character. He was the creation of Sir Arthur Conan Doyle, a strange Scotsman who believed in fairies, tinkered with science, helped the Italian long-distance runner Pietri across the finishing line of the Marathon at the London Olympics in 1908 (thereby costing the poor man a gold medal), was a good doctor and a dreadful poet, and gave the world the most famous detective in fact or fiction.

Conan Doyle was born in 1859. Sherlock Holmes first appeared in 1887 in a full-length story called *A Study in Scarlet*, published in *Beeton's Christmas Annual*. Dr Watson, the narrator of Holmes's adventures, is taken from the Criterion Bar in Piccadilly to a laboratory in Holborn, where Holmes has found "a re-agent which is precipitated by haemoglobin and nothing else".

The reader is immediately plunged into Conan Doyle's version of London in the 1880s – a city of gaslights, hansom cabs and their whimsical drivers, plump housekeepers, steam trains that always departed on time (despite the dense fogs), dim-witted policemen and obliging urchins.

It was a city of danger and mystery, the London of Dr Jekyll and Mr Hyde, Gilbert and Sullivan, Oscar Wilde and Lord Alfred Douglas, Aubrey Beardsley and Jack the Ripper. Men wore ulsters and deerstalkers, check trousers and bowler hats: women wore flowing capes and thick veils, *mousseline-de-soie* and fluffy pink chiffon. Royalty travelled incognito, everyone had something to hide.

At the centre of all this were Holmes and Watson, in their bachelor quarters at 221b Baker Street, with their landlady Mrs Hudson. Such an address never existed in Victorian times, though it is now the home of the Sherlock Holmes Museum at the top end of Baker Street, near the Clarence Gate entrance to Regent's Park. From here Holmes set out to visit museums and galleries, went to concerts and recitals, occasionally (and reluctantly) attended a reception. And all his journeys were by

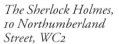

The Sherlock Holmes, 10 Northumberland Street, WC2

Devotees of Holmes also make their way to the Sherlock Holmes pub, a couple of minutes' walk from Trafalgar Square. In Victorian times it was known as the Northumberland Arms, and was the venue for the second meeting between Sherlock Holmes and Sir Henry Baskerville in *The Hound of the Baskervilles* – after Holmes had spent two hours in a Bond Street gallery admiring the works of the modern Belgian masters.

The pub contains a recreation of Holmes's study at 221b Baker Street, and the bar is full of relics from his famous cases, most of them supplied by members of Conan Doyle's family. Go early – it is a much-favoured tourist attraction.

cab or train – he never used the Underground, although
Baker Street Station was but a stone's throw away.

The Haunts of Holmes

Conan Doyle set the majority of the Sherlock Holmes
mysteries in London, from the opium dens of
Limehouse to the fashionable residences of the West
End. A frequent location is Brixton, then a thriving
upper-middle-class suburb, and there are other visits to
the southeast of London. In *The Man with the Twisted
Lip*, Holmes and Watson travel from the leafy purlieus of
Lee to Upper Swandham Lane, "a vile alley lurking
behind the high wharves which line the north side of the
river to the east of London Bridge". The investigation
into the doings of *The Red-Headed League* centres in and
under Aldersgate and King Edward Street in the City.
The action moves further east to the Pool of London for
The Five Orange Pips, and *A Case of Identity* takes place in
the hotels in the St Pancras area. Goodge Street and the
Alpha pub in Brixton Road provide the background for
The Blue Carbuncle. Holmes and Watson were back in
south London for *The Adventure of the Cardboard Box*,
finding relief from the furnace of Baker Street in the
refreshing atmosphere of Croydon and Wallington. Mrs
Warren, the heroine of *The Adventure of the Red Circle*,
was landlady of a high, thin, yellow brick edifice in Great

Orme Street, near the British Museum. You will search
in vain for such a house, or, indeed, for Great Orme
Street – but you could try Great Ormond Street.

The Paraphernalia of Holmes

The wardrobe of Sherlock Holmes was a mixture of the
formal, the comfortable and the disguise. He wore full
evening dress when the occasion demanded, a smoking
jacket or his famous purple dressing-gown to relax in, a
long grey travelling-coat and a close-fitting cloth cap
when the London weather was inclement, and (usually)
stained, filthy, smelly clothes when in disguise. He had a
ready supply of cocaine – not difficult to obtain in
Victorian London – and a Stradivarius violin, both of
which he turned to at moments of tension or misery.

He also had a collection of pipes, including "the long
cherrywood pipe which was wont to replace his clay
when he was in a disputatious rather than a meditative
mood", and in which he smoked "his before-breakfast
pipe, which was composed of all the plugs and dottles left
from his smokes of the day before".

Much of this, and a whole lot more, is on display at
the Museum.

One of the modern Baker
Street Irregulars guards the
entrance to 221b.

Capital Murders, Capital Punishment

Until late Victorian liberalism restricted capital punishment to murderers, traitors, pirates and those who set fire to the Royal Dockyards, far more people in London were killed by due process of law than by criminals. For hundreds of years no week passed without the spectacle of at least one public execution – the last in 1868, when Michael Barrett was hanged for his part in the Clerkenwell Explosion.

'The Whitechapel Murder - The Cry is Jack the Ripper'. A lurid reconstruction of one of the Ripper's evil deeds, as printed in the Illustrated Police News of 1889.

Martyrs, out of step with royal tastes in religion, were burnt at Smithfield, their clothes sometimes being stuffed with gunpowder to give them a comparatively merciful, swift death. Pirates were hanged with the "Devil's Neckcloth" and their bodies left in chains at Execution Dock, where the Neckinger River joined the Thames near Tower Bridge. Noble felons, traitors and fallen court favourites were beheaded on Tower Hill. Petty criminals, often guilty of nothing more serious than stealing a shirt or a handful of food, "took the journey westwards" to Tyburn, where they were hanged eight at a time.

This judicial slaughter attracted vast crowds. When Earl Ferrers was hanged at Tyburn in 1760 a crowd of some 15,000 gathered to watch. Mother Proctor, a cowkeeper who erected a grandstand to give some of the bloodthirsty a better view, made more than £500. It was always a dreadful spectacle. When the cart pulled away and the miserable victim was left hanging, relatives would rush forward and pull on his or her legs, to speed the end. If a condemned person was given a last-minute reprieve, the crowd often became violent, destroying the seats and rioting.

Tyburn was demolished in 1783, and from then on hangings took place at Newgate. The last beheading took place in 1747, when Lord Lovat, an old Jacobite warrior and rebel, was executed on Tower Hill. As he laid his head on the block, one of the stands collapsed, killing 12 spectators. The noble lord saw what had happened, and is said to have died with a bright smile of satisfaction on his face.

Newgate attracted even larger crowds. 100,000 people crowded to see Henry Hathaway hanged for forgery in 1824. A hundred people were trampled to death at a hanging in 1807. Reporting a hanging in 1864, *The Times* was shocked by the "robbery and violence, loud laughing, oaths, fighting, obscene conduct and still more filthy language [that] reigned round the gallows far and near". Dickens was appalled when he witnessed an execution on the roof of Horsemonger Lane Gaol in 1849 – "I felt for some time afterwards almost as if I were living in a city of devils."

Addresses to Avoid

Most murders are known by the name of the murderer (the Crippen Case, Jack the Ripper, the Ruth Ellis Case). A few are remembered by the name of the victim (WPC Yvonne Fletcher, Airey Neave). Occasionally, however, it is the site of the murder that gains long-lasting notoriety. Dotted about London are a few addresses that still have a blood-curdling resonance for Londoners with long memories. During the 1980s property boom, it was extremely difficult for estate agents to sell certain flats at 23 Cranley Gardens and 195 Melrose Avenue, north London. In these two flats, Dennis Nilsen murdered 15 young men in the early 1980s, and hid their bodies under the floorboards.

The most infamous of London addresses was 10 Rillington Place, Notting Hill. It was the home of John Reginald Halliday Christie, variously described as "unattractive and insignificant", "very much the gentleman", "repulsive" and "a marvellous bloke". Christie murdered at least eight women here between 1943 and 1953. Tragically it was also the home of Timothy Evans, Christie's lodger and a man of very limited intelligence. Although he was innocent, Evans confessed to the murder of his own wife and child and was executed at Pentonville in 1949. It was later discovered that Christie was responsible. 10 Rillington Place became the subject of books and a film. The street's name was changed to Ruston Close, in an attempt to put an end to the horror, and later to Wesley Square. It has now been demolished.

Jack the Ripper

Between August and November 1888, six women, most of them prostitutes, were murdered in a small area of Whitechapel and adjoining Aldgate. The murderer was never found, but was nicknamed Jack the Ripper. Rumour abounded. It was said that the Ripper was a doctor (because of his knowledge of anatomy), a sailor (because of his ability to slip away undetected), a member of the government or the Royal Family (because the police seemed less than eager to catch him).

The crimes received enormous publicity, because of their horrendous nature, and terror spread right across London:

> It seemed to be round the corner, although it happened in the East End and we were in the West; but, even so, I was afraid to go out after dark, if only to post a letter. Just as dusk came on we used to hear down our quiet and ultra-respectable Edith Road the cries of the newspaper-boys, in tones made as alarming as they could: "Another 'orrible murder!... Whitechapel! Murder! Disgustin' details... Murder!" One can only dimly imagine what terror must have been in those acres of narrow streets, where the inhabitants knew the murderer to be lurking…

M.V. Hughes, *A London Girl of the Eighties*

Jack Sheppard's Farewell to Mr Wood.

Blueskin cutting down Jack Sheppard.

The body of Jack Sheppard carried off by the Mob.

Three steps to immortality – George Cruikshank's record of the execution of Jack Sheppard in 1724: 1) Sheppard arrives at Tyburn, 2) Sheppard's body is cut down, 3) the crowd carry off the body.

London Prisons

There were criminals in London from the earliest days, and the punishments meted out to them were swift and vicious – a whipping or a spell in the stocks pelted with offal, rotting fruit and dead cats was, though, to suffice in most cases. Imprisonment is a comparatively new way of dealing with hardened felons in the city.

The Fleet Prison was one of the oldest, dating back to early in the reign of William the Conqueror. It was a large gaol, occupying at least an acre of land, run by crooks for crooks. Prisoners were charged for food and lodging, and other privileges, such as the right to stay out all night. The post of Keeper was hereditary – the Leveland family held it in unbroken succession from 1197 to 1558. But, though individual keepers came and went, the abuses continued. In 1691, a debtor named Moses Pitt complained that he was being charged eight shillings (40p) a week for a cell that should have cost only two shillings and four pence (12p). In the 18th century, the Fleet was inspected, condemned, "improved", inspected and condemned. It was closed in 1842 and demolished four years later. The site is now occupied by Blackfriars Station.

Newgate was a little younger. There was a prison on the site, near St Paul's, in the late 11th century, but the gaol was rebuilt several times – in 1423, at the end of the 16th century, and after the Great Fire. The new prison, completed in 1672, was magnificently decorated with statues and emblems, but, to a contemporary, "the sumptuousness of the outside but aggravated the misery of the wretches inside". Newgate had no adequate water supply, it stank, and it was host to frequent outbreaks of gaol fever (a virulent form of typhoid). Henry Fielding regarded it as a "prototype of hell", a place of bullying, robbery, extortion on the part of the warders, darkness and despair.

The Marshalsea in Southwark was founded some time in the late 13th or early 14th century. In Elizabethan times it became second only to the Tower as a place of incarceration, but later it became principally a prison for debtors. The father of Charles Dickens was imprisoned in the Marshalsea, and Dickens selected it as the birthplace of Little Dorrit: "an oblong pile of barrack building, partitioned into squalid houses standing back to back, so that there were no back rooms; environed by a narrow paved yard, hemmed in by high walls duly spiked on top".

The Clink, also in Southwark, dates back to the 15th century. It was a small prison in the Bishop of Winchester's Park, and most of its inmates were prostitutes from the brothels of Bankside, or those who had broken the peace nearby. Bridewell, on the banks of the Fleet River, was originally a royal palace built for Henry VIII. In the 1530s it was leased to the French Ambassador, and was the scene for Holbein's painting *The Ambassadors*. Edward VI gave the palace to the City for the reception of vagrants and homeless children, and for the punishment of disorderly women and petty offenders. It was a short-term prison, where whipping was almost invariably part of the punishment. It also had a ducking stool permanently ready on the river bank. The name "Bridewell" became synonymous with "prison", and other Bridewells were established in Westminster and Clerkenwell. It was finally closed in 1855, and the Unilever building now occupies the site.

Brixton Prison

When it first opened, in 1820, Brixton was called the Surrey House of Correction. It was a hard-labour prison, where most prisoners were sent to work on the treadmill, grinding corn. The treadmill was invented by Sir William Cubitt, whose other (and better) works included constructing the South-Eastern Railway from Charing Cross to Dover, and the Berlin waterworks.

The gaol closed in 1851, but reopened two years later as a women's prison when it was decided to substitute imprisonment for transportation to the colonies. The inmates of Brixton had to wash the clothes from other London prisons, including Pentonville and Millbank. It was converted into a military prison in 1882, but reverted to a civilian one in 1902. Overcrowding has long been the curse of Brixton. In 1991 it housed well over 1000 prisoners (mostly awaiting trial) in a gaol built for only 739.

Victorian Prisons

At the time when many of the older gaols were being closed and demolished, the crime rate was soaring in London, and the Victorian authorities set about building several new prisons. The older ones had been warrens of complicated design – one of the warders at Millbank Penitentiary still chalked his path through the building after he had been there for seven years. The new plan was

for buildings that were large, but of simple layout.

Pentonville was conceived as a model prison, based on one in Philadelphia. When it opened in 1840, Pentonville was said to have a "Dutch-like cleanliness" and the light and airy charm of the Crystal Palace. For a long time, it remained the Ritz of London prisons. Wandsworth was built ten years later. It's a grim and dismal place, stifling and dungeon-like, where freedom seems a million miles away. Poor Oscar Wilde spent the first six months of his sentence here in 1895. The Great Train Robber, Ronald Biggs, escaped from Wandsworth in 1965.

Wormwood Scrubs was for a long time the largest prison in Britain. It was built by prisoners in a novel rolling programme. Nine prisoners were originally kept here, and they built a block which could house 50. The 50 then built another block for another 50, and the 100 prisoners completed the prison. The process took 16 years, from 1874 to 1890, and gave a whole new meaning to the term "purpose-built". Its most famous escapee was George Blake, the spy, who went over the wall in 1966.

above:
Wandsworth Prison, a typical 19th century London jail.
opposite:
The 20th century view of custody – Belmarsh Prison in south east London.

Low-Life London

The Language of the Beggars

The London beggars of Tudor and Stuart times were well-organized, operating a society separate from the rest of the population, and speaking its own language. Horse thieves were called "priggers of prancers". Beggars who pretended to be insane were known as "abram-men". "Anglers" or "hookers" were those who stole clothes or purses from houses by pushing a stick with a hook on the end through an open window. Beggars so poor that they slept on straw in stables were known as "palliards". A "ruffler" was a proud, arrogant or swaggering fellow. The cream of the scrounging society were the "upright-men". London itself was "Rome-ville".

The rest of Britain has always seen London as the centre of crime, a hotbed of evil that attracted every cutpurse, ne'er-do-well and trickster. Criminal statistics go back less than 200 years, but London's criminal reputation is much older. In the medieval Court Rolls there are references to fights, killings, trading malpractices and all manner of lawlessness. In 1564 William Bullein warned of "the wild rogue and his fellows… with picklocks, handsaws, long hooks, ladders etc to break into houses, rob, murder, steal, and do all manner of mischief in the houses of true men, utterly undoing honest people… No man shall be able to keep a penny, no, scant his own life in a while. For they that dare attempt such matters in the city of London, what will they do in houses smally guarded, or by the highway?"

Once a city gets a reputation as a centre of crime, it attracts more criminals, and this is what happened to

Filth, stench and fever – the slums of London in 1820.

London. At the same time, it was reputedly a place of great wealth – where the pavements were made of gold – and this brought other desperate fortune-seekers to the city. In Tudor times armies of beggars drifted in. By the end of the 16th century there were reckoned to be over 12,000 beggars in the City alone. In 1569 they threatened to "loot" Bartholomew Fair.

Bartholomew Fair

The annual fair was founded at Smithfield by Rahere, court jester to Henry I and later Prior of St Bartholomew the Great. It quickly became the greatest cloth fair in the country, lasting for three days from St Bartholomew's Day (24 August). In 1445 the cloth fair joined forces with the rival cattle fair, and for 400 years this uneasy alliance was in charge of the celebrations. Rahere himself had been a juggler, and the fair attracted strolling players, wrestlers, dwarfs, fire-eaters, tight-rope walkers, pickpockets and shady characters. The Puritans lacked the courage to put an end to it, and as late as 1825 it was still going strong. William Horns recorded, in his account of a visit that year, seeing "four lively little crocodiles hatched from eggs at Peckham by steam, a menagerie, and a glass-blower in a glass wig blowing teacups for three pence each".

The fair constantly posed a threat to public order, however, and it was finally suppressed in 1855.

Low-Life Characters

By Victorian times there were hundreds of thousands of Londoners living on the borders of starvation or the threshold of crime. In *London Labour and the London Poor*, Henry Mayhew left eye witness accounts of some of the characters he met. There were the street-sellers of fried fish, hot potatoes, and ham sandwiches. The sandwich sellers reckoned they sold half a million sandwiches a year, "though a penny pie shop has spoilt us at the 'Delphi" (the Adelphi Theatre). There were men and women who ran coffee-stalls, where the coffee was adulterated with chicory, baked carrots and saccharine root. There were illegal distillers selling rot-gut gin, and purveyors of "soda-water" – made from Thames water mixed with acids and alkalis.

In the opening chapters of *The Water Babies*, Charles Kingsley described the life of a climbing-boy, one whose job it was to haul himself up chimneys, scraping the soot away as he went. Mayhew met many of them, and learnt that they were washed once every six months (or less), and that the operation was regarded as a punishment. Children were also sent out to sell matches, radishes, coat-studs, toys, steel pens, garters, lavender, firewood,

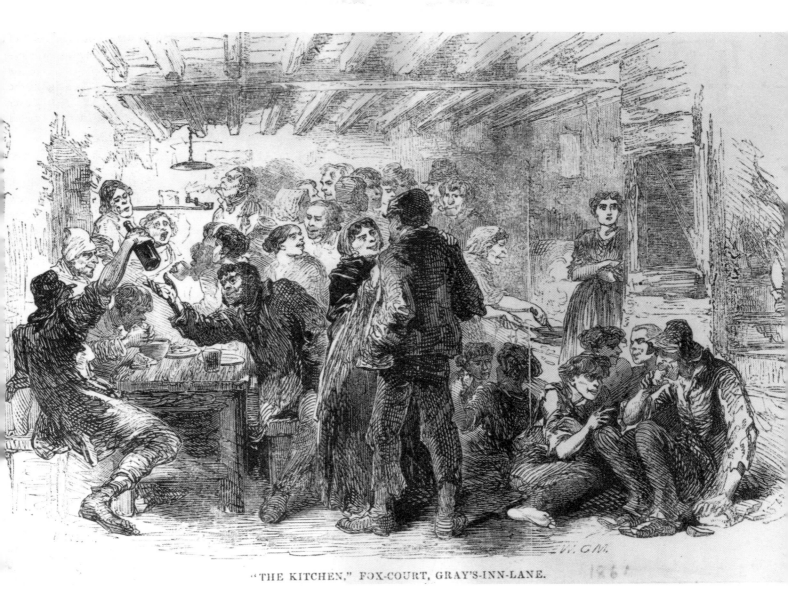

"THE KITCHEN," FOX-COURT, GRAY'S-INN-LANE.

flypapers, nuts, oranges, apples, nutmeg-graters and hundreds of other items. By the banks of the Thames, children known as "mudlarks" collected coal, bones, old tools, and the copper nails from ships. Gangs of children worked as crossing-sweepers, clearing the path through the horse manure and dust for people who wished to cross the road. They would cry out "two toffs" (two men) or "toff and a doll" (man and woman) as their customers approached, and whoever cried out first would get the money. It was reckoned that being a crossing-sweeper was the last step down before becoming a criminal.

Among the street entertainers were street conjurers, fire-eaters (notably "The Street Fire-King" or "Salamander"), street clowns (a sample joke – "Why is the city of Rome like a candle-wick? Because it's in the midst of

Greece"), blind pipers, dancing girls, English and German bands. Earnings varied from 12s 6d (63p) to less than a shilling (5p) a week. It was not uncommon for such artists to go to bed in the small hours having failed to raise the price of a hot pie for dinner.

A few made a reasonable living. Most barely survived. Many turned to crime.

Beggars, drunkards and thieves gather at Fox Court, Gray's Inn Lane in the early 1860s.

London's Organized Crime

In the 1950s the more sensational British newspapers often ran articles giving sordid details of organized vice in Soho. Gangs of Maltese men were alleged to be running brothels and living off the immoral earnings of prostitutes. Ten years later fashions in crime seemingly changed. The press were now concentrating on the evil doings of the East End "family" gangs – the Krays and the Richardsons.

By the 1970s, drug dealers were major public enemies – unscrupulous men from the Caribbean, the Far East or South America, whose aim was to create an entire population of addicts. By the 1980s attention had switched to the "tongs" that were said to operate in Chinatown and east London. Another ten years later, newspapers carried warnings about the gangs of Australian shoplifters known to be helping themselves in Oxford Street and the West End. Strange how often London's criminal problems are held to be the responsibility of foreigners.

It was not always so. Back in the 17th century London was capable of breeding and training its own criminal gangs. In Westminster, Whitefriars, Houndsditch, the Barbican and Smithfield there existed "rookeries", places of sanctuary for the hardened criminal, places of such violence and lawlessness that no law enforcer would dare approach them. In Billingsgate alehouses young boys were taught the craft of picking pockets. A school had been set up

to learn younge boyes to cutt purses. There were hung up two devices, the one was a pockett, the other was a purse. The pockett had in yt certen cownters and was hunge about with hawkes bells and over the topp did hange, a little scaring bell; and he that could take owt a cownter without any noyse, was allowed to be a publique Foyster; and he that could take a peece of sylver owt of the purse without the noyse of any of the bells, he was adjudged a judiciall Nypper… a Foyster is a pickpockett… a Nypper is a Pickepurse or a Cutpurse.

The Devil's Cabinet Broke Open, 1658

Jonathan Wild

No modern criminal has ever come near to matching the breathtaking exploits of Jonathan Wild, who virtually ran London's underworld during the early 18th century. At first Wild placed his talents on the side of the law, styling himself "Thief-Taker-General of Great Britain and Ireland". In this role he sent more than 100 wretches to the gallows, laughing and mocking them on their way.

At the same time, however, Wild was running gangs of thieves, pickpockets, prostitutes, highwaymen and burglars. He also had an army of "Spruce Prigs" – former servants who had been trained in the social graces, and whom he sent to balls, operas, plays and assemblies, suitably attired to mingle with the legitimate guests and take their pickings. In all, Wild was reckoned to have some 7000 criminals working to his orders. He filled warehouses with stolen goods, most of which were shipped out to Holland to be sold.

For roughly 13 years Wild's criminal empire brought him a fortune, but in 1725 the law caught up with him, and he was hanged at Tyburn for "receiving reward for restoring stolen property". Like Al Capone, it was a conviction for a petty crime that brought about his downfall.

Johnathan Wild, 'Thieftaker General of Great Britain and Ireland', circa 1710. Wild controlled many criminal gangs until he was hanged in 1725.

After Wild's death, his army split up into many small gangs. London was still a profitable, and in many ways a safe place for the thief. It was described by Henry Fielding, a magistrate and the author of *Tom Jones*, as "a Vast Wood or Forest, in which a Thief may harbour with as great Security, as wild Beasts do in the Desarts of Africa". By the late 18th century there were even more areas of London given over to the underworld. Smithfield and Saffron Hill were known as "Jack Ketch's Warren" – Ketch being the public hangman. Blackfriars was "the haunt of strolling prostitutes, thieves and beggars". Dick Turpin was a member of a band of highwaymen 40-strong known as the Gregory Gang. Forgers and counterfeiters flooded the market with "bad" money. Holywell Street, near the Aldwych, was the centre of a vast pornography industry – one dealer was found to possess "no less than 12,346 obscene prints, 393 books and 351 copper plates".

Ladies of the Night

Henry Mayhew and others recorded the staggering amount of prostitution on the streets of London in Victorian times. It was reckoned that one house in 60

was a brothel, and one woman in 16 a whore. In all there were 6000 brothels in the metropolis and 80,000 prostitutes, many of them children. The West End was one of the worst areas – Haymarket was renamed "Hell Corner" – but the women here were at least presentable, many of them launderers, milliners, servants and shop-girls who worked the streets part-time. By the Bank of England there were queues of prostitutes waiting for customers. In the poorer East End Mayhew met a prostitute with hands so filthy he believed mustard and cress could have grown on them.

The Shooting of George Cornell

In the 1960s two gangs ran most of the crime in London – the Richardsons operated south of the river, the Krays in the East End. Rivalry between the two gangs was kept to a minimum, but there was always trouble when a member of one gang encroached on the other's territory. In 1966 George Cornell of the Richardson gang refused to let the Krays in on money being made out of "blue" films. He is also said to have called Ronnie Kray "a big fat poof". Inexplicably, Cornell was sitting in the Blind Beggar in Whitechapel Road on 6 March, in the heart of Kray territory.

At 8.30 pm the door opened and Ronnie Kray entered. "Look who's here," said Cornell. Ronnie shot him at point-blank range. "Typical of the yobbo mentality of the man," said Ronnie later. "Drinking in a pub that was officially on our patch. It was as though he wanted to be shot."

above:
On 15th June 1982 the body of Roberto Calvi of the Banco Ambrosiano was found hanging here, beneath Blackfriars Bridge.
left:
The Blind Beggar, Whitechapel – where George Cornell met his end.

A Brief History of Protest in London

The centre of power in any society is usually the centre of discontent. Over the centuries London has had its share of political, religious, economic and social protest. Long ago the stage was reached where protest and the policing of protest run along well-worn grooves. If enough people feel strongly about an issue – even if the issue has nothing to do with London – they have only to apply for permission to stage a rally in Hyde Park, a march to Trafalgar Square, or a mass lobbying of Parliament. The chances are that permission will be granted.

But before tradition had established the regular route of protest, London was always thought to be at risk from the London Mob, which struck when and where it liked, destroying property, assaulting politicians and visiting statesmen, setting fire to the capital's treasure houses and bastions of control. The Mob reached the peak of its power in the late 18th century – before the poor were given the vote and before London had a disciplined and organized police force. In 1770 the Mob took to the streets in support of "Wilkes and Liberty" – Wilkes being a radical candidate in an election. The Duchess of Bedford was pelted with dirt, the Prime Minister fled to

above:
The arrest of a suffragette, outside Buckingham Palace, 1914.
below:
Anti-Serbian demo, 1998.

Newmarket, the Lord Chancellor fled to Bath. The windows of the Mansion House were smashed.

The Gordon Riots of 1780

Ten years later, far more serious rioting occurred. A deranged Protestant nobleman, Lord George Gordon, whipped up anti-Catholic feeling into a violent frenzy. There were plenty of bigots to support him, but, once the rioting began, a great many people joined in just for the hell of it. Looting and burning reached the point where the Prime Minister (the *same* Prime Minister, Lord North, as in 1770) and other leaders were terrified to set foot outside their houses. The Mob attacked the Bank of England, unsuccessfully, released all the prisoners from Newgate Gaol, set fire to the Fleet Prison and many houses, and plundered the Old Bailey. The military restored order, and Lord Gordon was dragged off to the Tower.

In 1833 troops attacked a crowd of some 7000 people demonstrating for the right to vote. The battle took place on Coldbath Fields, in the area where Mount Pleasant sorting office now stands. Fifteen years later one of the biggest protest meetings ever seen in London took place on Kennington Common, when supporters of the Chartist Movement gathered to demand universal suffrage and annual elections. The authorities feared the worst. Cannon were placed at the end of the Royal Mews, and 1500 Chelsea Pensioners were forced out of retirement for the defence of Battersea and Vauxhall. Louis Napoleon (later Emperor of France) was sworn in as a special constable. Post-office clerks were armed with rifles. But it started to rain, and the protesters melted away.

Bloody Monday, 1886

In the 1880s the Victorian economy entered a period of depression, which coincided with increased activity on the part of London trade unions. On Monday 8 February 1886 a crowd of 20,000 protesters (including many dockers and workers in the building

police-station inside Marble Arch), and in 1872 the authorities recognized the right of assembly here. Speakers' Corner isn't really a corner at all, but a stretch of the path where anyone who wishes may address passers-by on any subject, provided he or she is neither obscene nor blasphemous, and does not pose a threat to peace and good order. If you are lucky you may witness some good exchanges between speakers and hecklers. Over the years some great firebrands and some monumental bores have been heard on Sunday afternoons at Speakers' Corner.

trades) assembled in Trafalgar Square. The rally passed off peacefully enough, but when it ended a group of extremists headed for Pall Mall and the West End, smashing windows and looting shops, before marching home singing *Rule, Britannia*. For an hour, the West End was at the mercy of the mob.

It was a bitterly cold, brittle winter, and the next day a dense fog descended on central London. It was rumoured that a vast army of the unemployed and the shiftless was on the march. There were fears that London was about to experience a rising similar to that of the Commune in Paris 15 years earlier. But the fog lifted, and nothing happened.

Speakers' Corner

Just to the south of Marble Arch is the area of Hyde Park known as Speakers' Corner. Throughout the middle of the 19th century that part of the park had been the gathering point for many demonstrations (hence the secret

Brixton, 1981

For an entire weekend – from 10 to 12 April – much of Britain watched in horror as the Brixton Riots were displayed on television screens. Not for almost a century had there been such violence in peacetime on the streets of London. In the centre of Brixton a few hundred young people – not all of them black – repeatedly attacked the police who were seeking to establish order. No one knows for certain what sparked the riots – there were various stories of over-zealous and heavy-handed policing, and other stories of much drug-dealing and drug-use among locals.

A variety of weapons were used – stones, bricks, iron bars, petrol bombs. The fighting reached its peak late on the Saturday night. When the police finally restored calm – or when the rioters finally felt they had done enough – the centre of Brixton looked like a battlefield. For most Londoners it was a salutary experience.

above:
Brixton 1981.
left:
One of London's happier protests, in favour of legalising cannabis, Trafalgar Square, 1998.

right:
Four orators at Speakers Corner, Hyde Park: (from top) The End of the World is Nigh, Free Speech, The Martians are Coming, and The Voice of Jamaica.

Motorcycle courriers waiting impatiently for the 'green' in Picadilly.

How Safe is London?

London is an old and crowded city, full of alleys and side streets, narrow courts and footpaths. It has some appallingly badly designed and inadequately lit public areas. The old approach to North Acton Station used to be described as a "mugger's paradise", and it took a brave heart to march through the Bull Ring south of Waterloo Bridge late at night. George II was once mugged in Kensington Gardens. Belgravia used to be a swampland, infested with cut-throats. At the turn of the 18th century all well-off shopkeepers slept with loaded firearms by the bedside, and the garrotting and robbing of citizens reached epidemic proportions. A hundred and fifty years later, Reggie Kray often worried about what he perceived as the rising crime rate in London.

Geographically, it would seem ideal territory for the criminal. It has millions of houses, all well stocked with TVs and videos – the bread and butter of amateur crime. It attracts hundreds of thousands of visitors, people who don't know their way about and who have that air of preoccupied exhaustion that makes them readily identifiable as potential victims. The police seem to have their hands full dealing with traffic problems and guarding those premises deemed too important to be left to private security firms.

For all that, London is a remarkably safe city, and not simply because 85% of the centre is under constant video surveillance. In the Metropolitan Police area there are some 175 murders a year, but most of them are those tragic killings where murderer and victim are already known to each other. A little care and caution are all that are needed to guard against pickpockets and snatch thieves. The photographer of this book was advised by the local police in Brixton *not to* wander about with a case full of cameras – such items had "been known to disappear".

Safety is largely a matter of common sense. If you're withdrawing money from a cash machine at two in the morning, in a lonely stretch of street, it's a good idea not to hang about. On the other hand, although you may frequently come across signs warning you that beggars are operating nearby, few beggars constitute a danger. Most of them seem quite unreasonably satisfied by a polite refusal. Drunks can be a nuisance, especially the friendly variety. Those that appear to be making a career out of drunkenness on the London streets are either in a lager-induced state of euphoria or physically incapable of carrying out any threats they may mutter.

Not that crime is the only danger in any city. The biggest threat to personal safety in London probably comes from traffic. Hundreds of thousands of vehicles a day crawl into London, and, once there, many do their best to make up for lost time by jumping lights, cutting corners and driving as though on a race track. Motor-cycle couriers are among the worst offenders, with pedal cyclists a close second. Eternal vigilance is the price of safety when crossing any London street at any time.

There is little to fear from dogs in central London. You are unlikely to tread in any dog mess in Regent Street or Kensington High Street – though you should watch your step in most London parks and in all the suburbs. Attacks by dogs are rare, though you may find the odd unwelcoming Dobermann or Rottweiler if you try to force an entry into a pub outside licensing hours.

On the whole, London railways and the Tube network have a good safety record. Escalators seem to be out of action at an increasing and irritating number of stations, but walking up or down a long flight of stairs is hardly dangerous, unless you have a chronic heart condition. Bus accidents are extremely rare, too.

There has been no earthquake of any note in London since the mid-18th century, when the tremors that destroyed much of Lisbon were felt as far north as Scotland and as far south as the Caribbean. The nearest active volcano is Vesuvius, and London is unlikely to be in the path of any future hurricane or tornado. Flooding has been a threat in the past, and may be in the future, though the Thames Barrier is claimed to be more than a match for all but the worst possible combinations of wind, rain and tide that Nature can arrange.

Terrorism

Britain's imperial past made London a regular target for nationalist organizations that resented their homeland's subjugation. The Empire has all but disappeared, but there is now a bitterness in many parts of the world towards Western commercial interests that have their headquarters in London. In general, however, Londoners go their merry way, rightly (if subconsciously) believing that their chances of witnessing or experiencing a terrorist outrage are millions to one.

The exceptions throughout modern history have been actions by Irish terrorists. When the movement for Irish independence gathered strength and was balked in the 19th century, violence hit the London streets. The most effective perpetrators were the Fenians, forerunners of the IRA. Their organizational skills enabled them to set off three explosions within a few minutes in December 1867. Just over 100 years later, between March 1973 and December 1974, London seemed to lose some of its comfortable feeling of safety, with terrorist explosions near the Old Bailey, the Houses of Parliament and the Tower of London, Woolwich and Oxford Street. Since then, more hopeful times have prevailed.

The aftermath of a car bomb explosion outside the Old Bailey, 8th March 1973, at the height of an IRA bombing campaign in London.

Ethnic London

In the gentlemen's lavatory at the British Museum, a couple of years ago, there was a piece of graffiti that read: "Welcome to London, half-caste capital of the world." Although it was meant to be offensive, it is quite possible that it was unintentionally true. London has long been a melting-pot of hundreds of different nationalities and dozens of ethnic groups. Political, religious and financial refugees have sought asylum and a new life in London for centuries. And, once settled, they have freely mixed.

The variety of these peoples is staggering – Jews and Huguenots, fleeing from religious persecution; Italians, Russians and Germans, escaping political oppression; Africans, anticipating the monstrous misdeeds of General Amin in Uganda; Jamaicans, Trinidadians and Antiguans hoping to find regular work and a regular wage. Asian sailors came to the Port of London from China, Siam and Malaya, left their ships and found work in the shops and warehouses around the Docks. As early as 1858 a Strangers' Home for Asiatics, Africans and South Sea Islanders opened in West India Dock Road, Limehouse. Britain's first Indian MP, Dabadhai Naoroji, was elected to represent Finsbury in 1892. The main influx from India, Pakistan and Bangladesh came in the 1980s and 1990s.

The process has not been without its tragedies. Not all Londoners have been happy to greet the newcomers.

There are still areas of racial tension in London. Asians and whites clash in the East End. The racial storm that followed the murder of Stephen Lawrence, a black teenager, in southeast London has not yet blown away. In certain areas, the British National Party and other Fascist cliques still seek to do their evil work – though there is ironic justice in the fact that the Yorkshire Grey (a pub in Eltham that used to be a meeting-place for members of the BNP) has become a branch of McDonald's.

There is irony in all this, too. Many of the black immigrants were invited to London by right-wing members of the Conservative government. Workers were recruited from the Caribbean to run London's transport system and to staff London's hospitals. A prime mover in this was Enoch Powell, subsequently infamous for his "rivers of blood" speech. While Powell's political descendants were moaning about black immigration in the 1980s, many white South Africans, sensing that the "wind of change" was about to sweep over the land of *apartheid*, rushed to London. And for the last 50 years or more there has been a regular flow of white immigrants from the old colonies – Canada, Australia and New Zealand – descendants of those who left London for the best and worst of reasons in the 19th century.

Initially, each group tended to make their home in a

Members of the Sikh community in Southall, west London.

particular area of London. The Jews settled in the East End. The Huguenots opened their silk-weaving workshops in Spitalfields. The Italians congregated in Clerkenwell, the Jamaicans in Brixton, the Irish in Kilburn, Germans and Austrians in north London. It was an unplanned colonization. In many cases the New Londoners had intended merely to pass through on their way to the New World. But a family or two missed the boat, or decided to stay, and gradually other families joined them. They absorbed much of the culture of London, but never lost the culture they brought with them. Today you can see Sikhs in turbans driving mini-cabs in Southall, Arabs smoking hubble-bubbles outside cafés in Edgware Road, and young rabbis earnestly discussing scholarship on the platform at Golders Green Underground station.

These strong links to the homeland are often centred around places of worship. All over London there are mosques, temples and synagogues. In Moscow Road, just north of Bayswater Road, there is the Greek Orthodox Cathedral of St Sophia. In Soho there is a French Protestant church. Gradually, however, the mixture of cultures has trickled through the whole of London. There are Greek and Spanish restaurants from Battersea to Barking. There are Turkish grocers and Italian delicatessens from Deptford to Dollis Hill. There are Indian and Chinese restaurants everywhere.

Outsiders (and scribblers of graffiti in the British Museum) may see the process of immigration in purely black and white terms. By "immigrants", they mean "blacks". But there is nothing new about black people living in London. There is recorded evidence of black Londoners going back at least 300 years. In 1684 a black slave named Katherine Anker was brought to London by her master, one Robert Rich, a planter from Barbados. For six years she was ill-treated by the Rich family, until she successfully petitioned to be released from slavery. Thirty-seven years later, Benjamin and John Wood, printers of Whitechapel, were ordered to pay wages to John Caesar, a black slave who had worked for them for 14 years without earning a penny. Dr Johnson had a black servant named Francis Barber, brought to London from Jamaica as a slave in 1750. Barber later worked as an apothecary in Cheapside, and was left an annual payment of £70 in Johnson's will. Ignatius Sancho was born on a slave ship. He became butler to the Duke of Montague, set up business on his own as a grocer, and had his portrait painted by Gainsborough. In early Victorian times, a black crossing-sweeper left £500 in his will to a Miss Watchman – the equivalent of some £100,000 today.

In 1786 the wheel came full circle. Five hundred black Londoners embarked from Tilbury to establish the first free settlement in Sierra Leone.

Jewish London

More than any other race, the Jews have brought their faith, food, fashions and festivals to London. It's possible that the best bagels in town are to be found at J. Grodzinski and Daughters in Stamford Hill, but you can buy good bagels anywhere in London – even on the concourse of Waterloo Station. And there are still many who mourn the passing of Schmidt's, the monumental Jewish restaurant in Soho.

Although it's one of London's greatest strengths that it has been able to assimilate so many races in its history, the process has not been an easy one, and all immigrants have suffered. London has not always been kind to the Jews since they followed William the Conqueror from France in the late 11th century. In 1290 all Jews were expelled from England. A small group returned 200 years later, driven from Spain. Known as Marranos, they practised Judaism in secret, but ostensibly embraced Christianity. In 1656 Cromwell announced that Judaism was permitted, and Sephardi merchants, bankers and gem importers settled at Creelchurch Lane in the East End. The Bevis Marks Synagogue opened in 1701 and is still in use today.

George I encouraged Ashkenazi Jews to come to London from Germany, and they settled in Aldgate and Houndsditch. It was the Rothschilds and Montefiores who first moved from the East End to the West End, and in 1858 a special parliamentary resolution allowed Lionel de Rothschild to take his seat in the House of Commons as the first Jewish MP. By the 19th century there were

top right:
The Jewish market in Whitechapel, April 1952.
below:
The all-night beigel bakery in Brick Lane.

synagogues, Jewish schools, cemeteries and even stage-coach yards in London. The biggest community, however, was still in the East End – between 1881 and 1914 over 100,000 Jews arrived from Russia and Poland. In the 1920s and 1930s Jews moved into the expanding suburbs of Dalston, Stoke Newington, Finchley and Golders Green, many of them new arrivals from persecution in central Europe. In 1932 a Jewish Museum opened his doors in Tavistock Square – it is now in Albert Street, Canning Town.

The problem for many Jews in London has been that English literature and drama has so crudely misrepresented them. The creation of Fagin in *Oliver Twist* did little for their image. In 1873, on a visit to London, the French poet Paul Verlaine echoed Dickens when he described Jewish communities in Poplar and Whitechapel as "leprous little hovels on which hung signs written in Hebrew, and the Jews... who seemed figures from a picture by Rembrandt, with their livid yellow skin, their drawn and haggard features, their straggling beards and their skeleton-like claws."

Beatrix Potter in the East End
Verlaine was not the only anti-Semite in late-Victorian London. Beatrix Potter compiled an only slightly more balanced description of London's Jews when working as

a researcher for the social reformer Charles Booth in 1889. She visited an East End *chevras* (association):

It is a curious and touching sight to enter one of the poorer and more wretched of these places on a Sabbath morning… situated in a small alley or narrow court. To reach the entrance you pick your way over the rickety bridge connecting it with the cottage property fronting the street. From the outside it appears a long wooden building surmounted by a skylight. You enter; the heat and odour convince you that the skylight is not used for ventilation… A low, monotonous, but musical-toned recital of Hebrew prayers rises from the congregation… Your eye wanders from the men, who form the congregation, to the small body of women who watch behind the trellis. Here certainly you have the Western world, in the bright-coloured ostrich feathers, large bustles, and tight-fitting coats of cotton velvet or brocaded satinette. At last you step out, stifled by the heat and dazed by the strange contrast of the old world memories of a majestic religion and the squalid vulgarity of an East End slum.

Life and Labour of the People of London.

The Battle of Cable Street

In the 1930s anti-Semitism was whipped up in London by Oswald Mosley and his Blackshirts – a low-budget version of Hitler and the Nazis. The authorities turned a blind eye to Mosley's doings, at times ordering the London police not to intervene however his henchmen behaved. In 1934 Mosley hired Olympia, and thousands of his supporters flocked to attend a very stage-managed rally. Harry Daley, a London policeman, described Mosley's entrance: "The lights were lowered, a spotlight shone on the doorway and through it came Mosley with a thug bodyguard, all giving the Fascist salute. They strode like ham actors to the platform by an unnecessarily long route, whilst the cheering audience rose as one man to their feet" (*This Small Cloud*).

Mosley's power and ego grew, and by 1936 he believed his Blackshirts were strong enough to invade the East End of London, still seen as the Jewish heartland. On Sunday 5 October Mosley and his followers started their march. Communists and local residents (many of them Jews) barricaded the roads. The police began by helping the Blackshirts tear down the barricades, but were later ordered by the Home Office to halt the march, to avoid a riot. The Fascists retreated, but during the next week, windows of every Jewish shop in the Mile End Road were smashed.

East End, West End

Brick Lane Market – hustling and bustling for bargains in the East End …

Just as the antagonism between north and south London is based on a single bone of contention (accessibility to the Tube), so the rivalry between the East End and the West End centres round a single issue – the difference between wealth and wages.

The relationship between the two in the 20th century has been generally tolerant, which says much for the generosity of East Enders. Only during the Second World War was it marred by bitterness. The East End suffered greatly from bombing: the West End escaped with comparatively slight damage. It was widely believed in the East End, however, that most fire appliances for dealing with incendiary bombs were kept in the West End, to protect what was regarded as more valuable property.

The East End has long been one of the principal workshops of London, giving shelter and employment to the cheap labour that regularly arrived from Europe and the rest of the world. Many of these immigrants brought skills with them, many were unskilled. They settled to the east of the City – in the cottage workshops of Whitechapel and Aldgate, in the factories of Dagenham and Bow, in the laundries of Wapping and Shadwell, and in the Docks themselves.

For a hundred years or more, from the mid-18th century, the West End remained an odd mixture of rich and poor. Behind the grand squares and rich parades were slum districts inhabited by the chimneysweeps, washerwomen, dressmakers, flower-sellers, knife-grinders and all those who made life comfortable for the well-to-do. Gradually, however, the slums were cleared to make way for more salubrious development. The rat-catchers and cab-drivers, the clerks and porters were driven out of the West End, and found new homes in the East End. Many of them took their work with them. In Victorian times, the gowns that were stitched and embroidered in the attics of Poplar were sold in the shops and stores of Bayswater and Knightsbridge, and worn to balls and receptions in Mayfair and Grosvenor Square. The women who cut out and assembled the fine silks and brocades were paid a few shillings a week. The dresses they produced sold for several guineas. The bulk of the profit went west.

This process of creating wealth in the East End and harvesting it in the West End accelerated in the 18th century, becoming ingrained in London life. Grace, beauty, comfort and elegance were to be found in the West End. Squalor, ugliness, want and poverty were endemic to the East End. Some industries flourished in the East End, but jobs were never secure. In the early 19th century there were 30,000 silk weavers in Spitalfields alone. The ending of monopolies and the rise of Free Trade dealt the industry a death-blow, and almost every one of the weavers was thrown out of work. But, even when woven silk was imported ready-made from India and China, the industry continued to bring handsome profits to the West End.

Such changes, coupled with the decline of the London Docks in the late 19th century, destroyed the old East End. The old industrial and seafaring centre became a wasteland of destitution, inhabited by starving, ragged, hopeless hordes. At the same time, the West End began purging itself of the few industries that had survived: glue-boilers, match-makers, soap-makers, manufacturers of rubber and tar. A rise in rents forced the factories out of the West End, and they had to find cheaper accommodation in Bow, Old Ford and Hackney. The few wealthy people left in the East End moved west. The poor moved east.

For a few East Enders, the re-siting of factories created employment. For all East Enders it created pollution. The worst affected were men who worked in the white lead factories. They were hired a day at a time, and were limited to a three-day week, as conditions in these factories posed a threat to life. Women who worked in the Bryant and May match factory in Bow ran the risk of premature baldness and "phossy jaw", a slow but steady rotting of the jawbone through phosphorus poisoning. It was a time when opinions hardened. In February 1886 – the time of the Bloody Monday demonstration in Trafalgar Square – a piece of inflammatory graffiti appeared on the wall at the entrance to the West India Dock:

WANTED: 100,000 RIOTERS FOR THE WEST END.

Dinner at the Ritz
In the 1930s a few brave groups of the unemployed from the East End marched into the Ritz Hotel in Piccadilly and demanded to be fed. One of the daring diners was Chris Cansack:

> There was about 14 of us. We went in smartly, walked to the table, sat down. The waiter come up,
> "Gentlemen, what do you want?"
> "We would like a dinner please."
> "Dinner! Dinner! I'll get the manager."
> So he got the manager. Now they didn't want trouble, the Ritz, because the unemployed could wreck the place, that's what they thought. So the manager got on to the police and they were waiting outside, but we still said,
> "We're not going till we have something to eat."
>
> They didn't call the police in, they didn't want it in the papers… bad publicity, the big nobs go to the Ritz. So some dinners came up… meat and potatoes we had, and sweet afterwards, and tea. We thoroughly enjoyed it. We marched out and the police didn't touch us… and we marched all around Piccadilly, saying it was the finest meal we'd ever had. That was a great day for the unemployed.

Gavin Weightman and **Steve Humphries**,
The Making of Modern London

… discretely making a purchase in the West End – Asprey's in Bond Street.

Lottery London

London consumes money in vast quantities. There is never enough to go round – to maintain the superstructure, the transport system, the sewers, the ancient monuments. The rest of Britain complains that London receives a disproportionate amount of public money from central government, via the Arts Council, the Heritage Commission, and the National Lottery. When the Royal Opera House holds out its hand for another £78 million, cries of rage and despair are heard in Glasgow, Newcastle, Plymouth, Swansea and Belfast. Every city in the country has a list of worthy projects that could put such money to "more appropriate use".

London itself is a lottery, and few parts of London are secure. True, no one is likely to approve a road-widening scheme that slices through the Tower of London or Buckingham Palace, but you wonder how long humbler dwellings will last. As traffic grinds in and out of west London along Talgarth Road, few motorists turn their eyes to a handsome terrace of houses called St Paul's Studios. They are tall, narrow houses with large arched windows facing on to the street, built in Victorian times for a colony of artists. They are unique, but that may not be enough to save them as motorway madness creeps steadily eastwards.

The same commercial interests that blocked Wren's plans for the rebuilding of the City in the late 17th century are at work today – nibbling away wherever there's a square yard of land that isn't fulfilling its money-making potential. Over the centuries this process has destroyed much of London that was odd, beautiful or redundant, but it has also left many pockets of the city that present wonderful surprises.

You walk along the towpath of the Grand Union Canal, averting your gaze from the oily, scummy water at Westbourne Park. Behind you is the concrete nightmare of the Westway flyover. Raindrops laced with car exhaust splash down. Suddenly, a barge chugs by, with a small child helping her father steer. Twenty yards on, you come upon a row of Victorian houses, finely proportioned, backing down to the canal, with apple trees in their tiny gardens, and tubs top-heavy with tomato plants on the verandas. It all looks idyllic.

Often the lottery side of life in London is obvious. You have only to stroll down the Bishop's Avenue, Hampstead, then take the Northern Line 13 stops south

above:
Flats at the Elephant and Castle…
opposite:
… apartments in Eaton Square.

to the Elephant and Castle to appreciate that there is a rich and a poor side to living in London. But the lottery can be subtler than that. In Ladbroke Grove there is a fish bar that sells salmon and chips, Dover sole and chips. Just to the west of Catford, off the ugly, crowded South Circular Road, is a tiny cul-de-sac called Stanstead Grove. It contains half a dozen Regency cottages (one of which used to be inhabited by a white witch), some glorious trees, and a coach-house with a well. In the wasteland surrounding the shell of Battersea Power Station, between the river and the disused, overgrown railway marshalling yards, are two enormous gasholders. In their shadow is an imposing Victorian house, probably the home of the gasworks manager in former times, though it looks more like a parsonage from a novel by Trollope.

Gems like these have survived largely through luck. More valuable jewels have been carefully protected. Many London squares have secluded gardens surrounded by railings six feet (2 metres) high, with gates that are kept locked. Only local residents have the keys. When Euston Station first opened in July 1837, guarded barriers were erected at the top end of Gordon Street and Upper Woburn Place, to prevent such common personages as railway travellers invading these middle-class enclaves.

Sometimes a single square in London became a lottery winner simply through the eccentricities of residents. When the south side of Portman Square was built in the 1770s, it quickly became fashionable thanks to the rivalry between Henry Portman and Mrs Elizabeth Montagu. Both aspired to be the greatest host in London. Mrs Montagu emerged victorious by throwing breakfast parties for up to 700 guests. Portman Square has never looked back.

As such areas of wealth and fashion developed, slums grew up alongside, populated by those whose lot in life was simply to serve the wealthy – ostlers, servants, laundry-maids, needlewomen, messenger-boys and dozens more. The fine houses survived. The slums have all been destroyed, disinfected and dressed up.

Seven Dials

This area on the western edge of Covent Garden perhaps best illustrates the rise, fall and resurrection of London neighbourhoods. When the pillar known as Seven Dials was first erected in 1694, it stood in the middle of a fashionable part of London. A hundred years later it had become the rendezvous for rogues and villains. By the mid-19th century, it stood in the middle of one of the city's most notorious slums. It is now perfectly respectable – a modestly Bohemian settlement of coffee shops, health-food shops, a cheesemonger's and a greengrocer's selling organic fruit and vegetables. Seldom is resurrection so complete.

Madame Tussaud's

Madame Tussaud's is in Marylebone Road, a hundred yards east of Baker Street Station. It's a long, elegant building with a fine classical façade. At the western end, like a giant pimple, is the green-domed London Planetarium. It's easily identifiable in the summer by the enormous queues that stretch along the frontage and round the corner into Allsop Place.

The best way to approach Madame Tussaud's is from the Pâtisserie Valerie on the first floor of the Royal Institute of British Architects in Portland Place. Go there on a Wednesday morning, when your breakfast will be accompanied by music – or, if you prefer, by the gentle trickling of the water trellis on the terrace. When you've finished your croissant, cross Portland Place and go along Devonshire Street as far as the Devonshire Arms. Turn right along Devonshire Place Mews, the east side of which contains some charming houses, though many have been ruined by ugly replacement windows and hideous garage doors. The Mews will bring you to the Terence Conran shop in Marylebone High Street.

Cross the road and enter the charming circular garden behind St Marylebone Parish Church, in which Robert Browning and Elizabeth Barrett were married in 1746. A pedestrian alleyway leads round the church, past the St Marylebone Central National Schools, a lovely Regency building, well worth lingering to admire. All you have to do now is cross Marylebone Road, and there you are, at Madame Tussaud's.

By now a queue will have formed, for the waxworks are one of London's most popular tourist attractions. While you queue, however, you will have time to admire the golden figures round the top of the cupola of St Marylebone Church.

Cynics may find it hard to discern what it is that draws such crowds to Madame Tussaud's. A waxwork is not a thing of beauty, and putting a whole lot of waxworks together doesn't make them collectively more beautiful. There is no denying the skill of the wax sculptor – when subject and waxwork are photographed side by side, it is sometimes alarmingly difficult to tell which is which. But a waxwork can seldom be more than a three-dimensional snapshot. The figure of Pavarotti in the foyer of the museum is incredibly life-like, but does have no life.

Stars in Wax: The Beatles, Queen Elizabeth and the Duke of Edinburgh, David Attenborough, Yassar Arafat, Gerard Depardieu, 'spares', Michael Jackson, Pierce Brosnan, Madame Tussaud herself, Princess Diana.

So what is the attraction? Perhaps it is that Madame Tussaud's is like a pop chart. It tells us who are our top 100 celebrities of the moment, and who are the all-time greats. You have to be very high in the public eye to warrant a place here. So, you will find few Nobel prize-winners in Madame Tussaud's, but plenty of pop stars, sports stars and film stars. Some have only a temporary place – fame is a fickle jade. Others seem to rest in eternity. Jean-Paul Marat, whose death mask was moulded by Madame Tussaud herself, has been in the collection for over 200 years.

The Exhibition

The museum is divided into seven main areas: the Spirit of London, the Grand Hall, the Garden Party, 200 Years, Legends, Superstars and the Chamber of Horrors. The Grand Hall is the home of kings and queens, statesmen and stateswomen. Henry VIII is surrounded by all six wives – a happening that unfortunately never occurred in real life. The French Royal Family were modelled by Madame Tussaud from life, when she was art tutor to Louis XVI's sister.

The Spirit of London covers more than 400 years of London's history, though it is difficult to vouch for the accuracy of some of the earlier figures – Queen Elizabeth I looks less like Bette Davis than the animatronic Sir Christopher Wren does. The Garden Party, on the top floor, is a collection of glitterati. Legends and Superstars are largely what you would expect. The most interesting section is "200 Years", which reveals many of the tricks of the waxwork trade.

The Chamber of Horrors

The most famous section is, of course, the Chamber of Horrors, which had its origins in the Caverne des Grands Voleurs of Dr Philippe Curtius. The Caverne opened in Paris in 1783, and Curtius was Madame Tussaud's teacher and mentor. This collection formed the basis of the travelling exhibition which Madame brought to England in 1802. To avoid giving offence to "sensitive ladies", Madame removed the more unsavoury exhibits into what she called "The Separate Room", and this became the Chamber of Horrors – the name being invented by *Punch* magazine in 1846.

The chamber is horrific, containing scenes of torture and execution that may upset even modern sophisticates. It also houses such relics as the Old Toll Bell of Newgate (which rang to indicate a hanging had taken place), the original door to the condemned cell at Newgate, and the guillotine blade that beheaded Marie Antoinette.

The lighting is suitably dramatic, and the atmosphere one of nervous ghoulishness.

Madame Tussaud

Marie Grosholtz Tussaud was born in Strasbourg in 1761, the daughter of a soldier. Her father was killed in the Seven Years War two months before she was born, and for the first five years of her life she lived with her widowed mother in Berne. Her mother was housekeeper to Dr Curtius who took them both to Paris in the 1770s. Marie learnt the skills of wax-sculpting and made models of famous figures of the age, including Voltaire and Benjamin Franklin – still on display in the museum.

Marie was invited to the court at Versailles, a royal connection that nearly cost her her life in the Revolution. She was imprisoned, but later released and employed to prepare death masks of some of the more notable victims of the guillotine.

In 1795 she married François Tussaud, but seven years later she and her older son left France, her husband and her baby for England, never to return.

Painters' London

William Marlow,
Blackfriars Bridge and St. Pauls's Cathedral, London Guildhall Art Gallery, Corporation of London, UK

Every day of the year you will find artists at work in London. It is a city that often delights and sometimes inspires sketchers and painters, who see rich sources of encouragement for their talent in parks and bridges, sunsets over Camden Town, the Thames, railway stations, markets and almost every single paving slab.

However humble their efforts may be, they are in good company. For hundreds of years great artists have lived and worked in London. In many cases the best (and sometimes only) pictorial records of it are the works of artists like Claes Visscher, who visited in the early 17th century. In Visscher's panorama of London Bridge (1616) we see houses, churches, shops, carts, citizens, boats on the Thames, and even the heads of traitors on the gate leading to the bridge. It's one of the few paintings of that time that isn't concerned merely with the rich and famous.

In general we have plenty of pictures of kings and queens, courtiers and ministers, and some of the great events of Tudor and Stuart times. It wasn't until the 18th century, however, that artists began to paint ordinary people and ordinary streets on an ordinary day. The watercolours of Rowlandson and Hogarth, and the aquatints of Malton, between them cover the whole of London life – an execution at Tyburn and a cockfight in Dartmouth Street (Hogarth), the Tottenham Court Road turnpike and the first gas lighting in Pall Mall (Rowlandson), Temple Bar and Threadneedle Street (Malton). Rowlandson's portrait of a "Charley", or nightwatchman, and Hogarth's series *The Idle Apprentice* bring to life the characters of London in a way that had never been done before.

Not that every artist has loved London. William Blake, who had his first visionary experience at the age of nine when he saw a tree filled with angels on Peckham Rye, hated living in South Molton Street. Canaletto must have been homesick while in the city from 1746 to 1756, since all his paintings look more like Venice than London. Gainsborough took exception to the way the Royal Academy hung his pictures and withdrew them all. And James Whistler came to financial ruin…

James Whistler and John Ruskin

In the early 1870s, James Abbott McNeill Whistler was a highly successful artist. One of his most recent paintings – *Portrait of My Mother* – had been rapturously received in London and Paris. In 1877 Whistler painted a study of a firework display as seen across the Thames. He called it *Nocturne in Black and Gold: The Falling Rocket*. The art critic John Ruskin called it "throwing a pot of paint in the public's face". It was what might be called the art world's first brush with Impressionism.

Whistler sued Ruskin for libel, claiming £1000 damages. The case came before Baron Huddleston, an insensitive judge, who examined another of Whistler's works:

HUDDLESTON: Do you say that this is a correct representation of Battersea Bridge?
WHISTLER: I did not intend it to be a "correct" portrait of the bridge.
HUDDLESTON: The prevailing colour is blue?
WHISTLER: Perhaps.
HUDDLESTON: Are those figures on the top of the bridge intended for people?
WHISTLER: They are just what you like.

Whistler won the case but was awarded the derisory sum of one farthing (0.1p) damages. Within two years he had been declared bankrupt.

London and the French Impressionists

Whatever poor Whistler's experiences, many of the French Impressionists enjoyed their time in London at the end of the 19th and the beginning of the 20th century. Vincent van Gogh worked as a teacher at a school in Isleworth in 1876. He wrote to his brother Theo in October: "The suburbs of London have a peculiar charm; between the little houses and gardens there are open spots covered with grass and generally with a church or school or workhouse in the middle among the trees and shrubs. It can be so beautiful there when the sun is setting red in the evening mist."

Camille Pissarro came to London in 1870 at the age of 40, a refugee from the Franco-Prussian War:

I found myself in London with Monet, and we met Daubigny and Bonvin. Monet and I were very enthusiastic over the London landscapes. Monet worked in the parks, whilst I, living at Lower Norwood, at that time a charming suburb, studied the effects of fog, snow and springtime. We worked from Nature, and later on Monet painted in London some superb studies of mist… About this time we had the idea of sending our studies to the exhibitions of the Royal Academy. Naturally we were rejected.

In 1892 he wrote to his dealer in Paris:

I am now very busy at Kew Gardens where I have found a series of splendid motifs which I am trying to render as well as I can. The weather helps – it's quite exceptional, it seems… But the time is so short and the work takes so long that I'm driven to despair!

In the 1920s, looking back on his time in London, Claude Monet remembered similar difficulties to those experienced by Pissarro:

At the Savoy Hotel or at St Thomas's Hospital, where I had my viewpoints, I kept almost a hundred canvases on the go – for one subject. I would search feverishly through my sketches till I found one not too different from what I could see. Then in spite of everything I would change it entirely. When I finished work I would move the canvases and see that I had overlooked just the one which would have served… That wasn't very bright!

Still, he did stay at the Savoy Hotel.

Canaletto, *Procession of the Knights of the Bath.*
Courtesy of Dean & Chapter of Westminster Abbey, UK

Mapping London

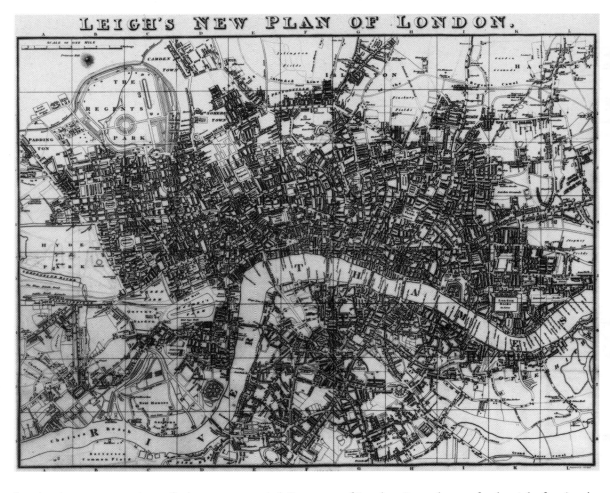

LEIGH'S NEW PLAN OF LONDON.

Leigh's Map of London in 1818.

London is not an easy city to find your way around. It doesn't have the grid system of streets that helps the logical visitor to New York. It isn't compact like Hong Kong. It doesn't embrace the demands of the motorist as Los Angeles does. It doesn't have the symmetry of Rome or the concentricity of Paris. It's huge, and it's rambling and difficult to disentangle. So a map has long been essential for locals and visitors alike.

Maps of London are a comparatively recent phenomenon. The first one to be of any use would seem to have been published in 1572 in Braun and Hogenberg's *Civitates Orbis Terrarum*. It was a large-scale map, roughly 27 1/2 inches (70 cm) to the mile. It covered the city as far north as Finsbury, as far south as the Thames, and as far west as St James's.

In the next 100 or so years a few more maps were published, none of them of much use. The Great Fire of 1666 made all of them redundant, and revealed the need for maps that were more detailed, to help establish title to land and boundaries. In 1676 John Ogilvy and William Morgan produced the first accurate

map of London. It was large – five by eight feet (150 by 240 cm) – and with a scale of 51 inches (130 cm) to the mile. The only copy of it still existing is in the Guildhall Library.

London mapmakers were busy in the 18th century, but it was a French immigrant called John Rocque who produced the best and most detailed survey to date in 1745. Fifty years later, Richard Horwood published the first maps of London to show every house and, where it had one, its number. The first Ordnance Survey maps of London came early in the 19th century – one each for Middlesex, Essex, Surrey and Kent.

Just as the Great Fire had led to better maps of London, other tragedies – the cholera outbreaks of the 1830s and 1840s – provided the impetus for the next improvement. Large-scale maps which showed the contours of land were needed for the Commissioners of Sewers to devise their drainage plan.

Today, the largest-scale maps of the whole of London are on the scale of 49 inches (125 cm) to the mile. These are reasonably easy to find. Full sets are in the British Museum Map Room and the Guildhall Library,

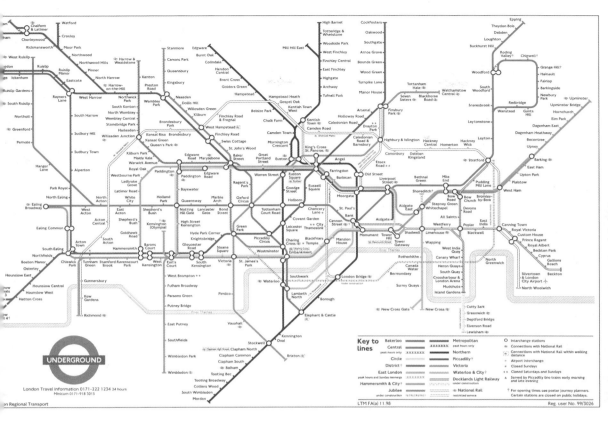

but you may also be able to track them down in local public libraries.

Charles Booth's Social Map of London

Booth was a shipowner and social reformer, and a pioneer of the movement to introduce old-age pensions. Towards the end of the 19th century he embarked on a street-by-street survey of London, later published as *Life and Labour of the People in London*. He used armies of researchers to gather information for the 17-volume work, which recorded everything from window-boxes to street lighting, from the condition of children to the number of drinking troughs for horses, from broken window-panes to brothels. The researchers, who worked in pairs, covered hundreds of miles.

Part of the survey was the mapping of every road and alleyway in London. The maps were large-scale, extremely accurate, and full of detail (important buildings, the size and shape of each house and garden, gas-holders, even individual trees). More than that, the maps were colour-coded to show the class structure of London

– where the rich and poor lived. More details of this are given in Chapter 5, "London and Class – History and Background".

Mapping the Underground

One of the most famous and most beautiful of all London maps is that of the London Underground. For the first 70 or so years of the Underground's existence, attempts were made to print maps that accurately followed the twists and turns of the underground routes. The problem was that such maps were not easy for the public to read, and didn't show clearly enough where different lines crossed or joined.

In 1931 Frank Peck commissioned a commercial artist named Harry Beck to design a completely new map – one that simplified finding the way through the Underground system. Two years later, Beck's map was published. Each line was given a different colour, and the layout didn't seek to show the exact course of a line, but merely to give a diagrammatic representation. It has become a classic.

The A to Z

The most popular map of London is the A to Z. It comes in several sizes, from pocket-size, to paperback-size, to large album. It was originally the work of a young woman named Phyllis Pearsall. Like many in the 1930s, she was unemployed. When she applied for jobs and was called up for an interview, she discovered there was nothing to help her find her way about London. What she wanted was a convenient set of maps that named every street, avenue, crescent, and mews. So she set about compiling her own. She decided a set of maps would be too bulky, and that a book would be better. She bought a large-scale Ordnance Survey map and walked all the streets in central London, noting down their names. It took her well over a year, but the book she created has become one of the biggest sellers of all time.

London's Character and Characters

The London Busker

Buddy, Chuck, Jimi… has it all come to this? Busking on the streets of London.

Backs to the wall as a cold wind freezes the fingers on your fife.

Good, bad and indifferent music has floated round the streets of London for centuries. five hundred years ago, John Lydgate compiled some of the cries of London streetsellers in a work called London Lackpenny. That was back in the days when hawkers sold everything from sweet lavender to hot sheep's feet. In 1738, Handel incorporated some of these cries in his opera Xerxes. Lionel Bart achieved a very different commercial and artistic success with the same kind of material in Oliver!, and the genuine article lasted well into the 1950s. Indeed, there is a rag-and-bone man still to be heard in the streets of Kentish Town, north London.

Queen Elizabeth I outlawed ballad singing (so much for the notion of Good Queen Bess). Early in Victoria's reign, Parliament gave London householders the right to require street musicians to withdraw on the grounds of "illness or other reasonable cause". A few years later, Michael T. Bass, head of the brewery company, led a campaign against London street musicians and published a book called Street Music in the Metropolis (so much for the notion of Good King Bass). He didn't see why Londoners should have to show cause why street musicians should move away. Nor did Professor Babbage, inventor of the first computers, who calculated that "one fourth of his entire working power had been destroyed by audible nuisances, to which his highly strung nerves rendered him particularly sensitive". In 90 days he reckoned he had been interrupted 165 times, by six brass bands and 96 street pianos and organs.

In late Victorian and Edwardian days there were large numbers of German bands in London. These bands were made up largely of Bavarians, who worked at home in the winter, but formed groups of up to 15 travelling musicians in various countries throughout the summer. Even well after the first World War there were plenty of barrel-organs and hurdy-gurdies to be heard on London streets. In the 1930s, many unemployed men brought their musical ability to London – Welsh choirs, bagpipers from Scotland, brass players from the North of England.

Busking Today

At any time of day you'll come across buskers in the entrance to Underground stations, or, more often, at the foot of escalators – it's much warmer there in the winter, and possibly cooler in the summer, and the acoustics can be very invigorating. And during shopping hours, Oxford Street as well as other commercial centres have buskers blowing, sawing and pounding away every few yards.

Everybody has heard at least one busking fairytale. It's like Cinderella – one moment the busker's blistering his fingers on a guitar and rupturing his larynx as he sings, the next moment he's been "discovered" and a glittering career has opened up for him in showbiz. Two years ago, a young woman was singing merrily in the grim subway at Hammersmith Broadway. A record producer came along, stopped and listened. Then he approached her, introduced himself, and invited her to a recording session. The rest is not yet history – but an awful lot of people have been singing their hearts out in Hammersmith ever since.

Better documented is the case of Robert Parker, a harpist. Back in 1987, Robert borrowed a stereo electric harp. Record companies didn't want to have anything to do with this somewhat iconoclastic instrument, and Robert tried in vain to get someone to give him a recording contract. So he made an album himself and then set about promoting it. In 1992 he managed to get a four-week stint in Harrods' music department to launch his album, and sold 1000 tapes and CDs. In the last four years he's sold over 100,000.

Unlike Paris, London is not an accordion city, but you will find at least one squeezebox in the subway complex at Charing Cross station, and there's often a blind accordionist in Oxford Street. A brave, kilted Scotsman (possibly an ancient hangover from the 1930s Depression) sometimes plays the saxophone outside Selfridges, and there's also a Highlander in full regalia (kilt, tam and sporran) who plays the bagpipes just outside HMV (west) in Oxford Street. He's very loud. You can hear him all the way down to the Classical Music and Jazz department in the basement, or alternatively all the way to the back of Debenhams, across the street.

There's the steel pan player in Piccadilly Circus Underground, who plays a knockout version of Chopin's Minute Waltz. There is a whole rota of guitarists who take it in turn to play in the tunnel approaching the Northern Line platforms at Charing Cross – mainly Beatles numbers and Simon and Garfunkel. In the underground walkway from South Kensington to Albertopolis, there's a red-headed Irishwoman who plays reels and jigs at devilish speed on the fiddle. At the top of Bond Street, there's an orthodox Jew who plays a diatonic xylophone on one leg – the xylophone, not the Jew. There's even a bold trombonist frightening commuters as his slide flashes in and out at King's Cross.

Around the South Bank you'll come across a great mixture of music. There are some really fine student players, fluttering their way through Bach or Vivaldi on flute, violin or cello. There's also an old geezer who sits, limpet-like, outside the Royal Festival Hall and grinds away at Porter and Gershwin evergreens on straight soprano sax. His tempo never changes. His volume never varies. He has no highs or lows, but there are those who stop and listen, and even buy the CDs he has to sell. Public reaction to London buskers is sharply divided. There are those who share the views of Charles Babbage – that all extraneous and unnecessary noise is a bad thing and should be discouraged – and those whose spirits are positively uplifted by the music of flute, sax or even bagpipes wafting along a street or echoing in a tube tunnel. You make your choice, and you pay your money – or not, as the mood takes you.

above:
A brace of pipers tune up for a night time session.

The London Red Bus

In 1829 the first London bus ran from Paddington to the Bank of England. Twenty-six years later, the Compagnie Générale des Omnibus de Londres was established in Paris, with both French and English directors. This became the London General Omnibus Company, a name revived by some of the London tour buses operating today. In 1933 the London Passenger Transport Board was set up, known to most Londoners as simply "London Transport". For almost a century, the scarlet double-decker bus has been a London icon. Now, however, different liveries have appeared on some routes.

There are now some 300 bus routes in London, crossing the city from all points of the compass or meandering along the main arteries. Some routes are more than ten miles (16 km) long, others barely five (8 km). There are local, circular routes, running round and round all day like rats in a transport maze. There are routes that cover many of the great tourist attractions, and routes that take you to parts of London known to few of its citizens. The most bus-packed road in London is Oxford Street. Since the privatization of London buses in the 1990s, eight different companies run buses along that thoroughfare, most of them operating more than one route. At rush hour, you could almost walk from Oxford Circus to Marble Arch along bus tops.

A Day in the Life of a London Bus

The bus garage has been open all night, with crews bringing in and taking out night buses, but at 4.22 am the first day bus leaves the garage. It's a single-operator bus on route 47, from Catford in southeast London to Shoreditch in the city. There is room for 88 passengers: 42 seated on the top deck, 26 seated "inside", and 20 standing. At this time of the day, however, there are few customers.

4.40 am

Opposite Docklands Car Auctions, Deptford, a few people board the bus. Of the dozen or so passengers, ten are black and most are women, which gives some idea of who works at this time of day. Five minutes later the bus passes Surrey Quays Shopping Centre. Not long ago this area was still called "Surrey Docks", but with gentrification has come a new and vulgar name.

4.50 am

The bus passes under the great mass of railway lines leading to London Bridge station and crosses London Bridge. There, on the right, is Tower Bridge, beautifully

floodlit, with its reflection twinkling in the water. North of the river most of the passengers leave the bus, hurrying away to the office blocks that they have to clean and tidy in the next three or four hours. The bus travels on through the City, past empty Leadenhall Market and the bright lights of Liverpool Street station, where the first rail commuters are trickling in.

5.05 am
Shoreditch High Street is the end of the line. The driver pulls into a bay and the bus empties. Driver and bus wait in this bay for eight minutes before beginning the journey back to Catford. It's still dark, and Shoreditch High Street has little to commend it – a couple of tramps, a cold wind and some lorries thundering past.

Most of London's buses are now running, and those heading for central London are beginning to fill. The next hour or so will be easy, with light traffic on the roads and seats for everyone on the buses. From 6 am onwards, the bus's progress will be slower, with more stops to make and congestion slowly building up along the route.

5.13 am
The bus pulls out of the bay and moves a hundred yards up the road to the bus stop. A few passengers climb aboard. The lights are now on in most of the large City office blocks, and the cleaners that the first buses brought into the City are hard at work. From the top of the bus, in Gracechurch Street, there's a fine view of the floodlit Monument. Gladstone believed that the best way to see London was from the top of a bus. In his day the top deck was uncovered, but the seats were cheaper there.

5.52 am
The bus arrives back at Catford Garage. The return journey took only 39 minutes. Eight minutes later, with a new driver, the bus is back on the street, for its second journey of the day to Shoreditch.

And so it goes on, hour after hour, always on the same route. The passengers will change – cleaners will give way to schoolchildren, white-collar workers, pensioners whose right to cheap travel doesn't begin until 10 am, shoppers, visitors and tourists. The driver will change. The time it takes to drive from Catford to Shoreditch will change, taking longer each journey until the evening rush hour is over. But the bus will travel the same streets, until it leaves Shoreditch High Street for the last time at one minute past midnight, and finally gets back to Catford for a few hours' rest.

The London Pigeon

Friend or foe? Two London pigeons take a break from feeding in Trafalgar Square.

There are those who love London pigeons – scattering loaves of sliced bread on pavements, in parks and under railway bridges; clasping their hands together in joy when they behold the mating dance of their feathered friends; mourning each mangled avian corpse they chance to find in the metropolis. There are those who hate them – accelerating rather than braking when a pigeon waddles on to the road; swatting or kicking at them on station concourses; viewing the courtship display as a neurotic little ritual in which the female feigns disinterest while the male gyrates and wipes his tail feathers along the ground.

The London pigeon is classified as *Columba livia*, the same species as the rock dove. The rock dove nests on cliff faces and rocks. The London pigeon nests on the sculptured friezes of Nelson's Monument in Trafalgar Square, in the crevices of arches and bridges, and on the ledges of empty buildings. It is not a bird that typifies London. The true London bird is *Passer domesticus*, the house sparrow – as of 1998 reported to be in steep decline. It used to be a term of endearment to call someone "me old Cockney sparrer". There are no terms of endearment about pigeons.

Parts of central London are infested by pigeons. No one knows how many there are in the city, though most Londoners think there are too many. The birds are not pretty, many of them are diseased, and a large proportion of them have damaged or deformed feet or eye defects. The most healthy specimens are to be found in and around the London Zoo, where they have a full complement of talons, sleek plumage and wide-awake eyes. They may well thrive on the very mixed diet that the Zoo provides, for they raid every cage and compound.

They are messy birds. When the roof of the Foreign Office in Whitehall was cleaned a few years ago, 50 tonnes of pigeon dung was removed. Nelson is never free of it, and you have to watch your step when walking under most London bridges. The dung is potent stuff. Researchers at the University of North London have discovered that, left untreated, pigeon droppings can strip the paint on some cars down to the metal.

Window cleaners and those who maintain the exterior of London's buildings loathe pigeons. Park-keepers detest them. Jeffrey Bernard, Soho character and writer, hated them, and called them "flying rats". In 1997, a council worker whose job it was to make office blocks at the Elephant and Castle "pigeon-proof" was so incensed by the birds' cunning that he applied to his local authority for permission to return at night and blast them away with a shotgun. It was felt, however, that the use of firearms in and around the Elephant and Castle should not be encouraged, at any time.

The Pigeons of Trafalgar Square

If you really must see London pigeons in all their alleged glory, go to Trafalgar Square. There are thousands of them here every day – so many that when 10,000 were stolen by unknown snatchers in the mid-1990s, nobody noticed. It was said that the stolen pigeons were sold as food, which is a most unpleasant thought, though that is why the poor things were first introduced to London in medieval times.

The pigeons of Trafalgar Square are perhaps the most pampered, overfed and photographed birds in the world. Tourists and visitors love them, and cover themselves with pieces of biscuit and cake so that the pigeons will graze on them. Every day at a stall in the square you can buy pigeon food for 25p per cup – the cup is about the size of a sherry glass. The food is a mixture of nuts and corn, and pigeons will do almost anything to stuff their crops with it. The moment you approach the stall, they land on your shoulders, lapels, head and arms, and if you try to shoo them away, they are likely to leave their mark on you, like a gypsy's curse.

Railway Pigeons

A state of war exists between Railtrack, the company which owns and operates London's railway stations, and the London pigeon. Pigeons love railway stations, especially the large termini, which have high roofs and lots of arches and were designed with a great deal of ornament and decoration, creating hundreds of cosy little corners in which the birds can roost.

Railtrack have tried anti-pigeon paint, suspending wires from the roofs in the birds' flight path, fixing wire grilles to ledges and balconies so that they find it difficult if not impossible to land. But pigeons are adaptable

creatures, with a steep learning curve, and they are holding their own in the war.

Railtrack's problems increased in 1997. Wandsworth Borough Council threatened them with legal action when no amicable agreement could be reached as to which organization should pay to clear the droppings that fell from the railway bridge on to Balham High Street. The matter has not yet been resolved.

For London Transport there is the added problem created by pigeons which travel on the London Underground. Along a section of the Hammersmith and City line, they regularly hop on to trains at Edgware Road station, waddle up and down the carriage looking for crumbs of food, and then hop out a couple of stops further on. All this without a ticket.

above:
Inspiration for Alfred Hitchcock, persecution of the pedestrians.
bottom left:
The Pigeon Food Stall in the Square – the most crowded eating place in London.

London's Wildlife

The Grey Squirrel – London's popular pest.

The ubiquitous buddleia grows on roofs, railway lines and brickwork in London.

Dotted about London are 60 nature reserves, most of them managed by the London Wildlife Trust. They are a mixture of wetlands, islands, woods, sandpits, meadows, ponds, marshes, sections of canal and even parts of a golf course. Though most of them are in the outer suburbs, often at the extremities of the Underground network – Uxbridge, Barnet, Wimbledon and Morden – several are much nearer the heart of the city, at Battersea Park, New Cross and King's Cross. Their purpose is twofold – to provide a natural habitat for as many species of plant and animal life as possible, and to help Londoners of all ages to get to know the natural world.

The reserves themselves, however, are only a small part of the city's wildlife habitat. As suburban London rapidly grew in the early part of the 20th century, animals, birds, insects, reptiles and flowers were forced into an unwelcoming countryside. But nature is stubborn, with an irresistible urge to recover and survive – witness the buddleia plants sprouting from the roof of St George's Church, Bloomsbury, or the crevices of Hungerford Bridge. The second half of the 20th century has seen flora and fauna re-establish itself throughout the suburbs and the inner city.

The most dramatic success story – to some, the most worrying – has been the rise of the urban fox. You can now see foxes in thousands of suburban gardens, along railway cuttings leading into London, in recreation grounds and parks, and loping along main city roads at night. The Queen has lost all her flamingoes to a fox in the grounds of Buckingham Palace. Cats have been killed and decapitated by foxes in Notting Hill; dustbins are regularly overturned near most London parks. On cold winter's nights, many Londoners are disturbed by the howling and barking of foxes as the mating season approaches. Some people would like to see a programme of culling put into operation. Others happily put out bowls of cat or dog food in their gardens, actively encouraging the offenders.

Other mammals thrive in London. Some 10 million rats have learnt to keep out of people's way, but you will often see mice scuttling along the lines of Underground stations. Grey squirrels come boldly up to passersby in most London parks, knowing that they will almost certainly be given bits of cake, sandwich, biscuits or even ice-cream cone. Hedgehogs survive in many suburban gardens, and moles ruin many a lawn. There are herds of deer in Richmond Park, bats in Catford, and rabbits in Hampstead. Toads, frogs and newts thrive in garden ponds and park lakes. Lizards and slow-worms scuttle and slide respectively in neglected scraps of land.

In the late 12th century, William Fitzstephen wrote of the Thames being "well-stocked with

fish". Over the next 750 years fish had to struggle hard to survive. By the 1950s the Thames was an obscenely polluted river, choked with silt and awash with poisonous chemicals. The last 50 years, however, have seen a miraculous recovery. There are now dozens of different species of fish in the Thames, and there are fishermen who catch salmon off the Isle of Dogs. The river is now so clean that seals can be seen in summer sunning themselves off Wapping Stairs.

The top ten bird sites for any London ornithologist are Regent's Park, Hampstead Heath, Brent and Staines Reservoirs, the Lea Valley, Epping Forest, Dagenham Chase, Docklands, Rainham Marshes and Barn Elms. As well as the sparrows, starlings, crows, robins and magpies that you would expect to find in London, you may also come across kestrels, sparrowhawks, owls, woodpeckers, herons, cormorants, and many others. In Hither Green and some other suburbs, flocks of wild parakeets are threatening to drive out the indigenous birdlife.

On wasteland and along railway lines there is a profusion of wild flowers. You can see ragwort and willowherb growing out of the ballast between the tracks at the entrance to Charing Cross and Blackfriars stations. In the railway cuttings of Camden and New Cross there are at various times of year daffodils, sweet peas, irises, bluebells and poppies. A mile or two further from the centre of London you will find wild marjoram, ox-eye daisies, clematis, broom, kidney vetch, goat's beard, cow parsley, shaggy soldier, purple toadflax and Canadian fleabane.

There are even one or two tiny farms in London. The Vauxhall City Farm, Spring Gardens, has several breeds of sheep, a Nubian goat, a calf, a ferret, chickens and ducks, cats, rabbits, guinea pigs, turkeys, geese and Bella the British Saddleback pig. As Eurostar trains whine past in the background, cocks crow and sheep bleat. The whole enterprise occupies a small strip of land, backed by some run-down 19th-century cottages complete with outside lavatories and lean-tos that are unchanged since the days of Charles Dickens.

And at the very heart of London's wildlife is the Camley Street Natural Park, surrounded by the main railway lines leading into King's Cross and St Pancras, overshadowed by giant gas-holders, circled by throbbing traffic. It is an inspiring oasis of greenery. There are ponds and coppices, tiny meadows, bog gardens, bramble and hawthorn thickets. Willows and silver birches shut out all signs of the city (save the spire of the glorious St Pancras Hotel). Coots ripple across the ponds. The scent of honeysuckle, wild roses and watermint and the hum of bees fill the air. In the 1980s it was scheduled to

be a coach park, but the Greater London Council (blessed be its memory) gave in to public pressure and sanctioned the creation of this beautiful place.

Bella's stall at the Vauxhall City Farm in Spring Gardens.

Canine City

Thanks to Walt Disney and the English media, the best-known London dogs are the 101 Dalmatians who lived in Primrose Hill, and the Welsh corgis who live in Buckingham Palace. Like their royal masters and mistresses, however, the corgis nowadays have a lower public profile.

Although there are hundreds of thousands of dogs out in the suburbs, ranging from pedigree lap dogs to snarling pit bulls, there are few pet dogs in the centre of the city. You may see a few poodles, Pekes and Yorkshire terriers being gently exercised in the parks of London before returning to their Mayfair or Kensington apartments for a little boiled chicken or poached salmon. You will certainly see, accompanying many of the homeless that sleep on the streets, woebegone and timorous mongrels on the end of short lengths of rope. Apart from that, the West End is mercifully free of stray dogs and of dog mess.

A lot of London's canines are working dogs – sniffer dogs looking for drugs or explosives at airports; police dogs with their handlers, ready to fight crime; guard dogs patrolling building sites and private grounds; and, once or twice a year, sheepdogs showing their skills in Hyde Park. The dogs with the poorest career prospects in the city are probably the greyhounds that race on the tracks at Walthamstow, Hackney and Catford. Their active racing life is a year or two, and many are then exported to Spain where their working conditions take a decided

top right:
One of the hopefully temporary residents at the Battersea Dogs Home.
below:
The 'Doggie Hilton' – the Battersea Dogs Home.

turn for the worse. One of the hardest-working of London dogs was Laddie, a golden Labrador who collected money on Wimbledon and Waterloo stations for a railway children's orphanage in Woking. When he died, his body was stuffed and placed in a glass case on Platform 7 at Wimbledon station. Today Laddie is kept in the National Railway Museum at York.

Two hundred years ago, London was not a safe place for any dog. A report in the *Morning Herald*, dated 28 January 1801, gave details of a ring of thieves who lured dogs to premises at the back of the Philanthropic Society in Webber Row, St George's fields, and there killed them for their skins. "In the course of the examination it appeared it was a common mode among the dog stealers to take small houses for the purpose of carrying on this abominable trade, and when they had collected as many carcasses as they could bury, and the house would contain, to abscond without paying any rent.... The neighbours were almost poisoned by the stench." There were always plenty of dogs to be found in St George's fields, for packs of spaniels hunted the duck that gathered there. Until 1811 a pub called the Dog and Duck stood on what is now the site of the Imperial War Museum.

A dog's life improved considerably in Victorian times. In 1880 some dogs were so highly prized and so much loved that the Dogs' Cemetery was opened in Kensington Gardens. Nowadays most Londoners are prepared at least to tolerate dogs, and the majority of citizens are actually fond of them. The greatest concern is reserved for the canine inhabitants of the Dogs' Home, Battersea Park Road.

Battersea Dogs' Home

In 1860 Mrs Mary Tealby opened the Temporary Home for Lost and Starving Dogs in Holloway, north London. Eleven years later the home moved to its present site in Battersea Park Road, and was renamed the Dogs' Home, Battersea. Each year the Home takes in over 8000 dogs, many of them strays, some of them brought in by owners who cannot cope with them. Of the 8000, roughly a quarter are claimed by their original owners, half are kept and eventually re-homed, and the remaining quarter are in such a pitiful condition that they have to be put down. The Home also takes in 1500 cats each year, and the Battersea cattery can house up to 130 cats at any one time.

If a dog is healthy, the Home will take care of it until a suitable new owner comes along, no matter how long it takes. There are dogs at Battersea that have been there for years. On arrival they are vaccinated, wormed and given a health check. Where appropriate and practicable, they are neutered. When they leave the home, they are microchipped for registration and identification purposes. Once a year the Home holds a Reunion Day in Battersea Park for ex-residents. It is a day of great good spirits and high emotion.

The Home is open to visitors every day of the week. You enter through the shop, pay your 50p, and proceed to a small courtyard. To the right is the multistorey Tealby Kennels, opened in 1991. It is spotlessly clean, with a strong but not overpowering smell of disinfectant. On each floor (named after London streets – Oxford

The most prestigious dog racing track in London – Walthamstow Stadium.

Street, Regent Street, Bond Street, etc.) there are several dozen kennels, each with stainless steel bowl, bone, rubber ball, blanket and one or two occupants. Some are noisy, standing on their hind legs, noses pressed through the bars, barking loudly. Others, sadder or wiser in their self-marketing, are simply curled up on the floor, gazing with big eyes at the parade of soft-hearted humans passing by.

The Home takes the re-housing of one of its dogs very seriously. It prefers all members of the family to attend for a searching interview, and the initial meeting between dog and family is carefully monitored. It is a place of great hope and eager affection. Occasionally an adoption doesn't work, and a dog is brought back, but over the 130 years of its existence the Home has provided shelter and care for nearly 3 million dogs.

The Greyhound Racing track at Wimbledon Stadium, south London.

Underneath the Arches

In the 1930s and 1940s two of the most popular variety stars in London were Flanagan and Allen, a couple of music-hall artists who combined comedy with overwhelmingly sentimental songs. The tune that played them on and off stage was called Underneath the Arches. It's a song about two tramps who spend their nights dreaming under the arches, with cobblestones for a bed and the pavement as a pillow.

In a city where every square yard is precious, however, a great deal more than sleeping and dreaming takes place under road and railway arches. There is a whole dark world to be found and explored as trains or traffic rumble overhead, though not all of it appears welcoming. It would take a brave heart to seek out the Cavern Auction Rooms beneath the railway approach to St Pancras station. A chalked sign on a grimy brick wall leads to a pitch-black tunnel, where water drips into sooty puddles and the air is dank and bitter. Both the London Dungeon and the Museum of the London Blitz are grimly sited under the arches of London Bridge station, and, in nearby Crucifix Lane, there is a series of painted panels commemorating some of the bloodier conflicts of the Second World War.

Not every arch houses something grisly and hair-raising. Under the arches of Richmond Bridge you will find Tide Tables, a vegetarian restaurant. When the weather is fine, there are tables by the river. When it rains, customers retreat beneath the bridge. In Cornwall Road, below Waterloo East station, there is a car engineering works that deals exclusively with old Citroëns – the sort that carried Inspector Maigret from one crime scene to another in the detective novels of Georges Simenon. On weekdays you will see these beautiful machines parked in the road, their gleaming paintwork catching what little sun penetrates this corner of London.

The arches beneath the railway tracks heading in and out of Waterloo Station.

A hundred yards along the same railway lines, towards the Thames and the Royal Festival Hall, there's a unique history of the 20th century in a series of murals by the artist Felix Topolski. The exhibition has erratic opening hours, but it's worth persisting in attempts to see it. A further three arches along, there's a fine restaurant, the Archduke (a clever musical as well as topographical pun), in which to recover from the dramatic images.

The spaces underneath the arches in St Pancras Road have been converted into a variety of enterprises. Among the shops are Layton's Wine Merchants, a picture framer's, bric-à-brac and antique dealers, and a snack bar. Across the river, in Vauxhall, there's even a small brewery called O'Hanlon's. The stouts, Irish ales and wheat beers brewed here are sold in O'Hanlon's pub at Tysoe Street, near Exmouth Market in Farringdon. Most of the businesses in the Vauxhall arches are more mundane affairs, typical of under-the-arches development – motorbike repair sheds, panel beaters and paint shops. It's also the place where taxis go when they're damaged – proof that just occasionally taxis do get involved in accidents.

In fact, in any parade of arches you are almost certain to come across a motor workshop, or an MOT Test station, or a body shop. There is clearly something about the troglodyte existence (perhaps the cheap rents) that appeals to those who make their living patching up old bangers.

The Players' Theatre
Under the arches supporting the railway lines leading from Charing Cross station, on the north side of the Thames, is the Players' Theatre. It's a 250-seat playhouse converted from Nos. 173 and 174 Villiers Street, long a home of the music hall. The Players' Theatre was founded in 1929 as Playhouse Six, but moved to the Villiers Street premises in 1946. By then music hall in London was on its last legs, and the theatre re-opened as a club in 1953 with a production of Sandy Wilson's *The Boy Friend*. Later it reverted to a revival of music hall, with a resident company known as "The Late Joys".

The Catacombs of Camden
An elaborate and extensive honeycomb of arched cellars runs from Euston to Camden Lock and Dingwall's. It passes under the goods depot at Primrose Hill, the bonded warehouse of Gilbey's the distillers on the Regent's Canal, and the canal itself. It's owned by Railtrack and is used for storage, but it was originally built as stabling for the horses and ponies that worked in the shunting yards

of Euston station. Taking care to avoid traffic, you can still trace part of the route taken by this labyrinth, for there are several series of cast-iron grilles in the roads between Euston and Camden. These supplied the only sources of light for the horses that lived in the catacombs.

The Adelphi Arches
Forty feet (12 metres) underground, leading eastwards from Charing Cross station to the Savoy Hotel car park, are the Adelphi Arches. They run the length of John Adam Street. They are all that remains of the splendid Adelphi, built by the Adam brothers in the 18th century, a riverside palace with vaults so magnificent that they were hailed as "a reminder of the Etruscan Cloaca of Old Rome". It had been intended to store gunpowder in them until it was discovered that they were liable to flooding. Instead, they were used as wine cellars and coal bunkers. When the Embankment was built in 1870, the Adelphi lost its riverside frontage and its fashionable charm. It declined in value and favour. In its vaults "the most abandoned characters often passed the night, nestling upon foul straw; and many a street thief escaped from his pursuers in these dismal haunts". The Adelphi itself was pulled down in the 1930s, but a section of the vaults remains.

A mixture of enterprises thrive underneath the arches at King's Cross.

Scotland Yard and the London Copper

The Metropolitan Police Force was founded in 1829 by Robert Peel, then Home Secretary in the Conservative administration of the Duke of Wellington. Three thousand officers were appointed and stationed in 16 divisions, all within a seven-mile (11-km) radius of Charing Cross. They were sworn in, given a uniform of blue coat,

The headquarters of the Metropolitan Police – New Scotland Yard in Broadway, Victoria.

white trousers and a top hat (to distinguish them from the military), and paid three shillings (15p) a day to combat crime in London. They were at first highly unpopular and regarded with great suspicion. "No doubt," said Peel, "three shillings a day will not give me all the virtues under heaven, but I do not want them. Angels would be far above my work."

At first, the new police were christened "blue devils", then came the more affectionate nicknames "peelers" and "bobbies", from Peel's own names. Others, kind and unkind, have followed: "bluebottles", "filth", "pigs", "rozzers", "the Old Bill", "flatfeet", "coppers". Over the years there have been scandals and revelations of dishonesty in the Metropolitan Police (known as "the Met"), greeted by the public with genuine shock and disgust. That such discoveries should surprise people is a tribute to the general run of London's police, for there are many cities in the world where police corruption is accepted as endemic.

From the beginning, the Met has had to maintain a precarious political balance. It was created largely to protect the rich from the poor, and working-class men and women still spend most of their time policing fellow members of the working class. On the other hand, the Met has always had to show that it is impartial in the struggle between rich and poor, not offering preferential treatment to the high and mighty. A Punch cartoon many years ago showed an irate "gentleman" angrily saying to a policeman, "Do you know who I am?", and the policeman replying "No, and I shall be wanting your address as well in a moment."

The bobby on the beat is one of the icons of London, to be seen on postcards in souvenir shops and on posters all over the city. For decades the image was of a strong, kindly, brave, unarmed father figure, full of wisdom and fairness, a servant and protector of his local community – women police officers did not appear until the first World War. With whistle and truncheon, the bobby faced all evil-doers, hauling them off to justice with a cautionary "Now then, my lad, are you coming quietly or do I have to snap the bracelets [handcuffs] on you?"

The image remains, though increasingly blurred at the edges. Many London police are armed, racing round the city in cars, relative strangers to the community in which they are stationed. There are still police officers walking the beat in the West End, but they are there more to reassure the public than to tackle criminals. The Met now has nearly 30,000 officers and polices some 786 square miles (2035 sq. km). It also has police jurisdiction over an area of 25 miles' radius (40 km) from the Queen, wherever she is, in Britain or the rest of the world.

Scotland Yard

The first headquarters of the Met was at 4 Whitehall Place, Westminster, with a police station and recruiting office attached which were entered from Scotland Yard. The station was soon nicknamed after the Yard. The old building was quickly outgrown, and became littered with books and documents, blankets, clothes and horse saddles. It was almost fortunate, therefore, that old Scotland Yard was blown up by Fenians in 1883. Norman Shaw designed a fine replacement, and New Scotland Yard opened in 1890. It was described by A.P. Herbert as a "very constabulary kind of castle", faced with granite that had been quarried by convicts on Dartmoor, and surmounted by turrets in the style of a French château.

It lasted as the Met's headquarters until 1967, when the police moved to new and ugly premises in Broadway, just off Victoria Street. The old New Scotland Yard is now called the Norman Shaw Building, to distinguish it from the new New Scotland Yard. The Met is housed in a 20-storey block with some 700 offices. It is the hub of London's police work, the home of the Criminal Investigation Department and the Black Museum. This is a grisly collection of criminal artefacts, not open to the public.

Once the site of a house presented to Kenneth III of Scotland by Edgar of England in 959, later the HQ for the Met.

Hendon Police College

In 1929, exactly 100 years after the establishment of the Met, two men met in the smoking room of Brooks's Club in St James's. They were Sir Arthur Dixon, from the Home Office, and Lord Trenchard, head of Scotland Yard. The conversation centred around the need to recruit more young policemen from the public schools and universities. By the time they left the smoking room, they had agreed on the idea of a police college, similar to the Army's Sandhurst, at which candidates with special potential would be trained to fill the higher ranks of the Metropolitan Police.

The College was opened on 31 May 1934 by Edward, Prince of Wales (later Edward VIII). Like the early force, it was initially unpopular, regarded by many as an upholder of the class system and an encouragement to Fascism. It closed in 1939, but a second training school was opened in Hendon in 1946. The present Metropolitan Police Training Centre was opened in 1974. You can see it clearly from a Northern Line train as you approach Colindale from the south. It looks like a well-appointed technical school, generously equipped with sports grounds and attended by very well-behaved students.

bottom left:
Old Scotland Yard, for 100 years the most famous police station in London.
below:
The City has its own police force.

London Graffiti

There is nothing particularly modern about graffiti. Scrawling protests on a wall is not a new phenomenon. In the 1940s, when food and clothes were rationed and luxury goods were in short supply, on many walls there appeared "Wot, no...?" slogans – "WOT, NO SUGAR?" "WOT, NO CIGARS?" "WOT, NO OFFAL?" or cheese, fruit, nylons, elastic, and so on. On a wall in Lewisham, you can still discern some scratches of 18th-century graffiti. Opponents of the phenomenon, however, see it as very much a problem of our times.

A piece of good graffiti is a slogan in a public place that is pithy and witty or wise. A piece of great graffiti is a slogan in an appropriate public place that is pithy and witty or wise. An example of good graffiti is that chalked on the outside of a pub in Lewisham in July 1998: "TIME IS A GREAT TEACHER. THE TROUBLE IS IT ALWAYS KILLS ITS PUPILS", an aphorism that was attributed by the anonymous dauber to the composer Hector Berlioz. There are all too few examples of great graffiti, though at least one is still remembered in London. In the late 1940s the playwright Christopher Fry erected a sign on the gate leading to his house in Little Venice that read "BEWARE OF THE DOGE".

London graffiti come in many different languages (including Urdu, Arabic, Cantonese and Australian). In 1998, in August, a time when examination results are published, "POS LUEGO" (the Spanish for "afterwards") followed by "I CAN'T BELIEVE IT" was written on the wall of the St Martin's School of Art. And there are messages from all over the world – "COMMUNISM IS ALIVE AND FIGHTING IN PERU". Most examples, however, are of a local, baldly informative and deadly dull nature – "KILROY WOZ HERE", "LEE LOVES TRACY TRUE", "EVERYBODY HATES MILLWALL!". There are also plenty of examples of the Inexplicable (BIG DAN'S GUSSET), the Cunningly Disguised (WELL'ARD, i.e. very tough), and the Blindingly Obvious (£1 WILL BUY THE WHOLE WORLD WHEN EVERYTHING IS FREE). Other graffiti seek to rouse people to action far away from London – "FREE THE BIRMINGHAM SIX!" or "SMASH THE H-BLOCKS NOW!", the latter lingering on into the very late 1990s on one of the arches in Electric Avenue to the rear of Brixton Market. The prob-

Art goes Pop on the streets of London.

lem is that painted words may well outlast the issue they seek to highlight. You can still see "GEORGE DAVIS IS INNOCENT" here and there, though most Londoners now have no idea what it is that George Davis is innocent of – he was convicted of armed robbery in 1975.

The art of decorating Underground trains in London with spray paint has not reached the advanced levels to be seen in New York. Most examples are no better than mere vandalism. The eye quickly tires of seeing the monosyllabic names of posses and loners repeated over and over again – ZONK, FAZZZZ, BRANES, FUNK, KRAN, MEFF, etc. – all useful words for a game of Scrabble, though they do little to raise the spirits. Finding something worth at least a few seconds' thought is not easy. You may search in vain even in the most promising public lavatories. The Gents at the British Museum has long been a bitter disappointment to connoisseurs of graffiti. Whole walls may be covered with small print, but the sentiments are either boyishly dirty, or of an extreme right-wing political nature, or both.

London's Most Famous Piece of Graffiti

On the night of 30 September 1888 the bodies of two women were found in Whitechapel. The murders of Elizabeth Stride and Catherine Eddowes had taken place within 45 minutes of each other – Stride in a backyard off Berners Street (now Henriques Street), Eddowes in Mitre Square. A message had been chalked on the wall of a building nearby – "THE JUWES ARE THE MEN THAT WILL NOT BE BLAMED FOR NOTHING".

The Police Commissioner gave orders for the wall to be wiped clean before the graffiti could be properly recorded or even examined, but it was presumed to be the work of Jack the Ripper himself. There have been those who claim that the Police Commissioner was part of a conspiracy to cover up the identity of the Ripper, and that the message hinted at a Masonic plot involving Lord Salisbury (the Prime Minister) and Sir William Gull (physician extraordinary to Queen Victoria). It has been further suggested that the Ripper was the Duke of Clarence, Victoria's own son, and that Mary Kelly (the Ripper's last victim) had assisted as midwife at the birth of the Duke's illegitimate child. Well over a hundred years later, nobody knows, but the Ripper's message has passed into history.

The Medium is the Message… but don't look too closely.

Geoffrey Fletcher and the Holborn Lavatory Attendant

> I made friends with the attendant… who told me that there were very few old lavatories left in London. He called old conveniences "Queen Victorias", a somewhat startling terminology. I was told that the lavatory in Charing Cross Road was the place to go if you want the writing on the wall… "make your blood run cold, it would".
> **Geoffrey Fletcher**, *The London Nobody Knows*, 1962

Unhappily, when Fletcher visited the public lavatories at the bottom of Charing Cross Road they had been cleaned up and he found no writing on the wall. Today they no longer exist. The Gents is closed, though you can still see the handsome black railings that marked the entrance. The Ladies is covered over by the House of Football – "eat it, sleep it, wake up and play it" – and there is not a trace of graffiti to be seen anywhere.

Haunted London

St James's Palace, home of the ghost of the Duke of Cumberland's valet.

The Adelphi Theatre is haunted by the ghost of an actor who was murdered there.

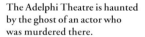

Many of those who have died in London seem reluctant to leave it. There are reported visitations or sightings of ghosts all over the city, the favourite haunts being palaces, pubs and theatres. London ghosts are a benign crowd. There are few records of mischief-making or evil-doings, but a few spirits are unquiet.

Three of the most miserable are the ghosts of Oliver Cromwell, Henry Ireton and John Bradshaw. After overthrowing Charles I and becoming Protector of the Commonwealth of England, Cromwell lived a further busy nine years before dying of a tertian ague in 1658. Ireton was a soldier and Cromwell's son-in-law. He was also one of the regicides who signed Charles I's death warrant. Ireton died of a fever while besieging Limerick in 1651. Bradshaw presided at the trial of Charles I and it was he who pronounced sentence of death on the King. Bradshaw died in 1659. The trio's spiritual restlessness began when Charles II was restored to the throne in 1660. The bodies of all three were exhumed, taken to Tyburn and there hanged. The remains of Cromwell's head were then severed from his body and placed on a spike in Westminster Hall. Since then, all three are said to haunt Red Lion Square in Holborn, though no one has come up with a reason why.

The Temple is said to be haunted by the ghost of Baron Brampton, better known as Henry Hawkins, and perhaps unfairly nicknamed "Hanging Hawkins" for his lack of leniency as a criminal judge. Vine Street Police Station is the beat of the ghost of Sergeant Goddard, a policeman who hanged himself in one of the station's cells during Edward VII's reign. Goddard's spirit is blamed for anything that goes wrong at Vine Street:

lights left on, papers wrongly filed, doors left unlocked.

Durward Street in the East End of London is the haunt of Mary Ann Nicholls, the first victim of Jack the Ripper. Her ghost takes the form of a pathetic woman, huddled in the gutter. Another young woman haunted 50 Berkeley Square in the West End for many years in the second half of the 19th century. It was said that she had killed herself rather than submit to the lecherous advances of her guardian. Visitors to the house fainted, two sailors who broke in looking for somewhere to sleep fled in panic when the ghost appeared, and Lord Lyttleton fired his pistol at the apparition. All is quiet there now, however.

Things are still quiet in Cock Lane, EC1. In the 14th century, the street was the only licensed "walk" for prostitutes, but "Scratching Fanny" didn't trouble residents until some 500 years later. She was a classic poltergeist who scratched on walls and hurled articles across rooms. Not far away, St Paul's Cathedral is still haunted, by an unthreatening male ghost who frequents the Kitchener Chapel. Westminster Abbey also has its own ghosts. John Bradshaw, when not busy in Red Lion Square, does a little haunting here. More pathetic is a spectral figure dressed in first World War khaki, who approaches visitors as if about to ask a question and then suddenly disappears.

Pub Ghosts

Several London pubs are haunted. The Grenadier in Wilton Row has the ghost of an army officer who was flogged to death after being caught cheating at cards. The old Nun's Head in Nunhead Green is visited by the spirit of the last abbess of the nunnery that stood on the site of the pub. She was beheaded during the Reformation and her head set on a stake – hence "Nunhead". A strange apparition manifests itself at the John Snow in Broadwick Street. Snow was the London doctor who established that cholera was caused by contaminated water in the 1840s, and identified the wells and pumps responsible. The apparition is the image of a water pump, which appears just outside the pub from time to time.

The spirits of some of those hanged at Tyburn haunt the Rose and Crown in Old Park Lane. In the 18th century a few felons on their way to the gallows at Tyburn were incarcerated in the cellars of the pub overnight. The Silver Cross in Whitehall is reputedly haunted by a Tudor maiden, and the Cheshire Cheese in Little Essex Street is home to a meddlesome spirit who pushes the fruit machine around at night, plays with the dumbwaiter and throws barrels about the cellar. The landlord doesn't seem to mind. Visitors are offered a ghost tour by one of the customers in 17th-century costume.

Palace Ghosts

Most palaces have ghosts. The Palace of Westminster was haunted by the doppelgänger of Mrs Milman, wife of one of the palace staff in the 1920s. The doppelgänger would appear inside and outside the palace, behaving in a most unladylike way. St James's Palace is still haunted by the ghost of Sellis, valet to the Duke of Cumberland, later King of Hanover in the 1830s. Sellis cut his own throat after a violent attack on the Duke, who may have seduced Sellis's daughter. George II's spirit appears at a window of Kensington Palace, its pale face awaiting news from Hanover that never came to him in life.

Catherine Howard was Henry VIII's fifth wife. She was beheaded on his orders for her promiscuity. Her ghost comes shrieking along the gallery in Hampton Court, towards Henry VII's Oratory, whither she raced in 1542 to plead for the king's mercy.

Theatre Ghosts

There are almost too many theatre ghosts to mention. Grimaldi's ghost appears in a box at Sadler's Wells. The dress circle of the Coliseum is haunted by an army officer from the first World War. St James's Theatre (sadly demolished in 1957) was the playground of the ghost of Oscar Wilde. The Adelphi Theatre in The Strand is home to the ghost of William Terriss, a theatrical idol in Victorian times. Terriss was murdered by another member of the cast of *The Secret Service,* jealous of Terriss's success. It is said that Terriss also haunts Covent Garden Underground station on his way to the theatre. Dan Leno's ghost haunts the Theatre Royal, Drury Lane. This theatre has a more famous ghost, however, who appears only when a production is going to have a long run. This ghost would appear to be the victim of an unsolved murder mystery, whose skeleton was discovered in the theatre in 1870 with a dagger embedded in its ribs.

Though all seems quiet today, there have been strange 'goings-on' at 50 Berkeley Square.

Refugee London

Over hundreds of years, London has provided an asylum for political and religious refugees. It has been seen as a haven by Jews and Protestants, anarchists and socialists, Europeans and Asians, those fleeing the wrath of, in turn, the Shah of Persia and the Ayatollah Khomeini of Iran, the Tsar of Russia and the Soviet Union, republicans and monarchists. To many, the city has given a warm welcome, to some a frigid reception.

From time to time some Londoners find this influx of fugitives hard to accept. They see such newcomers as people seeking homes, jobs or welfare benefits at their expense. In harsh economic times they believe there will be even less of the cake to be shared. This sometimes understandable but never acceptable view takes no account of the fact that the population of London has been steadily falling for the past 30 years, but provides an unwholesome fuel for the racist right-wing bandwagon.

There has long been a trickle of refugees across the Channel from France. In the 17th century Huguenots fleeing religious persecution came to east London. In the late 18th century émigré aristocrats and others came here to escape the worst excesses of the French Revolution. Among them was Cleopha Copp, a young woman of

right:
Each year the Italian community in Clerkenwell holds a festival to celebrate the Assumption of the Virgin Mary.
top right:
Italian flags on sale in Clerkenwell.

German parentage, who married John Nyren, a famous cricketer. She took a large house in West Ham, where she gave 50 young female French refugees employment in lace-making. She also employed a Jesuit priest to give them religious instruction two or three times a week.

Among other refugees was Charles Maurice de Talleyrand-Périgord. His first visit to London was as French Ambassador in 1792. Shortly after this he was discredited by the Revolution and fled to London for safety. He was followed half a century or so later by Prince Louis Napoleon, Bonaparte's nephew. Prince Louis was escaping the police of Louis-Philippe, the Citizen King of France. Soon afterwards, Louis-Philippe hurriedly left France after the Revolution of 1848. He settled in Orpington, south London, then a little village where locals drank too much at cricket matches and laid bets on the length of the Sunday sermon.

With comings and goings reminiscent of French farce, that left the way clear for Louis Napoleon to return to Paris and assume the throne as Emperor Napoleon III. After the defeat of the Franco-Prussian War in 1871, however, the Emperor rushed to London to join his wife in exile. He spent the rest of his life in Camden Place, Chislehurst, not far from Orpington. There was an old windmill nearby, and it was said that the new French Republic posted spies at the top of the windmill to make sure Napoleon wasn't planning a coup and a return to

France, and that Napoleon posted his counter-spies at the bottom of the windmill.

Meanwhile, leaders of the "Young Italy" movement were refugees in London, most notably Mazzini and Garibaldi. Their aim was to unify Italy and, in the case of Mazzini, to promote revolution throughout Europe. Mazzini was constantly on the run, sought sanctuary in Switzerland, but was banished from there in 1837. He came to London penniless, and sought to politicize the poor Italian organ-grinders who worked on the streets. Garibaldi, however, arrived in splendour, the hero of liberals everywhere. Hundreds of thousands of spectators, dressed in red hats and red blouses (the colour of Garibaldi's Army of Liberation in Italy), met his train at Vauxhall, and more than 500,000 lined the route from Wandsworth to the West End. While Garibaldi stayed with the Duke of Sutherland at Stafford House, St James's, the Duke's lackeys sold bottles of soapsuds alleged to have come from Garibaldi's washbasin.

Lenin and Trotsky were not as popular, and Lenin was disappointed in the English during his exile in London. "There are many revolutionary and socialist elements among the English proletariat," he wrote, "but they are all mixed up with conservatism, religion and prejudice, and somehow the socialist and revolutionary elements never break through the surface and unite." Karl Marx, on the other hand, enjoyed his time in London. He arrived in the city in 1849 and died there in 1883, spending much of his time brooding on the overthrow of capitalism in the Reading Room of the British Museum.

From the late 18th century onwards, there were regular influxes of Polish refugees, usually as a result of failed insurrections in their own country. White Eagle Hill in Highgate Cemetery is the resting-place of many of the leaders of the abortive rising of 1863–4. Joseph Conrad fled to London at this time and settled in Islington. By 1901 there were 42,000 Russians and Poles living in Stepney alone. At the beginning of the Second World War, some 30,000 Poles, including leaders of the government and military, arrived in London. After the war, a further 150,000 Poles sought asylum in London following the Soviet occupation of their country.

In detention in Hounslow today, there are those seeking asylum, awaiting Home Office ruling on whether they may stay or not, who would question London's hospitality, but on the whole London has kept its door open to those who needed succour.

A Day in the Life of London Beer

Five hundred years ago thousands of Londoners brewed their own beer from ingredients they grew themselves or obtained locally. Monks, tradesmen, housewives and even nuns brewed the good ale that the English maintaine was the finest in the world. One of the largest breweries in London was the Stag, at Westminster Abbey. One of the oldest was the City of London Brewery in Cannon-Street.

William Hogarth painted a picture in praise of beer in 1751 as a social commentary on the pleasures and virtues of this worthy beverage. The emergence of capitalism and the industrial revolution put an end to much of the home-centred brewing economy, and small neighbourhood breweries were established. As with most commercial enterprise, it wasn't long before the big fish swallowed the little fish. Breweries became fewer, bigger and better-known.

Among the best-known during Hogarth's day were the Albion Brewery in the Mile End Road (run by Charrington's), the Black Eagle in Brick Lane (run by the brothers Joseph and Benjamin Bucknall), the Woodyard at St Martin's-in-the-fields, and the Courage Brewery in Southwark Bridge Road, which according to Dr Johnson allowed one the chance to grow "rich beyond the dreams of avarice". In the early 1800s a brewery stood on the site of the Dominion Theatre in Tottenham Court Road. It was named after a nearby pub called the Horseshoe Tavern, whose successor you can still visit today.

As time has gone by the dozens of London breweries have been whittled down to a handful – Fullers (in Chiswick), Whitbread (in Chiswell Street, EC1), the Firkin chain of breweries-within-a-pub, and Young's Ram Brewery in Wandsworth.

A Working London Brewery
In 1581 Humphrey Langridge began brewing beer in Wandsworth. The fame of his beer spread and Queen Elizabeth I became a regular visitor, stopping off for a pint on her way to Hampton Court. The brewery changed hands in both the 17th and 18th centuries, and in 1831 was bought by Charles Alan Young. Since then it has remained in the continuous ownership of the Young family.

It's an old-fashioned brewery using traditional ingredients such as malt from East Anglia, hops from Kent and the west of England, yeast, and water which used to be supplied from an artesian well beneath the brewery itself.

A guided tour round its six and a half acres (2.5 ha) takes place four times a day, covering the entire brewing process – mashing, fermentation, filtering, bottling and barrelling, and loading on to the lorries and horse-drawn drays that deliver the beer to the 186 Young's pubs within the perimeter of the M25. The tour includes a free pint.

Little is wasted in the brewing process. By-products are sold to farmers as cattle feed or fertilizer, and the unwanted yeast is sold to Marmite, who used to have a pungent factory in nearby Vauxhall. On hot days, when the wind was in the right quarter, you could smell the savoury fumes drifting across the Oval Cricket Ground.

The Ram Brewery has its own museum. Among the exhibits are a length of elm-wood piping from the 17th century, copper vessels from 1869 (made by Pontifex and Wood in Shoe Lane, EC4), old bottles, and a notice threatening that "Any man found smoking in the Brewery will be immediately discharged". The brewery still has the steam-driven beam engines that worked 12 hours a day, every day, for 109 years until honourably retired in 1976. To the delight of many, it still employs heavy horses to deliver its beer to the Young's pubs in the neighbourhood. In the last Victorian working stables in London live Big Harry, the enormous shire; Sandy and Tim, a pair of Suffolk Punches; and Clydesdale and Percheron horses.

The brewery is surrounded by Young's pubs. The Alma Tavern in Old York Road is a lovely green-tiled Victorian pub with a gleaming brass and dark wood interior. It's a favourite drinking haunt for rugger fans on their way back to Waterloo after a match at Twickenham – you may wish to avoid it on such occasions. The Crane, in chocolate and cream, stands by the River Wandle, hinting at the charms of old Wandsworth village before the internal combustion engine ruined it. Its upstairs restaurant is reputed to be haunted. The Ship in Jew's Row is the best of the pubs to visit in summer, when you can sit on the patio that overlooks the Thames. It also holds spectacular firework displays on Guy Fawkes Night, 5 November. The grand Spread Eagle, opposite the brewery, is one of the last of London's gin palaces, and is the subject of a preservation order. Next door to the brewery is the Brewery Tap, where the tour starts and where you can help yourself to nibbles of roasted malt grains from dishes on the bar. Workers from the brewery tend to use the Grapes in Fairfield Street.

In the brewery yard there are tack rooms for the collars, brasses, reins and bridles of the working and show horses, for Young's carriages often take part in ceremonial occasions. There's also a small forge for the farrier who shoes the horses. Ducks and geese swim in the pond. Bonnie the donkey and a pair of goats called Danny and Daffodil munch contentedly on bales of hay. The tour is fascinating, and the pint of beer at the end is excellent.

Dustmen, Mudlarks, Flushers and Toshers

All cities make lots of rubbish. When London dustmen went on strike in October 1970, it wasn't long before the streets and squares of the West End were covered with bags of old food, empty packets, cardboard boxes, and piles of plastic, glass and paper. There were fears that this would lead to a plague of rats, and the smell of rotting meat, fish and vegetables was appalling. Troops were called in, but it wasn't until the dustmen went back to work that Londoners could literally breathe easily.

Whether dustmen are employed by a local authority or by private firms their work is the same – to remove the tons of litter that London produces every day, which they do with a mixture of good and bad humour, care and carelessness, skill and occasional ineptitude. Increasingly, London's rubbish is recycled or incinerated, but most of it is still used as landfill on the Essex shore of the Thames estuary. In all weathers you can see tugs pulling strings of barges downriver, loaded with the grit

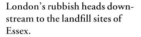

London's rubbish heads downstream to the landfill sites of Essex.

and grime of the city. It's a method that Londoners have used since Tudor times to dispose of their rubbish. Five centuries ago, when there were no dustmen, citizens had to take their refuse to barges moored in the Thames.

It took another 200 years before anyone realized that disposing of the city's rubbish could be a profitable occupation. Horse-drawn carts lumbered through London in the 18th century, collecting refuse from those willing to pay for the privilege. As the population grew, so did the number of refuse collectors. By 1850 the main task for London's 1800 dustmen was to collect the cinders from the 3.5 million tons of coal that Londoners burned each year on their domestic fires. The mixture of ash and clinker was taken to the nearest piece of waste ground, where it was dumped. Vast dustyards arose in Gray's Inn Road, Paddington, Lower Shadwell and other parts of London. Charles Dickens set several scenes of Our Mutual Friend in one. Here gangs of women were paid one shilling (5p) each per day to sieve the mixture and separate the breeze (clinker) from the dust.

At the same time, the 300,000 London dustbins were emptied by another squad of 150 men, each handling and emptying some 100 bins a day. The refuse then went by

barge to the brickfields of Faversham or Sittingbourne in north Kent, where the dust was mixed with clay to make the bricks and the breeze was used to fire the furnaces.

Sweep-Nightmen

Some 800 years ago, medieval London's cesspits were cleaned and emptied by "gong-fermors". They were an elite group of workers who were sometimes paid £2 for dealing with a single pit. The system had changed little by Victorian times, when many dustmen also worked at night, removing "night-soil" (urine and faeces) from the cesspools of the city. For this they were paid an extra ten shillings (50p) a week and a small allowance of beer. They were said to be immune to the plague.

Mudlarks

This was the name given to groups of young boys and girls and old women who combed the banks of the Thames at low tide, from Woolwich in the east to Vauxhall in the west. They spent the day in total silence, looking for anything of value washed up on the mud – coal, bones, copper nails, bits of rope, hammers and saws. Occasionally they would board and steal from an unmanned boat, but if caught this meant a week in the House of Correction. Some mudlarks preferred this to liberty, as they were clothed and fed while in prison. They sold the coal they collected to poor local households for one penny (0.5p) per 14 lbs (6.5 kilos). On average they earned three old pence (1.5p) per day, and started work at the age of six or seven years.

Sewermen

Beneath the streets of London lies a network of Victorian sewers. It's a world inhabited by rats, frogs, fungi, algae, eels and sewermen. The men who clean and maintain the city's sewers are called "flushers". They work in groups of five, led by a foreman called a "ganger". To protect themselves from the slime and ooze that they work in, they wear heavy waders that come up to the waist, and boots. Against the cold they wear thick, thigh-length socks. Theirs is not a pleasant job. In the winter of 1963–4 they killed over 650,000 rats in the London sewers.

Their work consists mostly in shovelling away the sediment that collects at the bottom of every sewer, threatening to block the system, and checking for signs of any build-up of dangerous gases. The sewers are all over 100 years old, and much of the brickwork is crumbling. Weil's disease (an infection from rats' urine that affects the brain) and hepatitis are occupational hazards. There is also the risk of suddenly finding yourself in the middle of a flood of, say, ammonia, released from a

London factory. The gangs carry two-way radios, so that they can be supplied with up-to-date weather forecasts, for a shower of rain can send a tidal wave sweeping through the sewers.

Toshers

While mudlarks combed the banks of the Thames, others grubbed through the sewers, searching for treasure. Toshers were the scavenging elite of London, men who spent up to 18 hours at a time underground. They wore long greasy coats with large pockets, canvas trousers and thick shoes. Their ambition was to find a "tosheroon", a ball of copper and silver coins that had fused together over decades. They entered the sewer system at low tide, through the tunnel openings at the riverside. When these archways were bricked up in the 1840s, the toshers of London disappeared.

Chucking it on the cart... one of London's dustmen on the weekly round-up of rubbish.

Recycled London

Not much of London gets recycled. If any part of it has ceased to have a profitable existence, it will probably be unceremoniously pulled down. Old theatres, office blocks and barracks, hospitals and hotels, prisons and palaces have all been demolished to make way for something more marketable, if less romantic. The original "Bedlam", the Bethlem Hospital near Broad Street Station, is now a National Car Park.

There have been exceptions. The Round House at Chalk Farm used to be the shed where crack locomotives were turned round so that they faced the right way to pull express trains out of Euston. Now it's a rock and pop concert venue. The Oxo Tower on the South Bank was originally a private power station for the Post Office, but was sold in the 1920s. It was then a meat warehouse for 60 years; now it's smart apartments crowned by a very smart restaurant. In the suburbs you can come across old churches that are now Community Arts Centres, or pine furniture showrooms, or the homes of ageing hippies.

The present Somerset House started life as government offices. Parts of it have been, in turn, the Royal Academy, the headquarters of the Navy, the Stamp Office, the office of the Hackney Coach and Barge Master, and the stronghold of the Inland Revenue. The Courtauld Institute Galleries took up residence in the 1990s. The Prince Regent's Victory Pagoda, built in 1814 to celebrate or at least anticipate the final defeat of Napoleon, blew up when lit with gas at a fireworks display. It was then transported to Woolwich, where it became part of the Royal Artillery Museum.

The old British Museum Underground station, closed in 1933, became the administrative office of the Brigade of Guards, and later the Flood Control Centre for the British Army. Only the military mind could conceive something as startling as having a flood control centre 80 feet (25 metres) underground. Another disused Underground station – the Bull and Bush under Hampstead Heath – became the nuclear bunker for London Transport in the 1950s. It's now empty. The Camden Town Underground shelter became one of the sets for BBC TV's Doctor Who series. The Woolwich Arsenal's own underground railway system housed hundreds of thousands of books from the old British Library.

The downstream building of the Shell Centre is now flats. County Hall, once the home of the LCC and the Greater London Council, has suffered a similar fate. The Floral Hall at Covent Garden is now the London Transport Museum. Less radically, lock-up garages become artists' studios, pubs become clubs, and clubs become cut-price stores. One building in Wandsworth had previously been an orphanage, a first World War hospital for men wounded at the battle of the Somme, a lunatic asylum and an internment camp for SS officers in the Second World War before it became a school. It's now (allegedly) a "luxury apartment block", boasting facilities that SS officers wouldn't even have dreamt of, let alone Victorian orphans.

When they no longer serve their original purpose, however, most London buildings are reduced to rubble. And that is why it's surprising that several old London power stations are being recycled. Indeed, it's hard to work out quite how or why they're surviving. They are huge buildings, and even when their guts have been removed and brand new interiors substituted, they will be extremely expensive to maintain. In some cases they have been redundant for a very long time. Although Lots Road Power Station (one of the oldest) has miraculously survived to provide power for the London Underground system, Battersea Power Station ceased to generate any heat or electricity in 1983. Bankside had a working life of 100 years and is now converted into an extension of the Tate Gallery. Once one of the largest power stations in Europe, Barking opened in 1925 and closed in 1981. It was demolished in the 1980s, and most of the site is now railway sidings for the freightliner services that transport bulk goods from Britain to mainland Europe.

Just over 100 years ago Deptford Power Station was the brainchild of Sebastian Ziani de Ferranti, who wanted to build the biggest power station in the world, one that would light two million lamps. Ferranti was a young man in his early twenties who was in love with electricity. He dreamed of 10,000-horsepower generators, but his bosses at the London Electricity Supply Corporation said "no", and Ferranti resigned. Now all trace of it has gone.

Battersea

Battersea was "the cathedral of power". It was designed by Sir Giles Gilbert Scott, the architect for Liverpool Cathedral, and opened in 1933. Its appearance has been compared to an upside-down table. The interior was so lavishly decorated as to be the wonder of the age. There were marble halls, wrought-iron stair-rails, art deco control rooms. The parquet floors were so beautifully made that staff had to wear carpet slippers as they padded to and fro.

Even the smoke from the enormous chimneys, 300 feet (92 metres) tall, was clean and white, already washed to remove any particles of sulphur or other impurities. And the Thames water used in the power station, heated to boiling point, was carried under the river to the radiators of Dolphin Square and the Churchill Gardens Estate in Pimlico.

It was a grand and glorious building. For almost 15 years there were unsubstantiated rumours that it was to become a film studio, a leisure park, a helicopter station, or that it would all be pulled down. Now it seems almost certain to become an enormous cinema complex.

A Day in the Life of the Notting Hill Carnival

Mixing, scratching and entertaining the crowds at the Notting Hill Carnival, 1997.

The Notting Hill Carnival takes place at the end of August, on the late summer Bank Holiday. It is said to be the biggest carnival in the world, taking well over a year to organize and attracting hundreds of thousands of people of all races, religions and terpsichorean abilities. It was founded in 1961 by West Indian immigrants, homesick for fun as much as sun. Over the years it has had its problems, though the worst race riots in Notting Hill took place in 1958. It lasts for more than a week, though the bulk of it is a three-day event with bands and processions, competitions and parades, much eating and drinking, and dancing in the streets.

8 am Sunday (second day of Carnival)

Along most of the Carnival route you get no sense of excitement or expectation. There are a few food stalls being erected outside churches and temples. If you breathe deeply you can smell goat or mutton being stewed, the main ingredient for cauldrons of curry later in the day. An old woman in a purple and pink floral frock down to her calves, DMs and a baseball cap advertising "Amos Eats" is stirring a saucepan of chicken wings on a camping stove. Here and there sound systems are being set up on the backs of lorries, and steel pans are being unloaded from elderly vans.

At this time the streets are almost deserted – police officers outnumber civilians by some ten to one. The illegally parked ice-cream van gets a friendly wave from passing patrols. A loudspeaker van drives by, warning of the Wrath to Come.

9 am

This is a multi-racial part of London, not just Afro-Caribbean. There are Hindu families walking about, Malaysians, French and Spanish. For the most part, people are sticking to their usual Sunday routines – sitting at pavement cafés, drinking coffee, munching croissants and reading the Sunday papers. It's only those seeking protection or escape from the carnival who are on the move – boarding up shops, phone boxes and gardens against pilfering, vandalism and litter respectively. Some of the residents of smart streets such as Arundel Gardens are loading their Volvo estates with suitcases and supplies for the weekend, seeking escape from the celebra-

far left:
Carnival floats edge through
the revellers in Ladbroke
Grove.

floats pound by, food sellers are doing a roaring trade in jerk chicken, rice and peas, ackee and saltfish, spicy oxtail and cow's foot stew, goat curry, mangoes, sugar-cane, water-melon, jellied coconut and the ubiquitous burgers and hot-dogs.

1 pm

There's no way out of the crowds, and the Tube stations are only letting people into the Carnival, not out of it. You have to go with the flow as the crowds shuffle round and round the Carnival route. Even the placid police horses find the vibrations of the powerhouse sound systems hard to withstand. But there's a great good humour about everything, and food and drink are never more than a dozen faltering steps away. There is, however, a premium on shade.

3 pm

Struggle into the side streets and rest your overheated body on the low wall of a churchyard. Eat and drink and let the world pass by. Now is the time to find a tree or bush or scrap of hedge and sleep if you can in its shade.

6 pm

If you don't mind crowds, this is a good time to arrive. There's still enough food to feed the entire city, and plenty to drink. The major venues for bands are beginning to swing into action. The sun is less unbearably hot. The dancing is about to begin.

8 pm onwards

To many, Carnival proper is only just starting. Sweat and fruit juices are pouring down the gutters. You may well find yourself dancing through coconut shells and melon rind. If you're wise, you will have left anything valuable at home. If you haven't, try to stay sober enough to avoid any pickpockets. Otherwise, remember tomorrow's still a holiday, and have a great time.

A young visitor to the Carnival in full costume.

tions. Council officials have offered free hotel rooms in faraway Bournemouth for the weekend, but reports suggest that few residents have taken up the offer. They prefer to take the traditional Londoner's stand – "I'd rather stay here and be miserable and complain than do something about it."

10am

Street-cleaning lorries go squelching by. Cooks are now crumbling barbecue fuel blocks on to the trays of charcoal. Buckets of ice begin to melt in the sun, cases of lager are warming nicely. The judging podium for the parade and procession is in Westbourne Grove, by the Texaco garage. This is North Kensington, a mixed rather than a posh part of London.

You can hear the first whistles piercing the air. There are salesmen and women everywhere, with trays and boxes of snakes on sticks, T-shirts, funny hats, whistles and balloons. The sound systems have started up, and a police helicopter clatters overhead.

12 noon

There's a stirring in the crowd, necks crane forward. In the distance, the whistles and the music increase in volume. Then, like a bird of paradise taking to the skies, the carnival bursts forth. Dancers in glittering costumes whirl and sway. The streets burn with Caribbean splendour. The whole area from Ladbroke Grove to Chepstow Road is filled with surging crowds. As the

Crowds throng the streets from midday to the small hours.

The London Marathon

The Fun Runners

Organizers claim that the London Marathon differs from all other marathons by virtue of the carnival atmosphere that the fun runners create. Many of them don fancy dress, running in animal costumes, fright wigs, inside large cardboard models of Big Ben, tied together like members of a chain gang, or playing the bagpipes as they jog along. In the 1997 Marathon, among others taking part were a rhinoceros, Superman, pirates, several versions of Enid Blyton's "Noddy" character, the Wombles of Wimbledon, badgers, Snow White and the Seven Dwarfs, giant clams, rabbits, cricketers with bats and pads, Stone Age men, pot-noodle runners, and numerous London policemen.

And there was a running chef, carrying a large frying pan and hoping to complete three marathons in one day – an extra three miles, all thanks to Princess Mary way back in 1908.

Every major city in the world has its marathon race, and every one is different save in its standard length of 26 miles 385 yards (42 km 196 metres). And any runner who has gasped curses at this distance while panting along the last mile or so has London to blame. Originally the Marathon was only 25 miles (40 km) long. It was lengthened expressly for the London Olympic Games of 1908 at the request of the Royal Family, who wished it to start directly beneath Princess Mary's bedroom window at Windsor Castle. Pity poor Dorando Pietri of Italy, who ran into the stadium with only a few hundred yards to go, well in the lead. He turned right when he should have turned left, was re-directed, stumbled, fell, picked himself up, stumbled and fell again. He crossed the line ahead of all the other runners, but was helped. He was disqualified, and the gold medal went to an American, Johnny Hayes. If the starting line had not been moved to accommodate the wishes of the Royal Family, Pietri would have cantered home.

The modern London Marathon is an annual, not an Olympic event, and the Royal Family is not involved. The race begins in Greenwich Park, flows past the Cutty Sark, crosses Tower Bridge, and heads east to make a circuit of the Isle of Dogs. It then doubles back westwards, past the Tower of London and along the north bank of the Thames to Westminster, where it turns away from the river to finish at the end of The Mall.

It is one of the big city marathons. Forty thousand people enter for the race each year, and approximately 29,000 actually take part. It takes ten minutes from the time the starting gun is fired for the last of the runners to reach the starting line, by which time the leaders will already have covered two miles (nearly 4 km). The race is subdivided into several sections – the men's elite, the women's elite, the wheelchair runners, the club runners and the fun runners. The main aim of the race is to raise money for charity, though each one of the entrants has something to prove personally.

This is perhaps most clearly seen in the wheelchair runners. They can cover the course in under one hour 45 minutes (20 minutes faster than the best of the men's elite). Although there are sections of the race where they can freewheel downhill, as in the first few miles, it's a gruelling, punishing course that includes racing over cobblestones as they pass the Tower. A regular entrant is a one-legged man who roller-skates his way round.

Over the past 20 years support for the London Marathon has grown enormously. Thousands of volunteers line the route, handing out bottles of water or wet sponges to the runners, administering first aid, controlling the crowds. Every step of the way there are fans, friends and families shouting encouragement, applauding in respectful wonder and urging the runners forward. Outside the many pubs along the route, bands play – Dixieland bands, jazz groups, rock groups, pan bands – though some of the runners may well be heartily sick of hearing Keep On Running by the end of the day. There are street parties, fairs, fêtes and festivals. It is in many ways the biggest sporting occasion in the London calendar.

The record time for the men's London Marathon is 2 hours 7 minutes 55 seconds. The peak finishing time is around 3 hours 30 minutes, when 140 runners a minute are crossing the finishing line. But there are those who need considerably longer. In 1997 the oldest male entrant took 6 hours 10 minutes. He was 87-year-old Abraham Weinthrop, who took up marathon running at the age of 81, and he was by no means the last to finish. The clock keeps ticking away at the finishing line. After 7 hours 45 minutes, 28,439 of the 29,000 starters had completed the course that year – the other 561 had either given up, been carried away on stretchers, or were still limping and hobbling through London as the April sky darkened and the streets lights came on.

As soon as the runners finish, they are wrapped in foil, handed a sandwich and sent on their way. For the rest of the afternoon and the evening, you will come across them wandering around the West End, for most of them do not come from London and find themselves in a strange city. The following day they have their moment of glory, when The Times prints a list of all those who completed the course.

Pounding the streets, hitting
the wall, pushing the body to its
limits in the London
Marathon.

Ten of the Finest

There is no definitive list of the finest buildings in London. There are those who love the modern, for whom the Lloyds building and the Millennium Dome represent a new path to beauty. There are those who glory in the ancient splendour of Westminster Abbey or Hampton Court Palace. There are those who believe the 18th-century architectural gems will never be bettered. There are those who love the cosy, and those who gaze in awe at the magnificent. Many are attracted to the bizarre and unusual – the Round House at Chalk Farm, Little Ben (the ten-yard-high version of Big Ben that stands in the forecourt of Victoria Station), or the few remaining warehouses at Shad Thames. Some see beauty in details – the lamp-posts along the Thames Embankment or the wonderful ironwork on the sides of Holborn Viaduct, the Hollywood Byzantine columns in the ticket hall of Battersea Park station. Any attempt, therefore, to pick the ten best buildings in London is doomed to failure in that it will please no one.

It seems foolish to offer any sort of list, for it is impossible to compare, say, Hanover Terrace with the Pagoda at Kew, or Ham House with Southgate Underground station, or the pavilion at Lord's with Downshire Hill, Hampstead. It doesn't really help if you try to pick one building from each century since the first millennium, though such a list is full of riches. Starting with the 11th century, in order, the joys could include the Tower of London; St Mary Magdalene, East Ham; Westminster Abbey; Staple Inn, Holborn; St Margaret's, Westminster; the Olde Mitre Tavern, Ely Place; the Apothecaries' Hall, Blackfriars; Leighton House, Holland Park Road, or Linley Sambourne House, Stafford Terrace; the Octagon Room of Orleans House, Twickenham; and Barclay's Bank, Piccadilly.

Immediately, however, the list is unsatisfactory. It should include Deptford Town Hall, Hoare's Bank in Fleet Street, Charterhouse Square, EC1, Chiswick House, 39 Frognal in Hampstead (the fairytale house designed by Norman Shaw for Kate Greenaway), the Sir John Soane Museum and Marble Hill House. It should contain at least three of London's railway stations – Marylebone, Liverpool Street and St Pancras – and several theatres – the Fortune, the Theatre Royal in Covent Garden, the Haymarket Theatre. There are dozens of beautiful churches that have been left out – St Paul's in Deptford, St Bartholomew the Great in Smithfield, St James the Less. Many palaces have been omitted – Buckingham Palace is not beautiful, but Kensington,

Greenwich, St James's and Hampton Court Palaces are. Above all, the list excludes too many worthwhile favourites – the Albert Hall and the Albert Memorial, St Paul's Cathedral, Carlton House, Tower Bridge and dozens of others.

Any list of the finest buildings in London will provoke argument, but, for what it is worth, here is a selection of lesser-known edifices, in no particular order of age, beauty or importance.

St Peter's Italian Church, Clerkenwell

The church was originally planned as a Roman Catholic cathedral in the 1850s, but the plans were scaled down, and the church was opened by Cardinal Wiseman in 1863. It's a fine, narrow-fronted building in white stucco and deep red brick, the front of which is decorated with brilliantly coloured mosaics of scenes from the life of Christ. This is not a classic building, but a wonderful shock of colour (inside and out) in a comparatively drab London street.

Hackney Empire

This is an unspoilt 19th-century theatre, with a lush interior of scarlet and gold. The tiers of seats for the audience rise dizzily into the roof, and the cheapest seats offer the best views of the ornate pillars and pilasters. Gloriously over-elaborate in decoration, the whole theatre has all the subtlety of a Victorian melodrama.

Blackfriars Bridge

The present road bridge was designed by Joseph Cubitt and H. Carr, built in 1860–9, and opened by Queen Victoria at a time when she was so unpopular that she and her famous ghillie, John Brown, were both hissed by the public. It's a beautiful bridge, wide, low and delicate, and worth walking across simply to admire the cast-iron rails.

Camden Town Gasholders

The paint is beginning to peel off these Martian monsters that tower above the railway marshalling yards of St Pancras, but they are still among the prime examples of industrial beauty in London. Close by is the site of the last fatal duel in the city, where Lieutenant Munro killed his brother-in-law Lieutenant-Colonel Fawcett in 1843.

The Porter's Lodge, Ely Place, Holborn

By one of those delightful quirks of London history, Ely Place is technically a part of Cambridgeshire. It is also a private road that belongs to the Crown – hence the porter and the porter's lodge. The lodge is a tiny building

of warm yellow brick and white stucco, perfectly proportioned.

Whittington Lodge

This is the original cattery at the Dogs' Home, Battersea. It was designed by Clough Williams-Ellis and was built in 1906. Lovingly restored to its former glory, it is now a listed building.

The Tower House, 29 Melbury Road, Kensington

A magnificent town house in terracotta brick, this has a hint of the medieval about the stained-glass windows and winged gargoyles, with a huge fig tree in the front garden. It was built by William Burges in the 1870s for his own use. No. 31, next door, is almost as good, though the modern monstrosity across the road does nothing to enhance an otherwise handsome road.

Abbey Mills Pumping Station

The flat wastelands of West Ham are an unusual setting for such a gem. This is Victorian Venetian architecture at its best. The best time to see it is at sunset, when the yellow, red and blue brickwork comes to life, and the splendour of Bazalgette and Cooper's design is thrown into high relief.

Finally, two oddities. 10 Hyde Park Place is no beauty. It is modern, built of a dark orange brick and very plain. It is, however, reputed to be the smallest house in London, two storeys high and no wider than a door.

24 Leinster Gardens, Bayswater, doesn't exist as a house. It is merely a façade with blind windows and a door with neither handle nor keyhole. It was built to hide the old locomotives of the Metropolitan Railway as they let off steam.

A Victorian symphony in cast iron – the gasholders of Camden Town.

Looking west over the City from the dome of St Paul's Cathedral.

The Best Views of London

As you jet into or out of any of London's airports, you seldom get a good view of the city. Heathrow is too far to the west, Gatwick too far to the south and Stansted too far to the north-east. The flight paths leading to any of these airports avoid London. There's even the same problem if you use the City Airport at Docklands. Although it's much nearer the heart of London, the flight path takes aircraft away from the centre, not towards it.

Unless you have a private helicopter or hot-air balloon it's impossible to get a satisfactory view of the whole of London. The city is too big and too scattered. Climb the hills of north London (Parliament Hill on Hampstead Heath is one of the best) and admittedly you can see across the 12-mile (20-km) plain to the hills of Camberwell and Clapham in the south. But it's an ill-defined view. The tallest of London's buildings (the

NatWest Tower, the Victoria Tower of the Houses of Parliament, the BT Tower and the dome of St Paul's Cathedral) stand out, but you get little or no idea of the scale of the city, how London has been put together, or of the character of its inner core.

So the finest views of London tend to be limited. You see only the parts that make up the whole – the swirling river, the financial palaces of the City, the splendour of Westminster, the rich cream of Kensington, the sparkling lights of the West End at night. No one vantage point can offer all these. For the best views of London you have to be prepared to do a little travelling, as Gladstone was when he remarked that the best view of London was from the top of a bus.

The Vauxhall Balloon

Bob the Balloon in Spring Gardens, Vauxhall, can offer better than that. The company has been flying balloons from Vauxhall for nearly 200 years. One of the pioneers of balloon flight in London was Charles Green, who in 1828 crossed the Channel in a balloon named the Royal Vauxhall. A panoramic engraving of London in 1859 shows a balloon floating over the same spot now used by the Great Balloon Experience, Bob's owners.

Bob is the largest tethered balloon in Europe. You climb aboard the walkway that runs round its base, and it slowly ascends to a height of 500 feet (154 metres). It's high enough to get some idea of the size of London, and what is staggering is how far London reaches in every direction, flowing over every horizon. Looking eastwards you see St Paul's Cathedral, Canary Wharf, the NatWest Tower, the Savoy Hotel, the Millennium Dome. To the north are the Houses of Parliament, Westminster Abbey and Cathedral, the BT Tower, Centrepoint, Buckingham Palace, and, in the distance, Parliament Hill fields and Hampstead Heath. To the south is the Oval, Crystal Palace and the hills of Surrey. To the west the railway runs like a fat snake over the landscape as it sidles into Waterloo, and beyond are Battersea Power Station, the Brompton Oratory, and New Covent Garden.

You are get some idea of the colour of London. It's a melange of grey, pale brown and white, tinged with blue and punctuated by many trees. In the morning the sun is in your eyes as you gaze to the east, and the city is blurred and indistinct. In the evening the west of London is silhouetted against the setting sun. At weekends you can go up in Bob until midnight, and a warm summer night is the best time to make the trip. In the words of the old Frank Sinatra song: "London by night is a fabulous sight…"

A Host of Towers

For those who prefer to be earthbound there are plenty of magnificent views across and along the Thames in central London. Wordsworth's sonnet On Westminster Bridge captures much of the glory of the river 200 years ago, but from the high-level footbridge of Tower Bridge there are finer views both upstream and downstream today. The view from the top of the Monument well repays the effort in climbing its endless spiral staircase. On the south side of the river, a lift will whisk you, free of charge, to the top of the Oxo Tower. Here you may either dine in the restaurant and exhaust your credit card, or simply sip a coffee on the balcony and gaze at one of the most charming stretches of riverside architecture in central London.

Both the dome of St Paul's Cathedral and the tower of Westminster Cathedral are open to the public, and in both cases the fee and the climb are well worth the sacrifice for the panorama of London that you see from the top. The view from St Paul's is all the more precious because few City institutions are prepared to let the public into their buildings. The BT Tower is no longer open to the public – sadly, as it is set in a part of London that lacks a bold and accessible public viewpoint.

Finally, it is worth taking the trouble to arrange a visit to the roof garden at what used to be Derry and Toms' department store in Kensington High Street. It opened in 1933, with over 500 shrubs and a stream trickling through one and a half acres (over 6000 sq. metres) of Spanish and Tudor gardens. The fountains and trees are a delight, but the view from the edge is wonderful, too.

A view of Vauxhall Station, with the Thames winding upstream, from Bob the Balloon in Spring Gardens.

A History of London Pub Signs

In Roman London signs depicting a bush of vines or ivy leaves were hung from buildings to denote wine-houses. By the Middle Ages, it was customary for every London alehouse-keeper to place a stake in front of his house as a sign that he had a brew ready for sale. This was a simple pole – it would have been pointless to use a written sign, as few people could read. There is believed to be a portrait of an ale-stake in the Bayeux Tapestry. Whereas most fellow tradespeople put up signs relevant to their trade (shears for a barber, shoes for a cobbler), alehouse-keepers used any sign of their choice to distinguish their premises from those of a rival (moon, stars, animals, and sometimes the coat of arms of the local Lord of the Manor).

As time went by the ale-stakes became bigger and bigger, and in 1375 an order was issued in London to prohibit any stake or sign projecting more than seven feet over the highway. Signs were made compulsory in 1393, by order of Richard II: "Whosoever shall brew in the town with intention of selling it must hang out a sign, otherwise he shall forfeit his ale."

The old problem returned. By the 15th century, the Common Council in the City of London stated that many ale-stakes were so heavy as to be dangerous. Two hundred years later, however, the streets of the City of London had become so cluttered that inn signs were banned altogether in Charles II's reign, unless they were fixed flat to wall or balcony. In 1719, a French visitor to London wrote:

> At London, inn signs are commonly very large, and jut out so far, that in some narrow streets they touch each other; nay, and run across quite to the other side. They are generously adorned with carving and gilding; and there are several that, with the branches of iron that support them, cost above a hundred guineas…

Modern signs, a mixture of words and picture, date from the late 18th century, and have vastly improved artistically in the last 50 years.

Who's Who

Alfonso XIII: King of Spain from 1886 to 1931. He died in exile.

Ambrose, Fred: British dance-band leader, especially popular with the Prince of Wales and the Bright Young Things of the 1930s. He was offered the post of musical director at the Mayfair Hotel in the 1920s for the astonishing salary of £10,000 a year.

Arnold, Dr Thomas (1795–1842): he was headmaster of Rugby School during the Tom Brown years.

Babbage, Professor Charles (1791–1871): English mathematician who spent much of his life seeking to invent a calculating machine.

Banks, Sir Joseph (1744–1820): English botanist who accompanied discoverer Captain Cook on his voyage round the world from 1768 to 1771.

Barnum and Bailey: American promoters who invented the Three Ring Circus.

Barry, Sir Charles (1795–1860): architect who designed the Palace of Westminster in the year 1840.

Bart, Lionel: London composer born in 1930 whose biggest success was *Oliver*.

Bazalgette, Sir Joseph (1819–91): engineer who designed London's drainage system and the Thames embankments.

Beardsley, Aubrey (1872–98): a leading figure among the Decadents, a group of artists that flourished in the 1890s.

Beecham, Sir Thomas (1879–1961): great and idiosyncratic conductor and founder of the Royal Philharmonic Orchestra.

Beerbohm, Sir Max (1872–1956): English writer and critic in the first half of the 20th century.

Behan, Brendan (1923–64): Irish author, playwright and lover of drink.

Bentham, Jeremy (1748–1832): English philosopher and social reformer. His clothed skeleton has been preserved on view at University College, London.

Bernard, Jeffrey: bibulous author and Soho *bon viveur* until his death in 1997.

Blondin, Charles (1824–97): French acrobat who crossed Niagara Falls on a tightrope in the year 1859.

Blyton, Enid (1897–1968): English children's author and creator of Noddy and the Famous Five.

Boswell, James (1740–95:) Scottish companion and biographer of Dr Johnson.

Bow Street Runners: forerunners of the police force, founded in the mid-18th century by John and Henry Fielding.

BNP: British National Party – unpleasant Fascist and racist group on the extreme right.

Brown, John (1826–83): not the one whose soul is marching on, but Queen Victoria's ghillie, confidant and much more.

Brummell, Beau (1778–1840): 18th-century dandy and dictator of fashion; friend of the Prince Regent.

Buck, Frank (1884–1950): American big-game hunter and collector of animals in the first half of the 20th century.

Burns, John (1858–1943): Labour MP who became the first working-class member of the Cabinet when he was made President of the Local Government Board in 1905.

Byron, George Gordon, Lord (1788–1824): poet and liberal, lover of Lady Caroline Lamb among others, who died in the Greek War of Independence.

Cade, Jack: Irish rebel leader of the insurrection against Henry VI in 1450.

Carnegie, Andrew (1835–1918): Scottish philanthropist and industrialist who made his fortune in the United States.

Caruso, Enrico (1878–1921): Italian singer, one of the greatest tenors of all time.

Chesterton, Gilbert Keith (1874–1936): London-born critic, novelist and poet, creator of Father Brown.

Chippendale, Thomas (1718–79): Maker of graceful, neoclassical furniture.

Christie, John Reginald Halliday (1898–1953): landlord of 10 Rillington Place, and mass murderer. The wrongful execution of Timothy Evans for one of Christie's killings played its part in the abolition of the death penalty in the 1960s.

Churchill, Clementine (1885–1977): long-suffering wife and lifelong support of Winston Churchill.

Coke, Thomas William, Lord (of Holkham) (1752–1842): Norfolk farmer and MP, and one of the pioneers of selective breeding of animals.

Conrad, Joseph (1857–1924): Polish-born British writer, whose novel *The Secret Agent* is set in London.

Conran, Sir Terence: English designer and entrepreneur, born in 1931. Founder of the Habitat company.

Cook, Captain James (1728–79): English navigator and discoverer.

Crippen, Dr Hawley Harvey (1862–1910): American-born doctor, notorious for the murder of his wife Cora at Hilldrop Crescent, Holloway.

Davis, Bette (1908–89): American actress and film star.

Desmond, Norma: character in the film *Sunset Boulevard*, the fading star who wishes to revive her career.

Diaghilev, Sergei (1872–1929): Russian impresario and founder of the Ballets Russes.

Dixon, Sir Arthur (1881–1969): civil servant of great reputation who was largely responsible for reform of both the police force and the fire service in the 1930s.

Douglas, Lord Alfred (1870–1945): English poet and lover of Oscar Wilde. In the end, Wilde could hardly decide which he disliked most – Douglas's poetry or his company.

Eco, Umberto: Italian novelist born in 1932, author of *Foucault's Pendulum*.

Eden, Sir Anthony (1897–1977): Churchill's heir apparent for many years, and Prime Minister at the time of the Suez Crisis in 1956. He resigned 1957 due to ill health.

Ellis, Ruth (1926–55): after shooting her lover outside a Hampstead pub, Ruth Ellis was the last woman to be hanged in Britain.

Escoffier, Auguste (1847–1935): French chef who was persuaded by César Ritz to take up residence in the kitchens of the Savoy Hotel.

Evans, Dame Edith (1888–1976:) London actress, most famous for her portrayal of Lady Bracknell in the film of Wilde's *The Importance of Being Earnest*.

Fawkes, Guy (1570–1606): one of the Catholic conspirators involved in the Gunpowder Plot to blow up Parliament, King James I and the Protestant bishops. After his arrest in the cellars of the Palace of Westminster, Fawkes was tortured, tried and executed for treason.

Ferranti, Sebastian Ziani de (1864–1930): engineer and inventor. In 1887 he was appointed chief electrician to the London Electric Supply Corporation which planned to supply electricity to the whole of London north of the Thames from the power station at Deptford.

Firman, Bert: American-born leader of a dance-band, very popular in London during the 1930s.

Fletcher, Yvonne: London policewoman who was killed on 17 April 1984 in St James's Square. Her murder was blamed on gunmen in the Libyan embassy, but this has never been proved.

Fox, Charles James (1749–1806): English gambler, drinker and MP, described by Edmund Burke (even though indisputably an opponent) as "the greatest debater the world ever saw".

Fox, Roy: American band-leader who led the resident band at the Café de Paris in London's West End during the 1930s.

Fox Talbot, William Henry (1800–77): pioneer of photography, which he described in 1839 as "photogenic drawing".

Galsworthy, John (1867–1933): English novelist and playwright, author of *The Forsyte Saga*.

Garibaldi, Giuseppe (1807-82): Italian patriot and soldier, largely responsible for the unification of his country; much adored by the people of London.

Garrick, David (1717-79): English actor, manager and dramatist, equally at home in tragedy or comedy.

Gibbon, Edward (1737-94): historian and author of *The Decline and Fall of the Roman Empire*.

Gladstone, William Ewart (1809-98): Four times Prime Minister, the "Grand Old Man" of British politics. Gladstone's unsuccessful life's work was the attempt to bring Home Rule to Ireland.

Gloucester, Richard, Duke of: born in 1944, grandson of George V, and an architect by training.

Grace, W.G. (1848–1915): doctor and the most famous cricketer of all time – Grace virtually invented the modern game.

Grey, Lady Jane (1537–54): married against her will to Lord Guildford Dudley, she became Queen of England for nine days in 1553 and the dupe in a foolish plot to deprive Mary Tudor of the throne. She and Dudley were executed on Tower Hill.

Hardie, James Keir (1856–1915): Scottish miner who became one of the founders of the Labour Party and an MP.

Harrison, Rex (1908–90): English actor, somewhat unfairly best known for his role on stage and screen as Professor Higgins in *My Fair Lady*.

Havisham, Miss: the old woman in Dickens's *Great Expectations* who has never changed her clothes nor cleaned her house since she was jilted by her fiancé.

Haw Haw, Lord (William Joyce) (1906–46): American-born political extremist. Joyce was expelled from Mosley's British Union of Fascists and founded his own British National Socialist Party. He worshipped Hitler and fled to Germany in 1939, whence he broadcast in English, bringing messages of gloom and despair to Britain. He was captured at the end of the war and executed for treason, wrongfully as he didn't have a valid British passport.

Hazlitt, William (1778–1830): English essayist whose last words were "Well, I've had a happy life".

Heath, Sir Edward: English politician, born in 1916. Although a Conservative Prime Minister from 1970 to 1974, he later became an outspoken critic of his party's policies.

Herbert, A.P. (1890–1971): wit, poet and novelist; independent MP for Oxford University from 1935 to 1950.

Hunt, Leigh (1784–1859): English essayist and poet, whose house at Hampstead became the centre of literary London.

Irving, Sir Henry (1838–1905): one of the great English actor-managers, and the first actor to be knighted.

Isis: Ancient Egyptian goddess of protection and healing whose cult persisted into the Roman Empire. Isis was the sister and wife of Osiris, and was represented wearing a cow's horns.

Jersey, Lady: 18th-century society hostess and wife of George Bussy Villiers, fourth Earl of Jersey.

John, Augustus (1878–1961): Welsh painter whose work has been perhaps as overrated as that of his sister (Gwen John) has been underrated.

Kipling, Rudyard (1865–1936): enormously popular English writer and poet, in many ways the chronicler of the British Empire.

Knights Templars: members of a military order founded in 1118 to protect pilgrims to the Holy Land. Resentment over their power and wealth led to their persecution and dissolution in 1314.

Lamb, Lady Caroline (1785–1828): wife of Lord Melbourne (q.v.) and for nine months (1812–13) passionately devoted to Byron (q.v.).

Landseer, Sir Edwin (1802–73): English painter, largely of animals. His most famous work is *The Monarch of the Glen*.

Langtry, Lillie (Lily) (1853–1929): a great beauty, an actress, a racehorse owner, and Edward VII's mistress.

Livingstone (1813–73): Scottish missionary and traveller who sought the source of the Nile. He died in Africa, but his body was embalmed, brought back to London, lay in state in what is now No. 1 Savile Row, and was buried in Westminster Abbey.

Macaulay, Thomas Babington, Lord (1800–59): poet and historian, author of *The Lays of Ancient Rome*.

Malton, Thomas (the Younger) (1748–1804): architectural draughtsman and illustrator who published *A Picturesque Tour Through London and Westminster* in 1792.

Marconi, Marchese Guglielmo (1874–1937): Italian physicist and inventor, best known for his experiments in wireless telegraphy.

Marlborough, John Churchill, Duke of (1650–1722): handsome soldier who led the British armies in the War of the Spanish Succession. Among his rewards was Blenheim Palace.

Marx, Groucho (1895–1977): one of the famous Marx Brothers, a vaudeville act that became famous through a series of comedy films in the 1930s and 1940s.

Mazzini, Giuseppe (1805–72): Italian patriot and leader of the Risorgimento who found refuge in London in 1837.

McGill, Donald (1875–1962): English comic postcard artist whose red-nosed humour was first brought to the attention of the discerning by George Orwell.

Melbourne, William Lamb, Lord (1779–1848): statesman, MP and the young Queen Victoria's favourite Prime Minister.

Millais, Sir John Everett (1829–96): artist and founder member of the Pre-Raphaelite Brotherhood. His most enduring work has been Bubbles, used to advertise Pears soap.

Mithras: Zoroastrian god of light and wisdom was adopted by Roman soldiers as the ideal comrade. The cult declined in the third century.

Monmouth, James, Duke of (1649–85): illegitimate son of Charles II and Lucy Walter. On the death of his father, Monmouth claimed the throne of England for the Protestant cause, but was captured after the battle of Sedgemoor and executed.

Montagu, Lady Mary Wortley (1689–1762): writer and society hostess who played a part in the introduction of vaccination.

Montagu, Mrs Elizabeth (1720–1800): the first of the "bluestockings", she established a famous salon in Mayfair.

Morland, George (1763–1804): painter who first exhibited in the Royal Academy at the age of ten, but whose life of debt and drunkenness led to death in destitution.

Mosley, Sir Oswald (1896–1980): leader of the British Fascists in the 1930s, and husband of the Hon. Diana Mitford.

Nash, John (1752–1835): architect who was responsible for much of the most beautiful 18th-century development of London.

Neave, Airey: Conservative politician and MP, killed by an IRA car bomb as he was leaving the underground car park of the House of Commons, 30 March 1979.

Nelson, Admiral Horatio, Lord (1758–1805): the most famous sailor in British history, commander of the British fleet at the battle of Trafalgar, in which he died.

Nightingale, Florence (1820–1910): nurse and hospital reformer who accompanied the British expedition to the Crimea in 1858.

Noddy: small lovable and perhaps equally loathable brainchild of Enid Blyton (q.v.); also a nickname for a policeman.

North, Oliver: American soldier born in 1943, deeply involved in the Iran-Contragate affair of 1986.

Nyren, John (1764–1837): giant of a man and one of the most famous of the early English cricketers.

Oakley, Annie (1860–1926): stage name of Phoebe Annie Oakley Moses, rodeo star and sharp-shooter, immortalized in Irving Berlin's *Annie Get Your Gun*.

Palmerston, Henry John Temple, Lord (1784–1865): statesman and not one of the young Queen Victoria's favourite Prime Ministers. He objected to her frequent interference in foreign policy.

Pankhurst, Emmeline (1857–1928): founder of the Women's Franchise League and the Women's Social and Political Union (with her daughter Christabel).

Pankhurst, Sylvia (1882–1960): like her mother Emmeline, a leading figure in the movement for women's suffrage.

Parry, Sir William Edward (1755–1822): Arctic navigator and explorer who subsequently became Governor of Greenwich Hospital.

Peel, Sir Robert (1788–1850): statesman, MP and Prime Minister. As Home Secretary he organized the first London police force, members of which were called "Peelers" or "Bobbies".

Pitt, William (the Younger) (1759–1806): youngest ever Prime Minister (at the age of 24), who died so heavily in debt that the House of Commons raised £40,000 to pay off his creditors.

Porter, Cole (1891–1964): brilliant lyricist and composer of immortal songs such as *I've Got You Under My Skin, Night and Day, Begin the Beguine*.

Powell, Enoch (1912–98): controversial Conservative politician and MP, with views that verged on the racist if they did not actually qualify as such.

Priestley, J.B. (1894–1984): English novelist, playwright and critic, best known for his novel *The Good Companions* and his play *An Inspector Calls*.

Princes, the Little: the two sons of Edward IV (Edward V and his brother Richard) who were murdered in the Tower of London, possibly on the orders of their uncle Richard III, in 1483.

Quant, Mary: English fashion designer born in the year 1934. She opened a boutique in Chelsea in 1955 but became famous some ten years later, very much as part of the swinging London scene.

Rhodes, Cecil (1853–1902): diamond hunter, maverick statesman and highly controversial figure in history whose dream was that Britain should rule Africa from Cairo to Capetown.

Robey, George (1869–1954): English comedian, dubbed the "Prime Minister of Mirth".

Rogers, Ginger (1911–95): dancing partner of Fred Astaire in a series of movie musicals.

Who's Who

Who's Who

Roy, Harry (1900–71): clarinet player and popular leader of the resident dance-band at the Embassy Club, London, for much of the 1930s and 1940s.

Rushdie, Salman: author born in 1947, victim of an Iranian fatwa for his 1988 novel *The Satanic Verses*, which Muslims claimed was blasphemous.

Rutherford, Baron Ernest (of Nelson) (1871–1937): physicist who led research into the atom and was awarded the Nobel Prize for chemistry in 1908.

Sandwich, John Montagu, fourth Earl of (1718–92): not a very good politician, but the brilliant inventor of the sandwich.

Sargent, John Singer (1856–1925): American painter born in Florence. Most of his work was done in England, where he became the most celebrated portrait painter of his age.

Scott, Sir Giles Gilbert (1880–1960): architect grandson of Sir George Gilbert Scott, who planned Waterloo Bridge and the reconstruction of the House of Commons after the Second World War.

Shaw, George Bernard (1856–1950): Irish dramatist, playwright, critic, vegetarian and outstanding wit, best known for *Pygmalion* and *St Joan*.

Sickert, Walter Richard (1860–1942): German-born British artist much influenced by Whistler and Degas. Member of the Camden Town group, later called the London Group.

Sinatra, Frank (1915–98): perhaps the most famous entertainer of all time, Sinatra was a singer and film actor of tremendous class – we shall not hear his like again.

Smith, Sydney (1771–1845): clergyman, essayist and acerbic wit who never really fulfilled his potential.

Soyer, Alexis (1809–58): the most famous French chef of his time. Soyer fled to London in 1830 and was chef at the Reform Club for 13 years.

Stanley, Albert Henry (Lord Ashfield) (1874–1948): MP and chairman of the London Passenger Transport Board. Stanley came to London in 1914, as late successor to the Underground empire of Charles Tyson Yerkes (q.v.).

Stephenson, Robert (1803–59): engineer son of George Stephenson who assisted his father in the construction of the Stockton to Darlington railway in 1823.

Stevenson, Robert Louis (1850–94): Scottish author, best known for *Treasure Island* and *The Strange Case of Dr Jekyll and Mr Hyde*.

Stone, Lew (1898–1969): London-born pianist who led the dance-band at the Monseigneur Club in the West End for much of the 1930s. He was also the musical director for British and Dominion Films.

Terry, Dame Ellen (1848–1928): English actress and professional partner of Sir Henry Irving. Irving wished to keep her as second fiddle in his company, and denied her the chance to play such roles as Portia and Rosalind.

Thackeray, William Makepeace (1811–63): prolific novelist, best known for *Vanity Fair*.

Thomas, Dylan (1914–53): poet, writer and drinker, whose most famous work is the radio play *Under Milk Wood*.

Trenchard, Hugh Montague, Lord (1873–1956): Marshal of the Royal Air Force and prime mover in the creation of the Police College at Hendon.

Turpin, Dick (1705–39): butcher's apprentice, cattle-lifter, smuggler, housebreaker, highwayman, horse thief and murderer who was hanged in York for the murder of an Epping keeper. His horse was the famous Black Bess, but the story of their ride together from London to York in less than 16 hours is sheer invention.

Tyler, Wat: English rebel leader of the Peasants' Revolt in 1381, England's first popular rebellion, wounded by William Walworth (q.v.) and subsequently beheaded.

UFA (Universum Film Aktiengesellschaft): German film production company that made many masterpieces of the silent cinema, the most famous of which was probably Fritz Lang's *Metropolis*.

Walpole, Horace (fourth Earl of Orford) (1717–97): essayist and gossip who wrote first-hand accounts of the execution of Jacobite leaders in London in 1746 and of the Gordon Riots in 1780.

Walworth, William: Lord Mayor of London who rode out with young King Richard II to face the peasants at Blackheath in 1381. Played a dastardly part in the killing of Wat Tyler. He died in 1385.

Wanamaker, Sam (1919–97): American actor and director who devoted much of his later life to the establishment of the New Globe Theatre on the South Bank.

Watts, Alaric (1797–1864): English journalist and poet, best remembered for his alliterative poem "An Austrian Army awfully arrayed", in which all the words in each subsequent line begin with the next letter of the alphabet.

Wellington, Arthur Wellesley, Duke of (1769–1852): soldier, statesman and Prime Minister, victor of the battle of Waterloo, and known as "The Iron Duke", "Old Conky" and other less salubrious names.

Whistler, James Abbott McNeill (1834–1903): American artist who became the best known of the "British" impressionist painters.

Whistler, Rex (1905–44): English artist and illustrator, no relation to the above. Best known for pastiches and recreations of 18th-century style.

Whitbread, Samuel (1758–1815): MP, son of the founder of the great Whitbread brewery.

Wilberforce, William (1759–1833): philanthropist and MP who played a large part in the abolition of the British slave trade.

Wilde, Oscar (1854–1900): Irish wit, dramatist, essayist, poet and scourge of the "establishment", whose heady life ended in imprisonment and disgrace.

Wilkes, John (1727–97): Firebrand MP and member of the Hell Fire Club, which indulged in orgies in Medmenham Abbey. Wilkes was in and out of trouble for most of his life, but was seen by many as a champion of liberty.

Wilkie, Sir David (1785–1841): Scottish painter in the Dutch style who became painter-in-ordinary to King William IV.

Wilson, Keppel and Betty: a music-hall act of the 1920s and 1930s that has subsequently acquired cult status. The act consisted of a strange, eerily comic "sand" dance in mock Egyptian style.

Wilson, Richard (1714–82): Welsh landscape painter who anticipated Gainsborough and Constable.

Windsor, Edward (David), Duke of (1894–1972): popular heir to the throne in the 1930s (he became Edward VIII in 1936 on the death of his father). From then on all was downhill. His love for the twice-divorced Wallis Simpson and his admiration for Nazi leaders led to his abdication and his virtual exile from Britain.

Wolseley, Sir Garnet (1833–1913): soldier and commander-in-chief of the expedition to Egypt in 1882 to quell the followers of the Mahdi and avenge the death of General Gordon.

Wombles of Wimbledon: heroes of a series of children's books (by Elisabeth Beresford) and television programmes, these furry creatures were supposed to inhabit Wimbledon Common.

Wood, Sir Henry (1869–1944): English conductor and co-founder (with Robert Newman) of the annual Promenade Concerts.

Woolf, Virginia (1882–1941): English critic, novelist and essayist and key member of the Bloomsbury Group in Edwardian London.

Yerkes, Charles Tyson: American financier and speculator who funded three London Tube lines (Bakerloo, Piccadilly and Hampstead). He died in 1905 before any of the lines was completed.

Yorkshire Ripper (Peter Sutcliffe): born in Yorkshire in 1946, convicted of 13 murders and seven attempted murders in 1981.

The one indispensable book is *The London Encyclopaedia*, edited by Ben Weinreb and Christopher Hibbert. It's a great thick work of reference with an enormous amount of detail. If you can afford only one book on London, this is the one to buy.

Historical

Peter Ackroyd *Blake*.
A biography of the poet and painter that contains many descriptions of 18th-century London.
Paul Bailey (ed.) *The Oxford Book of London*.
A collection of eye-witness accounts from the 12th to the 20th century.
Felix Barker *Edwardian London*.
One of the best accounts of London's Golden Age, with many stunning contemporary photographs.
A.C. Benson *Diaries 1898–1909*.
Delightful memoirs of late Victorian and Edwardian London.
Charles Booth *Life and Labour of the Poor of London*.
Later version of Henry Mayhew's survey of London's workers.
James Boswell *The Life of Samuel Johnson*.
The high style and low life of 18th-century London.
Alan Bott *The Londoner's England*.
Beautifully illustrated series of short essays on central London, the suburbs and the city's surroundings.
Ivor Brown (ed.) *A Book of London*.
A collection of literary and historical descriptions of London life and London characters.
François René Chateaubriand *Memoirs*.
Entertaining account of the French statesman's visits to London in the late 18th and early 19th centuries.
Kellow Chesney *The Victorian Underworld*.
Rogues, villains and victims in garish detail.
Harry Daley *This Small Cloud, A Personal Memoir*.
Graphic descriptions of London's poor and destitute in the first half of the 20th century.
Daniel Defoe *A Journal of the Plague Year*.
The most graphic and terrifying account of the Great Plague of 1665, written by a man who witnessed the Plague as a five-year-old.
Eric de Marny *London 1851*.
Beautifully illustrated account of London in the year of the Great Exhibition.
John Farley *The London Art of Cooking*.
Cook book written in 1783.
Richard Findlater *Lilian Baylis: The Lady of the Old Vic*.
Biography of the woman who revived London's theatre in the 1930s.
Geoffrey Fletcher *Pocket Guide to Dickens' London*.
Slim, small volume that identifies and describes some two dozen London locations used by Dickens. Fine illustrations.
Ford Madox Ford *The Soul of London*.
An impressionistic account of life in London in Edwardian times.

Alethea Hayter *A Sultry Month*.
The trials and tribulations of Carlyle, Browning, Elizabeth Barrett and Robert Haydon during June 1846.
Christopher Hibbert *London: The Biography of a City*.
A general history of London from Roman times to the 20th century.
Christopher Hibbert *The Tower of London*.
Detailed history of the part played by the Tower in the history of London and Britain.
Molly Hughes *A London Family 1870–1900*.
A highly readable account of everyday life for a London family.
Simon Jenkins *Landlords to London*.
The story of how the rich and aristocratic laid down the pattern of streets and squares that today make up central London.
David Kynaston *The City of London* (2 vols).
A very detailed history of the financial centre of London.
Norman Longmate *King Cholera*.
Graphic description and account of the plagues that hit London in the 19th century.
Raymond Mander and Joe Mitchenson *The Lost Theatres of London*.
History of some of the theatrical gems that have disappeared from the capital.
Henry Mayhew *London Labour and the London Poor*.
An abridged version of the four-volume study of the struggles of the London poor during the second half of the 19th century.
Arthur Morrison *A Child of the Jago*.
Description of the East End of London in late Victorian times.
Ian Nairn *Nairn's London*.
Wonderfully written book on the architecture of London.
Samuel Pepys *The Diary of Samuel Pepys*.
The finest eye-witness descriptions of life and events in Restoration London.
Liza Picard *Restoration London*.
An extremely well-researched recreation of what it was like to live in the London of Charles II.
Roy Porter *London: A Social History*.
The lives of ordinary citizens in London through the centuries.
Thomas de Quincey *The Nation of London*.
Contemporary description of London in the 1830s.
George Rude *History of London: Hanoverian London*.
Largely eye-witness account of events and personalities 1714–1808.
George Sims *Living London*.
Sims was much moved by the struggles and suffering of the poor in London at the end of the 19th and beginning of the 20th centuries.
John Stow *A Survey of London*.
A systematic survey of the city of London, first published in 1598 and still available.
Reay Tannahill *Regency England*.
Not strictly a book about London, but with many fine reproductions of old prints of the Thames, the Fleet Prison, Somerset House, etc.

J. Timbs *Curiosities of London*.
The little-known London of the 1860s.
Rosalind Vallance (ed.) *Dickens' London*.
Essays by Dickens on many aspects of London life in the 1850s and 1860s better than the descriptions to be found in his novels.
Gavin Weightman and Steve Humphries *The Making of Modern London* (2 vols).
Well illustrated books that accompanied a television series in 1983. The first volume covers 1815 to 1914, the second 1914 to 1939.
A.N. Wilson (ed.) *The Faber Book of London*.
An anthology of London life and London people in history and literature through the centuries.

Contemporary or Near-Contemporary

Julian Barnes *Letters from London*.
A collection of letters and reports on what exactly was happening in London from 1990 to 1995.
Jeffrey Barnard *Low Life*.
The confessions of an alcoholic who enjoyed life to the full in Soho from the 1950s to the 1980s.
Harry Blacker *Just Like It Was*.
East End memories.
Mark Edmonds *Inside Soho*.
One of many accounts of Soho in its heyday.
Daniel Farson *Never a Normal Man*.
A colourful account of life in Soho and the East End in the 1950s.
Geoffrey Fletcher *The London Nobody Knows*.
Wonderful book, illustrated by the author, that reveals many charming secrets of London.
Geoffrey Fletcher *London at My Feet*.
A personal journey through the city from Vauxhall to Wapping by one of the finest writers on London, a man with immense knowledge of the city.
Roger Jones and Thomas Lowry *Walking London's Royal Parks*.
A very slim volume outlining and describing seven walks through London parkland.
A.B. Levy *East End Story*.
A rich description of one of the most colourful parts of London.
Henrietta Moraes *Henrietta*.
More first-hand accounts of Bohemian life in Soho in the 1950s.
Debra Shipley and Mary Peplow *London Theatres and Concert Halls*.
A 32-page encyclopedia of London places of entertainment.
Ian Sinclair *Lights Out for the Territory*.
A mixture of travelogue, history book and memoir, written largely in anger.
Descriptions of London *Felix Barber and Denise Silvester-Carr – The Black Plaque Guide to London*.
A lively tour round some of the less salubrious parts of London.
Andrew Duncan – *Secret London*.
Fascinating guide to many of the hidden gems of London.

Books on London

Diana Howard – *London Theatres and Music Halls 1850–1950.*
The spicy side of London's entertainment.
Andrew Kershman – *The London Market Guide.*
Compact and indispensable guide to the many markets of the city.
Mervyn Miller and Stuart Grail – *Hampstead Garden Suburb.*
The world-famous experiment in housing.
The Nicholson Pub Guide.
Well-produced guide to over 500 of London's best pubs – it may help to bear in mind, however, that Nicholson's own many of them and their descriptions of their own pubs may be a touch generous.
Julian Paget – *Discovering London Ceremonial and Traditions.*
Enthusiastic guide to everything from Trooping the Colour to Beating Retreat. Tremendously patriotic.
James Pope-Hennessy – *The Houses of Parliament.*
Short and well-written guide to the Mother of Parliaments – perhaps a little dry for modern tastes.
James Roose-Evans – *London Theatre.*
Detailed account of London's theatreland.
B. Rosen and W. Zuckerman – *The Mews of London.*
An interesting investigation of some of the most charming byways of London.
A. Saunders – *Regent's Park.*
The history of one of London's largest open spaces.
Desmond Shawe-Taylor – *Covent Garden.*
The story of the Covent Garden in good and bad times.
Edward Sullivan – *The London Pub and Bar Guide.*
Excellent guide to over 700 London watering-holes.
Foil Thompson – *Hampstead.*
A portrait of London's most desirable suburb – as far as those who live in Hampstead are concerned.
Richard Trench and Ellis Hillman – *London Under London.*
Wonderful account of everything to be found beneath the streets of London.
Linda Zoff – *Jewish London.*
The part played by the city in the history of the Jews and by the Jews in the history of the city.

Films on London

The following is a list of films set in London and made in Britain (with one American exception). They have not been selected for their quality, but even the worst of them will include a few shots of historic interest. Almost all the films are set at the time they were made – with the exception of *The Mudlark*, I have tried to avoid historical reconstructions.

Against the Wind (1947)
Second World War thriller centred around the training of British saboteurs in London.
The Arsenal Stadium Mystery (1939)
Murder mystery set in pre-war Highbury.
Battle for Music (1943)
The story of the ups and downs of the London Philharmonic Orchestra in wartime.
The Bells Go Down (1943)
Adventures of a London firefighting unit during the Second World War.
The Bespoke Overcoat (1956)
Set in the East End of London and possibly the best short drama filmed in Britain.
Les Bicyclettes de Belsize (1969)
Short, whimsical romance set in Hampstead.
Black Joy (1977)
Problems between a Guyanan and a Jamaican in Brixton.
Blackmail (1929)
Hitchcock's first talkie, in which the girl-friend of a Scotland Yard detective is in-volved in a murder.
Blind Date (1959)
A young Dutch painter gets out of his depth in London.
Blitz on Britain (1960)
Semi-documentary record of the effect of the Blitz on the lives of ordinary people.
Blondes for Danger (1938)
A Cockney taxi driver is involved in a deep, dark deceit.
Blow Up (1966)
Antonioni's weird mystery set against the swinging London of the 1960s.
The Blue Lamp (1949)
The film that created the archetypal London policeman, P.C. George Dixon of Dock Green.

The Boy and the Bridge (1959)
A boy who believes he committed a murder hides in Tower Bridge.
Bunny Lake is Missing (1965)
A four-year-old American girl disappears in London.
Burning an Illusion (1981)
A black secretary in London becomes a political militant.
Connecting Rooms (1969)
Dismal melodrama set in a seedy Bayswater boarding house.
Contraband (1940)
A Danish sea captain and his girlfriend ex-pose a gang of spies in London.
Crime over London (1936)
Gangsters hide out in a London department store.
Crossplot (1969)
Yet another spy ring in London. The film ends with an assassination in Hyde Park.
The Day the Earth Caught Fire (1961)
The approaching end of the world seen through the eyes of workers on the Daily Express. Realistic and suspenseful sci-fi.
Death at Broadcasting House (1934)
Murder mystery set in what was then a very new headquarters of the BBC.
Derby Day (1952)
The interweaving stories of four visitors to Epsom Racecourse on Derby Day.
East of Piccadilly (1940)
A murderer is tracked down by a newspaper reporter and his girlfriend.
84 Charing Cross Road (1986)
Film version of the best-selling book by Helene Hanff.
Expresso Bongo (1959)
Not very successful attempt at a British musi-cal centred around Soho.
The File of the Golden Goose (1969)
Scotland Yard on the trail of a counterfeiter, with lots of shots of "touristy" London.
The Final Test (1953)
Poor low-key drama with some good shots of the Oval cricket ground during a Test match.

Fires Were Started (1943)
Documentary about a day and a night in the lives of members of the National Fire Service at the height of the Blitz.
Four in the Morning (1965)
Four stories about four people during one night in London.
Frenzy (1972)
One of Hitchcock's worst films, set in and around the old Covent Garden.
Front Page Story (1953)
A day in the life of a Fleet Street newspaper.
Goodbye Gemini (1970)
Fantasy and murder set in swinging London.
The Happy Family (1952)
Amiable comedy set at the time of the Festival of Britain on the South Bank.
A Hard Day's Night (1964)
The adventures of the Beatles in London.
The Horse's Mouth (1958)
Light drama about a painter, with a back-ground of the River Thames.
Hue and Cry (1946)
Delightful Ealing comedy set among the bombsites of London.
It Always Rains on Sunday (1947)
An escaped convict seeks asylum in the East End of London.
It's Not Cricket (1946)
The adventures of two bumbling, cricket-loving ex-Army officers in and around London just after the Second World War.
John and Julie (1955)
Sentimental story of two children who run away to London at the time of the Coronation of Queen Elizabeth II.
The Lavender Hill Mob (1951)
The most famous Ealing comedy, with many London locations.
The League of Gentlemen (1960)
Ex-army officers set out to rob the Bank of England.
Let's Be Famous (1939)
Adventures of a stage-struck Lancashire lad in London.
The London Nobody Knows (1967)
Wonderful documentary narrated by James

Mason and based on the book by Geoffrey Fletcher.

The Long Arm (1956)
A Scotland Yard detective grapples with a series of robberies.

The Long Good Friday (1980)
Melodramatic violence set in the East End of London.

The Long Memory (1952)
Excellent footage of the Thames estuary and some fine shots of Shad Thames near Tower Bridge and the Lower Pool of London.

The Man Who Knew Too Much (1934)
Lots of London locations (East End, Albert Hall, Westminster Cathedral) in a film about a kidnapped boy.

The Man Who Knew Too Much (1956)
Hitchcock's remake of the above with similar locations.

Mrs Brown, You've Got a Lovely Daughter (1968)
Adventures of a young singer and a prize greyhound in swinging London.

The Mudlark (1950)
Sentimental tale of a street urchin who breaks into Windsor Castle and sees Queen Victoria.

My Beautiful Laundrette (1985)
Adventures of a young Asian in south London.

My Old Dutch (1934)
The son of an old Cockney couple dies a hero.

Nil by Mouth (1997)
Heavy and violent drama set in Catford and other parts of south London.

The Optimists of Nine Elms (1973)
An old busker is befriended by children from a London slum.

Otley (1968)
Spoof version of the James Bond genre, set (as ever) in swinging London.

Out of the Clouds (1954)
Dramatic tales of passengers and staff at London Heathrow Airport.

The Party's Over (1963)
One of the worst of the "swinging London" films, about Chelsea beatniks.

Passport to Pimlico (1949)
Comedy whose premise is that ancient documents prove that Pimlico belongs to Burgundy.

Piccadilly (1929)
Murder in the West End.

Piccadilly Third Stop (1960)
Average thriller, redeemed by excellent final chase through the Underground.

A Place to Go (1963)
A young man turns to crime amid London's low life.

Pool of London (1950)
A tale of smuggling set in and around London docks.

Poor Cow (1967)
Realistic drama set in run-down inner-city suburbs of London.

Say Hello to Yesterday (1970)
Romantic drama, with the then compulsory background of swinging London.

Seven Days to Noon (1950)
Excellent thriller about a mad scientist who threatens to destroy London.

The Shakedown (1959)
Dreadful drama set in the sleaze and vice of 1950s Soho.

Smashing Time (1967)
Another dreadful film which sets out to be a comedy about two young girls from the North who visit swinging London.

So This is London (1939)
Comedy set in London at the end of the 1930s.

The Strange Affair (1968)
An honest London policeman discovers his superiors are "bent". Another bad "swinging London" film.

Street Corner (1953)
Competent drama about the work of police-women working in Chelsea police station.

Sunday, Bloody Sunday (1971)
Finely acted drama with many location shots in and around Blackheath and Greenwich.

Terminus (1951)
Documentary about 24 hours in the life of Waterloo Station.

Three Hats for Lisa (1965)
Generally sad attempt at a "swinging London" musical, relieved by lots of scenes of London and the pleasant personality of Joe Brown.

Twinky (1969)
Unattractive sex comedy set in the last gasps of swinging London.

Up for the Cup (1931)
The adventures of a Yorkshire man who comes to Wembley for the FA Cup Final.

Up the Junction (1967)
Unsuccessful attempt at realistic drama set among the workers of Clapham.

Variety Jubilee (1942)
Memories of the grand old days of London music hall.

Wanted for Murder (1946)
The son of the public hangman becomes a murderer. Interesting London locations.

Warn London (1934)
London copper thwarts international gang.

The Waterloo Bridge Handicap (1978)
Interesting short film that focuses on London commuters.

Films on London

Glossary

ackee and salt fish: one of Jamaica's most famous dishes – ackee is a red-skinned fruit that is safe to eat only when it is fully ripe

After Eight Mints: dark chocolate-coated peppermints – considered by some the ultimate petty bourgeois end to a meal

baron of beef: two sirloins left uncut at the backbone

black-balled: barred from membership of a club – the origin of the phrase comes from the days when voting was done by placing little balls in a cloth bag; the presence of a black ball in the bag meant that the candidate was not selected

bosky: woody

chalybeate well: a well where the water is impregnated with or tastes of iron

Cheddar: a town in Somerset long famous for the hard strong cheese produced there

clip joint: a club where the customers are over-charged for food and drinks

clog dancer: a dancer, usually from the north of England, who performed in wooden clogs

coaching inn: an inn where stagecoaches stopped to allow their passengers time to eat or even to spend the night

coir: fibre of the husk of the coconut, used for making ropes and mats

copper: policeman or woman; also old penny or halfpenny

coster: short for "costermonger" – now used to describe anyone who sells fruit and vegetables from a stall, but originally "one who sold apples"

crack locomotives: locomotives that hauled the most important passenger trains

crossing sweepers: men, women, boys and girls who swept a pathway across the road clear of mud, dust and horse manure so that pedestrians could cross in comfort

dandy: an excessively smartly dressed man

delved: dug

Dirty White Candy: unrefined sugar cane, sold in lumps or as a "loaf"

dodgy: suspect

Earl Grey: fine, scented blend of tea

flagstone: a paving stone

flunkey: servant, usually a footman

fly-by-night: someone or something that has a very temporary existence, usually suspect

Gable Worm Seed: treacle wormseed, a plant used to treat children infested with worms

Gentlemen's Relish: a savoury pâté in which anchovies are the strongest ingredient

Guardian reader: the phrase means more than simply "one who reads The Guardian newspaper" – it implies someone who is sensitively liberal in his or her views, perhaps too much so

hart's-horn: powdered antler of a deer – once a principal source of ammonia

haunch of venison: leg and loin of a deer

Glossary

hawkers: door-to-door salespeople
heckling: interrupting a performer on stage
hotch-potch: rough and ready mixture
inexpressibles: 18th- and 19th-century colloquial word for "trousers"
jamboree: a noisy revel
jerk chicken: dried chicken meat
kilt: pleated thick woollen skirt worn by Scotsmen
Labrador: a variety of the Newfoundland dog, originally used in hunting
lackey: servant
lightermen: workers on a lighter, or flat-bottomed barge used to take cargo from large ship to shore
little bash: a party, not necessarily a small party
local: neighbourhood pub
Marmite: savoury spread made from vegetables and yeast
mashing: mixing malt with hot water to form wort in beer-brewing
Meccano: very popular toy construction kit first made by Lines Brothers of Liverpool in the 1930s
muffler: scarf
muzak: piped music, usually appalling, heard in shops, lifts, precincts, restaurants and so on
neat's tongue: the tongue of an ox or bullock
Ordnance Survey: government department that produces accurate and highly detailed large-scale maps of Britain
ostler: servant whose job it was to look after horses, usually at an inn
pea-souper: a very thick London fog
penny gaff: a very cheap lodging house

penny plain, twopence (tuppence) coloured: a series of cut-out model theatres, scenery and characters, so called because they cost one penny uncoloured, and twopence coloured by hand
pigtail tobacco: tobacco twisted into a thin rope
pilfering: stealing
posh: smart, expensive, refined – some say the word originated from those people who could afford cabins on the expensive (cool) side of the ship when sailing to India and back: "Port Out, Starboard Home"
Proms: series of promenade concerts at the Royal Albert Hall, held every summer
pub: public house, inn
pukka: genuine or thorough
pusher: new word for bouncer in London clubs
Roller: a Rolls Royce car
saddle of lamb: two loins of lamb joined together by the backbone
semi: a semi-detached house, joined to its neighbour on one side only
short back and sides: a traditional haircut for boys and men – literally cut short at the back and sides of the head
skivvies: servants, usually female
sling yer 'ook (hook): go away
smart lad: a young man or boy, one likely to work hard at the job being offered
smog: a mixture of fog and smoke
snifter: a small measure of alcoholic spirits
snooty: with a superior air
snuff: powdered tobacco
sprogs: young children
squeezebox: accordion

squint: a quick look at something or someone
span: past tense of "to spin"
sporran: a leather wallet worn on the front of a Scotsman's kilt
spree: a happy and often wild outing involving much consumption or spending
stevedores: men involved in loading or unloading cargo ships
stews: brothels
Stilton: a town in Leicestershire famous for its strong blue-veined cheese
sweatshop: a small workshop where the labour force is overworked and underpaid – usually in the clothing trade
sweep smelters: those who comb through piles of soot to see what they can find
tam: a Scotsman's bonnet
toffs: rich, often well-bred people – a term of awe or abuse from the poor
ulster: a long loose overcoat
utter: to express oneself with great affirmation
wannabee: someone who hopes to make a career, often in show-business
well bulled: well polished
wet bobs: students who spend their summers rowing rather than playing cricket
whelks: small molluscs, boiled and eaten with vinegar
whiff: a small Thames rowing boat for one oarsman
wide-awake boys: young men who are difficult to fool
Wolfenden Report: a seminal report in 1957 which recommended decriminalizing homosexual relations between consenting adults.

Index

Index

Photographic Credits

All photographs are taken by Rupert Tenison except those listed below:

© Bridgeman Art Library, London/New York, p. 310, 311
© Hulton Getty, London, p. 53 top, 68, 70 top, 78, 79, 81, 85 top right, 89, 90, 92, 93, 105 bottom left, 106, 107 top right, 109 bottom left, 120, 135, 137 top left, 152, 155, 156 bottom right, 176 top left, 186 top right, 187 top right, 203 top, 205 bottom, 214, 239, 242, 249, 260, 261, 263/64, 268, 270, 271, 272, 273, 276, 277, 288, 289, 292, 293, 294, 296 top left, 297 top left, 299, 302 top right, 303, 312
© London Regional Transport, p. 313 top left
© Mander & Mitchenson, Beckenham, p. 12